M000278571

Rational Theory of International Politics

Rational Theory of International Politics

THE LOGIC OF COMPETITION AND COOPERATION

Charles L. Glaser

PRINCETON UNIVERSITY PRESS
PRINCETON AND OXFORD

Copyright © 2010 by Princeton University Press

Published by Princeton University Press, 41 William Street,
Princeton, New Jersey 08540
In the United Kingdom: Princeton University Press, 6 Oxford Street,
Woodstock, Oxfordshire OX20 1TW

All Rights Reserved

Library of Congress Cataloging-in-Publication Data

Glaser, Charles L. (Charles Louis), 1954–
  Rational theory of international politics : the logic of competition and cooperation /
Charles L. Glaser.
      p. cm.
  Includes bibliographical references and index.
  ISBN 978-0-691-14371-2 (hardcover : alk. paper) — ISBN 978-0-691-14372-
9 (pbk. : alk. paper   1. International relations—Philosophy.   2. Competition,
International.   3. International cooperation.   I. Title.
   JZ1305.G555 2010
   327.101—dc22   2009038211

British Library Cataloging-in-Publication Data is available

This book has been composed in Sabon

Printed on acid-free paper. ∞

press.princeton.edu

Printed in the United States of America

10 9 8 7 6 5 4 3 2 1

To Carol and Adam

Contents

Preface

THE QUESTIONS THAT led to this book first puzzled me when I was working on nuclear strategy and policy in the 1980s. I could not find a satisfactory answer to the basic question, "Is the nuclear arms race dangerous?" Most of the arguments that saw grave dangers in the Cold War nuclear competition were internally inconsistent. The arguments on the opposite side of the debate, which held that the nuclear arms race was necessary to preserve U.S. security, were even less satisfactory. Especially in need of development was analysis of the relationship between the military competition and the politics of U.S.–Soviet relations.

Thinking about arms races led me to structural theories of international politics, as a means for understanding when states should compete and when they should cooperate. To evaluate whether arms races are dangerous, we need to be able to assess the alternatives that were available to states. Arms races might increase the probability of war, but not racing might have made war even more likely. The rational theory that I develop in this book enables us to separate the impact of the international environment from the impact of the strategies that states choose; we can use it to assess whether arms races themselves were dangerous, or instead whether the international situation facing states was the true source. More broadly, my theory helps us understand the impact of the international environment on states' strategies and argues that international anarchy does not generate a general tendency toward competitive international strategies; under a wide range of material and information conditions, cooperation is a state's best option for achieving security.

My work on these questions played out in a series of articles over many years in *International Security* and *World Politics*. The articles were written to stand on their own and without the next article in mind. And I did not set out from the start with the idea of writing a book on grand international relations theory. When I did decide to write a book that pulled together and integrated these articles, I imagined that this would be a rather quick project. In the end, this book took a number of additional years to write and includes many arguments and chapters that I had not envisioned at the outset.

My greatest intellectual debt may well be to the University of Chicago, where I benefited from the scholarly energy and intensity for which the university is famous. At Chicago, the Program on International Security

Policy (PISP) provided an ideal forum for faculty and graduate students to interact, learn from each other, and work together. During most of this time, I codirected PISP with John Mearsheimer and Bob Pape. I especially valued their commitment to this enterprise, their deep concern about the theoretical and policy issues we addressed, and their friendship; I believe that the community we created over more than a decade was a great success. In my early years at the university, I also benefited from close interactions with several other Chicago colleagues who focused on international security—Jim Fearon, Alex Wendt, and Steve Walt.

Many individuals contributed to the evolution of my thinking about international relations theory. I have thanked many for help with my articles on international relations theory, and I am not repeating those thanks here. I apologize in advance to anyone I failed to thank here for help with this book and related unpublished articles.

During the spring of 2008 the Program on Political Institutions at the Harris School at Chicago sponsored a day-long workshop on my book that was tremendously helpful. Chaim Kaufmann, Bob Powell, and Jack Snyder launched sessions with excellent comments and criticisms that fueled discussions throughout the day. I thank them for taking the time to thoroughly read my manuscript and to travel to Chicago for the workshop. I also thank the many Chicago faculty and graduate students who attended that day. My book benefited from presentations at a number of scholarly workshops, including PISP; the Program on International Politics, Economics and Security at the University of Chicago; the Olin Institute National Security Studies Group at Harvard; and the Woodrow Wilson School Research Program on International Security at Princeton. In addition, I thank the graduate students in my seminar on Military Policy and International Relations, who provided valuable reactions to early versions of some chapters.

For comments on my entire manuscript, I thank Andy Kydd and Steve Brooks, who provided exceptionally detailed written comments; and Jon Caverley, Matt Evangelista, Daragh Grant, Rose Kelanic, Negeen Pegahi, and John Scheussler, who also provided excellent guidance. For comments on chapters of the manuscript and related unpublished papers, I thank Michael Barnett, Steve Brooks, Barry Buzan, Jasen Castillo, Dale Copeland, Alex Downes, David Edelstein, Colin Elman, Matt Evangelista, Jim Fearon, Sven Feldmann, Michael Glosny, Lloyd Gruber, Ted Hopf, Seth Jones, Paul Kapur, Dong Sun Lee, Chaim Kaufmann, Jennifer Lind, John Mearsheimer, Takayuki Nishi, Bob Pape, Bob Powell, Sebastian Rosato, John Schuessler, Randy Schweller, David Siroky, Duncan Snidal, Jack Snyder, Celeste Wallander, and Alex Wendt. This feedback and advice helped me sharpen my arguments and develop new ones. For able research assistance I thank Jon Caverley and Jon Schuessler. For helping me improve the presentation and clarity of the final draft of my manuscript, I thank Negeen Pegahi.

The book draws on my arguments in the following articles: "When Are Arms Races Dangerous? Rational versus Suboptimal Arming," *International Security*, Vol. 28, No. 4 (Spring 2004); "What Is the Offense-Defense Balance and Can We Measure It?," *International Security*, Vol. 22, No. 4 (Spring 1998), which I coauthored with Chaim Kaufmann; "The Security Dilemma Revisited," *World Politics*, Vol. 50, No. 1 (October 1997); "Realists as Optimists: Cooperation as Self-Help," *International Security*, Vol. 19, No. 3 (Winter 1994/95); and "Political Consequences of Military Strategy: Expanding and Refining the Spiral and Deterrence Models," *World Politics*, Vol. 44, No. 4 (July 1992). This material is included by permission of the publishers.

My son, Adam, slowed down progress on this book and I am grateful for the richness he has added to my life. My wife, Carol, gracefully endured and supported my more than occasional preoccupation with this project. I dedicate this book to them.

Rational Theory of International Politics

CHAPTER ONE

Introduction

TERRORISM, NUCLEAR PROLIFERATION, and regional instability currently top the list of international dangers facing the United States largely by default. Until recently, war with other major powers posed the greatest danger, with the Cold War Soviet threat providing the most recent and vivid example. Now, however, the prospect of war between the globe's major powers is widely viewed as insignificant, and even competition between these powers is muted. The contrast to the previous century is stark, with concern about major-power war dropped from its historical pride of place. While some observers worry that a growing China may eventually challenge U.S. security, most see at worst a distant threat, dwarfed by concerns about economic competition. Conflict within Europe is seen as still more unlikely, a past danger, not a current or future one.

A future of peaceful and relatively tranquil major-power relations would have significant implications for U.S. policy. If conflict is sufficiently unlikely, the United States should give lower priority to maintaining its unipolar military advantages and global reach, and higher priority to increasing its economic growth and prosperity. If confident that good political relations will continue, the United States would be free to adopt otherwise provocative foreign policies—knowing that the United States was not a threat, major powers would neither respond aggressively nor begin to question the United States' benign motives. If not threatened by other technologically advanced countries, the United States should invest less in cutting-edge military forces and possibly give greater weight to forces designed for regional intervention and counterterrorism.

Assessing whether future major-power relations are, in fact, likely to be peaceful, and how if at all this depends on U.S. strategy, requires us to address the most basic questions of international relations (IR) theory. What is the impact of the international system on states' behavior? More specifically, does the combination of international anarchy and states' military requirements consistently favor competitive policies? Or instead, can a state's concern about its military capabilities sometimes make cooperation its best option? What is the impact of states' motives and goals on their behavior? Is it the international system and the insecurity that it generates, or instead the nonsecurity motives of "greedy" states, that drives international competition? What is the impact of states' political relations on the likelihood of conflict? More specifically, how does states' information about other states' motives influence the likelihood of competition and conflict? Does uncertainty about others' motives require states to adopt competitive policies?

Although extensively studied, these questions require further investigation. None of the major theories of international relations provides a framework for building an integrated, balanced answer to these questions. Instead they tend to emphasize one variable at the expense of others. As a result, their arguments overlook important aspects of international relations and fail to capture interactions between factors that should significantly influence states' decisions. Moreover, some prominent theories suffer deductive flaws that underpin key disagreements about the nature of international politics.

THE THEORY

Type of Theory

The theory developed in this book is a rationalist, strategic choice theory. It takes the perspective of a state that faces an international environment that presents constraints and opportunities. The international environment is assumed to be anarchic, that is, it lacks an international authority that can enforce agreements and prevent the use of force. The state is assumed to be rational—it makes purposive decisions that take reasonable account of its interests, and the international constraints and opportunities that it faces.

The theory analyzes the strategies a state *should* choose—which is essentially the same as assuming that the state is a rational actor. I focus on cases in which the opposing state is also rational (and in which the state accurately believes this is the case). Evaluation of this rational-state versus rational-state interaction lies at the heart of the entire neorealist/ structural-realist international relations theory project, as the major works incorporate either a rationality assumption or an evolutionary mechanism that selects out states that behavior irrationally. Although more general, a substantial portion of the theory I develop in this book can therefore be viewed as working within this realist tradition.

I am, however, skeptical that as a general rule states actually act rationally. Over the past few decades, scholars have developed a range of theories—including domestic politics arguments that focus on state structure and regime type, organizations and bureaucratic politics, and theories of individual decision making that focus on cognitive misperceptions—to explain states' decisions that were seriously flawed. This scholarship provides strong grounds for concluding that states often fail to act rationally. When states do act rationally, my theory will succeed in explaining much of their behavior. In contrast, when states choose suboptimal policies, the theory will do less well at explaining past state behavior but will remain an essential building block of a more complete IR theory. The rational theory would be necessary to tell us how well a state can do—for example, how much security it can achieve—in the face of the constraints and opportunities imposed by the international system. In other words, understanding the impact of the international system on states' behavior requires a rational theory, even if states do not always act in line with its constraints.

In addition, my theory provides a rational baseline against which actual state behavior can be evaluated. We cannot evaluate whether a state is acting rationally/optimally without such a theory. Bad outcomes—for example, arms races and war—could simply reflect a dangerous international security environment, not flawed policy decisions. Therefore, theories of suboptimal behavior, whether built on arguments about domestic politics or errors in individual decision making, rely at least implicitly on a rational theory. Moreover, if the opposing state is believed to be a rational actor, the theory can provide policy guidance, prescribing strategies based on the state's understanding of its international environment.

Independent Variables

To adequately depict the state and the international situation it faces, I identify three types of variables that are essential to include in an evaluation of states' security policy choices. The decision-making state is characterized in terms of its *motives*. Motives embody what a state values, capturing its fundamental interests and goals. Types of states are distinguished by their motives. The state's international environment is characterized by two types of variables that can significantly influence the opportunities and constraints the state will face for using military force to achieve its goals. *Material* variables largely determine the military capabilities a state can build. *Information* variables, both what the state knows about its adversary's motives and what it believes its adversary knows about its own motives, influence the reactions a state anticipates to its actions and, therefore, the strategy it should choose.

Basic intuition suggests that each of these types of variables—motives, material potential, and information about others' motives—should influence a state's choice of strategy. Motives translate into the benefits states see in maintaining the territory they possess and in acquiring more, and therefore can influence their strategies. A state that is satisfied with the status quo is less likely to see benefits in changing it and, therefore, is less likely than a dissatisfied state to try to change it. More precisely, a state that is motivated only by security, and therefore would accept the status quo if secure within it, should be more inclined toward cooperative policies than a state with more ambitious motives. Nevertheless, under certain conditions a security-seeking state will value changing the status quo—if more territory would increase its ability to defend itself—and value war—if fighting would reduce its adversary's current or future ability to attack it. In contrast, states with the more ambitious motives, which I term "greedy" states, are fundamentally dissatisfied with the status quo, desiring additional territory even when it is not required for security.[1] These nonsecurity goals result in a fundamental conflict of interests that makes competition the only strategy with which a greedy state can achieve its goals.

Material variables should influence a state's choice of strategy because they influence its ability to acquire military capabilities, which in turn influence the outcome of efforts to deter and coerce, and to defend and attack. A state must consider not only the military forces it can build, but also the forces its adversary can build in reaction; the overall result of both states building determines a state's military capability, that is, its ability to perform relevant military missions. A state that is more powerful than its potential adversary—that is, has more resources—is more capable of winning an arms race and, if fully armed, winning a war. Consequently, a more powerful state is more willing to adopt these competitive policies. Closely related, power should influence a state's assessment of the danger posed by potential adversaries—more powerful adversaries have greater potential to damage and conquer it. During the Cold War, the U.S. decision to defend against and compete with the Soviet Union, which was the only other superpower, partly reflected these basic power considerations. Current concerns about a future China largely reflect its growing power.

In addition to power, a state's ability to acquire military capabilities also depends on the relative effectiveness of forces deployed to defend (hold) territory compared to forces deployed to attack (take) territory, a comparison that is captured in what is termed the "offense-defense balance." When defense is easier than offense, equally powerful states should have better prospects for defending against each other and be more secure. If the advantage of defense is large, even a much weaker state should be able to effectively defend itself, which could change the strategies of both the more and less powerful states. Nuclear weapons are the clearest example of a technology that provides a large advantage to defense: at

---

[1] A state can be both security seeking and greedy; I explore this issue in chapter 2. I will often refer to these mixed-type states simply as greedy.

least for major powers, the nuclear forces required for deterrence by retaliation are much less expensive than the forces required to deny these
retaliatory capabilities, which would be required for offense. This fact lies
at the heart of the theory of the nuclear revolution, which explains why
nuclear weapons should lead to a reduction in military competition between the major powers, an increase in their security, and a reduction in
conflict and war.[2]

A state's options will also be constrained by the nature of military capabilities. A state that can deploy forces that are good for defending, but
are of little value for attacking, has different options than if the available
forces are equally good for both types of military missions. In the former
case, when offense and defense are "distinguishable," a state can defend
itself without threatening an opposing state's ability to defend itself, while
in the latter it cannot. Offense-defense distinguishability has significant
implications for states' political relations, as well as their military capabilities. Consequently, the material situation a state faces depends on
both of these offense-defense variables, as well as power.

Finally, a state's information about its adversary's motives should affect its choice of strategy because this information influences its expectations about the adversary's behavior, including reactions to its own policies. A state that believes it likely faces a security seeker should find
defending itself to be less necessary and valuable than if the adversary is
believed to be a greedy state because the greedy state would be more determined than a security seeker to alter the status quo. Closely related,
beliefs about others' motives influence the proper balance between cooperative and competitive strategies. When the adversary is likely motivated
by security, the state should anticipate that cooperation is more likely to
be reciprocated than when the adversary is likely motivated by greed and,
therefore, has larger incentives to take advantage of the state's restraint.
When uncertain about the adversary's type, the state needs to balance the
merits of cooperative and competitive strategies. Post–Cold War reactions to U.S. power are most easily understood in terms of other states'
beliefs about U.S. motives. The United States' tremendous advantage in
material power has generated little if any reaction from other major powers, certainly from European powers, at least largely because they believe
the United States will respect the major-power status quo.[3] Similarly, the
United States' understanding of the danger posed by opposing nuclear
forces is heavily colored by its assessment of others' motives—small Iranian or North Korean forces generate great concern, as such states are

[2] Robert Jervis, *The Meaning of the Nuclear Revolution: Statecraft and the Prospect of Armageddon* (Ithaca: Cornell University Press, 1989).

[3] Kier A. Lieber and Gerard Alexander, "Waiting for Balancing: Why the World Is Not Pushing Back," *International Security* 30, 1 (Summer 2005): 109–130.

viewed as driven by nonsecurity interests, while much larger Russian forces now receive little attention because Russia is believed to be motivated by security alone.

While the intuitive case for including all three types of variables in the theory is strong, whether they should influence a state's strategy is a different question. It is possible one or more of the variables do not matter, that is, variation should not lead the state to choose different policies. Deciding which variables to include is therefore essential for starting to build a theory, but it is only a beginning. To answer the question of which variables should influence a state's policy, we require a deductive theory. Whether certain variables have substantial influence and others have little or no influence will be a finding of the theory. In contrast to this approach, influential strands of international relations theory have been built on the assumption that the impact of a single type of variable far exceeds that of all others. Most prominent is Kenneth Waltz's structural realism, which focuses almost exclusively on material power and argues that the international environment created by the distribution of power leads states to adopt competitive policies, even when they are motivated only by security.[4] Largely in response to this material emphasis, Alexander Wendt, a structural constructivist, focuses on ideas, which for him include information about others' motives, in making possible cooperation as well as competition.[5] Other scholars have emphasized the role of states' nonsecurity (greedy) motives as the key source of international competition.[6]

Deductive Arguments

The deductive theory that I develop demonstrates that all three types of variables should in fact influence a state's policy, and that in general one type of variable is not more important—should not play a greater role—in determining a state's strategy than the others. Furthermore, a state's strategy should often depend on the combined effect of different variables. The result is greater complexity and less parsimony than theories that argue for the importance of a single type of variable. The price is warranted, however, because it turns out that theories that emphasize one

[4] Kenneth N. Waltz, *Theory of International Politics* (Reading, MA: Addison-Wesley, 1979). John J. Mearsheimer, *The Tragedy of Great Power Politics* (New York: Norton, 2001), also emphasizes the importance of material variables; while dealing explicitly with uncertainty about motives, he argues it should not influence variation in states' choices.

[5] Alexander Wendt, *Social Theory of International Politics* (Cambridge: Cambridge University Press, 1999).

[6] See, for example, Randall L. Schweller, *Deadly Imbalances: Tripolarity and Hitler's Strategy of World Conquest* (New York: Columbia University Press, 1998), who emphasizes motives but also gives weight to power in determining states' strategies.

of these types of variables at the expense of the others risk misevaluating states' options and prescribing the wrong policies, under a range of conditions. Moreover, by starting with a more general framework, we can see that battles between theories that emphasize one type of variable or another have been unproductive or misleading because they fail to provide an adequate deductive foundation for reaching their conclusions.

To analyze the impact of the international environment on a state's behavior, I focus on the decisions facing security seekers. If these states choose competitive policies, the international environment must be the source of this competition because such states lack fundamental conflicts of interest that could drive arms races, opposing alliances, crises, and war. I find that although competition is a security seeker's best choice under some conditions, cooperation is preferable under other conditions. The international system does *not* consistently favor competitive policies. Variation reflects both material and information variables. Defense advantage reduces pressures for competition by making effective deterrent forces relatively easy to acquire, creating the possibility that two states can simultaneously possess the ability to perform the military missions required for their security. Information that the adversary is likely to be a security seeker can make cooperation a state's best strategy for two reinforcing reasons: cooperating is less risky because it is more likely to be reciprocated; and cooperation is more valuable because restraint can lead the adversary to conclude that the state is more likely to be a security seeker, which increases the adversary's security, which in turn increases the state's own security. The state's strategy should depend on the combined impact of material and information variables. For example, there are cases in which material conditions would favor competition, but a high probability that the opposing state is a security seeker makes cooperation a state's best option.

At the core of competition between security seekers is insecurity, which can create incentives for states to build up arms to acquire military advantages and to deny them to potential adversaries, and to weaken opposing states by taking their territory and destroying their military forces. As a result, a security seeker should be interested not only in being capable of defending itself, but also in increasing its adversary's security. The state can do this by reducing or forgoing the military forces it can use for attack, thereby making its adversary less vulnerable. The state can also increase its adversary's security by taking actions that convince the adversary that the state is more likely to be a security seeker and therefore less likely to attack it. This requires the state to send a "costly signal"—to take an action that a security seeker would be more likely to take than would a greedy state because the action would be less costly for a security seeker. An effective costly signal convinces the adversary to revise its information about the state, reducing its estimate that the state is greedy, thereby increasing the willingness of an opposing security seeker to cooperate.

States should not, however, always find that policies designed to increase their adversary's security are their best option. Increasing the adversary's security will sometimes require the state to increase its own vulnerability to attack and will therefore be too risky. This trade-off occurs when the state faces a security dilemma. The security dilemma is usually described as a situation in which the measures that a state takes to increase its own security reduce its adversary's. Closely related, a state faces a security dilemma when the actions it would take to increase its adversary's security would increase its own vulnerability to attack and, therefore, might decrease its own security. This increased military vulnerability is a barrier both to reducing its adversary's military vulnerability and to signaling its benign motives, and it can therefore lead a security-seeking state to pursue a competitive strategy instead of a cooperative one. The security dilemma lies at the core of competition between security seekers: when the security dilemma is mild or ceases to exist, avoiding competition should be relatively easy.

The magnitude of the security dilemma depends on both material and information variables. The standard formulation focuses on material variables—the offense-defense balance and offense-defense distinguishability. For example, when offense and defense can be distinguished, a state can choose not to acquire offensive capabilities while deploying defensive ones, thereby reducing the adversary's vulnerability without increasing its own, and signaling its benign motives because a greedy state would be less willing to forgo offense. When offense has a large advantage, security seekers face large incentives to adopt competitive military strategies that resemble those that greedy states would choose.[7]

However, although they have received relatively little attention in this context, information variables also influence the severity of the security dilemma.[8] If both states are sure that the opposing state is a security seeker (and if both also know that the other knows this), the security dilemma is eliminated and neither state has incentives to compete, even if

[7] Robert Jervis, "Cooperation under the Security Dilemma," *World Politics* 30, 1 (January 1978): 167–214; Charles L. Glaser, "The Security Dilemma Revisited," *World Politics* 5, 1 (October 1997): 171–201; and Stephen Van Evera, *Causes of War: Power and the Roots of Conflict* (Ithaca: Cornell University Press, 1999), chap. 6.

[8] The key exception is Andrew H. Kydd, *Trust and Mistrust in International Relations* (Princeton: Princeton University Press, 2005), who develops game-theoretic models of the effect of these information variables. In contrast, costly signaling has received extensive attention. The information variables I am focusing on here refer to the information that a state has prior to a given strategic interaction, not to signaling, which is designed to lead its adversary to revise the information it has about the state's motives as a result of the interaction.

material conditions would otherwise fuel insecurity and competition. And certainty is not required to moderate the dilemma—under uncertainty, higher estimates that the adversary is a security seeker make cooperation less risky, increasing the range of material conditions under which a state can afford to adopt strategies that would reduce the adversary's insecurity. As a result, the information that states have at the beginning of their interaction can determine the future path of their political relationship. A state that believes that its adversary is likely to be greedy should be more inclined to adopt competitive policies, which could signal malign motives and fuel a negative spiral in political relations. Similarly, initial beliefs that the adversary is likely to be a security seeker can support policies that set in motion a positive political spiral. A history of international conflict, if it informs states' beliefs about their adversaries' motives and intentions, will therefore create a tendency toward competition; likewise, a history of international peace will fuel cooperation.

In short, the anarchic international environment does not create a general tendency toward competition: under some conditions it can fuel rational competition between states that lack a fundamental conflict of interests; under other conditions, the international environment can encourage cooperation between such states. Both information and material variables play important roles in establishing the international environment, and in turn the security dilemma, that a state faces, and they can determine the relative merits of cooperation and competition. When the security dilemma is severe, states will be insecure and competition may be less risky than cooperation. In contrast, a mild security dilemma can moderate or eliminate pressures for competition, making cooperation a state's best strategy. Depending on their values, both information and material variables can favor cooperative or competitive strategies; neither type of variable consistently overshadows the other and a state's strategy should often reflect their combined impact.

The end of the Cold War provides a useful illustration of the combined effect of material and information variables, and the limitations of theories that envision the international environment more narrowly. The Cold War ended without a reduction in the Soviet strategic nuclear capabilities that were commonly viewed as the most dangerous component of the Soviet military machine. The Soviet Union retained not only forces capable of annihilating the United States many times over, but also the advanced forces required to destroy much of the U.S. nuclear force, which had generated great concern, particularly among American hard-liners, during the 1970s and 1980s. In addition, although the Soviet Union did announce significant reductions of its conventional forces in Europe, these reductions had only begun and were reversible. Yet arguably the Cold War was over by the spring of 1989 and almost certainly by the end of that year, following the collapse of the Soviet empire in Eastern Europe but preceding the dissolution of the Soviet Union.[9] U.S. security increased disproportionately relative both to the reductions in Soviet deployed forces and to Soviet military potential.

This increase in U.S. security was driven largely by the changed U.S. understanding of Soviet motives.[10] During the Cold War, the vast majority of American experts believed the Soviet Union was dangerous, but there was not a consensus on the reason. Views of Soviet motives ranged from pure security seeking to high levels of greed (nonsecurity motives) and included the view that the Soviets had mixed motives (security plus greed). Even those who believed that Soviet motives were likely to be benign saw danger due to Soviet insecurity and the competition they believed it fueled. U.S. policy reflected a mix of these views, which shifted across time during the Cold War. In contrast, by the end of the Cold War a strong consensus had emerged that the Soviet Union was unlikely to be greedy. The result was a dramatic increase in U.S. security that reflected its new security environment. In response, the United States reduced its force posture, including the cancellation of nuclear modernization programs, deep reductions in theater nuclear forces, significant decreases in U.S. conventional forces in Europe, and large cuts in its overall conventional force structure.[11] The United States and NATO continued to rely on nuclear deterrence, but now the previously most worrisome and risky Soviet attacks were considered implausible, which eased U.S. force requirements; nuclear weapons became a type of insurance policy against future unpredictability. Theories that focus only on material variables face a daunting challenge in explaining the U.S. understanding of its increased security at the end of the Cold War and the policies it adopted as a result.

At the same time, a theory that focuses only on information misses a key piece of the explanation for Soviet decisions that led the United States to revise its assessment of Soviet motives. Existing material conditions enabled the Soviet Union to adopt a number of policies that would likely have been too risky under different material conditions. Specifically, nu-

[9] Making the case for the earlier date is John Mueller, "What Was the Cold War About? Evidence from Its Ending," *Political Science Quarterly* 119, 4 (2004–05): 606–631.

[10] On the key events and their impact, see Raymond Garthoff, *The Great Transformation: American-Soviet Relations and the End of the Cold War* (Washington, DC: Brookings Institution, 1994); Matthew Evangelista, *Unarmed Forces: The Transnational Movement to End the Cold War* (Ithaca: Cornell University Press, 1999), esp. part 4; Richard K. Herrmann and Richard Ned Lebow, eds., *Ending the Cold War: Interpretations, Causation, and the Study of International Relations* (New York: Palgrave Macmillan, 2004); and Kydd, *Trust and Mistrust in International Relations*, chap. 8.

[11] The United States did, however, pursue a number of potentially provocative policies in subsequent years, including NATO expansion and withdrawal from the ABM Treaty.

but these material
conditions were consistent
what explains shift?

Introduction • 11

clear weapons provided the Soviet Union with a highly effective deterrent capability for protecting its homeland. This reduced the value the Soviet Union placed on maintaining Eastern Europe as a buffer against Western attack, which in turn reduced the risks of accepting some increased weakness in its conventional forces.[12] Consequently, the Soviet Union was able to signal its security motives without having to accept large risks in its ability to deter attacks against its homeland.[13] In addition, material considerations played an important role in U.S. decisions, although this may be less obvious because such considerations were more in the background. Nuclear weapons reduced how confident the United States had to be that Soviet motives were benign; if an increasingly unlikely dangerous scenario nevertheless occurred, the United States retained formidable deterrent, and potentially coercive, capabilities. As a result, the case for not reciprocating restraint in deployed military forces and instead actively pursuing military advantages was weak.

In addition to the international environment, a state's own motives can influence its choice of strategy. All else being equal, a greedy state that also values its security will place greater value on additional territory than will a comparable pure security seeker and, therefore, should be willing to run greater risks and accept greater costs to acquire it. As a result, for a given international environment, this greedy state will have larger incentives for adopting a competitive strategy than will the pure security seeker. For greedy states, material variables are more important as a barrier to expansion, and less important as a source of insecurity. Although greedy states will adopt competitive policies under a wider range of conditions, material conditions that promise to make competi-

[12] This argument is made by Kenneth A. Oye, "Explaining the End of the Cold War: Morphological and Behavioral Adaptations to the Nuclear Peace," in Richard Ned Lebow and Thomas Risse-Kappen, eds., *International Relations Theory and the End of the Cold War* (New York: Columbia University Press, 1995).

[13] This leaves open the question of why the Soviet Union did not pursue these policies earlier. Three strands of argument, all of which lie outside the bounds of the strategic-choice theory but influence its variables, contribute to the answer: (1) New ideas about the security dilemma and defensive defense were accepted by the new Soviet leaders, who then adopted more cooperative and defensive policies. See Evangelista, *Unarmed Forces*; and Thomas Risse-Kappen, "Ideas Do Not Float Freely: Transnational Coalitions, Domestic Structures, and the End of the Cold War," *International Organization* 48, 2 (Spring 1994): 185–214. This line of argument implicitly includes an important material dimension because it requires that the Soviet Union had military options that could signal information without being too risky. (2) Severe economic decline required Soviet leaders to find conciliatory policies; Soviet leaders then adopted ideas to support this shift. See Stephen G. Brooks and William C. Wohlforth, "Power, Globalization, and the End of the Cold War: Reevaluating a Landmark Case," *International Security* 25, 3 (Winter 2000/01): 5–53. And (3) Soviet motives and preferences changed, providing the foundation for policies that made this clear; see text below and note 15.

tion ineffective should still lead to restraint. Moreover, for greedy states that also value security (which seems likely to be most all greedy states), there are conditions under which they should choose cooperative policies that reduce their ability to attack because these policies also reduce their military vulnerability.

The paradigmatic example of a greedy state is Hitler's Germany. Hitler's unrelenting pursuit of hegemony in Europe is hard to explain as driven by insecurity, but relatively easy to explain as a reflection of the nonsecurity value he placed on expansion, which supported a risky set of military and diplomatic policies. A number of material considerations contributed to Hitler's successes, but these created permissive conditions, not the deep source of competitive expansionist policies.[14] Depending on one's understanding of the Cold War, it too can require including states' motives as part of the explanation. As sketched above, explanations that focus on the international environment can explain much about the end of the Cold War. However, hard-line and deterrence model arguments that emphasize greedy Soviet motives as the source of the Cold War reject these explanations as at best incomplete and giving too much weight to the security dilemma.[15] Given this reading of the Cold War, changed Soviet motives, from greed to security seeking, become a central element of the explanation.[16]

The theoretical importance of greedy states is increased by my conclusion that the international system does not consistently favor competition. If the international system did consistently make competition a security seeker's best option, greedy states (including states that have a mix of greedy and security-seeking motives) would matter relatively little. Across the full range of international conditions, both security seekers and greedy states would adopt competitive policies. From a theoretical perspective, focusing on greedy states would be less important. The sim-

[14] For an assessment of the debate over Germany foreign policy, see Ian Kershaw, *The Nazi Dictatorship: Problems of Perspective and Interpretation*, 4th ed. (London: Arnold, 2000), esp. chap. 6; on the role of Germany's revisionist motives in combination with polarity, see Schweller, *Deadly Imbalances*; on perceptions of the offense-defense balance generating alliance behavior that created opportunities, see Thomas J. Christensen and Jack Snyder, "Chained Gangs and Passed Bucks: Predicting Alliance Patterns in Multipolarity," *International Organization* 44, 2 (1990): 137–168. For dissenting views and more extensive discussion, see chapter 8.

[15] One the deterrence model and the opposing explanation, the spiral model, see Robert Jervis, *Perception and Misperception in International Politics* (Princeton: Princeton University Press, 1976), chap. 3; and Charles L. Glaser, "Political Consequences of Military Strategy: Expanding and Refining the Spiral and Deterrence Models," *World Politics* 44, 4 (July 1992): 497–538.

[16] Reviewing work on the impact of ideological changes on Soviet policy is Jeremi Suri, "Explaining the End of the Cold War: A New Historical Consensus?," *Journal of Cold War Studies* 4, 4 (Fall 2002): 60–92, esp. 73–81.

pler, more purely structural theory would offer greater parsimony at little cost. This is essentially the claim that Waltz's structural realism makes. However, because the theory developed here shows that security seekers should pursue cooperative policies under a range of material and information conditions, greedy states gain theoretical importance because they might prefer competition when a security seeker facing the same international environment should choose cooperation.

Relationship to the Realisms

A substantial body of international relations theory grapples with the questions I address in this book and explores them from a broadly similar perspective. Taking a moment here to place my book in that literature helps to clarify its goals and define its contributions.

In many ways, my theory is the logical extension of Waltz's structural realism. The strategic-choice perspective has much in common with Waltz's structural approach, which envisions states as largely separate from the international environment they face and analyzes their options for achieving their goals in light of the constraints their international environment imposes.

In the end, however, my theory is radically different from Waltz's *Theory of International Politics*: it adds material and information variables that are essential for characterizing the state and its international environment; identifies missing types of interaction—most importantly, signaling; corrects flawed deductions; and reaches quite different conditional conclusions about the prospects for international cooperation. Although Waltz's structural realism did a great deal to advance IR theory, his characterization of the international environment is too thin, focusing solely on power. In combination with deductive flaws, this limitation undermines what is probably Waltz's key conclusion—his contention that international anarchy generates a strong general tendency for international politics to be competitive.

Defensive realism corrects many of the limitations of Waltz's structural realism and can be viewed as a way station along the route to the full theory I develop in this book. Defensive realism puts the security dilemma at the center of its explanation for international competition, adds offense-defense variables that explain variation in the security dilemma, and explains that states can provide information about their motives by employing costly signals. It is important to note here that I am using "defensive realism" more narrowly than has become common in the literature. Defensive realism is often used to refer to a theory that combines the rational theory that flows from the security dilemma with unit-level theories that are designed to explain states' suboptimal policies. In contrast, I am using defensive realism to refer only to the rational security-dilemma foundation.

Although the two theories share many key similarities, my theory is significantly more general and complete than is defensive realism. It broadens defensive realism by including variation in states' types and by making more explicit the importance of information that states have about others' motives when they choose their strategy. Defensive realism assumes that the state making a decision is a security seeker, whereas the theory developed here allows for variation in the state's motives, addressing both security seekers and greedy states. And although defensive realism does suggest the importance of information about the adversary's motives, by the significance it places on the signaling of information, it is silent about the importance of the presignaling information that partially defines the state's international environment. As a result, although defensive realism makes prescriptions that match my theory's over much of its range, it yields divergent prescriptions when information or motives play a decisive role. For example, when a state is not militarily secure but believes that its potential adversary is highly likely to be a security seeker, I find greater opportunities for restraint and cooperation than defensive realism does.

My theory can also be understood partly as integrating defensive realism with neoclassical realism, which can be defined by its focus on the decisions of greedy states.[17] Neoclassical realism, however, in contrast to my theory finds that rational security seekers should be able to avoid competition, which leads to its emphasis on the central role of greedy states. My theory provides a more balanced picture of how both the international environment and a state's motives should influence its decisions between cooperative and competitive strategies.

Whether my theory is a realist theory is open to debate, at least over terminology. Letting the motives of the decision-making state vary—that is, including greedy states as well as security seekers—puts the theory clearly beyond the boundaries of structural realism, including defensive realism, but might leave it within the larger realist family. Whether a realist theory can include information about motives as a defining component of a state's international environment is more controversial. Realist theories are frequently described as defining the international environment entirely in terms of material variables. I would emphasize, however, that information about motives emerges as an organic element of the

---

[17] As with defensive realism, neoclassical realism has a rational foundation that has been combined with a variety of unit-level explanations of states' limitations. My discussion here refers only to the rational foundation; chapter 6 provides a fuller discussion.

theory, not simply as an additional variable: the security dilemma is necessary to generate competition between rational security seekers; uncertainty about states' motives is an essential element of the security dilemma; and variation in this information leads to variation in states' preferred strategies. From this perspective, therefore, there is not a logically coherent structural-realist theory that does not include information about states' motives as a key variable. Another common characterization of realism focuses on its findings that the international system is highly competitive and that institutions can play little role in moderating this competition. If realism must have these features, my theory clearly is not a realist theory. However, given its realist lineage and, closely related, the extent to which its analysis begins from many similar premises, one could argue that my theory must be realist. In the end this will be a debate over terminology, not the substance of the analysis of rational international politics that this book provides.

STRUCTURE OF THE BOOK AND SUMMARY OF ADDITIONAL FINDINGS

Chapters 2 and 3 develop the points summarized above at greater length. Chapter 2 describes the type of theory I am building, lays out the theory's key assumptions, and explores its variables in some detail. It locates the theory as the middle layer of a more complete explanatory theory: a preceding layer would explain the inputs to the strategic choice theory; a following layer would explain the types and sources of suboptimality that have led states to deviate from the theory's rational baseline. Although these types of theory are frequently characterized as competitors to the strategic choice theory, I view both these other layers as complementary.

Chapter 3 presents the core of the deductive portion of the theory. It begins by explaining why states should not always cooperate. The chapter next sketches why states should not always compete and compares this argument with the divergent one offered by standard structural-realist arguments (Waltz and what is termed "offensive realism"). The chapter then examines the ways in which a state's choice of strategy can influence its political relationship with an opposing state, exploring both how cooperative policies can serve as costly signals that provide reassurance and generate positive spirals, and how competitive policies can convince a rational state that its adversary is more likely to have greedy motives and generate a negative spiral. The following section looks in some detail at how material and information variables combine to influence the magnitude and nature of the security dilemma and a state's strategy. The chapter ends with a discussion of the importance and decisions of greedy states.

Chapter 4 adds breadth and depth to the theory by exploring a range of simplifications and extensions. The chapter begins by exploring a number of simplifications that were useful for building the core theory but now deserve further attention. The theory has characterized states in terms of their type, either security seeking or greedy (or mixed). However, variation within these types is also possible and important. The first section explores how variation in the value that security seekers place on protecting their territory can influence states' interaction. If the adversary is uncertain about this value, the state will want to communicate its resolve to protect its interests, which can require competitive policies. Competitive policies can serve as a costly signal of resolve because states that place greater value on protecting their interests are willing to invest more in military forces, which is costly because they have to forgo more consumption. This incentive for adopting competitive policies is a defining feature of the deterrence model and an element of the security dilemma, adding to the already complicated balance that a security seeker must make between cooperative and competitive policies. The next section addresses variation within greedy states, including variation in both the extent of a state's greediness and the scope of its aims—whether they are limited or unlimited. Following sections relax other simplifications. The theory has emphasized the importance of uncertainty about information variables but has not addressed the implications of uncertainty about material variables—power and the offense-defense balance. And the theory has characterized the state's material environment in static terms, not tackling the implications of a changing material environment, in which, for example, a state's power is declining. These sections explore the implications of moving beyond these simplifications.

The chapter then addresses two major topics—war and international institutions. The theory has been cast in terms of the broad categories of cooperation and competition, with most of the more specific arguments focused on states' decisions between arming and restraint, ranging from formal arms control to unilateral restraint. This section begins by addressing a different type of outcome—war. It draws on arguments from offense-defense theory and from formal theories of bargaining and war to explore how the probability of war varies with my theory's key variables. In line with basic intuition, war becomes more likely when the state is greedier and when the offense-defense balance favors offense. The impact of power is less clear, with different formal models and assumptions providing different results; probably the most convincing result is that the probability of war increases as the gap increases between a state's power and its share of benefits in the existing status quo.

However, these formal models have not yet captured some key features of the theory developed here, including those that have their roots in neo-realism and security-dilemma theories, and these limitations could undermine their results. Prominent formal models take the value of territory as exogenous; in contrast, my theory understands the value that a security seeker places on territory to be endogenous, reflecting the international situation that it faces. States that are more secure place less value on acquiring additional territory (and, more generally, on weakening their adversary). Once this perspective is built into the argument, there are conditions under which the probability of war should decrease as a state's power increases. These bargaining models have also not adequately included information about motives. Following their basic setup, including uncertainty about the adversary's type produces a somewhat counterintuitive result—higher estimates that the adversary is greedy could result in a lower probability of war because the higher probability leads the state to make larger concessions. However, broadening the perspective of this analysis to more fully capture the key features of my theory draws this result into question. High estimates that the adversary is greedy would influence not only crisis bargaining, but also the value the state places on territory, the military doctrine that it chooses during peacetime, and the military and political interactions that precede a crisis. All of these tend to push in the opposite direction, with the probability of war increasing with estimates that the opposing state is greedy. One broad point that emerges is that the key bargaining models of war have not yet captured many of the central key features of the theory developed here. This is somewhat surprising given that many of these arguments have roots in neorealist and security dilemma theories, which the bargaining models are often considered to reflect.

On institutions, my theory finds that they "matter" but does not establish a central role for them that is comparable to the one identified by neo-institutionalism. The theory understands institutions as primarily endogenous, reflecting states' motives and their international environment, and providing states with a means for achieving their goals. They are first and foremost policy choices to be evaluated. As a result, the theory finds the deep sources of international security cooperation in the states' international environment and their motives, not in the international security institutions that they create.

Chapter 5 evaluates some of the key arguments that challenge my theory's findings. Many of these arguments hold that the theory underestimates the barriers to cooperation because, among other reasons, (1) the possibility of cheating on agreements makes cooperation in the security domain too risky because falling behind can have dire consequences; (2) states' concern about how the relative gains of cooperation are distributed adds significantly to their reluctance to engage in security coopera-tion; (3) a host of problems with the offense-defense variables—including the vagueness of key concepts, the indistinguishability of offense and de-fense, and the difficulty of measuring the balance—undermines their util-ity, thereby eliminating the possibilities they create for cooperation; and (4) states should assume the worst about others' motives, which elimi-nates their incentives to cooperate by signaling benign motives and leads them to focus solely on others' capabilities. This chapter shows that at a minimum each of these critiques suffers important shortcomings, and consequently they do not require modifying the theory's central findings.

Chapter 6 explores how the theory I have developed compares with other leading IR theories that address essentially the same questions in broadly similar ways. These include Waltz's structural realism, offensive realism, defensive realism, neoclassical realism, and neo-institutionalism. The chapter also compares the theory with structural constructivism—al-though different in significant ways, the questions the two theories ad-dress, the arguments they employ, and the answers they offer overlap more than is generally recognized. These comparisons are valuable for better understanding both the theory itself and some of its strengths rela-tive to these other IR theories.

Because I have already commented briefly on most of these theories in the preceding section, here I only summarize my arguments about offen-sive realism and structural constructivism. The theory finds serious prob-lems with offensive realism, which holds that the international system is still more competitive than does Waltz's structural realism. John Mearsheimer argues that states face uncertainty about others' intentions and, given the pressures created by international anarchy, should there-fore assume the worst about them.[18] Given this decision-making crite-rion, he concludes that states should maximize their power as a means of increasing their security. The problem is that states should not, as a gen-eral rule, employ worst-case assumptions—doing so means always forgo-ing the potential benefits of cooperating with a security seeker, including when the state believes the opposing state is likely to be one. In effect, assuming the worst requires the state to ignore a key aspect of the secu-rity dilemma—the costs and risks of arming—while giving undue weight to the benefits of competition.

Alexander Wendt's structural constructivism, although different from my theory in important respects, shares some striking similarities. This is surprising given the supposed gap between constructivism and realism, with my theory having deep roots in the latter. Constructivists describe their theory as ideational, which is a broad category that includes infor-

---

[18] Mearsheimer, *The Tragedy of Great Power Politics*, p. 45.

mation (as well as norms and identities) in contrast to material, which is their characterization of realism. However, the rationalist theory I develop emphasizes that information about motives is an essential component of a strategic choice theory. Consequently, the material versus ideational distinction fails to characterize the difference between these theories. In addition, my theory emphasizes the possibility that interaction can lead states to revise their estimates of each others' motives and thereby reduce insecurity and competition, which parallels key arguments in Wendt. Moreover, in line with one of Wendt's central claims, the theory finds that a wide range of state behaviors is possible under anarchy; in contrast to Waltz, anarchy does not have a single logic. Although narrower in significant ways than Wendt's, my theory has important advantages, including providing a fuller analysis of the combined effect of material and information variables, and an explanation of sustained major-power peace that does not rely on his more demanding assumptions about collective identities and shared interests, but instead requires only states that seek security.

Chapters 7–9 evaluate the theory from three complementary perspectives. Chapter 7 addresses a challenge that flows from the rational/normative character of the theory combined with my skeptical position on whether states consistently act rationally. The standard approach for evaluating an international relations theory (and a social science theory more generally) is to explore how well the historical data support its hypotheses. If, however, a state fails to choose optimal policies, a rationalist theory will not do well at explaining its strategic behavior. International relations research over the past few decades supports the possibility of frequent suboptimal behavior. Thus, we need to be careful not to discard a rational theory too quickly simply because it does not excel at explaining state behavior. The lack of a tight fit between the theory and some state behavior might reflect suboptimal decisions, not flaws in the rational theory. And as discussed above, even if states sometimes act suboptimally, the rational theory remains valuable for a variety of reasons, including providing a rational baseline against which actual behavior can be compared and prescribing strategies for a state that faces a rational adversary. This raises the question of how to evaluate the rational theory.

The chapter adopts an unconventional approach to dealing with this challenge: it explores the theory *from within*. To perform this evaluation, it explores the theory's key components, including its explicit assumptions about how to characterize states and their international environment; its implicit assumptions about states' abilities to understand their international environment, utilize their resources, and analyze their options; and its deductions. If the theory's assumptions are sufficiently accurate, its variables sufficiently complete, and its deductions logically sound, then the theory will effectively identify the trade-offs facing rational states and the strategies they should choose.

This evaluation provides substantial confidence in the quality of the theory. Key assumptions, including that the state faces an anarchic international environment and acts rationally, do not raise serious problems. Anarchy is an accurate description of the international environment. Rationality is central to the theory—because it is designed to analyze the choices states *should* make, the theory needs to assume the state acts rationally.[19] The assumption that the state is a unitary actor is trickier. Although states certainly are not unitary, characterizing a state in terms of a single set of motives and situational preferences is appropriate and productive for answering the key questions the theory is designed to address. For example, when we ask, "What strategy should a state choose?," we are usually concerned about (and envision) an actor that knows what it wants and is simply trying to decide how best to achieve these objectives given the international environment it faces. We are not primarily concerned with the politics of domestic preference formation and bargaining. Moreover, even if we wanted to address these issues, we would first need a theory that understood the relationship between the motives and the strategic-choice preferences of each of the various domestic actors. In other words, the first order of business is to understand how a single unitary actor should act. In comparison, assuming the adversary is a unitary actor is potentially more problematic. In cases in which a state's choice between competitive and cooperative policies can significantly influence the balance of domestic power in an opposing state, and in turn the adversary's reactions, a state should not overlook this possibility. Recognizing this limitation suggests the need for caution in applying the theory to certain types of cases.

The chapter goes on to explore whether modern major powers have the resources required to act as the theory requires: for example, are they capable of measuring power and the offense-defense balance, and assessing an opposing state's motives, sufficiently well to influence their choices? Although states sometimes fail in these efforts, the chapter finds that they nevertheless are often capable of these essential judgments. Overall, while making clear that further evaluation is required, the chapter provides grounds for confidence that the theory can provide valuable insights into the basic international politics questions it is designed to address.

Chapter 8 employs a complementary, more standard approach to eval-

---

[19] The chapter addresses a number of potential complications that concern the stage in the decision-making process at which we assume rationality. For example, there is little question about assuming rationality in the evaluation of military options, but greater leeway concerning states' extraction of resources.

uating the theory. It looks briefly at a number of important cases and shows that my theory both explains them well and performs better than the key alternative theories. Although research on suboptimality provides an important caution, it does not suggest that states usually or always adopt flawed military and foreign policies. When states do act rationally, the theory should do well at explaining their behavior. Thus, we gain further confidence in the theory by exploring these cases of rational behavior. In addition, identifying important cases in which the theory does explain state behavior raises the question of whether the theory performs better at explaining these cases than similar theories that include fewer variables. If this were not the case, the theory's additional complexity might not be warranted—the standard argument is that the simpler theory would be preferable, explaining as much but with greater parsimony. To this end, the chapter extends the brief discussion of the end of the Cold War presented above and presents a comparison of current security politics in Europe and Asia. Both cases explore the central role of information and its interaction with material variables; although defensive realism captures some of what is most important, exploration of these cases demonstrates the advantages of my more general rational theory. The chapter then looks at the case of Hitler's Germany, showing that greedy motives are an essential component of this case and therefore that it cannot be dealt with adequately without including variation in states' motives in the theory.

Chapter 9 applies my theory to the question of whether arms races are dangerous and employs a third approach for evaluating the theory—considering whether states that according to the theory adopted suboptimal arming policies would in fact have done better if they had chosen alternative policies. This long-standing question in security studies is usually framed in terms of whether arms races increase the probability of war and studied by exploring their historical correlation with war. The chapter begins by explaining that the question needs to be reformulated—whether an arms race is dangerous depends not on whether it ends in war, but instead on whether building up arms was the best option available to both states for achieving their goals. The theory provides a rational baseline that enables us to make a distinction between a state's international security environment and its decision to build arms. If a state's international environment necessitates an arms buildup, then arming, as well as the competition that ensues if the adversary responds, is rational and the state's best available policy option. For these types of cases, even if arms races correlate with war, they do not cause it. Instead, the state's international environment causes the arms race and in turn war.

Policies that diverge from this rational baseline are suboptimal, that is, dangerous in the sense just described—the state could have better achieved its goals if it had chosen a different arming policy. The chapter employs the theory to assess many of the past century's key arms races, as well as cases of cooperation. It finds that a number of these arming decisions were suboptimal, including the German decision to build a large battleship fleet in the decades before World War I, the Japanese decision to build up its naval forces in the intrawar period, and the U.S. decision to build multiple independently targeted reentry vehicles (MIRVs) during the late 1960s and early 1970s.

For these divergent cases, the chapter considers the counterfactual possibility that the state would have been better off had it pursued more cooperative policies. In each of these cases the counterfactual analysis shows that cooperation had better prospects than the competitive policies that the state chose for achieving its goals. According to the theory, a state should do less well when it fails to choose the strategy that the theory prescribes. Therefore, the counterfactual finding that states would have been better off adopting cooperative strategies instead of engaging in suboptimal arms races provides additional support for the theory.

Chapter 10 concludes, providing a short summary of the book's central arguments and exploring implications for current U.S. international security policy. It addresses the likely impact of a rising China and how U.S. policy can reduce (or, if misguided, increase) the potential dangers.

CHAPTER TWO

Setting Up the Theory

THE BASIC SETUP of a theory—where it cuts into a question and the variables it includes to answer the question—will have a crucial influence on the theory's insights, prescriptions, and explanations. These choices reflect the features of the world that we decide to focus on and the ones we decide to simplify away. The understandings and intuitions that inform these basic choices may be more important than the results of detailed deductive arguments, which often depend on more specific and limiting assumptions. Therefore, before getting involved in deductive arguments, we need to consider carefully the theory's basic design.

TYPE OF THEORY

This book develops a rational theory—a theory of what states should do to achieve their goals, given the constraints they face; in this sense, it is a prescriptive, normative theory.[1] To assess the policies a state should pursue, the theory adopts a strategic-choice approach in which a state chooses a strategy that is designed to achieve its goals, given the constraints and opportunities it faces. The state understands that other states will respond to its policies and may also make choices in anticipation of its policies, and it takes this interaction into account in making its own choices.[2]

This approach reflects a simple and intuitively reasonable starting point: both a state's basic goals and the international situation it faces should influence the state's choice between cooperative and competitive military strategies. The state's international situation influences what is

[1] "Normative" is often used in a distinctly different way, referring to arguments about appropriate behavior and often related goals; see, for example, Jack Snyder, "'Is' and 'Ought': Evaluating Empirical Aspects of Normative Research," in Colin Elman and Miriam Elman, eds., *Progress in International Relations Theory: Appraising the Field* (Cambridge: MIT Press, 2003). In contrast, the theory developed here does not address what goals a state should have, nor does it address the role of norms in influencing these goals; rather, it takes goals as given.

[2] On this type of theory more generally, see David A. Lake and Robert Powell, "International Relations: A Strategic-Choice Approach," in David A. Lake and Robert Powell, eds., *Strategic Choice and International Relations* (Princeton: Princeton University Press, 1999).

possible, that is, sets the constraints and opportunities the state faces. Therefore, we expect that the same state in different international situations should sometimes choose different strategies because its options, their prospects for success, and their costs will vary across situations. For example, the international environment influences the costs of trying to expand. We expect that if the costs of acquiring territory are sufficiently high, even a state that places great value on the territory should not fight to acquire it; in contrast, if the costs were lower it would be more willing to fight. Similarly, we expect that states with different basic goals should sometimes choose different strategies. For example, whether a state that could win an arms race should choose to compete depends on whether the state's goals require military advantages—a state that wants only to defend the status quo is less likely to find competition to be its best option than is a state that values changing the status quo.

This framing leaves open the question of how to characterize a state and its international environment. Later in this chapter I explain that states should be characterized in terms of their motives, which reflect their fundamental interests and goals. The international environment should be characterized in terms of both material variables and information variables. Material variables determine the state's potential military capabilities. Information variables reflect the state's understanding of its adversary's motives and the state's beliefs about the adversary's understanding of its motives, both of which influence the risks of cooperative and competitive strategies.[3]

The theory takes these components of the analysis—a state's motives and its international environment—as given, that is, as inputs to the theory that are not explained by it. The central question then becomes: given its motives and international environment, can a state best achieve its goals with a cooperative military policy or a competitive one?

The theory combines two traditional levels of analysis—what are commonly termed the unit level and the structural level.[4] Unit-level theories attempt to explain state behavior in terms of variation in a state's motives and goals. They often go a step further by explaining this variation in

---

[3] Although both of these information variables are important, to reduce complexity in the analysis and the text, I tend to focus on and refer only to the first.

[4] These levels are also commonly termed the state and international levels, and the second and third images. On levels of analysis, see Kenneth N. Waltz, *Man, the State and War* (New York: Columbia University Press, 1959); J. David Singer, "The Level-of-Analysis Problem," in James N. Rousenau, ed., *International Politics and Foreign Policy* (New York: Free Press, 1969), pp. 20–29; and Jervis, *Perception and Misperception in International Politics*, chap. 1. Explaining that strategic choice theories integrate across levels of analysis is Arthur A. Stein, "The Limits of Strategic Choice: Constrained Rationality and Incomplete Explanation," in Lake and Powell, eds., *Strategic Choice and International Relations*, pp. 201–202; and Stein, *Why Nations Cooperate: Circumstance and Choice in International Relations* (Ithaca: Cornell University Press, 1990), esp. pp. 175–184.

terms of states' regime types, or the balance of economic or political interests within the state; but the theory developed here does not include this type of within-level explanation. Structural-level theories attempt to explain state behavior in terms of the constraints and opportunities presented by a state's international environment.[5] International relations theories typically describe structure in terms of material variables, with the distribution of power often the variable that determines the type of structure.[6] In contrast, the theory developed here defines the state's international situation in terms of information variables—specifically, what states know about others' motives—as well as material variables. Nevertheless, the basic approach has much in common with these structural theories, with my theory designed to understand how variation in the international situation a state faces should influence its strategy.

These types of theories—structural- and unit-level—are often cast as offering competing explanations. As I have already noted, however, including variables from both levels of analysis makes intuitive and analytic sense. In fact, from the perspective of a strategic choice theory, including both types of variables is not optional. A state's goals influence the benefits of achieving various outcomes;[7] a state's international situation influences both the probability and the risks of achieving these outcomes and can also influence their value. Both are required to analyze a state's broad options.

Prominent strands of structural realism adopt a different approach, privileging structure—specifically the distribution of power—and paying little attention to variation in states' motives. According to these arguments, states motivated by security combined with the pressures created by international anarchy are sufficient to generate the competitive behav-

[5] There is not, however, agreement on what is entailed in a structural theory. Even structural realism, as developed in the seminal work, Waltz, *Theory of International Politics*, has been criticized for not meeting the requirements of a structural theory. See, for example, John Gerald Ruggie, "Continuity and Transformation in the World Polity," *World Politics* 35, 2 (January 1983): 261–285; Richard K. Ashley, "The Poverty of Neorealism," in Robert Keohane, ed., *Neorealism and Its Critics* (New York: Columbia University Press, 1986); and Wendt, *Social Theory of International Politics*, chap. 4. In addition, there is disagreement about the variables that can be included in a structural theory. To avoid becoming entangled in this debate, I instead characterize this part of the theory in less restrictive terms— "international situation" and "international environment."

[6] Waltz, *Theory of International Politics*; and Mearsheimer, *The Tragedy of Great Power Politics*. See also Stephen Van Evera, *Causes of War: Power and the Roots of Conflict* (Ithaca: Cornell University Press, 1999), who includes other aspects of power in what he terms the fine-grained structure of power.

[7] As discussed below, a state's goals do not determine the benefits of outcomes because benefits can depend on the state's international environment, as well as its fundamental motives/goals. For example, a state that values only security will see benefits in taking territory if this increases its security, but not otherwise; and whether taking territory has this effect can depend on the state's international situation.

iors that best characterize international relations. Therefore, continues this argument, an adequate and powerful theory can focus solely on the structure of the international system.[8] To demonstrate this conclusion, however, we first need a theory that allows states' types to vary and then have to show that this variation should not result in variation in their strategy choices.[9] A theory's deductions may show that some variables turn out to play a smaller role than our initial intuition might suggest. Counterintuitive results will then be a key finding of the theory. Achieving this type of result, however, is quite different from leaving out variables that are integral elements of a theoretical perspective, in which case the relative insignificance of the excluded variables is essentially assumed. The following chapter shows deductively that, in fact, neither variation in motives nor in information drops out of the theory. On the contrary, both states' motives and their information about others' motives should under some conditions influence their choice between cooperative and competitive policies.

My theory is a theory of foreign policy—it evaluates a state's choice among the basic options for achieving its international objectives—as well as a theory of international politics. Most generally, states choose between cooperative and competitive strategies; more specifically, yet still broadly defined, states can choose between building up arms, acquiring allies, negotiating arms control agreements, making concessions, and launching wars. International political outcomes are the direct result of these foreign policy choices; consequently, evaluation of state's foreign policy choices underpins a theory of international politics.[10] A sharp distinction between theories of international politics and of foreign policy therefore does not seem possible.[11]

these are not mutually exclusive

---

[8] Waltz, *Theory of International Politics*; and Mearsheimer, *The Tragedy of Great Power Politics*. A parallel error is made by Andrew Moravcsik, "A Liberal Theory of International Politics," *International Organization* 51, 4 (Autumn 1997): 513–553, who privileges states' interests and preferences relative to material and information variables.

[9] Emphasizing this point is Robert Powell, "Game Theory, International Relations Theory, and Hobbesian Stylization," in Ira Katznelson and Helen V. Milner, eds., *Political Science: State of the Discipline* (New York: Norton, 2002), pp. 765–770.

[10] Waltz has argued otherwise; see *Theory of International Politics*, pp. 119–121; and Waltz, "International Politics Is Not Foreign Policy," *Security Studies* 6, 1 (Autumn 1996): 54–57. Emphasizing the position that I present here is James D. Fearon, "Domestic Politics, Foreign Policy, and Theories of International Relations," in Nelson W. Polsby, ed., *Annual Review of Political Science*, vol. 1 (Palo Alto, CA: Annual Reviews, 1998), pp. 292–298; see also Colin Elman, "Horses for Courses: Why Not Neorealist Theories of Foreign Policy?," *Security Studies* 6, 1 (Autumn 1996): 7–53.

[11] This is not to imply that other theories, including those that focus on domestic politics, are not also helpful for understanding states' foreign policies; for example, these theories can help to resolve indeterminacy in the strategic choice theory, incorporate path dependence, and explain suboptimality.

In a couple of key ways, the theory developed in this book is a partial theory. First, as already noted, it takes key independent variables—motives, material variables, and information variables—as given. For example, the theory does not explain what determines whether a state is a greedy state or instead a state that is motivated only by security. Similarly, it does not address the information that a state has about its adversary's motives at the beginning of their interaction. Although sometimes characterized as competing, theories that explain these independent variables complement a strategic choice theory and can be combined with it to provide a more complete theory. For example, liberal theories of the democratic peace include arguments about both the motives of democratic states—they tend to be interested in security but to lack greedy, nonsecurity motives—and the information that democratic states have about others' motives—they believe that opposing democracies are interested only in security.[12] Combining these liberal arguments with the strategic choice theory would produce a theory that explains both the inputs to democratic states' decisions and the strategic interaction that follows given these inputs. More generally, in its full version, a theory that combines these layers of theory would explain the types of states and their international environment, and their interaction that leads to choices of strategy.

Second, the theory is a partial theory when judged from the perspective of a positive, explanatory theory because it assumes that states act rationally, when in fact they may not, instead choosing suboptimal policies. The theory should do well at explaining states' strategies when they do act rationally. If, however, one or more states choose suboptimal policies, the rational theory alone will be unable to explain their policies. In these cases the rational theory provides the foundation for a more complete explanatory theory if it can be combined with theories of suboptimal behavior that explain elements of the state's failure to act rationally. These theories of suboptimality can focus on a state's failure in assessing the material variables and information variables that define its international situation, or on a state's failure to make rational decisions given its assessment of these variables. The combination of defensive realism (which is a rational theory) with theories that explain why states have misevaluated the offense-defense balance provides a prominent example of research that combines these two layers of international relations theory. This work has explored why states often exaggerate the advantage of

---

[12] For a brief overview of the democratic peace debate, see Miriam Fendius Elman, "Introduction: The Need for a Qualitative Test of the Democratic Peace Theory," in Miriam Fendius Elman, ed., *Paths to Peace: Is Democracy the Answer?* (Cambridge: MIT Press, 1997).

the offense and then explained why this leads to increased insecurity, competition, and war.[13]

In short, the strategic choice theory can be envisioned as sitting in the middle of three layers of theory[14]—between those that explain the inputs to the strategic choice theory and those that explain departures from it.[15] Theories in each layer are valuable in their own right. They do not compete against each other but instead are linked logically and are potentially complementary. In combination, they hold the promise of providing a more complete explanatory theory. The strategic choice layer plays an essential role, exploring the outcomes that should be produced by the interaction of states with their international environment.

BASIC ASSUMPTIONS

My theory starts with four basic assumptions. Key strands of IR theory— including neorealism and neo-institutionalism—are built on similar as-

---

[13] This body of research includes studies of biased military organizations, including Jack L. Snyder, *The Ideology of the Offensive: Military Decision Making and the Disasters of 1914* (Ithaca: Cornell University Press, 1984); and Barry R. Posen, *The Sources of Military Doctrine* (Ithaca: Cornell University Press, 1984); and studies of the impact of misperceptions, including Christensen and Snyder, "Chain Gangs and Passed Bucks"; and Van Evera, *Causes of War*. Also in this layer would be studies of flawed decisions that reflect individual cognitive limitations, including Jervis, *Perception and Misperception*; and Deborah Welch Larson, *Anatomy of Mistrust: U.S.–Soviet Relations during the Cold War* (Ithaca: Cornell University Press, 1997); and studies of the domestic structure of states, including Jack Snyder, *Myths of Empire: Domestic Politics and International Ambition* (Ithaca: Cornell University Press, 1991); and Stephen Van Evera, "Why States Believe Foolish Ideas: Non-Self-Evaluation by Government and Society" (1998).

[14] This terminology should not be confused with two other categorizations of theories: (1) the middle layer I am referring to here is not the same as what are typically called mid-level theories; rather, this strategic choice theory fits squarely into what is commonly termed "grand theory"; and (2) this image of layers does not map into the standard levels-of-analysis descriptions; as I noted above, the strategic choice theory combines two of these levels.

[15] We should also note that these layers do not capture the full range of types of theories. For example, the strategic choice theory assumes that states and their environment are separable and that international interaction does not change the type of state. In contrast, second-image reversed theories address how interaction can lead to change; see, for example, Peter A. Gourevich, "The Second Image Reversed: International Sources of Domestic Politics," *International Organization* 32, 4 (Autumn 1978): 881–912; and Robert Powell, "Anarchy in International Relations Theory: The Neorealist-Neoliberal Debate," *International Organization* 48, 2 (Spring 1994): 321–324. Constructivist theories challenge the assumption of separability and address the implications for change; see Alexander Wendt, "The Agent-Structure Problem in International Relations," *International Organization* 43, 3 (Summer 1987): 335–370; Wendt, *Social Theory of International Politics*, chap. 7; and David Dessler, "What's at Stake in the Agent-Structure Debate," *International Organization* 43, 3 (Summer 1989): 441–470.

sumptions; differences between these theories and the one I develop here result primarily from different independent variables and different deductive arguments, not from these basic assumptions.[16] Because the theory is designed as a normative theory, which may not do well at explaining states' actual behavior, the accuracy of these assumptions is more important than if it were a positive theory. I address the question of accuracy and its implications more thoroughly in chapter 7.

First, states live in an international environment characterized by anarchy—the lack of an international institution or authority that can prevent a state from using military force against another state, or that can enforce international laws and agreements.[17] As a result, states must rely on their own resources to achieve their objectives.[18] In Waltz's words, anarchy results in a "self-help system."[19] Anarchy is a key source of what is termed a "commitment problem"—a situation in which states would be better off if they could credibly commit not to pursue an action; because they cannot, the state or its adversary (or both) adopts policies to achieve its interests that are inefficient and result in making the state worse off.[20] We need to keep in mind that anarchy describes the nature of the international environment that states face, not their behavior—as used here, anarchy does not refer to a chaotic international environment or competitive state behavior.

[16] The foundational neo-institutionalist work is Robert O. Keohane, *After Hegemony: Cooperation and Discord in the World Political Economy* (Princeton: Princeton University Press, 1984). Key neorealist works include Waltz, *Theory of International Politics*, and Mearsheimer, *The Tragedy of Great Power Politics*; neither's assumptions are exactly the same as mine, but in key ways they are quite similar. On rationality in Waltz's theory, see Waltz, "Reflections on *Theory of International Politics*: A Response to My Critics," in Robert O. Keohane, ed., *Neorealism and Its Critics* (New York: Columbia University Press, 1986), pp. 330–331; and Miles Kahler, "Rationality in International Relations," *International Organization* 52, 4 (Autumn 1998): 924–925. Powell, "Game Theory, International Relations Theory, and the Hobbesian Stylization," characterizes the approach that underpins this wide range of theories as "Hobbesian stylization."

[17] For a critical assessment of the concept, see Helen Milner, "The Assumption of Anarchy in International Politics," *Review of International Studies* 17, 1 (January 1991): 67–85. Although much of this critique emphasizes the ambiguity of the basic concept, establishing a clear understanding that is well matched to its purpose in the theory does not seem problematic.

[18] This actually requires a further assumption—states are selfish egoists that care about their own goals and interests, but not others; for example, if states were instead altruistic, there would be the possibility that other states would come to the defense of a state that had been attacked, even when their own security and other interests were not in jeopardy.

[19] On the nature and implications of self-help, see Waltz, *Theory of International Politics*, pp. 105–107, 111–112.

[20] James D. Fearon, "Rationalist Explanations for War," *International Organization* 49, 3 (Summer 1995): 379–414; Robert Powell, *In the Shadow of Power: States and Strategies in International Politics* (Princeton: Princeton University Press, 1999); and James D. Morrow, "The Strategic Setting of Choices: Signaling, Commitment, and Negotiation in International Politics," in Lake and Powell, eds., *Strategic Choice and International Relations*.

The assumption that the international environment is anarchic is not problematic—it is an accurate description of the international situation that states, at least major powers, face when addressing their principal security policy choices. There is no international institution that has the resources to come to the defense of a country attacked by a major power.[21]

Second, the theory assumes that states act rationally. Acting rationally means that states are purposive actors that make at least reasonable efforts to choose the strategy that is best suited to achieving their goals. States are assumed to be able to identify and compare options, evaluating the prospects that they will succeed, as well as their costs and benefits. Rationality also imposes some additional requirements. States must hold beliefs and understandings that are well matched to the evidence that is available about their international situation; without holding these beliefs, a state would be unable to choose an optimal strategy.[22] These understandings would concern the state's material situation and the nature of other states in the system. A state's understanding of its material environment should include the available relevant military and technical knowledge about how its resources can be utilized to achieve its goals. The state should also have at least a basic understanding of how other states might interpret its strategy and react to it. For example, a rational state should consider how an adversary would respond to its military buildup, considering both actions that the adversary might take to offset the buildup and inferences the adversary might make about why the state launched the buildup. Rationality further requires that states invest an appropriate amount of effort in collecting and evaluating information that would inform them about their environment.[23]

Assuming that the state making decisions is rational is necessary for a prescriptive, normative theory—in taking the state's motives and goals as inputs and then asking what a state *should* do, we are asking what behavior would be rational or optimal.[24] Although real states may not always act rationally, the questions that the theory is designed to answer require assuming that the state making decisions does.

[21] The claim here is not that all international relations are necessarily characterized by anarchy; see, for example, David A. Lake, "Between Anarchy and Hierarchy: The Importance of Security Institutions," *International Organization* 50, 1 (Winter 1996): 1–33.

[22] These understandings are exogenous to the theory; how states develop and revise these understandings lies outside its boundaries. On the role of causal ideas, see Judith Goldstein and Robert O. Keohane, eds., *Ideas and Foreign Policy: Beliefs, Institutions, and Political Change* (Ithaca: Cornell University Press, 1993).

[23] Jon Elster, *Solomonic Judgements: Studies in the Limits of Rationality* (Cambridge: Cambridge University Press, 1989), pp. 3–7.

[24] On rational choice theory as first and foremost a normative theory, see ibid., p. 3.

It is true, however, that the strategy a state should pursue could depend on whether the *opposing* state is acting rationally. For example, if the adversary misunderstands the international situation it faces and therefore is going to choose the wrong strategy, the best option available to the decision-making state could differ from the rational-versus-rational case. Thus, if in fact states do sometimes choose suboptimal strategies, a prescriptive theory, while assuming that the decision-making state is rational, should not assume that the opposing state always is. Consequently, while my theory analyzes the case in which both states are assumed to be rational—which has held center stage in the neorealist debate and is arguably the combination of greatest interest—a natural extension is to cases in which the state believes its adversary will (or might) adopt suboptimal policies.

Third, the theory assumes that states can be envisioned as unitary actors. Obviously, this is a huge simplification—states are composed of elites with divergent preferences over ends and/or means, populations that may be similarly divided, and domestic institutions that aggregate preferences and implement policies.[25] And it is potentially a problematic simplification: for example, there may not be a satisfactory way of aggregating divergent preferences such that policies guided by the aggregation will satisfy all individuals; and, the policy a state chooses can depend on the specific relationship of domestic actors' preferences and institutional rules.[26] Nevertheless, the unitary-actor assumption is well matched to the central purpose of the theory. When we ask what strategy a state should pursue, we usually want to know about a state that has well-defined goals; this assumption is often implicit but is nevertheless appropriate to the purpose of the analysis. The focus of the inquiry is not about managing divergent domestic policy preferences, but instead analyzing a state's options for achieving its goals. In practice, a leader may be constrained by domestic actors with different interests and beliefs, and by institutions designed to influence the policy process. These constraints might prevent a leader from adopting his preferred strategy, but it is nevertheless important, and arguably the first order of business, to understand what strategy would be best if these domestic constraints did not exist. From this perspective, the unitary-actor assumption is much less

[25] Even when elites agree on international goals, a state's preferred strategy could depend on the composition of its leadership, reflecting leaders' preferences over domestic issues. See, for example, Kevin Narizny, "Both Guns and Butter, or Neither: Class Interests in the Political Economy of Rearmament," *American Political Science Review* 97, 2 (May 2003): 203–220.

[26] Helen V. Milner, *Interests, Institutions, and Information: Domestic Politics and International Relations* (Princeton: Princeton University Press, 1997), chap. 3.

problematic for a normative theory than it is for a positive theory of states' actual policy choices.[27]

Fourth, the theory assumes that states "black box" their adversaries— once a state is involved in strategic interaction, its policy choices are influenced by its adversary's actions but are not influenced by the adversary's domestic structure or the characteristics of its leaders. This is essentially equivalent to assuming that the adversary is a unitary actor. Again, this is a major simplification. This assumption neglects potentially significant strategic implications of features of the adversary, including the impact the state's policy could have on the relative influence of domestic groups that are competing to determine the adversary's strategy and the impact of the adversary's regime type on the information that its actions communicate.[28] The implications for the theory are potentially larger than the assumption that the state is a unitary actor. Whereas assuming a domestically unconstrained decision maker with clear preferences is consistent with the central purpose of the theory, simplifications that might result in overlooking significant interactions between the state's strategy and the adversary's domestic balance of power are potentially more problematic; these issues are explored in chapter 7.

Nevertheless, it is essential to emphasize here that not looking within the adversary's state is not nearly as restrictive as is frequently suggested. First, the black-box assumption does not mean that the theory assumes states lack all knowledge of others' motives. Rather, the theory assumes that preceding their strategic interaction states gather information about their adversary's motives. As discussed above, this initial information is not explained by the theory, but is instead an input that partially defines the state's international environment; other theories attempt to explain how states acquire this information, some of which address unit-level features of the opposing state, including ideology and regime type.[29] It follows from these arguments that if regime type is stable, making the black-box assumption does not result in a loss of information as the states' interaction unfolds. Second, the theory does not assume that a state cannot revise its estimate of the opposing state's motives. In fact, the theory emphasizes the possibility that an opposing state's actions can communi-

[27] This said, even with well-defined preferences and no domestic political constraints, unit-level features that are precluded by the unitary-actor assumption—for example, regime type—could influence a state's preferred strategy. This issue is addressed in chapter 7.

[28] On second-image reversed arguments, see Gourevich, "The Second Image Reversed"; and Jack Snyder, "International Leverage on Soviet Domestic Change," *World Politics* 42, 1 (October 1989): 1–30.

[29] David M. Edelstein, "Choosing Friends and Enemies: Perceptions of Intentions in International Politics" (Ph.D. diss., University of Chicago, 2000), chap. 2; and John W. Owen IV, "Transnational Liberalism and U.S. Primacy," *International Security* 26, 3 (Winter 2001/02): 117–152.

cate valuable information about its motives. Consequently, strategic interaction can lead a state to update its assessment of an opposing state, but only based on the opposing state's actions, not its internal characteristics.

It is important to note here that the theory does not make assumptions about the motives and fundamental goals of states that populate the international system (which I will use to define their type) or about the international environment that they face. These features are treated as variables and discussed in the following section. The result is a theory that is consistent with the broad perspective of structural realism (and neo-institutionalism) but at the same time more general, addressing the implications of variation in states' motives, states' information about other states' motives, and material variables in addition to power.

INDEPENDENT VARIABLES

To analyze a rational state's choice between cooperative and competitive military policies we need to compare the expected costs and benefits of available strategies. The theory needs to identify the variables that influence the strategies that are available to a state, the prospects that a strategy will succeed, and the costs and benefits of the potential outcomes.

What a state wants and the value it places on achieving this outcome can depend on both its motives and its international situation. I define a state's type in terms of inherent features—motives and fundamental interests—that are separate from the international situation it faces. As explained below, I define different types of states in terms of security-seeking and greedy motives. However, the value that a state places on outcomes can depend on the international situation it faces, as well as its motives; as a result, outcomes must be evaluated in specific international situations. Probably most important, a security seeker may, as a consequence of the international situation it faces, have the objective of territorial expansion.

The strategies that are available to a state and their prospects for success depend on the opportunities and constraints created by the state's international environment. To identify the variables that determine the impact of the international environment, we need first to understand the potential means (strategies) available to the state for achieving its objectives. This understanding is unavoidably part of the theory and necessarily precedes the identification of the variables that define the state's environment. These understandings reflect our insights into the nature of interaction between states; they are taken as given by the theory, not developed by it. As noted above, a rational state will possess these understandings of how the world works.

Described broadly, a state can attempt to achieve its objectives in two ways. First, and most obvious, the state can acquire military capabilities to achieve its objectives. Depending on the type of state and its international situation, these military capabilities could include the ability to deter attacks, to coerce concessions, to defend territory and to take territory.[30] Second, a state can attempt to achieve its objectives by influencing its adversary's objectives, bringing them in line with the state's own objectives. Most important, an adversary that is motivated by security can have competitive military objectives and expansionist territorial objectives that result from its insecurity and that thereby increase the state's own insecurity. In this case, the state may be able to increase its own security by increasing its adversary's security.[31]

Given these ways in which a state can achieve its objectives, what variables capture the relevant features of the international environment? The state's ability to acquire military capabilities depends on two material variables: power—the ratio of the state's resources to its adversary's resources; and the offense-defense balance—the ratio of the investment cost of the military forces required for offensive and defensive missions. The state's ability to increase its adversary's security depends on both material and information variables. Offense-defense distinguishability— the degree to which military forces that contribute to offensive missions also contribute to defensive missions—determines the extent to which the state can deploy defensive capabilities without threatening the adversary's ability to defend itself. The offense-defense balance affects the state's willingness to engage in cooperative military policies by influencing the risks if its adversary fails to reciprocate cooperation. In addition, the state's estimate of the adversary's motives will influence its choice of strategy—the more likely the adversary is a security-seeking state, the more willing the state should be to exercise restraint and run risks to increase the adversary's security. Furthermore, the state's estimate of the adversary's estimate of the state's own type should influence the state's

[30] Robert J. Art, "To What Ends Military Power?," *International Security* 4, 4 (Spring 1980): 3–35; Glenn H. Snyder, *Deterrence and Defense: Toward a Theory of National Security* (Princeton: Princeton University Press, 1961); Thomas C. Schelling, *Arms and Influence* (New Haven: Yale University Press, 1966).

[31] A third possibility arises when facing a greedy state that has limited expansionist aims; in this case, concessions might satisfy the greedy state, thereby reducing the probability of a war that would result in greater losses of territory or other costs. Strategies that take advantage of this possibility are labeled appeasement; although appeasement is commonly viewed as a flawed strategy, in fact it can be a state's best option; see Robert Powell, "Uncertainty, Shifting Power, and Appeasement," *American Political Science Review* 90, 4 (December 1996): 749–764. This type of concession could also be a state's best option when facing a security seeker that has limited territorial aims; this case fits under the broad description in the text. For more on the implications of limited vs. unlimited objectives, see chapter 4.

choice of strategy: if the adversary believes the state is motivated by greed, the adversary will be more inclined toward competition, which makes restraint less attractive because the adversary is less likely to reciprocate.

In short, the independent variables that flow from this view of states and their interactions are: a state's motives; three material variables— power, the offense-defense balance, and offense-defense differentiability; and two information variables—the state's estimate of the adversary's motives, and the state's estimate of the adversary's estimate of the state's motives. This is a substantial number of variables,[32] many more than included in ultraparsimonious strands of structural realism, which focus only on power. However, a quite basic understanding of states' decisions suggests that each of these variables should influence their choices. The following chapter explores how a state's choice of strategy should depend on these variables, including their combined impact. It is possible that certain variables may dominate the influence of others, at least over part of their empirical domain. But as mentioned above, this should be a deductive finding, not an incoming assumption. The remainder of this section explores these variables more thoroughly.

Motives

The theory defines types of states in terms of two different types of motives—security and greed.[33] I will refer to states that are motivated only by security as "security seekers." Security measures the state's prospects for preserving control of its territory, avoiding war to protect its territory, and suffering low costs in fighting if war occurs.[34] All else being equal, a state is more secure when it possesses the military capabilities required to protect its territory from attack. These capabilities could include those required to deter attack, thereby making war less likely. They could also include those required to directly protect the state—by defeating an invasion and/or protecting against attacks that would damage the state, thereby leaving it susceptible to coercion—which make war less costly. A

---

[32] Nevertheless, the theory includes many significant simplifications; I note some of them below and address them in chapters 4 and 7.

[33] Discussions of this type of distinction include Arnold Wolfers, *Discord and Colloboration: Essays on International Politics* (Baltimore: Johns Hopkins University Press, 1962), pp. 81–102; Jervis, *Perception and Misperception*, pp. 48–54 and chap. 3; and Randall L. Schweller, "Neorealism's Status-Quo Bias: What Security Dilemma?," *Security Studies* 5, 3 (Spring 1996): 92–108.

[34] A broader definition of security would include the state's ability to protect its prosperity and way of life more generally, and therefore could require not only the ability to protect territory, but also the ability to prevent coercion and competition that would transform the state or undermine its prosperity.

state's security is not, however, determined entirely by its military capabilities. A state that does not face any states interested in attacking it (assuming it knows this) would be very secure, even if it lacked the military capabilities required to defend and deter. It is the combination of these factors—the state's capability to deter and defend, and the opposing states' interest in challenging and attacking the state—that determine the state's security.

Although security is a benign motive, a state seeking security could find territorial expansion to be desirable and therefore be willing to engage in an arms race and start a war to change the status quo.[35] Expansion could increase a state's security in a variety of ways, including increasing its resources and resource autonomy;[36] decreasing its adversary's resources and in extreme cases eliminating its adversary as a sovereign state; and improving its ability to employ its resources effectively by, for example, providing a buffer zone against invasion, strategic depth, or more defensible borders. Similarly, even if it did not desire additional territory, a security seeker might start a war to weaken its adversary, thereby increasing its own security.

A state can also have nonsecurity motives for expansion, which can include the desire to increase its wealth, territory, or prestige, and to spread its political ideology or religion, when these are not required to preserve the state's security. I use the term "greed" to refer to these nonsecurity motives.

States can have both types of motives—security and greed. Consequently, this framework identifies four different types of states—pure security seekers, greedy security seekers, greedy non–security seekers, and nongreedy non–security seekers. I use "security seeker" to refer to a pure security seeker, that is, a state that is motivated only by security.[37] In con-

[35] Along these lines, Wolfers, *Discord and Colloboration*, p. 92, argues, "To preserve possessions does not mean merely to defend them when they are actually under attack. *Status quo* powers regularly demand that the threat of such an attack be reduced at least to the point of giving them a reasonable sense of security. Thus the quest for security—the preservation goal par excellence—points beyond mere maintenance and defense. It can become so ambitious as to transform itself into a goal of unlimited self-extension."

[36] Whether acquiring more territory increases a state's wealth/resources depends on the cumulativity of resources. See Van Evera, *Causes of War*, chap. 5; Peter Liberman, *Does Conquest Pay?: The Exploitation of Occupied Industrial Societies* (Princeton: Princeton University Press, 1996); and Stephen G. Brooks, *Producing Security: Multinational Corporations, Globalization, and the Changing Calculus of Conflict* (Princeton: Princeton University Press, 2005).

[37] However, an actual state may not have to entirely lack greedy motives to be productively categorized as a security seeker; if it values security much more than expansion for nonsecurity reasons and places a low value on the latter, then categorizing a state as a pure security seeker can be a productive approximation for evaluating its choices between cooperative and competitive strategies.

| | | Greedy | |
		Yes	No
Security- seeking	Yes	Greedy	Security seeker
	No	Purely greedy	Unmotivated

Figure 2.1. Types of States

trast, to simplify the terminology I use "greedy state" to refer to a state that is motivated by both greed and security; that is, "greedy state" actually refers to a state with mixed motives, a security-seeking greedy state. When referring to a greedy state that is not motivated by security I use "purely greedy state."

We do have theoretical reasons for expecting that most states are motivated by at least security:[38] security is required to enable a state to pursue any other motives and goals over the long term, including domestic goals such as prosperity.[39] In contrast, we expect greater variation in whether states are greedy (and as I discuss in chapter 4, in how greedy they are)—there does not appear to be a general reason to expect states to place value on nonsecurity expansion. In the end, the relative frequency of types is an empirical question. Robert Jervis has identified states that could fit into the non–security-seeking categories—Hitler's Germany as not valuing security while placing great value on greedy expansion, and France in the 1930s as valuing neither its security nor nonsecurity expansion—but notes that these cases are likely to be exceptions.[40] Because they appear likely to be most common and therefore most important, the theory focuses on states that are motivated by security, including states that are motivated by both security and greed, but addresses the non–security-seeking types as well.

I focus on motives (as opposed to policy objectives and intentions) because *why* a state wants to expand matters. The value that a security

[38] This is not to imply that these security-seeking states are always insecure. A security seeker can be secure either because material conditions provide confidence that it can protect itself against attack or because information conditions provide confidence that the adversary has no interest in attacking.

[39] See, for example, Waltz, *Theory of International Politics*, pp. 91–91, who argues, "Survival is a prerequisite to achieving any goals that states may have, other than the goal of promoting their own disappearance as political entities. The survival assumption is taken as the ground of action in a world where the security of states is not assured." This does not mean, however, that states will continue to invest in security until they have achieved as much security as possible, because they also value consumption.

[40] Jervis, *Perception and Misperception*, pp. 50–51.

seeker places on expansion varies with the international environment it faces. The more insecure the state is, the larger the potential benefits and therefore the larger the costs—in arming and fighting—that it will be willing to pay to expand. A security seeker that is very secure will see little or no value in expansion; in this situation, the security seeker would accept the status quo, even if the costs of changing it were quite small. Consequently, changes in the international environment, some of which its adversary may be able to influence, can affect the benefits the state sees in expansion. Specifically, a state that wants to expand to increase its security could be induced to forgo policies necessary for expansion if its adversary pursues policies that increase its security. In contrast to security seekers, a greedy state is willing to run risks and incur costs to expand, even if it is entirely secure.[41] A purely greedy state would not respond positively to strategies designed to increase its security.

From the perspective of the strategic choice theory, the distinction between motives and intentions is important and deserves to be emphasized. Much work in international relations, however, conflates the two and creates confusion as a result. Motives are primitive, that is, they are inherent features of states. In contrast, intentions—what a state intends to do—result from the interaction of a state with its international environment. Motives are useful for distinguishing types of states; intentions are far less useful. This is because different types of states can in certain situations choose the same behaviors; that is, they may have the same intentions. Nevertheless, the type of state is key because it is its motives that influence how a state reacts to another state's strategy.

The problem is evident in commonly used terminology. The states that I refer to as security seekers are often instead referred to as "status quo." The confusion arises because used this way a status quo state may in fact be unwilling to accept the status quo—it is satisfied with existing international borders and thus uninterested in expansion, *except* if necessary to protect its security in the status quo. As a result, a status quo power may be willing to launch wars, and a state facing a status quo state may therefore need to deter it. If instead status quo refers to intentions and therefore a state that is willing to accept the status quo, security seekers will often not qualify. For example, Mearsheimer holds that there are no status quo powers in the international system. His argument is clear—although survival is the primary goal of great powers, the international system leads states to have revisionist intentions—but nevertheless risks

---

[41] Much of this discussion can be recast in terms of the level at which we define a state's preferences, including the distinction between intrinsic and situational preferences. For discussion of related issues see Jeffrey Frieden, "Actors and Preferences in International Relations," in Lake and Powell, eds., *Strategic Choice and International Relations*.

Intentions

		Status Quo	Revisionist
Motives	Security	Secure or deterred	Insecure and not deterred
	Greed	Deterred	Not deterred

Figure 2.2. Explanations for Intentions

confusion if readers take "no status quo powers" to be a statement about states' types.[42]

For similar reasons "greedy" is a more accurate description of states that are frequently categorized as "revisionist" and "aggressive." A greedy state could be deterred from pursuing the territory that it desires and therefore act like a status quo power, not a revisionist one. And a security-seeking type could choose revisionist, aggressive policies, albeit for quite different reasons than a greedy state that decides to try to revise the status quo. Figure 2.2 captures these basic points.

While the categories of greedy and security seeking effectively distinguish key types of states, variation within these categories is also possible and potentially important. Security seekers could vary in the value they place on security, that is, the value they place on protecting what they already possess. This variation will translate into differences in the states' resolve to protect their interests. Similarly, although I have characterized greed as a dichotomous variable, there could be a spectrum running from not greedy to extremely greedy states. Where a state lies on this continuum could influence its choice of strategy because greedier states are willing to pay higher costs to achieve their objectives.[43] To keep the core of the theory relatively simple, I assume for the time being that states' motives can be treated as dichotomous variables. However, while the core of the theory is sufficient to capture much of what is most important about international politics, relying on these simplifying assumptions does risk overlooking issues that deserve attention. Maybe most significant among these is the requirement, in a world of incomplete information, for states

---

[42] Mearsheimer, *The Tragedy of Great Power Politics*, pp. 2, 29, 31; he does, however, sometimes appear to conflate inherent motives and strategy choices; see, for example, p. 18, and p. 31, n. 7.

[43] Furthermore, defining a state's greed with a single variable could be problematic. For example, consider a case in which a state places great value on acquisition of specific limited territory but little value on other territory; how would the extent of this state's greed compare to a state that places moderate value on much more territory?

to choose strategies that communicate their resolve to protect their interests. In this chapter and the following one, I flag places where the assumptions I am using could lead us to overlook issues that deserve further analysis. I then begin chapter 4 by exploring the implications of richer assumptions about security-seeking and greedy motives.

Finally, for the sake of clarity, a couple of common misconceptions about the term security seeker deserve to be addressed.[44] First, the categorization of states refers to their international motives, not their domestic motives and goals. A pure security seeker could value prosperity and consumption, as well as security, and therefore see a trade-off between investing in military forces that would increase its security and instead consuming the resources required to acquire these forces. Consequently, models that include a trade-off between security and consumption are consistent with this categorization. In fact, an alternative but complementary formulation identifies consumption as the end that states value and understands security as a derivative objective that is valued only because it is necessary to ensure consumption.[45]

Second, by focusing on security and greed, the theory does not intend to imply that states do not actually have other types of international motives and goals, including possibly humanitarian interests in other states. The theory is designed to address states' key strategic choices for dealing with potential adversaries and therefore does not address these other motives. While this limits the theory's reach, state behavior that lies outside its boundaries does not undermine the core of the theory. For example, the claim that states' interests in humanitarian intervention undermine realism reflects a misunderstanding of this point. However, if a state values security far more than these other goals, the theory does predict that as a state's security increases it will have greater leeway to pursue humanitarian and other nonsecurity objectives.[46]

Material Variables

A state's ability to achieve its objectives—whether driven by security or greed—depends on its military capabilities, specifically its ability to perform military missions. Protecting territory depends on the state's ability

[44] On ambiguities in the closely related term "survival," which I do not address here, see Powell, "Game Theory, International Relations Theory, and Hobbesian Stylization," pp. 773–777.

[45] See, for example, the guns vs. butter model in Powell, *In the Shadow of Power*, chap. 2. However, this does mean that states that have different values for security relative to consumption could have different optimal strategies; this potential variation is not captured by the theory developed here.

[46] Charles L. Glaser, "Structural Realism in a More Complex World," *Review of International Studies* 29 (2003): 412–413.

to deter attacks and to defend if deterrence fails.[47] Taking territory requires the state to be able to coerce other states into making territorial concessions or to attack, conquer, and control territory if coercion fails. Increasing an adversary's security requires a state to reduce its ability to coerce and attack, or to convince its adversary that its own motives are benign; the state's willingness to pursue these policies depends on its ability to protect its territory without possessing the ability to conquer others' territory.

I use the term "military capabilities" to refer to the ability to perform military missions. Some authors use "military capabilities" to refer to military forces, that is, as a measure of the forces a country has deployed, not as a measure of the ability of these forces to perform missions against an adversary's forces.[48] The distinction is important because a state's ability to perform military missions is not determined by the size, type, and quality of its own forces or resources, but instead by how these forces compare with and would fight against the adversary's forces.[49] Given this terminology, an arms race can result in a reduction in a state's military capability, even though it increases the size or quality of its military forces. This section explains that a state's prospects for acquiring different types of military capabilities depends on its power and two offense-defense variables—the offense-defense balance and offense-defense distinguishability.

POWER

A state's power—the ratio of the state's resources that can be converted into military assets to the adversary's resources—plays a central role in determining its ability to acquire military capabilities.[50] As used here, power is an inherently relational concept—it is measured relative to other states—not a "property concept," that is, one that is inherent to a single

[47] On the distinction between deterrence and defense, see Snyder, *Deterrence and Defense*; for seminal works on deterrence and compellence, see Thomas C. Schelling, *The Strategy of Conflict* (Cambridge: Harvard University Press, 1960) and Schelling, *Arms and Influence*. On the current status of research on compellence, see Robert Art, "Introduction" and "Coercive Diplomacy: What Do We Know?" in Robert Art and Patrick M. Cronin, eds., *The United States and Coercive Diplomacy* (Washington, DC: United States Institute of Peace Press, 2003).

[48] See, for example, Waltz, who explains that "capabilities are attributes of units [states]" and includes "military strength" among the components of overall capability; Waltz, *Theory of International Politics*, pp. 98, 113.

[49] On the advantages of this use of "capability," see Glenn H. Snyder, "Process Variables in Neorealist Theory," *Security Studies* 5, 3 (Spring 1996): 180–183.

[50] On defining and measuring power, see Mearsheimer, *The Tragedy of Great Power Politics*, chap. 3; William Curti Wohlforth, *The Elusive Balance: Power and Perceptions during the Cold War* (Ithaca: Cornell University Press, 1993); and Klaus Knorr, *The War Potential of Nations* (Princeton: Princeton University Press, 1956).

state.[51] The factors that contribute to a state's overall resources include its wealth, population, and level of technological development.[52] Overall resources in turn influence the potential size and sophistication of a state's military forces. A state's power determines how its potential military compares to the military that an adversary could build. The more powerful a state, the larger and/or more sophisticated its military can be relative to its adversary's military. Although power is sometimes used as a measure of a state's ability to influence other states, I am using power more narrowly here. Power—relative resources—may affect a state's ability to influence, but this would be a finding of the strategic choice theory, not a direct property of power itself.

Power indicates the *potential* relative size and quality of states' military forces, not the actual forces that states have deployed. I am using power to refer to what is sometimes termed "latent power"; in contrast, a state's military forces are sometimes termed "military power."[53] Which type of power is appropriate to focus on depends on the questions being addressed. My theory is designed to assess the military policies a state should pursue during peacetime, including how large its military should be and whether it should engage in competitive, arms-racing policies or instead cooperative, arms-controlling policies to meet its military requirements. Power is an element of the international situation that the state faces in making these choices. The theory understands power as a constraint or, closely related, as an input to the state's choice.[54] If power were instead to refer to the military forces the state had deployed, power would be an outcome of the state's policy choices, which is what the theory is designed to explain, and not an element of the situation the state faces. If instead I were focusing on questions of crisis bargaining and war, focusing on military power would be more appropriate, especially if states anticipate that war would be short and fought primarily with the forces they had already deployed. Theories that use power to refer to deployed military forces, instead of potential, and then address the probability of war are in certain ways closer to theories of deterrence than to theories that emphasize the impact of a state's fundamental international situation.[55] In chapter 4, I discuss the relationship of my theory to theories

[51] On this distinction, see David A. Baldwin, *Economic Statecraft* (Princeton: Princeton University Press, 1985), pp. 18–24.

[52] The resources that a state has available to it would also depend on its ability to extract resources from its society. Although states can vary in this ability, the theory views this as unit-level variation and therefore assumes that states have equal extraction capabilities. For more on extraction, see chapter 7.

[53] Mearsheimer, *The Tragedy of Great Power Politics*, pp. 55–56.

[54] Another way of putting this is that power is an independent variable, while military forces are a dependent variable.

[55] In terms of explanatory ability, we expect that this type of theory will be more success-

about war and explain the relationship of states' peacetime arming choices to their crisis interactions.

OFFENSE-DEFENSE VARIABLES

Although standard structural-realist arguments are cast entirely in terms of power, this formulation is problematic because power does not translate directly into a state's ability to perform relevant military missions. Power matters, but it only begins to define the material dimension of a state's international situation.[56] For example, under certain conditions, two equally powerful states might have good prospects for defending against each other, while under other conditions their prospects might be poor. Compare two states that share a border to two states that are separated by a large ocean—all else being equal, the states in the second pair are better able to defend against each other because distance and water make attack more difficult. Similarly, compare two states that have nuclear weapons to two nonnuclear states—nuclear weapons enhance deterrence, thereby moderating competition and reducing the probability of war between the nuclear states.

To shift from a theory cast in terms of power to one cast in terms of military mission capabilities we need to include a variable that reflects how effectively a state can convert its power into different types of military capabilities. The offense-defense balance—defined as the ratio of the cost of the offensive forces the attacker requires to take territory to the cost of forces the defender has deployed—is the necessary variable.[57] Defense enjoys a larger advantage when the investment in offense that is required to defeat the defense is larger. The offense-defense balance depends on a variety of factors, including the nature of military technology and geography, which are not included in power but could significantly influence a state's ability to defend.

A state's power multiplied by the offense-defense balance indicates the defender's prospects for successful defense. All else being equal, the larger

---

ful because it takes key variables as exogenous that the more structural theory attempts to explain.

[56] Other critiques of Waltz have identified additional factors that should be included in characterizing a state's international environment; on interaction capacity, see Barry Buzan, Charles Jones, and Richard Little, *The Logic of Anarchy: Neorealism to Structural Realism* (New York: Columbia University Press, 1993); and Ruggie, "Continuity and Transformation in the World Polity."

[57] On this definition of the offense-defense balance, Charles L. Glaser and Chaim Kaufmann, "What Is the Offense-Defense Balance and Can We Measure It?" *International Security* 22, 4 (Spring 1998): 44–82; see also Jervis, "Cooperation under the Security Dilemma"; Van Evera, *Causes of War*, chap. 6; and Powell, *In the Shadow of Power*, pp. 49–51. There is an extensive debate over the definition and significance of the offense-defense balance; these issues are addressed in chapter 5.

this product, the greater the defender's prospects for success. Put slightly differently, the offense-defense balance determines the power (ratio of resources) that a state requires to maintain the military capabilities that are required for defense and deterrence. As the advantage of defense increases, the defender requires less power. As a result, the offense-defense balance can sometimes overcome disparities in states' resources. When defense has a large advantage, even a state that is much weaker than its adversary may still be able to afford effective defense. Conversely, power imbalances can sometimes overwhelm the offense-defense balance. Even if defense has a large advantage, a much wealthier attacker might still be able to outspend a defender by a sufficient margin to gain an effective offensive capability.

The offense-defense balance therefore provides a general way to understand the specific impact of nuclear weapons. Nuclear weapons create a large advantage for deterrence, which in this context is the functional equivalent of defense.[58] By shifting the offense-defense balance heavily toward defense, nuclear weapons enable states that are much less powerful than their adversaries to satisfy their defense requirements and increase their security.

The above claim that power and the offense-defense balance combine to determine a state's potential military capability includes simplifications that are important to note. A state's military potential also depends on its military skill and the will of its soldiers to fight.[59] Military skill refers to a state's ability to effectively employ military technology, including designing military strategy and assessing an adversary's forces and strategy. To maintain a focus on the constraints imposed by a state's international situation, and to simplify by overlooking variation in states' unit-level institutional capabilities, my theory does not include these variables, assuming instead that states are roughly equal along these dimensions. States are assumed to have high levels of military skill; within reasonable limits of analysis, states make the best possible decisions about military

---

[58] Jervis, "Cooperation under the Security Dilemma," pp. 198–199; on how different views of the requirements of nuclear deterrence influence assessments of the offense-defense balance, see Charles L. Glaser, *Analyzing Strategic Nuclear Policy* (Princeton: Princeton University Press, 1990), pp. 94–99.

[59] A variety of literatures bear on military skill, including work on military tactics and doctrine, of which the most important is Stephen Biddle, *Military Power: Explaining Victory and Defeat in Modern Battle* (Princeton: Princeton University Press, 2004); on states' evaluative capabilities, such as Van Evera, "Why States Believe Foolish Ideas"; on organization theory, for example, Snyder, *The Ideology of the Offensive*; and Posen, *The Sources of Military Doctrine*; and, on culture, including Elizabeth Keir, *Imagining War: French and British Military Doctrines between the Wars* (Princeton: Princeton University Press, 1997); and Stephen P. Rosen, "Military Effectiveness: Why Society Matters," *International Security* 19, 4 (Spring 1995): 5–31. On will, see Jasen J. Castillo, "The Will to Fight: Explaining an Army's Staying Power" (Ph.D. diss., University of Chicago, June 2003).

strategy. Thus, the offense-defense balance is the cost ratio of the attacker's best available offense to the defender's best available defense.[60] This optimality assumption is a natural extension of the theory's broad rationality assumption to the specific area of military policy choices.[61]

A second offense-defense variable that the theory needs to include is offense-defense distinguishability. Including offense-defense distinguishability enables the theory to address whether states have the option of converting their power into different types of military capability, specifically offensive or defensive mission capability. When offense and defense are completely distinguishable, the forces that support offensive missions do not support defensive missions, and vice versa; when offense and defense are entirely indistinguishable, the forces that support offensive missions can be used as effectively in defensive missions, and vice versa. Varying degrees of distinguishability lie between these extremes.[62] The extent of offense-defense distinguishability is important for answering a set of questions about whether a state can avoid having offensive mission capabilities while maintaining defensive ones. As discussed in chapter 3, distinguishability influences the risks a state must run to avoid threatening its adversary and to signal its motives, and the possibility of qualitative arms control, all of which influence the severity of the security dilemma.

Two basic points about this formulation of material variables should be emphasized. First, the basic analytic perspective that underpins purely power-oriented theories (for example, structural realism) is not altered by adding offense-defense variables to shift from a focus on power to a focus on military capabilities. Indeed, capturing the central logic of structural realism requires that we assess how much and what type of military capability a state can produce with its power, because security seekers should evaluate their international situation and policy options in terms of military capabilities, specifically the capability to defend. Bringing in offense-defense variables is not optional but necessary.

Second, because including these offense-defense variables significantly increases the theory's ability to capture variation in a state's material environment, the theory is much better equipped to determine whether a

[60] See Glaser and Kaufmann, "What Is the Offense-Defense Balance," pp. 55–56; and Charles L. Glaser and Chaim Kaufmann, "Correspondence: Taking Offense at Offense-Defense Theory," *International Security* 23, 3 (Winter 1998/99): 200–202.

[61] This is not to deny, however, that states may face different constraints because they have different levels of skill that cannot be changed within the time frame that is relevant to their choice of strategy.

[62] Critics of offense-defense theory have argued that the difficulty of distinguishing weapons makes the balance impossible to measure and the theory's guidance impossible to implement. However, this line of criticism suffers significant flaws; see Glaser and Kaufmann, "Correspondence," pp. 79–80; and Glaser, "The Security Dilemma Revisited," pp. 198–199.

state should pursue cooperative or competitive policies. As the following chapter demonstrates, holding polarity and the distribution of power constant, variation in offense-defense variables can determine whether a state should engage in competitive arms-racing policies or instead cooperative arms-control policies. The results diverge significantly from the standard structural-realist formulation, which distorts the policies that flow from its assumptions by focusing exclusively on power.

Information about the Adversary's Motives

The basic purposes of a state's military policy should depend on its adversary's motives. We can appreciate this by considering the role of the state's own motives in influencing its policy choices. As sketched above, there are conditions under which two states facing the same international situation should choose different strategies and make different decisions because they have different motives. A state should expect that its adversary's policy could vary for the same reason. Consequently, for example, a state could require greater military capabilities if facing a greedy state than if facing a security seeker because its adversary might then be harder to deter; similarly, a state should be more inclined to make concessions to a security seeker than to a greedy state because increasing its adversary's security is then more important.

A state, however, may not know what type of adversary it faces; instead, states are likely to face uncertainty about opposing states' motives.[63] Variation in this uncertainty—that is, in its information about others' motives—could be quite substantial; near one end of the spectrum, the state believes that the probability that it is facing a greedy adversary is high, while near the other end the probability is low.[64] Intuitively we anticipate that where the state believes its adversary lies on this continuum could, and depending on the values taken by the other independent variables should, have quite significant implications for its strategy. Therefore, the theory does not simply assume that a state faces uncertainty about the other's motives, treating it as a constant condition facing states, much like anarchy. Instead, the theory includes a state's information about its adversary's motives as a key variable.

[63] As discussed briefly below, a variety of factors contribute to this uncertainty.

[64] I use "information" and "beliefs" interchangeably. This creates two potential objections that I note briefly. First, a state's information reflects extensive interpretation; it is not purely objective. Some analysts prefer to reserve information for uninterpreted data. Second, a concern from the opposite direction is that states often suffer misperceptions, so their beliefs are not necessarily closely related to the information (raw data) available to them. As a rational theory, my analysis assumes that states do not misperceive, so information and beliefs do not diverge. My use of "information" is quite similar to the recent use of the degree of "trust" in Kydd, *Trust and Mistrust in International Relations*.

One way to appreciate the central role of incomplete information (uncertainty) is to recognize that uncertainty about motives is necessary to generate competition between security seekers. Without uncertainty, a security seeker facing another security seeker would not need to invest in military forces to achieve security because it would know that the opposing state had no desire or need to attack it. Any forces that were deployed would not generate insecurity—which, as discussed in the following chapter, would essentially eliminate the security dilemma[65]—and cooperation and peace would easily prevail.[66] Once the central role of uncertainty is made explicit, including variation in this uncertainty is the natural next step. It appears to be an essential component of a state's international environment that needs to be captured and fits naturally in a strategic choice theory.

Closely related, a state's information about the adversary's beliefs about the state's own motives should also influence its choice of strategy. Mirroring the logic outlined above, the adversary's decision about whether to reciprocate cooperation would depend on this belief. For example, when the adversary believes that the state is likely to be greedy, the adversary is less likely to cooperate because it expects that the state will be less likely to continue cooperating. As a result, in this case, even if the state believes its adversary is likely to be a security seeker, the state's understanding of its adversary's information should make it more inclined to compete.

The theory developed here diverges from the family of structural-realist theories, including defensive realism, which defines variation in the international environment entirely in terms of material variables. Although not emphasized by Waltz, uncertainty about other states' motives must lie at the core of structural realism—which emphasizes the ability of the international environment to generate competition between security seekers; without it, security seekers would always cooperate. Defensive realism does suggest the importance of differences in information about the adversary's motives. For example, exercising restraint to signal one's own benign motives is a potentially valuable strategy only because the adversary's improved knowledge of the state's benign motives would positively influence its choice between cooperative and competitive strategies. But defensive realism does not identify the information that the state has at

---

[65] Glaser, "The Security Dilemma Revisited"; and Andrew Kydd, "Game Theory and the Spiral Model," *World Politics* 49, 3 (April 1997): 371–400.

[66] As I explain in the following paragraph, this would actually require that all states were also certain about what others knew, since otherwise states could still have incentives to attack. It would also require confidence that others' motives would not change. On the impact of future intentions, see Dale C. Copeland, *The Origins of Major War* (Ithaca: Cornell University Press, 2000).

the time of its decision as a key variable. In the more complete theory developed here, both material and information variables combine to define the state's international situation and establish the constraints that the state faces. As we will see in some detail in the following chapter, variation in a state's information about its adversary's motives can be decisive in determining its preferred strategy.

I should note here that the state's strategy could depend on yet another information variable—the state's information about the adversary's information about the state's resolve. I have not included this information variable here because, as discussed above, the core of the theory does not include variation between security seekers. Chapter 4 addresses this type of information and its implications for communicating resolve, competitive strategies, and the deterrence model.

ENDOGENEITY OF INFORMATION

A complication that arises with including this information variable is that a state's information about its adversary's motives might reflect prior interaction between the states, which could itself be influenced by the theory's other key variables. At a given time, therefore, this information may not be independent of material variables and the state's own motives.

This is a potential problem, if we want the theory to preserve a boundary between the state and the international situation it faces. Structural realism is built from this perspective.[67] The theory developed here adds information to the variables that define a state's international situation but ideally would preserve this separation. This would be possible if the theory used only the information that states have when they initially start their strategic interaction. By definition, this information is independent of the states' material environment and their own motives. Handled this way, initial information is parallel to the material structure that structural realism emphasizes, which keeps structure separate from states. Given this material and information environment, the theory would then explain the evolution of the state's information about others' motives based on the logic of costly signaling. States would then rely on this revised, postsignaling information in making their next choice of strategy.

Although modern states never have true first interactions, major changes in the international system may come relatively close to creating first interactions by placing states in sufficiently new strategic situations that they are required to consider their knowledge of others' motives from a very different, essentially new perspective. Major wars, domestic

---

[67] On related aspects of this issue, see Wendt, "The Agent-Structure Problem in International Relations Theory."

revolutions, and the dissolution of empires could have this impact. For example, the end of the Cold War and the dissolution of the Soviet Union can be viewed as creating this type of new start for the states of Western Europe. These states use the knowledge acquired in their prior strategic environment to create the initial information about motives that they use in their new strategic environment. As a result, initial information does not necessarily mean states have no information.

However, because such major changes in the international system occur infrequently, as time passes, it becomes increasingly difficult to trace a state's information about others' motives back to this type of initial information. Therefore, a more pragmatic approach to including information about motives accepts this difficulty and simply envisions a state's information as the information it has at the time of its decision. This compromise, which leaves the theory squarely within the family of strategic choice theories but somewhat blurs the line between states and their international situation, is certainly preferable to ignoring the information that states do have about others' motives. It is also important to note that we often deal with material factors in a similar fashion. Prior strategic choices can influence states' power, including decisions about territorial expansion and economic cooperation that results in unequal gains.[68] In addition, some analyses focus on deployed military forces and industrial capabilities instead of raw power, taking them as given although they reflect prior strategic choices.

A STATE'S INFORMATION VS. THE ADVERSARY'S ACTUAL TYPE

When a security seeker faces a security seeker but is uncertain about the opposing state's type, uncertainty can play an essential role in generating competition. Critics of this argument (focusing on structural realism, which parallels my theory when the state's type and its information take on these values) have argued that if there were only security seekers in the international system, rational states would know this and, therefore, that greedy states are necessary to generate competition.[69]

The point that needs to be stressed here is that there is nothing logically inconsistent about positing information about motives that does not match the states that are actually in the system. As explained in the following chapter, and especially important from the perspective of our strategic choice theory, the constraints imposed by the state's international

---

[68] On debate over states' willingness to engage in cooperation that yields unequal gains, see David A. Baldwin, ed., *Neorealism and Neoliberalism* (New York: Columbia University Press, 1993); and Peter Liberman, "Trading with the Enemy: Security and Relative Economic Gains," *International Security* 21, 1 (Summer 1996): 147–175.

[69] Schweller, "Neorealism's Status-Quo Bias"; and Jeffery W. Legro and Andrew Moravcsik, "Is Anybody Still a Realist," *International Security* 24, 2 (Fall 1999): 13–16.

environment can prevent a security seeker from fully signaling its benign type, thereby preventing it from eliminating uncertainty about its motives. This is one way in which the security dilemma constrains states.

In addition, although a state's (initial) information about others' motives is exogenous to the theory, available scholarship does shed light on this question of continuing uncertainty. Research shows that while states invest substantial effort in determining others' types and do make judgments, they often remain uncertain.[70] This may reflect the sheer complexity of states' motives or, maybe related, that states lack the theories and knowledge required to determine others' types with certainty. While an adversary's regime type and ideology, and the history of its foreign and security policy, may provide valuable information about its motives, these considerations often leave uncertainty and leeway for alternative explanations.

The stark case of a system with only security seekers does raise an interesting question about the relationship between the actual types of states and the states' information about them. Given that a state's choice of strategy depends on its information about the opposing state's type, not on its actual type, one might worry that actual types do not matter at all. This conclusion is unwarranted. Even if states rarely become certain about others' types, they often do make judgments about the probability that adversaries are greedy, and these judgments are informed by a variety of factors that correlate with the adversaries' actual types. In short, neither extreme characterization appears appropriate—instead, states may often be uncertain about others' types, yet at the same time make useful judgments about the probability that other states are security seekers.

The following chapter builds on the setup presented in this chapter to explore why states should sometimes prefer cooperative strategies and under other conditions prefer competitive strategies. It demonstrates that variation in a state's motives, variation in the state's material situation—including in power and offense-defense variables—and variation in the state's information about the adversary's motives and about the adversary's information about the state's motives should all influence the state's strategy.

---

[70] Edelstein, "Choosing Friends and Enemies"; and David M. Edelstein, "Managing Uncertainty: Beliefs about Intentions and the Rise of Great Powers," *Security Studies* 12, 1 (Autumn 2002): 140.

CHAPTER THREE

The Theory

HAVING LAID THE foundation in chapter 2, we are prepared to analyze the interaction between states and their international environment. This chapter develops the core of my theory. I focus on states' military-policy options during peacetime. In this context,[1] cooperation refers to coordinated policies designed to avoid arms races and improve political relations;[2] competition refers to unilateral military buildups, which can generate arms races, and the formation of alliances.[3] Although my focus is on arming decisions, the theory has significant implications for war as well. The conditions that make military cooperation a state's best option also tend to enable states to be secure and to support peace.[4] Related, cooperative policies often play a central role in taking advantage of these peace-supporting conditions, enabling states to moderate causes of war that exist in the international environment and to avoid competition that would intensify them.

The chapter begins by addressing two major questions of international relations theory. First, can a state's international situation generate competition? Put another way, why should security seekers ever compete? In broad terms, insecurity and the security dilemma provide the answer—

[1] In other contexts, cooperation can refer to decisions to make concessions during a crisis and to decisions to forgo launching a war, while competition then refers to the opposite.

[2] Cooperation—including both formal and informal reciprocated restraint—is not the only alternative to competitive policies. Uncoordinated but unthreatening, and therefore noncompetitive, policies can sometimes be a second key alternative. For example, if defensive forces can be distinguished from offensive ones, then a country could sometimes choose defense independent of others' choices. For simplicity in presentation, I usually do not separate out these two types of noncompetitive policies, but keeping the distinction in mind is important. On situations characterized by this second possibility—situations of harmony—see Keohane, *After Hegemony*, pp. 51–55.

[3] I consider alliances to be a type of competition because, although the allies are cooperating with each other, their behavior is driven by their need to compete with a common adversary. Since balancing in the form of alliance formation is probably the most prominent and widely accepted prediction of structural realism, the pessimism about cooperation that is commonly associated with structural realism presumably does not count alliances as cooperation. The key questions about cooperation therefore focus on cooperation between adversaries. However, because today's ally could be an adversary in the future, the line between allies and adversaries is not always sharp, and under certain conditions concern about relative gains could inhibit cooperation between allies.

[4] Van Evera, *Causes of War*, vol. 1: *Power and the Roots of Conflict*; and chapter 4.

competition can result because a state finds the policies required to reduce its adversary's insecurity to be too risky; insecure states then compete for security.

Second, should a state's international situation always generate competition? *Why should not security seekers always compete*? The deductive arguments developed in this section show that the international environment does not create a general tendency for states to adopt competitive policies; cooperation will sometimes be a state's best option. Although cooperation can be risky, competition can also be risky—a state could launch an arms buildup to avoid falling behind but then lose the arms race that ensues. Consequently, a state might prefer cooperation to competition simply because cooperation would be more likely to preserve its military capabilities than would an arms race.[5] Moreover, the state could become more insecure, even if it does not lose, if the competition is in offensive systems that provide both countries with enhanced offensive capabilities. And the state could become more insecure if the competition signals that it has malign motives, thereby making its adversary more insecure.

Having provided broad answers to these initial questions, the chapter develops important elements of the theory more fully. The third section addresses the question: *How can a state's military policy influence political relations*? The possibility that a state's strategy can communicate information about its motives plays a central role in the theory's analysis. A state may be able to signal its benign motives by sending a costly signal—choosing a strategy that a security seeker finds less costly than would a greedy state. The risks vary with the security dilemma—when the security dilemma is mild, a state will be able to signal its benign motives at lower risk. The result can be a positive spiral in which signaling becomes easier and relations continue to improve. In contrast, negative spirals can result from a somewhat different process. For example, when states face uncertainty about force requirements, their strategy choices can indicate that they have malign motives even when they are only pursuing security. If some security seekers believe larger forces are required for deterrence and others believe smaller forces are sufficient, a state that opts for larger forces can signal that it is a greedy state. The result can be a negative spiral in which a security seeker comes increasingly to believe that its adversary is a greedy state and competitive policies become increasingly attractive. This spiral can be rational, involving states that fully appreciate the security dilemma and are making sound decisions; it reflects the constraints imposed by their international environment.

---

[5] Recall that I use "capabilities" specifically to refer to a state's ability to perform military missions, not to refer to the state's military forces; see chapter 2.

The fourth section analyzes the security dilemma and a state's choice of strategy in greater detail, asking: *What determines the magnitude of the security dilemma and a security seeker's optimal strategy?* As this brief introduction makes clear, the security dilemma plays a central role in the theory's arguments. Security seekers want to maintain the military capabilities required to deter and defeat adversaries, but also to preserve other states' security by signaling benign motives and avoiding policies that undermine opposing military capabilities. The severity of the security dilemma influences the difficulty a state will have in balancing these potentially conflicting strategic objectives. I explain that the security dilemma depends not only on the offense-defense variables that are the usual focus of attention, but also on a state's power and its information about its adversary's motives at the time of their interaction. Cooperation is less risky when a state believes its adversary is more likely to be a security seeker, which reduces the severity of the security dilemma and makes cooperative policies designed to reduce military vulnerabilities and signal its benign motives more desirable. As a result, with material conditions constant, variation in a state's information can change its preferred strategy. Material conditions also matter, and the state's strategy should depend on the combined impact of material and information variables. For example, either defense advantage or high estimates that the opposing state is a security seeker can make cooperation a state's best strategy; the combined effect of these conditions would be to reinforce the case for cooperation. Similarly, offense advantage or high estimates that the adversary is a greedy state could make competition the state's best option. By comparison, countervailing material and information conditions would leave a state's choice between cooperation and competition more complicated, and possibly indeterminate.[6]

Finally, having focused so far on the impact of material and information variables, the chapter asks: *Why isn't the international situation sufficient to prescribe a state's strategy?* The theory demonstrates that focusing exclusively on the decisions of security seekers cannot be justified theoretically—greedy states need to be addressed as well. In previous sections, the possibility that a state faces a greedy adversary is captured in the information variable. Here the focus shifts to the state that is making decisions and faces the international environment. If the incentives created by the international environment consistently made competition a security seeker's best option, greedy states would matter relatively little. In this case, across the full range of international conditions, pure security seekers and greedy states should adopt similar and competitive poli-

[6] On indeterminacy in rational choice theories, see Elster, *Solomonic Judgements*, who argues that indeterminacy is a serious problem, but that such a theory can still have substantial value.

cies. This deductive finding would begin to lay the foundation for a theory that focused exclusively on the impact of a state's international situation and assumed that all states had the same motives and goals (in this case, security seeking).[7] This is essentially the position offered by key strands of structural realism, including Waltz's theory and offensive realism. According to these arguments, even if some states have motives in addition to security, this variation does not matter in that it does not influence their strategies; the drive for security is all that really matters.[8] However, because the theory I have developed shows that security seekers should pursue cooperative policies under a range of material and information conditions, greedy states gain theoretical importance because competition could be a greedy state's best option when a security seeker facing the same international conditions should choose cooperation.

The questions analyzed in this chapter have been extensively debated; key strands of international relations theory are defined by the answers they offer. Structural realists argue that the international environment can generate competition between security seekers; neoclassical realists have disagreed, holding instead that greedy states are necessary to generate competition. Waltz's structural realism, as well as offensive realism, push the structural argument a step further, arguing that the international environment creates a general tendency toward competition; defensive realists have disagreed. As the preceding summary suggests, the theory developed in this chapter rejects key aspects of most of these arguments—Waltz, offensive realism, and neoclassical realism—on deductive/logical grounds. The theory can be viewed as a generalization of defensive realism, significantly broadening it by including variation in states' types and by making explicit the importance of the information that states have about others' motives when choosing their strategies.[9] The overall result, however, is a theory that is significantly different. Chapter 6 explores these differences in some detail.

[7] As explained in chapter 2, to provide a fully structural/situational explanation, the theory would need in addition to show that variation in motives should not lead states to choose different strategies. Even if all types of states should choose competitive policies, the possibility remains that greedy states and security seekers should choose different types or intensities of competitive policies.

[8] Waltz, *Theory of International Politics*; and Mearsheimer, *The Tragedy of Great Power Politics*. Waltz argues that states may have motives beyond security but suggests for theory building that their behavior can be predicted without focusing on these nonsecurity motives. Waltz, *Theory of International Politics*, esp. pp. 118, 121.

[9] On defensive realism, see Charles L. Glaser, "Realists as Optimists: Cooperation as Self-Help," *International Security* 19, 3 (Winter 1994/95): 50–90; Snyder, *Myths of Empire*, esp. pp. 11–12, 21–26; and Van Evera, *Causes of War*. The latter two present multilevel theories that combine a defensive-realist foundation with other levels of analysis. For additional citations and a more complete comparison, see chapter 6.

WHY SHOULD SECURITY SEEKERS EVER COMPETE? INSECURITY AND THE SECURITY DILEMMA

A basic question is whether the international environment that a state faces can be the source of international security competition. If all states were security seekers, should a state ever adopt a competitive security policy? If not, states' motives and goals, not the international environment, would have to be the source of international competition. A range of structural-realist theories have argued that the international environment can drive states into international competition.[10] In contrast, critics hold (incorrectly) that if states lack fundamental conflicts of interest, the international environment cannot lead rational security seekers to choose competitive policies.[11]

Although a security seeker will accept the military and political status quo if it is secure, it may adopt competitive policies if it is insecure. Competitive policies will under some conditions provide military advantages that enhance the state's deterrent, ensure that the state does not fall behind if its adversary launches a military buildup, provide offensive capabilities that are necessary to protect the status quo, communicate the state's resolve by demonstrating its willingness to expend resources to protect its security interests, and/or provide a hedge against the possibility that the adversary will become more malign and therefore harder to deter.

The key to explaining why security seekers should ever compete lies in understanding why a state could be insecure when all other states in the system are also security seekers. A state may not know that others are security seekers. This uncertainty plays a central role in creating its insecurity—if facing an adversary that has the military capability (deployed or potential) to challenge it, the state must worry about being attacked and plan its military forces accordingly. This possibility immediately raises the question of why a state might not know that the opposing state was in fact a security seeker. The answer lies in the constraints facing its adversary. Its adversary—a security seeker whose security would be increased if the state knew its type—may be unwilling to adopt the policies that would convince the state that it faces a security seeker. This is be-

---

[10] In addition to Waltz and Mearsheimer, see Glaser, "Realists as Optimists"; Van Evera, *Causes of War*; and Copeland, *The Origins of Major War*.

[11] Schweller, "Neorealism's Status-Quo Bias"; and Legro and Moravcsik, "Is Anybody Still a Realist," pp. 13–16. Andrew Kydd, "Sheep in Sheep's Clothing: Why Security Seekers Do Not Fight Each Other," *Security Studies* 7, 1 (Autumn 1997): 114–154, also reaches this conclusion but importantly bases it partly on unit-level arguments and related empirical observations.

cause the policies that would convince the state may be too risky for the adversary to adopt. As I discuss in more detail in a following section, signaling that it is a security seeker may require the adversary to adopt policies that increase its vulnerability to attack. This will be the case when the types of military forces that a state deploys for defense are also useful for offense; under this condition, policies that reduce the state's ability to attack will also reduce its ability to defend. The adversary may be unwilling to accept this increased vulnerability because it does not know that the state it faces is a security seeker and therefore is concerned about its ability to defend against attacks. Of course, this problem could be eliminated if the state were willing to demonstrate that it was a security seeker, but it may face the same constraints as its adversary does.

What is at work here is the security dilemma. The security dilemma is usually described as existing when a state's efforts to increase its security would have the unintended effect of reducing its adversary's security.[12] Looked at from a somewhat different angle, a state facing a security dilemma cannot reduce its adversary's insecurity without increasing its own vulnerability to attack; therefore, the net result of such an action could be a reduction of the state's security. A security seeker facing a security dilemma thus may find that the dangers of cooperative policies are greater than the dangers of competition.

In sharp contrast, if there were no security dilemma, the international environment should not generate competition between security seekers. If a state knew all others were security seekers, opposing military capabilities, even if they would be effective for attacking, would not create insecurity.[13] If a state could reduce its ability to attack without increasing its own vulnerability, the state could signal its benign motives with no risk to its security. If states could deploy forces that were effective only for defense, all states could simultaneously be militarily secure, eliminating the need to compete for security. Consequently, although it does not appear to play a central role in Waltz's structural-realist theory, the security

---

[12] On the definition of the security dilemma, see Jervis's seminal article, "Cooperation under the Security Dilemma." Jervis also addresses the security dilemma in *Perception and Misperception*, chap. 3, esp. pp. 62–76. Earlier work on the security dilemma includes John H. Herz, "Idealist Internationalism and the Security Dilemma," *World Politics* 2, 2 (January 1950): 157–180; Herz, *International Politics in the Atomic Age* (New York: Columbia University Press, 1959); and Herbert Butterfield, *History and Human Relations* (London: Collins, 1951). This discussion draws on more recent work in Charles L. Glaser, "The Security Dilemma Revisited"; and Kydd, "Game Theory and the Spiral Model." See also Ken Booth and Nicholas J. Wheeler, *The Security Dilemma: Fear, Cooperation and Trust in World Politics* (New York: Palgrave Macmillan, 2008).

[13] This would actually require that other states knew the state was a security seeker and that the state knew this; and that states had confidence that others' motives would not change.

dilemma must be included if the international environment is going to generate competition between security seekers. For this reason, defensive realism has given the security dilemma a central role in its explanation of competition, and its importance continues in the expanded theory developed here.

WHY SHOULDN'T SECURITY SEEKERS ALWAYS COMPETE? RISKS AND THE SECURITY DILEMMA

The preceding discussion could lead one to conclude that states should always compete. Indeed, this is the broad conclusion offered by Waltz's structural realism and by offensive realism.[14] However, contrary to the picture presented by these theories, the international environment does not create a general tendency toward competitive policies. Instead, across a range of material and information conditions, a state's international environment creates countervailing pressures for cooperative and competitive policies; under some conditions, cooperation will be a state's best option. This section starts with a brief summary of the standard structural-realist case for competition; given its extensive influence, reviewing this argument helps in appreciating the significance of my theory. The section then sketches the arguments that identify the benefits of cooperation. Following sections develop these arguments more thoroughly.

Summary of the Standard Structural-Realist Pessimism

Based on a cursory examination, the case for generally adopting a competitive strategy might appear to be an easy one. The standard structural-realist argument combines a number of reinforcing elements.[15] First, as discussed above, there are strong military rationales for competition. Due to their insecurity, security seekers find military advantages especially valuable and thus compete to acquire them. If its adversary does not respond, arming provides the state with military advantages that increase its ability to defend and deter. If its adversary also decides to build, arming guarantees against initially falling behind. Moreover, arming communicates the state's resolve to protect its security. And even if arming was

---

[14] Chapter 6 provides a more extensive comparison of these arguments.

[15] The following description of the standard argument does not include some important nuances and blurs some differences between authors that I have lumped together as contributors to the standard argument. Nevertheless, I believe that it captures the argument's basic thrust. For a good summary of the realist literature, see Stein, *Why Nations Cooperate*, pp. 4–13; for a broader assessment, see Michael W. Doyle, *Ways of War and Peace: Realism, Liberalism, and Socialism* (New York: Norton, 1997).

unnecessary, the state is still no worse off, except for the economic expense of the arms race. Further supporting competition, cooperation is risky because the adversary can cheat on agreements. Either failing to compete or cooperating and then having the adversary cheat can carry extremely high costs: military inferiority invites war, and, in the worst case, a major power can lose its sovereignty.

A second factor said to reinforce this inclination toward competition is uncertainty about the adversary's motives and intentions. Intentions are unknowable and, even if known, could be different tomorrow. This uncertainty works against cooperation.[16] States must not overlook the possibility that potential adversaries will use their full capabilities against them, and they must therefore focus on their adversaries' capabilities instead of their intentions.[17]

Third, international anarchy creates what Waltz termed a "self-help" world—without an international authority capable of protecting them, major powers must look out for themselves.[18] Self-help is usually equated with pursuit of unilateral competitive policies.[19] Waltz agues that self-help systems "make the cooperation of parties difficult. . . . Rules, institutions, and patterns of cooperation. . . are all limited in extent and modified from what they might otherwise be."[20]

In its most succinct version, the standard structural-realist argument

[16] Waltz; *Theory of International Politics*, p. 105; Mearsheimer, *The Tragedy of Great Power Politics*, p. 45; and especially on the implications for preventive war, Copeland, *The Origins of Major War*.

[17] Mearsheimer, *The Tragedy of Great Power Politics*, chap. 2, esp. p. 45.

[18] On the nature and implications of self-help, see Waltz, *Theory of International Politics*, pp. 105–107, 111–112. The necessity of self-help also depends on the assumption that states do not believe that other states are highly altruistic—specifically, that they would be willing to risk their own security to guarantee others' security. If they were, then even under anarchy states would not have to rely entirely on self-help; instead, they could count on others coming to their aid, even when the other states' security was not in jeopardy. However, altruism is not the key issue for structural realists; under anarchy, the pressing concern is the probability and extent of opposing states' current and future malign motives; states cannot count on others being benign, let alone altruistic.

[19] For example, Christopher Layne, "The Unipolar Illusion: Why New Great Powers Will Rise," *International Security* 17, 4 (Spring 1993): 11, argues that "Because it is anarchic, the international political system is a self-help system in which states' foremost concern must be with survival. In an anarchic system, states must provide for their own security and they face many real or apparent threats. International politics is thus a competitive realm." In his critique of structural realism, Alexander Wendt, "Anarchy Is What States Make of It: The Social Construction of Power Politics," *International Organization* 46, 2 (Spring 1992): 392, argues that "The self-help corollary to anarchy does enormous work in neorealism, generating the inherently competitive dynamics of the security dilemma and collective action problem."

[20] Waltz, "Reflections on *Theory of International Politics*," p. 336. See also p. 329: "In self-help systems, the pressures of competition weigh more heavily than ideological preferences or internal political pressures."

sees the search for security that flows from anarchy as sufficient to explain competition: "realists argue that states are preoccupied with their security and power; *by consequence*, states are predisposed toward conflict and competition."[21] Mearsheimer describes realists as "pessimistic when it comes to international politics. . . . they see no easy way to escape the harsh world of security competition and war."[22] Competition is the norm and tends to be intense; cooperation is rare and limited to areas of secondary importance.

This conclusion is implicit in Waltz's focus on arms competition and alliance formation. In broad terms, states can choose from three approaches for acquiring and maintaining the military capabilities required to meet their security needs: building arms, gaining allies, and agreeing to limit the deployment of arms.[23] In principle, these approaches could be equally valuable. Waltz, however, excludes cooperation with adversaries from his description of the basic alternatives available to states in a self-help system: "States, or those who act for them, try in more or less sensible ways to use the means available in order to achieve the ends in view. Those means fall into two categories: internal efforts (moves to increase economic capability, to increase military strength, to develop clever strategies) and external efforts (moves to strengthen and enlarge one's own alliance or to weaken and shrink an opposing one)."[24] He does not explain why these competitive options dominate the cooperative alternative. Analysis of how these cooperative and competitive options compare is the focus of much of the remainder of this chapter.

Overview of Countervailing Considerations: Eliminating the Competition Bias

Although perhaps superficially compelling, the foregoing description of the incentives created by a security seeker's international environment is exceedingly incomplete, biased toward competition by overlooking the

[21] Joseph M. Grieco, *Cooperation among Nations: Europe, America and Non-tariff Barriers to Trade* (Ithaca: Cornell University Press, 1990), p. 4.

[22] Mearsheimer, *The Tragedy of Great Power Politics*, p. 17.

[23] "Agreeing to limit the deployment of arms" is used here to refer to the full range of restraint in the deployment, operation, and monitoring of military forces; it is not restricted to formal agreements. On this broader understanding, see Thomas C. Schelling and Morton H. Halperin, *Strategy and Arms Control* (New York: Twentieth Century Fund, 1961), pp. 2–5; on the relative strengths of formal agreements and tacit bargaining, see George W. Downs, David M. Rocke, and Randolph Siverson, "Arms Control and Cooperation," in Kenneth A. Oye, ed., *Cooperation under Anarchy* (Princeton: Princeton University Press, 1986), pp. 118–146.

[24] Waltz, *Theory of International Politics*, p. 118; see also Waltz, "The Origins of War in Neorealist Theory," in Robert I. Rotberg and Theodore K. Robb, eds., *The Origin and Prevention of Major Wars* (Cambridge: Cambridge University Press, 1989), p. 43: "Their individual intentions aside, collectively their actions yield arms races and alliances."

potential benefits of cooperation while underplaying the risks of competition. This bias is the result of several mistakes.

First, although cooperation can be risky, competition can also be risky. While deep concern about the adequacy of their military capabilities could create incentives for states to compete, it is also true that this concern should sometimes lead states to cooperate. If military advantages are extremely valuable, military disadvantages can be extremely dangerous. Because a state's military buildup is likely to generate a reaction (because it decreases the adversary's security, because the state faces a security dilemma), the state must consider the net effect of competing.[25] It might initially appear that the net effect of this action-reaction process would be to leave both countries' military capabilities unchanged—equal increases in forces would simply offset set each other.[26] However, the state's military capabilities could be reduced in a number of ways, which could create incentives to cooperate.

A state could lose the arms races that its military buildup provokes. If its adversary responds with a buildup that exceeds the state's buildup and that the state cannot match, the state's military capabilities would be reduced. The adversary's reaction would depend partly on its power. A state that is uncertain about whether it enjoys a power advantage might therefore prefer accepting the military status quo to competing. The adversary's response would also depend on its assessment of the state's motives. If the state's arms buildup signals that it has malign motives (which, as discussed below, is possible), the adversary could conclude that it requires more effective deterrent capabilities to protect its interests and that it should shift to a strategy designed to communicate its resolve from one designed to signal its benign motives. As a result, the adversary would devote a larger percentage of its resources to military assets, thereby reducing the state's prospects for winning the arms race. Therefore, when uncertain about the outcome of an arms race, which it would like to win,

[25] Throughout this chapter, for the sake of simplicity I focus on decisions to buy arms. However, other types of actions could fuel reactions through security-dilemma logic, including the decisions to take territory and to acquire allies to increase security. Regarding territory, an action-reaction process could be expansion into part of a buffer zone that leads one's adversary to expand into the remainder of the zone, or the acquisition of territory that increases the state's power, creating pressure for the adversary to expand to increase its power.

[26] Of course, even if the security dilemma does not result in a reduction in the state's security, the state can be worse off because the security dilemma results in an expenditure of resources that does not bring benefits. Glenn Snyder, "The Security Dilemma in Alliance Politics," World Politics 36, 4 (July 1984): 461–462, emphasizes wasted resources, arguing that alliance formation is similar to arming, in that all states would be better off remaining outside the alliance; action and reaction nevertheless generate alliance blocks that are costly but fail to increase security.

a security seeker could prefer an arms control agreement that accepted the current military status quo over gambling on prevailing in the arms race.[27]

Moreover, cooperation could be a state's best option for maintaining its military capabilities even when it is confident that it would not lose the competition. The state's military capability—that is, its ability to perform military missions—could be reduced, even if it wins a race, if the race involves a new military technology that favors attacking over defending, that is, that shifts the offense-defense balance toward offense.[28] If the state deployed a new weapons system that favors offensive missions and if its adversary responded by deploying this system, the state's ability to defend itself would be reduced, leaving it less secure than before this round of arming.[29] In this case, a security seeker determined to maintain its military capabilities could prefer arms control to an arms race. For example, multiple warhead nuclear missiles are usually considered to be this type of offensive innovation; initially deployed by the United States and then by the Soviet Union, MIRV made it more difficult for the United States to meet its requirements for deterrence.[30] In contrast, if the state deploys an innovation that favors defensive missions and its adversary matches it, the net result would be an increase in the

[27] Doubts about the outcome of the race could reflect uncertainties about which country has greater resources, is better able to extract resources for military purposes, or is better able to develop and exploit military technologies.

[28] The ability to perform offensive and defensive missions can also vary with force size. Thus, an action-reaction process that results in larger forces (as distinguished from different types of forces) can increase or decrease the state's military capability for defense. For example, equal increases in the size of conventional ground forces can result in an increase in the state's ability to defend, by enabling it to increase the density of forces along the front. Similarly, equal increases in the size of nuclear forces can increase both countries' retaliatory capabilities, thereby enhancing their deterrent capabilities. See Glaser and Kaufmann, "What Is the Offense-Defense Balance and Can We Measure It?," p. 66. In such cases, the action-reaction process shifts the offense-defense balance toward defense and increases states' military capabilities. However, even when larger forces are desirable, it is unclear that states should prefer competitive policies; an alternative is simply to coordinate increases in force size.

[29] This insight precedes offense-defense theory; the complementary observation that adversaries can have a mutual interest in reciprocating arms restraint is one of the core insights of modern arms control theory, which was developed during the late 1950s and early 1960s. See, for example, Schelling and Halperin, *Strategy and Arms Control*, esp. pp. 1–2; and Donald G. Brennan, ed., *Arms Control, Disarmament and National Security* (New York: Brazilier, 1961). Thomas C. Schelling, "A Framework for the Evaluation of Arms-Control Proposals," *Daedalus* 104, 3 (Summer 1975): 187–200, explores the implications of a country's preferences for an arms race, an unmatched unilateral buildup, and the military status quo.

[30] On MIRV, see Ted Greenwood, *Making the MIRV: A Study in Defense Decision Making* (Cambridge, MA: Ballinger, 1975); and chapter 9.

state's capability to defend itself and an increase in its security. The precision-guided munitions deployed on the central front during the Cold War appear to have been this type of innovation.[31] If facing the first type of innovation, a state should prefer cooperation; if facing the second, it should prefer competition.[32]

Second, although uncertainty about the adversary's motives creates incentives to compete, uncertainty can also create powerful incentives for states to cooperate. Uncertainty about the state's motives can make its adversary insecure, which is dangerous because insecurity can be a key source of international conflict. Making an adversary more insecure will often increase the value it places on expansion because expansion can have the potential to increase its security. For example, a more insecure adversary will find expansion more desirable when it can provide secure borders, strategic depth, or control of resources that are valuable for building military capabilities; and it will see war as more valuable when fighting can disproportionately destroy the adversary's power/resources. Consequently, a state's military buildup that makes its adversary less secure—by reducing its military capabilities and/or by signaling that the state has malign motives—could make the adversary more dangerous by increasing its willingness to run risks to restore its security. Therefore, even when arming would increase a state's military capability, the net result could be a reduction in its security. On the one hand, the state would enjoy the enhanced deterrent and defense capabilities provided by its improved military capability. On the other hand, because the adversary is now harder to deter, it might not be deterred by these enhanced capabilities, even if it would previously have been deterred by less effective military capabilities. Thus, a state that can achieve military advantages should not always seek them. This is a particularly stark trade-off that can be created by the security dilemma.

There is no general answer to whether sustainable military advantages that leave one's adversary less secure will increase or decrease a state's security. However, policy analyses that grapple with this trade-off in specific cases—including whether NATO should have acquired a conventional retaliatory capability during the 1980s, whether the United States should have pursued meaningful nuclear superiority during the Cold War, and whether NATO should have expanded into Central Europe following the Cold War—sometimes judge that these political costs exceeded the narrow military benefits.[33]

[31] John J. Mearsheimer, *Conventional Deterrence* (Ithaca: Cornell University Press, 1983), chap. 7.

[32] However, even here there could be a case for cooperation that allowed and coordinated the shift toward defense advantage; as with force size, the more precise statement is that the state should prefer deployment of the system, possibly cooperatively.

[33] Richard K. Betts, "Conventional Deterrence: Predictive Uncertainty and Policy Confi-

The danger posed by the adversary's insecurity can make cooperation preferable to competition for a couple of reasons. Cooperation is valuable if it reduces the military threat the state poses to its adversary, even if it does not reduce the adversary's estimate that the state harbors malign motives. Moreover, cooperation is valuable if it can shift this estimate, convincing the adversary that the state is less likely to be motivated by greed than it previously believed. If successful, this cooperative effort to "reassure" the adversary would increase the state's security. In contrast, competition can have the opposite effect, leading the adversary to believe the state is more likely to be greedy, and thereby reduce the state's security.

Third, although self-help is regularly equated with pursuit of competitive policies, in fact cooperative policies are an important type of self-help. For example, an adversary will engage in reciprocal restraint only if arms control promises to provide greater security than would the competitive alternatives. This is possible only if the adversary believes that an arms race would be risky. Consequently, a state gets an adversary to cooperate by relying on its own resources—through self-help—since the state's ability to engage in an arms race is a central condition for its adversary's judgment that arms racing is risky, and thus for its willingness to cooperate. In short, by itself, self-help tells us essentially nothing about whether states should prefer cooperation or competition.

In sum, a security seeker's international environment can create a variety of countervailing pressures for cooperation, as well as for competition. Launching an arms buildup may provide military advantages but may also make the adversary more insecure and, therefore, harder to deter. And pursuing military advantages forgoes the possibility of avoiding an arms race in which the state could fall temporarily or permanently behind. When the risks of competition exceed the risks of cooperation, states should direct their self-help efforts toward achieving cooperation. Therefore, we need to replace blanket conclusions with a more nuanced understanding of the impact of a state's international environment: under what conditions should a state cooperate and when should it compete? I return to this question toward the end of this chapter.

How Can a State's Military Policy Influence Political Relations? Positive and Negative Signaling

An important theme in the preceding discussion is the possibility that a state's military policy will influence its political relationship with its ad-

---

dence," *World Politics* 37, 2 (January 1985): 172–177; Glaser, *Analyzing Strategic Nuclear Policy*, chap. 5; and Michael E. Brown, "The Flawed Logic of NATO Expansion," *Survival* 37, 1 (Spring 1995): 34–52.

versary, which can in turn increase or decrease the state's security. This set of concerns runs counter to the standard structural-realist logic, which focuses entirely on power and military capabilities, and implies that states acting within the constraints imposed by international structure cannot communicate information about their motives or that this information would not matter. This section examines how a state's military policy can influence its adversary's information about its motives and explores the state's basic options for engaging in this type of tacit communication.[34]

The following discussion focuses specifically on sending information about the state's type—whether it is a security seeker or a greedy state. As I explained in chapter 2, if there is also uncertainty about the value a security seeker places on protecting its interests, it will also be concerned with communicating information about its resolve. To keep the number of variables relatively small, I have chosen not to address carefully variation between security seekers in this chapter, although I do refer to communicating resolve a number of times. Chapter 4 provides a more systematic exploration of the implications of uncertainty about resolve; the logic of communicating resolve is similar to the signaling logic that I describe in the section below.

Signaling Benign Motives

A key challenge facing a security seeker is simultaneously to meet its military requirements and increase its adversary's security, or at least not decrease it. One way to accomplish this is for the state to communicate that it has benign (security-seeking) motives, which makes its military capabilities less threatening. But this raises the question of how the rational security-seeking states posited by my theory can communicate information about their motives. The challenge is to convince a skeptical adversary, who must worry that it faces a greedy state that is trying to mislead it. A greedy state would like to mislead other states into believing that it is interested only in security, thereby convincing them to adopt policies that increase their military vulnerability, thus enabling the greedy state to meet its expansionist objectives.

Because a greedy state has incentives to misrepresent its motives, a pure security seeker can communicate information about its motives only by adopting a policy that is less costly for it than the policy would be for a

---

[34] The question of whether information and changes in it are possible or matter is frequently seen as establishing the divide between realist theories—which are characterized as material—and constructivist theories—which are characterized as ideational. Although important realist works may support this characterization, the material-information/ideational divide does not provide a useful contrast of realist/rationalist and constructivist theories. I address this issue in chapter 6.

greedy state; such a policy is a "costly signal."[35] The difference in costs means that a security seeker is more likely to adopt such a policy and, therefore, by doing so can communicate information about which type of state it is, that is, about its motives. Having received this costly signal, the security seeker's adversary should update its estimate of the state's type, shifting to a higher probability that it is a security seeker.

Cost here is measured in terms of the impact on the state's ability to achieve its goals. A policy that reduces a state's ability to take territory will often be more costly for a greedy state than for a pure security seeker because the security seeker places less value on taking territory. A policy need not reduce a security seeker's ability to defend to be costly because security seekers value protecting the territory they possess as much as greedy states do. However, a security seeker facing a security dilemma will often have to reduce its ability to defend if it wants to reduce its ability to attack. Consequently, signaling can require a security seeker to increase its vulnerability to attack, which could make cooperation too risky.

States can try to communicate their benign motives via three types of military policies: arms control, defense emphasis, and unilateral restraint. Arms control can be especially valuable when offense and defense are distinguishable. When offense has the advantage, agreeing to limit offensive capabilities can increase the adversary's assessment that the state's motives are benign. Although a greedy state might accept this arms control agreement because the limits on the state's offense would increase its security, the agreement is costly for a greedy state because it reduces its prospects for expansion. (A purely greedy state—one that does not value what it currently possesses—would not see this benefit in limiting offense and, consequently, is still less likely to cooperate.) Thus, although both pure security seekers and greedy states might accept such an agreement, the costs of agreement are higher for the greedy state. Consequently, al-

[35] The literature on costly signaling, which developed in economics, started to play a role in IR theory in the 1990s. Jervis used similar concepts earlier—see Robert Jervis, *The Logic of Images in International Relations* (Princeton: Princeton University Press, 1970); and Jervis, "Cooperation under the Security Dilemma." For an informal treatment that addresses signaling of motives, see Glaser, "Realists as Optimists," pp. 67–70. For formal treatments see Kydd, "Game Theory and the Spiral Model"; Kydd, *Trust and Mistrust*; and George W. Downs and David M. Rocke, *Tacit Bargaining, Arms Races and Arms Control* (Ann Arbor: University of Michigan Press, 1990). Other analyses of costly signals include James D. Fearon, "Threats to Use Force: The Role of Costly Signals in International Crises" (Ph.D. diss., University of California, Berkeley, 1992); and James D. Morrow, "The Strategic Setting of Choices: Signaling, Commitment, and Negotiating in International Politics," in Lake and Powell, eds., *Strategic Choice and International Relations*. On the possibility of communication without costly signals, see Anne E. Sartori, "The Might of the Pen: A Reputational Theory of Communication in International Disputes," *International Organization* 56, 1 (Winter 2002): 121–149.

though the state's acceptance of the arms agreement should not entirely convince the adversary that it does not face a greedy state, it does nevertheless provide valuable information. Moreover, the greedier the state was, the less likely it would be to accept the agreement. As a result, the agreement can also signal that the state is less greedy. By comparison, agreeing to limit offense when defense has the advantage provides less information because an arms race is less likely to provide a state with the offensive capabilities required for expansion. Consequently, a greedy state would then find an arms control agreement less costly, narrowing the cost differential between greedy and security-seeking states, and thus limiting the information conveyed by such a policy.

The 1972 Antiballistic Missile Treaty between the United States and the Soviet Union is a good example of this type of cooperation. In the context of the Cold War nuclear competition, antiballistic missile defense of cities and industry was a type of offense because it was intended to protect against opposing retaliatory deterrent (defense) capabilities. Therefore, agreeing to limit ABMs was a costly signal. However, this signal was relatively small because defense (retaliation) dominated offense. Nevertheless, because ABMs could be combined with other offensive systems, when evaluated through the highly risk-averse security lens of the Cold War, the signal was significant.

Arms control can also send a costly signal when offense and defense are indistinguishable. In this case, the agreement limits the size, not the type, of forces. If both states have some chance of gaining an offensive military advantage in a quantitative arms race, the costs of accepting limits on force size would be greater for a greedy state than for a security seeker. The largest signal would come from a state that had good prospects for winning the race (that is, a state with a power advantage) but nevertheless agrees to limit the size of its forces. The Washington Conference naval agreements, which were reached in the early 1920s, are an example of this type of cooperation—the United States agreed to a ratio of naval forces that was much smaller than its power advantage over Japan, with the goal of increasing Japanese security.

A second possibility for signaling benign motives is a policy of defense emphasis—a security seeker decides on its own to give priority to meeting its military requirements with a defensive strategy, even if it costs more than an offensive one. It is not cooperation in the form of arms control that is required to send a costly signal—in the arms control policy described above, it is the state's restraint, not the bilateral cooperation, that is costly. For a policy of defense emphasis to be feasible, offense and defense must be distinguishable. When offense has the advantage, a state that decides unilaterally to meet its military requirements with defensive means will have to make larger investments in military forces than if it had chosen the offensive route. Compared to the arms control approach, this state would then have indicated not only its willingness to forgo offensive capabilities, but also its willingness to invest greater resources to send this message. Because states value consumption, as well as security, this sacrifice makes the state's signal larger.

The feasibility of the defense emphasis approach relative to arms control will decrease with the advantage of offense (and the severity of the security dilemma) because the financial cost of a defensive policy increases and could become prohibitive. In contrast, arms control limits both states' offense, thereby reducing the financial cost of effective defense and possibly providing the state with defensive capabilities that it could not achieve unilaterally. Consequently, security seekers should usually prefer arms control to defense emphasis; defense emphasis becomes more attractive if arms control is infeasible due to political constraints (for example, the adversary believes the state is too likely to be greedy and, therefore, is unwilling to pursue arms control) or strategic constraints (for example, monitoring that provides timely warning of cheating is not technically feasible).

The debate over the German war plan in the decades preceding the First World War provides a possible example. If it had pursued a policy of defense emphasis, Germany would have replaced the Schlieffen Plan, which required a major offensive attack against France, with plans to remain on the defense on both the Western and Eastern fronts. This option was probably feasible because defense had the advantage in the West.[36] A second example comes from the debate over U.S. Cold War nuclear policy. Proponents of an offensive nuclear strategy argued that the United States required counterforce systems to redress the ratio of nuclear forces that would survive a Soviet counterforce attack. In place of this offensive policy, defense emphasis would have attempted to meet U.S. nuclear requirements without forces that threatened Soviet deterrent capabilities; instead, the United States would have increased the survivability of its own nuclear forces, thereby eliminating the Soviet ability to shift the ratio of forces.

Finally, a state can try to communicate benign motives by employing unilateral restraint—that is, by reducing its military capability below the level that it believes would otherwise be necessary for adequate deterrence and defense.[37] This strategy should send a clear message for two reasons: the state has reduced its offensive capability, which a greedy state would be less likely to do; and the state has incurred some risk to

[36] On the feasibility of a defensive option, see Snyder, *Ideology of the Offensive*, pp. 116–122, who argues that the best option might have included a limited offensive in the East.

[37] The uses of unilateral restraint are emphasized by Charles E. Osgood, *Alternative to War or Surrender* (Urbana: University of Illinois Press, 1962). Downs and Rocke, *Tacit Bargaining, Arms Races and Arms Control*, pp. 41–51, assess Osgood's arguments.

its security, due to the shortfall in its defensive military capabilities, which the adversary could interpret as a further indication of the value the state places on improving political relations. Gorbachev's unilateral reduction of Soviet conventional forces is a clear example of this type of restraint.[38]

Of course, this security risk will make states reluctant to adopt an ambitious policy of unilateral restraint. A state can try to manage this risk by starting the policy with small reductions, with the hope that the adversary will reciprocate, thereby making possible following rounds of restraint, which eventually send a large signal. Nevertheless, states are likely to turn to unilateral restraint only when the other options are precluded, for example, when arms control is impossible because the adversary refuses to negotiate, or when defense emphasis is impossible because offense and defense are indistinguishable or because offense has such a large advantage that defense emphasis is unaffordable. The risks of unilateral restraint will grow with the state's assessment of the probability that the adversary is greedy; a high probability that the adversary is greedy can make competition preferable to this form of cooperation. Therefore, a high probability that the adversary is greedy can make a state unwilling to signal its benign motives via unilateral restraint and, as discussed more fully below, can thereby increase the severity of the security dilemma.

If a security seeker can signal its benign motives, it may be able to set in motion a positive spiral. As its adversary concludes that the state is less likely to be greedy, the adversary should be more willing to signal its own benign motives, which could enable the state to engage in additional costly cooperation, which further improves relations. The interaction between states' estimates of others' motives and their decisions to cooperate is explored in the section below on the magnitude of the security dilemma.

Signaling Malign Motives

The standard security-dilemma/spiral-model story is rather the opposite of the one described above—states trying to achieve security choose policies that nevertheless reduce their security, partly by communicating that they have greedy motives.[39] This type of action-reaction process is the

---

[38] For analysis of this case, see Evangelista, *Unarmed Forces*, chap. 14; and Kydd, *Trust and Mistrust*, chap. 8.

[39] The adversary could also become less secure if it concludes that the state places a higher value on security, demands a higher level of security because it places lower value on consumption, or is greedier than previously believed. To keep the theory relatively simply, I do not add these types of variation, but analysis of these possibilities would be similar.

focus of the "spiral model," in which states that are seeking only security come to have increasingly strained political relations as their interacting policies signal that they are greedy states instead of security seekers.[40] Although the spiral model is often understood to result from misperceptions, my discussion focuses entirely on rational spirals.

The possibility of this type of interaction between rational states presents something of a puzzle. How could the arms policy of a state that seeks only security convince its adversary that the state is more likely to be greedy than it previously believed? The answer is not obvious because the adversary should understand that the state's arms buildup could be motivated by security, not greed. Recognizing that the state does not know its motives, the adversary should appreciate the state's desire for adequate defense capabilities, which could require more or improved military forces. In addition, appreciating the security dilemma, the adversary should understand that the forces the state requires for increased security could reduce its own security. A rational adversary will therefore have reason to expect a pure security seeker to engage in a threatening arms buildup and consequently will not automatically conclude that such a buildup reflects greedy motives. For example, in the years leading up to World War I, both Russia and France appreciated Germany's security requirements and therefore did not impute malign motives in reaction to Germany's decision to build up its army.[41]

The question then is, when would a security seeker's military buildup signal greedy motives? As with the positive signaling described above, part of the answer lies in actions that are not equally likely to be taken by a greedy state and a pure security seeker. Then when a state launches a military buildup that is more likely to be taken by a greedy state than by a security seeker, an adversary that is making sound inferences will update its assessment of the state's motives, concluding that the state is more likely than previously believed to be greedy. Running parallel to the cooperative policies considered above, different types of competitive arming policies can help distinguish greedy states from security seekers. A greedy state is more likely than a security seeker to deploy forces that

---

[40] The original description of the spiral model is Jervis, *Perception and Misperception*, chap. 3; for an earlier discussion of this type of interaction, see J. David Singer, "Threat-Perception and the Armament-Tension Dilemma," *Journal of Conflict Resolution* 2, 1 (March 1958): 92–105. Jervis states that the spiral can be rational but emphasizes the role of misperceptions. On rational spirals, see Glaser, "Political Consequences of Military Strategy"; Glaser, "The Security Dilemma Revisited"; Kydd, *Trust and Mistrust*, esp. chap. 3; and Snyder, "The Security Dilemma in Alliance Politics," pp. 468–470, who argues that firm alliance politics can generate reactions that are comparable to a spiral generated by an arms buildup.

[41] David G. Herrmann, *The Arming of Europe and the Making of the First World War* (Princeton: Princeton University Press, 1996), pp. 174, 191–192.

are larger than required to defend its territory adequately. If offense and defense are not distinguishable, the extra forces would not only provide some additional capability to defend, but also some additional capability to attack. A state interested only in security would see less value in these forces than would a greedy state because it does not value the additional offensive capability and, therefore, would be less willing to pay for them. A buildup to gain an advantage in force size can therefore signal greedy motives. The Soviet Union's large conventional forces and offensive doctrine had this effect during the Cold War, especially in light of the smaller forces and more defensive doctrine that NATO chose to defend itself.[42] Choosing different types of forces might also help distinguish types of states. For example, when a state has a choice between forces that add more to offensive capabilities or defensive capabilities, a greedy state is more likely than a security seeker to choose the type of force that favors offense. The greedy state sees both greater value in offense and sometimes less value in not provoking others, since it anticipates conflict anyway.[43]

However, different probabilities that security-seeking and greedy states will choose a policy are not sufficient to generate a negative spiral. In addition, there must be competitive policies that would be taken by greedy states that also would be chosen by some security seekers. If this overlap did not exist, a security seeker should never be mistaken for a greedy state. The increased fear and insecurity described by the spiral model, specifically the insecurity that results from believing the adversary is more likely to be greedy, would have to be the result of misperception, not interaction between rational states.

This type of overlap can occur if the states are uncertain about the size or type of forces required to maintain a given level of security or, related, if they disagree about force requirements. For example, consider the simple case in which some security seekers would be satisfied with a lower level of forces, but some would require a higher level to have an adequate defense, and in which all greedy states would require the higher level. A security seeker that builds to the higher level would then convince its adversary that it is more likely to be greedy because only some security seekers but all greedy states would build to this level. Similar interactions can occur if there is uncertainty or disagreement about whether security seekers require offensive capabilities to support an adequate deterrent

---

[42] On the dangers of Soviet doctrine, see Richard Ned Lebow, "The Soviet Offensive in Europe: The Schlieffen Plan Revisited?," *International Security* 9, 4 (Spring 1985): 44–78.

[43] There are, however, situations in which a security seeker requires offensive capabilities to defend its interests; see Jervis, "Cooperation under the Security Dilemma"; and Van Evera, *Causes of War*, pp. 152–160. As a result, a state's choice of offense would not always send a signal that would entirely separate different types of states, which as noted below can support a rational spiral.

and also if security seekers differ in the degree of security that they believe is adequate.[44] An example of this type of overlap is Cold War nuclear counterforce—although critics argued otherwise, U.S. doctrine held that the United States required nuclear counterforce systems to deter Soviet conventional and nuclear attacks; at the same time, U.S. leaders worried that the Soviet Union had acquired counterforce to destroy the U.S. nuclear deterrent and thereby gain military advantages that would enhance its ability to coerce the United States. Although the two states were buying similar forces, U.S. leaders were not necessarily inconsistent in concluding that the Soviet nuclear forces indicated that they were more likely to be greedy.[45]

A security seeker that prefers the larger or more offensively oriented forces faces a trade-off, which is captured by the security dilemma: acquiring the more threatening forces signals malign motives, while acquiring the less threatening forces avoids this provocation but leaves the state with forces that it believes are inadequate, or at least less effective. Unlike the case of positive signaling, the problem here is not a greedy state that wants to misrepresent its motives, but instead a security seeker whose true motives will be misunderstood if it satisfies its force requirements. To avoid sending this misleading information, the state must adopt a policy that is costly, leaving it short of its military requirements. When the costs of this military shortfall are too high—that is, preserving existing political relations is not worth the military vulnerability—the state should acquire the more capable forces and a negative spiral will result.

A negative political spiral can also result from an adversary's uncertainty about the state's understanding of its motives. For example, when the adversary believes that the state believes there is only a small probability that the adversary is greedy and, therefore, that the state does not fear it, the adversary will conclude that the state's buildup is largely unnecessary for security and therefore that the state is motivated by greed. If the adversary's initial estimate of the probability that the state is fearful

[44] For a discussion of related issues concerning subjective security requirements, see Jervis, "Cooperation under the Security Dilemma," pp. 174–176. An alternative explanation for disagreements is based in the analytic complexity of military strategy and bounded rationality.

[45] The United States did, however, exaggerate the differences in U.S. and Soviet nuclear policy, both underestimating its own capabilities and inflating Soviet capabilities; the result supported flawed assessments of Soviet motives. See Glaser, "Political Consequences of Military Strategy," pp. 517–518; Warner R. Schilling, "U.S. Strategic Nuclear Concepts in the 1970s: The Search for Sufficiently Equivalent Countervailing Parity," *International Security* 6, 2 (Fall 1981): 49–79; and Michael Salman, Kevin J. Sullivan, and Stephen Van Evera, "Analysis or Propaganda? Measuring American Strategic Nuclear Capability, 1969–1988," in Lynn Eden and Steven E. Miller, eds., *Nuclear Arguments: Understanding the Strategic Nuclear Arms and Arms Control Debates* (Ithaca: Cornell University Press, 1991).

is too low, this increase in its assessment that the state is greedy will be too large, resulting in a negative spiral. Formal analysis of this interaction shows that under a wide range of conditions a rational adversary will find the state's buildup to be provocative and that updating of beliefs is sensitive to prior estimates of the state's motives.[46]

What Determines the Magnitude of the Security Dilemma and a Security Seeker's Optimal Strategy?

Previous sections of this chapter have explored how the security dilemma plays the central role in generating competition between rational security seekers. We have seen that the security dilemma helps explain both why competition between security seekers can be their best option and also why they should sometimes cooperate. We have also seen that the severity of the security dilemma influences the willingness of security seekers to signal their motives and, closely related, the likelihood of positive and negative political spirals.

This section provides a closer look at the security dilemma, focusing on variation in its magnitude and nature. Although international anarchy is a constant condition, the international situation that states face can vary quite substantially. The extent of competition generated by a state's international environment depends on the magnitude of the security dilemma. When the security dilemma is mild or nonexistent, security seekers will be able to adopt cooperative and defensive policies, and peace between security seekers is likely; in contrast, when the security dilemma is severe, security seekers face much greater pressure to adopt competitive and offensive policies, and conflict and war are more likely. The possibility of variation in the security dilemma has dramatic implications, making possible a much wider range of competitive and cooperative policies than predicted by Waltz's neorealism.

The severity of the security dilemma is usually understood to depend on offense-defense variables. This section explains that these standard security-dilemma arguments are sound but incomplete. An additional material variable—power—also influences the magnitude of the security dilemma. In a larger departure, this section explains that the security dilemma also depends on information variables—the state's information about its adversary's motives, as well as the state's information about the adversary's information about its motives. The severity of the security dilemma therefore depends on the combined effect of material and infor-

---

[46] Kydd, "Game Theory and the Spiral Model"; see also Downs and Rocke, *Tacit Bargaining, Arms Races, and Arms Control*, chap. 4.

mation variables. This more complete formulation of the security dilemma helps to explain why a state should sometimes pursue cooperative policies when the material conditions it faces favor competition and, alternatively, why a state should sometimes compete even when material conditions make defense relatively easy.

This section also explores the closely related question of how a state's strategy should vary with the international situation it faces. This choice of strategy and the magnitude of the security dilemma are closely related. The security dilemma is a property of the international situation the state faces. Its magnitude and nature capture the incentives and constraints created by the international environment. A state's strategy reflects, and in some cases is determined by, these pressures. We see the effect of the nature and severity of the security dilemma in the rational outcomes the international situation produces.

Because a state's strategy should depend on both material and information variables, there are a large number of potential combinations. The following discussion lays out the basic logic of how a variable should influence a state's options and explores key combinations.

Material Variables

OFFENSE-DEFENSE VARIABLES

The standard security-dilemma arguments hold that the severity of the security dilemma depends on the offense-defense balance and on offense-defense-distinguishability.[47] The severity of the security dilemma decreases as the offense-defense balance—which, as described in chapter 2, reflects the relative difficulty of converting resources into offensive and defensive military mission capabilities—shifts toward greater defense advantage. When defense has an advantage, a state will usually be better able to protect its interests with a defensive doctrine than an offensive one. The larger the advantage of defense, the smaller the ratio of forces required for an adequate defensive capability, which reduces the state's incentive to build larger forces and decreases the difficulty (cost) of responding to its adversary's buildup. When defense has the advantage, the state's deployment of forces increases its ability to defend more than it decreases the adversary's ability to defend. Action-reaction cycles and arms races should peter out, and equal-size forces should be sufficient to provide both states with reasonable levels of security. Moreover, once a state achieves an adequate defensive posture, it has incentives for restraint because continuing its arms buildup could suggest that the state desires an offensive capability and thus signal malign motives. This re-

---

[47] Jervis, "Cooperation under the Security Dilemma."

straint would not be very risky because it would not require the state to compromise its defensive capability, but it would nevertheless send a costly signal because a greedy state would see greater military costs in restraint than would a security seeker. Therefore, defense advantage creates reinforcing military and political rationales for restrained arming policies.

In contrast, when offense has the advantage, the security dilemma will be more severe. Arms races will be more intense because when a state adds forces its adversary will have to make larger additions to restore its ability to defend, which would in turn require the state to make a still larger addition to its own forces.[48] Related, states face larger incentives to build up arms because small advantages in force size (which can be generated by falling a step behind in an arms race or by out-of-sync arms buildups) can translate into large military advantages. Agreeing not to build up forces could signal benign motives, but states will tend to find cooperation too risky because offense advantage creates large first-move advantages, so the adversary will be able to achieve significant military advantages by cheating on an arms control agreement.[49] Consequently, offense advantage will tend to prevent security seekers from improving their political relations. Equal-size forces will be insufficient to provide a state with a high degree of security and states will be inclined to adopt offensive strategies to protect their territory, so two equally powerful states would likely both end up insecure. Offense advantage makes war more likely for a variety of reasons, including making states more insecure, which increases the value of expansion, and increasing the advantage of striking first, which increases the probability of crises escalating via preemptive attacks and accidents.[50]

[48] For related analysis, see Malcomb W. Hoag, "On Stability in Deterrent Races," *World Politics* 13, 4 (July 1961): 505–527. If the advantage of offense is large, however, neither state can achieve its security with a defensive doctrine. As a result, both will adopt offensive doctrines, and the key to success will lie in fighting on the offense. Relative force size will matter relatively little, so arms races should not be intense, but war will be likely.

[49] The benefits of cheating will depend on the quality of monitoring and the state's ability to respond once cheating is observed. The effectiveness of monitoring will depend partly on technology; consequently, the capability of monitoring technology might need to be added as a variable to adequately characterize the state's material environment. In addition, however, the effectiveness of monitoring will reflect states' choices about openness and their willingness to agree to intrusive inspections. Van Evera, *Causes of War*, pp. 137–142, argues that offense advantage leads states to be more secretive, which undermines openness and reinforces the dangers created by offense advantage. The implications of cheating for cooperation are discussed more thoroughly in chapter 5.

[50] The relationship between the offense-defense balance and war is more complicated and controversial than I address here; see chapter 4 for more extensive discussion. On the relationship between first strike advantages, preemption, and accidents, see Schelling and Halperin, *Strategy and Arms Control*, pp. 14–16.

Nevertheless, even when offense has the advantage, states should sometimes prefer the military status quo to an arms race. Although the military status quo is unsatisfactory, a buildup could further reduce the state's security. If the state is not confident of maintaining a lead in an arms race, which is likely when states are comparably powerful, cooperating could reduce the probability of still more unsatisfactory outcomes.[51] In addition, an arms control agreement could help avoid some of the "dynamic risks" that an arms race itself could generate. When defense does not have the advantage, falling temporarily behind in a race, which creates a "window" of disadvantage, becomes more dangerous.[52] At the same time, by agreeing not to build when it has some chance of acquiring a meaningful advantage, the state can signal its benign motives; and, because the risks of cooperation are larger, the positive signal will be larger.

The severity of the security dilemma also depends on whether offense and defense can be distinguished—that is, whether the forces that support offensive missions are different from those that support defensive missions. Offense-defense differentiation has the potential to eliminate the security dilemma: if completely differentiated, a country can deploy forces that are useful for protecting itself, but not for attacking its adversary. Moreover, offense-defense differentiation enables a country to more easily signal its type—forgoing forces with offensive potential can signal benign motives because a greedy state would see costs in forgoing offense, while a security seeker would not.

The differentiation of offense and defense makes possible qualitative arms control agreements that ban weapons that are especially useful for offensive missions, thereby increasing both states' ability to defend. The value of qualitative arms control depends on the offense-defense balance. When defense has the advantage, arms control is less important because states can choose unilaterally to deploy defensive forces, adapting a policy of defense emphasis, independent of whether their adversary does. Even if one state decides to pursue offense, the competition should be relatively mild due to the advantage of defense. In contrast, qualitative arms control has more to contribute when offense has the advantage. Because defense then costs more than offense, a state might be unable to afford a defensive posture that could counter its adversary's offense; therefore, cooperation would likely be necessary to make effective defensive capabilities feasible.

States, however, face an increasingly severe trade-off as the advantage

[51] In addition, if the long-term economic consequences of an arms race promise to create domestic political instability or undermine the state's ability to compete, the state should accept still greater risks in the military status quo.

[52] On windows, see Van Evera, *Causes of War*, chap. 4.

of offense increases. This is because cheating poses a greater danger: as the advantage of offense grows, a given amount of cheating would provide a larger advantage; therefore, allowing one's adversary to gain a head start in a renewed arms race would be more dangerous. This makes satisfactory monitoring of an agreement more difficult, which makes it harder for arms control to increase the states' security.

Therefore, in addition to clear benefits that qualitative arms control could provide with regard to the military status quo, states must compare the dynamic risks of arms control and arms racing. States could reduce the dangers of cheating, and therefore the requirements for monitoring, by allowing large defensive forces while banning offensive forces, which would form a defensive barrier to cheating. However, there is no general resolution of the trade-off between these dynamic considerations; it will depend on the specifics of monitoring capabilities and the rates at which states can break out of agreements, as well as the effectiveness of a defensive barrier.[53]

POWER

In addition to these offense-defense variables, the severity of the security dilemma also depends upon power—the ratio of states' resources that can be converted into military assets.[54] The greater a state's power advantage, the less severe the security dilemma. This is because the state's power advantage reduces its adversary's ability to counter a military buildup; all else being equal, the greater a state's power, the more likely an arms buildup is to increase the state's military capability. A state with a large power advantage is likely both to win the arms race and to acquire large military advantages. Because the outcome of an arms race is clear, on-going competition may be unnecessary; the state may be able to acquire and sustain military advantages without provoking a reaction. In contrast, when states are equally powerful, an arms buildup is more likely to generate a reaction. There is some chance that the state would win the competition, but there is also a comparable probability of losing; a draw may be the most likely outcome. Both states may see the possibility that

[53] A defensive barrier increases the time required to gain an offensive advantage but does not necessarily reduce the benefits of cheating. However, if there are uncertainties about relative rearmament rates, then defensive barriers would increase uncertainty about whether breaking out of an agreement would provide military advantages, which could contribute to deterrence. See Schelling, *Arms and Influence*, pp. 248–259; and Glaser, *Analyzing Strategic Nuclear Policy*, pp. 178–179.

[54] To keep the analysis reasonably simple, the following discussion assumes that power is constant. When power is shifting, the declining state will have additional incentives to launch a buildup and initiate a war. These issues are addressed briefly in chapter 4; for citations on preventive war, see notes 19 and 20 in that chapter.

the arms race will provide benefits, but also worry about its risks. Consequently, whether arms racing or cooperating will be a state's best option depends on other variables, including both material and information variables. A weaker state faces a severe security dilemma because efforts to improve its military capabilities are unlikely to succeed and could generate reactions that leave it less capable.

The impact of power on the security dilemma becomes more complicated once we include signaling, but the basic conclusions stand under a wider range of assumptions. Launching a military buildup that provides large military advantages is likely to signal malign motives because a greedy state will tend to be more likely than a security seeker to require military advantages.[55] Consequently, although an arms buildup would increase a more powerful state's military capability, the dangers of reducing its adversary's security do create incentives for the state to limit its arms buildup.[56] A state with a power advantage may want to restrain its buildup, forgoing or at least limiting military advantages to avoid undermining the adversary's military capability and to signal its benign motives.[57] The signaling should be effective because the state's power advantage makes clear its potential to win a quantitative arms race and therefore its restraint. Recent arguments that the United States can best manage its unipolar position by adopting restrained military and foreign policies reflect this basic logic, applied to a situation in which there are a number of less powerful states that could balance against the United States.[58] As discussed below, how a state should resolve the trade-off between acquiring military advantages and reducing the adversary's insecurity depends on the offense-defense balance and its information about its adversary's motives.

[55] More precisely, whether there is a signal will depend on the match between the state's military capabilities and the requirements for protecting its interests in the geopolitical status quo. Military advantages should not signal malign motives if they are required to defend the status quo; in contrast, they will signal malign motives if the advantages are larger than this, or if there is disagreement about the requirement for defending the status quo or about the status quo itself.

[56] The extent of the state's power advantage, however, influences the impact of this signal in countervailing ways: on the one hand, signaling malign motives creates more insecurity when the state has greater power; on the other hand, signaling malign motives would be less dangerous because the adversary would be less capable of challenging a more powerful state. Arguably, these countervailing effects tend to cancel each other out.

[57] This consideration also generates incentives for cooperation between equally powerful states, but these political/signaling benefits are then smaller, while the military benefits of cooperation are larger.

[58] For example, Stephen M. Walt, "Keeping the World 'Off-Balance': Self-Restraint and U.S. Foreign Policy," in G. John Ikenberry, ed., *America Unrivaled: The Future of the Balance of Power* (Ithaca: Cornell University Press, 2002).

COMBINED EFFECT OF POWER AND OFFENSE-DEFENSE VARIABLES

The severity of the security dilemma and a state's choice of strategy—
whether to compete or cooperate and, related, whether to rely on an offensive or defensive doctrine—depend on the combination of these material variables. The state's power multiplied by the offense-defense
balance—the ratio of the cost of forces required to take territory to the
cost of the forces deployed by the defender—indicates its prospects for
acquiring an effective defensive capability. A state that suffers a power
disadvantage will be able to preserve its defensive capability if this disadvantage is smaller than the extent of defense advantage. Under these
conditions, the more powerful state should recognize its poor prospects
for acquiring an offensive capability and therefore adopt a cooperative
policy that accepts the limited value of pursuing an arms buildup. For
example, this logic explains why a medium power should be able to
maintain an effective nuclear deterrent against a superpower without
generating an intense arms competition. In contrast, a sufficiently powerful state can acquire an offensive capability, even when defense has the
advantage.

Although defense advantage favors a defensive strategy, a security-
seeking state could nevertheless require an offensive capability for a variety of reasons.[59] A state could require an offensive capability because it
has geographical interests that are separated from its homeland. For example, during the 1920s and 1930s the United States required an offensive naval capability to protect its interests in East Asia and had to decide
whether to engage in an arms race with Japan over this capability. A state
could also value an offensive capability because it faces a two-front war
and needs to fight its adversaries sequentially. This rationale underpinned
Germany's Schlieffen Plan in the years leading up to World War I. In addition, a state could choose an offensive capability and engage in the
arms competition that this generates to communicate its resolve to protect its interests in the political status quo. This rationale played a prominent role in the U.S. debate over Cold War nuclear policy.[60]

Whether a security seeker that values an offensive capability and is sufficiently powerful to acquire one when defense has the advantage should
exercise this option depends on a potentially complex trade-off. The benefits depend on the value of the interests at stake and the marginal deterrent value of an offensive capability. The costs include the provocation
generated by acquiring a threatening military capability, which tends to
be large when defense has the advantage. For example, during the Cold

[59] See Jervis, "Cooperation under the Security Dilemma" on the need for offense; see Van
Evera, *Causes of War*, pp. 152–160, on when offensive doctrines cause peace.
[60] Glaser, *Analyzing Strategic Nuclear Policy*, pp. 63–67, 240–242.

War opposition to NATO's acquisition of a conventional offensive capability focused on the high quality of its defensive capabilities, which reduced the deterrent value of offense, and on the threat the Soviets would impute to an offensive capability that was arguably unnecessary for protecting the status quo.[61]

How strenuously the weaker state should attempt to offset this offensive capability depends on the interests that are threatened. If its interests are greater than its adversary's, the state may be willing to devote a larger percentage of its resources to acquiring arms, which would increase its prospects for prevailing in the arms race.[62] Even if prevailing is infeasible, the weaker state may prefer to compete to enhance its deterrent by deploying forces large enough to increase the costs of war and demonstrate its resolve. As discussed below, the weaker state should also consider the opposing state's motives—if it requires offense for security, racing is less likely to be successful and more likely to strain relations.

In contrast to the situation described above, as the advantage of defense decreases, or if offense actually has the advantage, a state will increasingly find that equal-size forces are inadequate to support a defensive strategy and that it requires an advantage in force size.[63] Consequently, arms competition becomes a more attractive option, especially for states that enjoy a power advantage.[64] If sufficiently large, a power advantage enables a state to achieve an effective defensive capability, in addition to an effective offensive capability. Although larger forces decrease the adversary's military capability, the adversary should appreciate the security pressures that make them necessary, which should reduce the political provocation they generate.

Figure 3.1 summarizes the preceding discussion of how different combinations of power and the offense-defense balance should influence a state's decision to build up arms and engage in an arms race.

---

[61] For the case in favor of acquisition, see Samuel P. Huntington, "Conventional Deterrence and Conventional Retaliation in Europe," *International Security* 8, 3 (Winter 1983–84): 32–56; for the case against, see Betts, "Conventional Deterrence." For the case against nuclear superiority even if it were feasible, see Glaser, *Analyzing Strategic Nuclear Policy*, chap. 5.

[62] Another reason that the weaker state might engage in an arms competition instead of simply accepting military inferiority is that the states disagree about their power, although this is less likely when the difference is large. On this type of interaction, see Andrew Kydd, "Arms Races and Arms Control: Modeling the Hawk Perspective," *American Journal of Political Science* 44, 2 (April 2000): 222–238.

[63] If states knew the value of the balance with certainty, they might require an advantage in force size only under offense advantage. In practice, however, states face uncertainty about the offense-defense balance. In addition, uncertainty about the quality of forces and the scenario that leads to war further support the case for superiority.

[64] However, see the caveat in note 48.

Power	Offense-Defense Balance: Defense > Offense	Offense-Defense Balance: Offense > Defense
Power advantage	• No need to build—defensive doctrine without force advantage is adequate; action-reaction peters out • Exceptions if geopolitical rationales generate offensive requirements ♦ Must then compare political costs against military benefits (depends on information about adversary's motives)	• Arms buildups and offensive doctrine often best, unless ♦ power advantage is large enough to make defense possible ♦ power advantage is too small to guarantee success; weigh risks of losing a race ♦ offense and defense are different; weigh the benefits of limiting offense against risks of cheating
Power disadvantage	• If defense advantage is greater than power disadvantage, defensive doctrine is still feasible; arms buildups can be avoided or should peter out • If defense advantage is less than power disadvantage, cannot prevent adversary from acquiring offensive capability ♦ Weigh arms competition to retain some deterrent capability against cooperating to improve relations	• Buildup holds little prospect of producing a defensive capability • Might buildup to preserve an offensive capability

Figure 3.1 Material Variables and the Choice of Arming Policies

Information Variables

The preceding arguments are sound but incomplete, because the effectiveness of cooperative and competitive strategies depends on the opposing state's type. As a result, as argued in the previous chapter, a state's information about its adversary's motives should be included as a key variable defining its international situation. In addition, a state's information about its adversary's information about its motives should also be included. This section explores how the severity of the security dilemma and a state's choice of strategy should depend on these information variables, focusing on the impact of former.

A basic point to start with is that security-seeking states face a security dilemma only if they face uncertainty about their potential adversary's motives.[65] If a potential adversary knew that the state was a security seeker (and if the adversary also knew that the state knew that it was a security seeker), policies that the state pursued to increase its security would not reduce the adversary's security. The adversary would know that the state had no reason to attack it, and therefore would not be more insecure, even if the state had increased its offensive military capability. From the state's perspective, if it had the same information about its adversary, it would lack reasons for pursuing policies to increase its security in the first place. As a result, certainty about states' types would eliminate the security dilemma in reinforcing ways—by eliminating the need to pursue security and by eliminating the insecurity that security-driven policies would otherwise generate.

The impact of a state's information on the security dilemma does not stop as soon as there is some uncertainty about the adversary's type. Instead, a high probability estimate that the adversary is a security seeker results in a less severe security dilemma, while a high probability estimate that the adversary is greedy results in a more severe security dilemma.[66] To understand this relationship, we need to consider how a state should choose its strategy when faced with uncertainty about its adversary's type.

For a variety of reasons, cooperating with a security seeker will often

[65] This observation depends on the assumption that the states are pure security seekers. In contrast, if some states have mixed motives, then even certainty about motives would not eliminate the security dilemma. For example, an insecure greedy state could pursue a military buildup to increase its security; however, if its buildup increases its offensive potential, then its adversary will be made more insecure, which could generate security-dilemma reactions. To keep things simple, the discussion in the text does not address states with mixed motives; see chapter 2 for some discussion.

[66] The discussion here assumes that the adversary is in fact a security seeker; if the adversary is actually a greedy state, then the insecurity results partly from the adversary's greed and should not be attributed to the security dilemma.

be preferable to cooperating with a greedy state. A security seeker is more likely than a greedy state to reciprocate cooperation and to abide by arms control agreements because it places less value on gaining military advantages, because they are often not required for protecting its security in the status quo. In contrast, a greedy state often requires military advantages to pursue its agenda of changing the territorial status quo. In addition, a failure of cooperation with a greedy state is more dangerous than a similar failure with a security seeker. A greedy state is harder to deter than a security seeker because it places greater value on expansion and therefore is willing to incur higher costs in war. As a result, the advantages acquired by not reciprocating when the state cooperates or by cheating on an arms control agreement are more likely to lead to war when facing a greedy state. Moreover, cooperating with a security seeker can signal one's benign motives, which will increase the adversary's security, which in turn makes it more likely to cooperate and easier to deter. In contrast, the benefits of signaling benign motives to a greedy state are smaller because increasing its security is less important and because cooperating could signal that the state lacks resolve, which is more dangerous when facing a greedy state.[67] For similar reasons, competing with a greedy state is often preferable to competing with a security seeker: military advantages are more valuable because deterrence is more difficult, building arms to avoid military shortfalls is more important because the adversary is likely to pursue a military buildup independent of the state's policy, and signaling resolve is more important because the adversary is harder to deter.

If a state is certain that its adversary is purely greedy, it can focus solely on acquiring the military capabilities required to prevent its adversary from attacking its territory and on signaling its resolve.[68] On the other hand, if the state knows its adversary is a security seeker, the state must also consider the impact of its military policy on its adversary's security because reducing the adversary's security can generate reactions that reduce the state's own security.

However, when uncertain about its adversary's type, the state must draw upon its information about the opposing state's motives because this determines how likely the various outcomes would be. The state

[67] This signaling of resolve requires that there be differences among security seekers. For example, if two security seekers place different value on protecting their interests, and if this translates into higher military requirements for the state that values its interests more highly, then cooperation that accepts a reduced military capability—to avoid the military and/or political risks of competition—could signal a lack of resolve. Chapter 4 explores this issue in some detail.

[68] This raises the question whether there are states that are not made insecure by offensive capabilities, which I do not address here. The possibility of secure greedy states is central to the deterrence model; see Jervis, *Perception and Misperception*, chap. 3; Glaser, "Political Consequences of Military Strategy"; and chapter 4.

needs to weigh the outcomes that would be produced if facing a security seeker by the probability that the adversary is a security seeker, and the outcomes that would be produced if facing a greedy state by its probability. The overall effects of competition and cooperation can then be compared. Cooperation would be more attractive the more likely it is that the state faces a security seeker since in this case the positive results of cooperation are more likely to occur and the dangers of cooperating are less likely to occur. Put another way, the higher the probability that the adversary is a security seeker, the more likely that the expected benefits of cooperation with a security seeker will outweigh the expected risks of cooperating with a greedy state. Similarly, competition will be more attractive when it is more likely that the state faces a greedy state because the positive results of competition are then more likely to occur.

The state's evaluation should also take into account the adversary's beliefs about the state's own motives because the adversary's decision about whether to reciprocate cooperation should depend on this information.[69] For example, when the adversary believes that the state is likely to be greedy, the adversary is less likely to cooperate since it expects the state will be less likely to continue cooperating. As a result, even if the state is certain the adversary is a security seeker, the state's understanding of the adversary's information makes it more inclined to compete.[70]

When the probability that the opposing state is a security seeker is high enough (and when the adversary's information that the state is a security seeker is high enough), cooperation will be the state's best option. As discussed below, "high enough" depends on the material conditions facing the state. The key point to emphasize here is that variation in the state's information about the opposing state's motives can produce variation in the severity of the security dilemma and in the state's choice of strategy.

The American debate over U.S. Cold War strategy provides a clear example of the role of information in driving strategy preferences. Hawks favored competitive policies largely because they believed that the Soviet Union was motivated by greed and that it knew the United States was a security seeker; the danger was not a security dilemma, but rather that

---

[69] More precisely, what actually matters is the state's beliefs about the adversary's beliefs about the state's motives.

[70] With reasonable assumptions about payoffs, this discussion can be formalized as a state that faces uncertainty about whether it faces a prisoners' dilemma (if facing a greedy state) or a stag hunt (if facing a security seeker); if the adversary is uncertain about the state's type, then the state faces the additional uncertainty for both types of adversary about the game the adversary believes it is in and therefore that adversary's reaction. See Glaser, "The Security Dilemma Revisited," pp. 184–185; and Kydd, "Trust, Reassurance, and Cooperation," which also includes a treatment of two-sided uncertainty. However, other games are possible, depending on material conditions.

cooperative U.S. policies would enable the Soviets to gain military advantages and encourage them to underestimate U.S. resolve. In contrast, doves favored cooperative policies because they believed that the Soviet Union was motivated by security and that the Soviets failed to appreciate America's benign motives. Doves therefore concluded that the United States faced a security dilemma in which competitive policies would be self-defeating.[71]

The preceding discussion yields two broad insights about the implications of information about the adversary's motives that deserve to be highlighted. First, the information a state possesses can determine the evolution of its political relationships with other states: high estimates of benign motives help preserve good relations and may contribute to improving them, while low estimates tend to have the opposite impact. Information that one's adversary is likely to be a security seeker can lead the state to adopt cooperative policies, which can signal that it has benign motives, which can in turn lead other states to revise their information about the state's motives, which can make cooperative policies their best option, setting in motion a positive spiral. In contrast, under similar material conditions, but starting instead with higher estimates that the adversary is greedy, the state is more likely to choose a strategy that produces the opposite result—the state's best option is more likely to be competitive policies, which its adversary reacts to with competitive policies, thereby generating a reinforcing negative spiral.

Consequently, a world history that has experienced high levels of conflict and results in states often starting their interactions with information that opposing states are likely to have malign motives creates a tendency for a continuation of conflictual relations. The point here is not that states will necessarily be locked into conflict indefinitely, but rather that escaping it will be harder, requiring larger changes in the material environment or riskier cooperative signaling policies. On the other hand, once relations improve dramatically, as they have between the major powers since the early 1990s, the prospects for their continuation are also improved. The possibility of continuing peace in post–Cold War Europe, which I explore briefly in chapter 7, illustrates this point.

A second important result is that a state may need to mix or combine cooperative and competitive strategies. To simplify the analysis, the preceding discussion assumed that the state has two options—compete or cooperate. States, however, will often have a spectrum of options, ranging from very competitive to very cooperative. The extent of cooperation and competition can vary along a number of dimensions. For example, as

[71] See Jervis, *Perception and Misperception*, chap. 3; and Jervis, "Was the Cold War a Security Dilemma?," *Journal of Cold War Studies* 3, 1 (Winter 2001): 36–60.

described above, certain cooperative strategies accept some vulnerability to attack in order to increase the adversary's security, while other cooperative strategies are designed to be nonprovocative but avoid accepting military vulnerabilities. The risks and benefits of these strategies depend on the type of adversary that the state faces. Beyond these cooperative strategies are a range of more competitive ones that can enhance deterrence, including strategies that provide retaliatory offensive capabilities and that provide military capabilities designed to attack with limited aims. A state's information about its adversary's motives should influence its choice along this multidimensional spectrum, shifting toward more cooperative and riskier strategies when the probability that the adversary is a security seeker is higher.

This point reflects an insight that emerges from analysis of the spiral and deterrence models, which are defined largely by the behavior of different types of states. The deterrence model prescribes competitive policies to communicate resolve and enhance deterrence when facing an adversary that is motivated by greed; in contrast, the spiral model calls for cooperative policies because the adversary is motivated by security and locates the sources of competition in the adversary's uncertainty about the state's motives and a material security dilemma. The theory presented here is more general—it takes the adversary's motives as uncertain instead of known. Consequently, the theory calls for states to search for a mix of spiral and deterrence model policies, except in extreme cases of near certainty.[72]

Combined Effect of Material and Information Variables

The severity of the security dilemma depends on the combined effect of material and information variables. For example, as explained above, while offense advantage increases the severity of the security dilemma, information that the opposing state is likely to be a security seeker reduces its severity.[73] To appreciate the combined effect of these variables, consider the different reactions of security seekers and greedy states to offense advantage. Although offense advantage creates pressures for competition, a security seeker places less value on gaining military advantages and relatively greater value on avoiding the risk of falling behind in the ensuing arms race and of signaling malign motives. Therefore, if a state cooperates, a security-seeking adversary would be inclined to reciprocate this cooperation, unless the military value of competing instead is

[72] On the impact of uncertainty, see Edelstein, "Managing Uncertainty"; and Jervis, *Perception and Misperception*, pp. 111–112.

[73] Note, however, that this assumes the opposing state is actually a security seeker; if the adversary is a greedy state, this information does not reduce the state's security.

very large. In contrast, the military incentives created by offense advantage would reinforce the inclination of a greedy state to compete in response to cooperation. Consequently, the risk of cooperation, which tends to be higher when offense has the advantage, and the severity of the security dilemma are reduced if the state believes the adversary is likely to be a security seeker. If the probability that the adversary is a security seeker is sufficiently high, a state's best option is to cooperate, even when offense has the advantage. The probability that is necessary to make cooperation the state's preferred strategy depends on the offense-defense balance. Because the costs of cooperating with a greedy adversary increase as the advantage of offense increases, for cooperation to be a state's best option requires that its estimate that the adversary is a security seeker must be greater when the advantage of offense is larger.

Information and the offense-defense balance combine in similar ways to determine the severity of the security dilemma when defense has the advantage. Defense advantage makes cooperation less risky and states more secure for essentially the reverse of the arguments presented above. As a result, high estimates that the adversary is a security seeker are not required to make cooperation a state's best option. However, if the adversary is likely to be greedy, cooperation may not be a security seeker's best option, unless defense has a large advantage. Greedy states tend to be more willing to fight costly wars and wars that they have a low probability of winning. Consequently, a security seeker will desire a more favorable balance of forces when facing a greedy adversary, will find the possibility that its adversary would cheat on arms control agreements not only more likely but also more dangerous, and may even require an offensive capability to achieve an adequate deterrent.[74] Therefore, a state that believes its adversary is likely a greedy state will see dangers in cooperation even when defense has the advantage, and will see greater value in competition that might provide military advantages and signal resolve. As a result, unless defense has a large advantage, a state that believes it likely faces a greedy adversary may prefer competition to cooperation, even though this risks making its adversary less secure. Although defense has the advantage, the security seeker would face a moderate security dilemma. Competition would be even more attractive if the state enjoys a power advantage because this further reduces the risks of military competition.

Figure 3.2 illustrates the combined effect of information and material variables on the severity of the security dilemma.[75]

[74] Barry R. Posen, "Crisis Stability and Conventional Arms Control," *Daedalus* 120 (Winter 1991): 217–232.

[75] The relative levels in the figure are illustrative; a more precise ranking would depend on the specific values of the variables and would require a theory that translates material conditions into war outcomes and places values on them.

Information about Motives

Material Conditions		Likely greedy	Equally likely greedy or security seeker	Likely security seeker
	Offense advantage	Very severe	Severe	Moderate
	Defense advantage	Moderate	Mild	Essentially eliminated

Figure 3.2. Severity of the Security Dilemma

WHY IS THE INTERNATIONAL ENVIRONMENT INSUFFICIENT FOR PRESCRIBING STRATEGY? GREEDY STATES

So far, this chapter has focused on the impact of the international environment on a security seeker's choice of strategy: the state choosing a strategy is a security seeker. In fact, all states in the system are security seekers, although this is not common knowledge. All the action/variation is produced by the international environment, which includes uncertainty about the adversary's motives and type as a key variable. However, a key broad finding of the theory developed to this point—that security seekers should pursue cooperative policies under a wide range of material and information conditions—demonstrates that my theory needs to be expanded to include variation in the type of state making strategic choices, adding greedy states and analysis of their decisions.

If the international system should consistently produce competition, as some leading structural realists have argued, greedy states would matter relatively little.[76] According to this view, security seekers should adopt competitive policies across the full range of material and information variables; competitive policies would characterize the behavior of both greedy states and security seekers. Therefore, from a theoretical perspective there would be relatively little reason to distinguish between types of states.[77] The simpler theory that focused entirely on a state's international situation would offer greater parsimony at little explanatory and prescriptive cost. This supposed finding supports a key divide in interna-

[76] Waltz, *Theory of International Politics*; Mearsheimer, *The Tragedy of Great Power Politics*. Waltz does argue that what states want matters, explaining, for example, that a large advantage in power allows states to pursue other (nonsecurity) objectives. His key point, however, is that the international system leads all states into competition.

[77] This level of generality does underplay some possible differences; for example, under a range of conditions, greedy states might choose more competitive policies, have a greater propensity to balance versus bandwagon, and be more likely to initiate war. Nevertheless, the thrust of this broad observation remains sound.

tional relations theory over whether the international system (structural realism) or states (neoclassical realism) are the driving force behind states' international behavior. In contrast, the theory developed here shows that we cannot deductively demonstrate that either states' motives or their international environment has a dominant influence on the international strategies that they should choose.

A greedy state should under some conditions want to take territory when a security seeker should not.[78] A security seeker that is secure will be satisfied with the territorial status quo, whereas a greedy state will be interested in expansion. Even when a security seeker is interested in expansion, a greedy state will often be more interested—that is, willing to pay a higher price to take territory—because it sees nonsecurity value, as well as security value, in the territory. Because they place a higher value on taking territory, greedy states should be willing to run risks to their security that security seekers should reject.

As a result, greedy states will under a range of conditions choose competitive policies when a security seeker would choose cooperative ones. We have already considered these divergences from a different perspective, because a security seeker facing uncertainty about whether its adversary is greedy needs to include them in its assessment of strategies. Now we are simply shifting perspective, considering a greedy state that is making decisions—looking out at its international situation and choosing between cooperative and competitive strategies.

Possibly most obvious, a greedy state could prefer competitive policies even when it is confident that its adversary is a security seeker. Because its interest in expansion goes beyond security, these information conditions, which make the greedy state secure, do not make competitive policies unnecessary, as they would for a security seeker. A second example focuses on material conditions: when defense has the advantage, a security seeker will usually be able to meet its security requirements with a defensive doctrine and parity in military forces. In contrast, a greedy state will require an offensive military doctrine, which to be effective will require an advantage in force size. Consequently, the greedy state will be inclined to compete for military advantages. A greedy state with a sufficient power advantage will be able to acquire an offensive capability while maintaining a defensive capability and should be more inclined to pursue it than would a security seeker. Another example hinges on the options made possible by differences between offense and defense: a security seeker will value an arms control agreement that limits forces that favor offensive missions; in contrast, a greedy state will be reluctant to accept this type of limit because it requires these forces for expansion. Although a greedy

---

[78] The importance of this type of unit-level variation is emphasized by Schweller, *Deadly Imbalances*.

state might accept a qualitative arms control agreement that greatly increased its security, it would nevertheless see smaller net benefits in this cooperation; and in some cases the security risks would be smaller than the benefits of nonsecurity expansion, making competition the greedy state's best option. In effect, what we see in this example is that the value a greedy state places on expansion reduces the severity of the trade-off that lies at the heart of the security dilemma.

A similar logic explains why greedy states will be more inclined than security seekers to bandwagon—that is, to ally with a more powerful state (or alliance)—than to balance—that is, to ally against the more powerful state (or alliance). A state that has an effective balancing option runs a greater security risk when it chooses to bandwagon with a more powerful state—its alliance partner is more likely to turn on it, both because the ally is more capable of defeating the state and because the state is less important to the ally's security. A greedy state is more willing to run these risks because it places greater value on being in a more powerful coalition that has greater potential for expansion.[79]

A number of considerations broaden further the conditions under which a greedy state will find competition to be its best option. First, a greedy state that places higher value on taking territory should be willing to fight with a lower probability of winning and/or with the expectation of incurring higher costs of fighting. Consequently, it requires smaller military advantages to expect fighting to be successful. This in turn means there is a broader range of conditions under which a greedy state could expect competition to provide the military capabilities it requires; for example, it would require a smaller power advantage to expect to succeed in an arms race. Second, a greedy state should often be less concerned about provoking its adversary because it expects to engage in conflict anyway. Therefore, although a greedy state will have some incentive for restraint (if its adversary's reaction would pose a serious threat and especially if it believes its adversary is a security seeker), these incentives will be smaller and will tend to vanish as the greedy state prepares for war.[80]

Greedy states should not, however, always pursue competitive policies. A first concern is feasibility—a greedy state should not pursue competitive policies that have poor prospects for providing the military capabilities it requires for expansion. Although a greedy state may have less demanding military requirements than a security seeker, under a range of conditions competitive policies would not enable it to meet even this

---

[79] Waltz, *Theory of International Politics*, p. 127, uses these considerations to explain why states balance; on the logic of bandwagoning, see Randall L. Schweller, "Bandwagoning for Profit: Bringing the Revisionist State Back In," *International Security* 19, 1 (Summer 1994): 72–107.

[80] If, however, appearing threatening will contribute to the formation of an opposing balancing coalition, the greedy state will have continuing incentives for restraint.

lower standard. For example, when defense has a large advantage, a greedy state that lacks a power advantage will have poor prospects for achieving an offensive capability, making competition unattractive. At a minimum, competition promises to be economically draining, while offering little promise of enhanced military capabilities.

A second concern is security—as some of the preceding examples already suggested, greedy states can be motivated by security, as well as greed, which can create incentives for restraint and cooperation. Recall that I am using the term greedy to refer to states with mixed motives—greed as well as security; I use the term purely greedy state to refer to a state that entirely lacks security motives. Although there is a strong analytic rationale for identifying purely greedy states, we have theoretical reasons for expecting that most greedy states would value what they possess and therefore be interested in security; in the end, the frequency is an empirical question.[81] A greedy state can face a trade-off: if the policies required to achieve its greedy aims would provoke a reaction that reduces its ability to defend the status quo, the greedy state must weigh its security and nonsecurity objectives. A greedy state might prefer forgoing an offensive capability to allowing its adversary to acquire one and, therefore, prefer an arms control agreement that limited offensive weapons, even though this cooperation would reduce its ability to expand. As noted above, a greedy state would see less value in such an agreement than would a pure security seeker; it might nevertheless prefer the agreement to competition. The trade-off facing a greedy state will also depend on how much value it places on expansion. Consider a greedy state that wants to expand into peripheral areas in which it has secondary interests. If competition promises to provoke reactions that would reduce this state's ability to protect vital interests, for example, its homeland, this expansion, even if feasible, is likely to be undesirable. In contrast, a greedy state that has nonsecurity objectives that it values highly will face a more difficult trade-off.

SUMMARY AND IMPLICATIONS

In deciding between cooperative and competitive strategies, a state should consider their impact on both its own military capabilities and its adversary's security.[82] The state needs to ask how the alternative strategies should influence its adversary's security because decreases in the adversary's security can decrease the state's own security. All else being equal,

[81] Jervis, *Perception and Misperception*, p. 51.

[82] As noted above, a state may also need to consider the impact on its adversary's assessment of the state's resolve. Chapter 4 addresses this requirement.

a state's prospects for achieving security increase with its ability to perform the military missions required to deter attacks and, if deterrence fails, to defend; a state's prospects for achieving greedy goals increase with its ability to coerce opposing states and, if coercion fails, to take territory. Considering military capabilities requires the state to ask: if both states build, would its military capability—the capability to perform necessary military missions—increase or decrease?[83] Considering the adversary's security requires the state to ask both whether its arms buildup (combined with its adversary's reaction) would decrease its adversary's military capability and whether its arms buildup would lead its adversary to conclude that the state's motives are more likely to be malign, which would make its military capabilities more threatening. Under a wide range of conditions, both arming and not arming will be risky.

In broad terms, the security dilemma provides the theory's core logic and frames its analysis of these questions. Variation in power, offense-defense variables, and a state's information about its adversary's motives influences the magnitude and nature of the security dilemma and the strategy a state should choose. The theory shows that variation in the state's international situation should lead to variation in its strategy—under a wide range of conditions, cooperation will be a security seeker's best option; under other conditions, competition is more likely to provide security. Either information variables or materials variables can be the key to cooperation; under a wide range of conditions, neither alone will determine a state's strategy. A state's own motives should also influence its strategy. There are conditions under which a security seeker should cooperate, but a greedy state should compete.

A possible criticism is that the theory is too complicated. Unlike those realist theories that focus solely on power, my theory also includes variation in the type of states and in the information they have about other states' types, as well as additional material variables, specifically offense-defense variables. A key conclusion, however, that we can draw from the argument developed in this chapter and the preceding one is that simpler theories are suspect. The theory's setup has a clear analytic rationale and is intuitively sensible: the theory's variables (with the possible exception of offense-defense variables) are all essential components of a strategic-choice analysis. Moreover, it is intuitively reasonable that what a state wants, its capability to achieve what it wants, and what it knows about what its adversaries want should all be included in its choice of strategy. As explained in chapter 2, offense-defense variables make intuitive and logical sense, providing the necessary conceptual link between power and

[83] As discussed more fully in chapter 9, if the state decides that both not building would be preferable, the state must then also consider whether the adversary would build if it does not, as well as the risks of the adversary cheating on an arms agreement.

military capabilities. In fact, chapter 4 explains that still more variation is necessary to capture key arguments about international politics. And, as we will see in chapter 7, the more difficult question is actually whether the theory is too simple, not whether it is too complicated.

Given this starting point, one way to reduce the number of variables (and thereby the theory's complexity) would be to show deductively that variation in the one or more variables should not change a state's optimal strategy. This chapter demonstrates, however, that this is not the case—basic deductive arguments show that all these variables matter, that is, should significantly influence a state's strategy choices.

A possible rejoinder is that more parsimonious theories can explain international politics as well as this more complicated theory and, therefore, are preferable; this criterion is often used as a measure of IR theories. Even if this claim about explanatory power is correct (which I doubt), we should not necessarily prefer the simpler theory. First, and most important, the greater explanatory power might result because the states being studied and the international situations they faced have not varied across the full range of the independent variables. Unless we have powerful reasons for concluding that this degree of variation will not occur, different international behaviors are possible and a theory of international politics should make clear the conditions under which they will be a state's best strategy. The simpler theory risks overlooking these possibilities, even if it does well at explaining the past. Major power relations after the Cold War, including the lack of competition within Europe and the lack of balancing against U.S. unipolarity, illustrate this point. Earlier major power competition could have reflected a combination of states' high estimates that other powers were greedy or assessments of the offense-defense balance that did not heavily favor defense. Not recognizing these variables would lead to prescriptions (and predictions) of continuing future competition. Such a theory, although it did well at explaining the past, would overlook the implications of changes in information about motives and military technology, failing to recognize their implications for extensive cooperation and peace. Second, we need to be open to the possibility that states' behavior has often not been rational/optimal and that an overly simple (or deductively flawed) theory that does well at explaining states' behavior may be inadvertently benefiting from biases that wash out variation. For example, a history of competitive international relations could reflect organizational or cognitive biases that have led states to compete when they should have cooperated. A more complete, deductively sound theory is required to begin sorting out this possibility.

CHAPTER FOUR

Extensions of the Theory

THIS CHAPTER EXTENDS the theory in a number of ways. The chapter first increases the theory's complexity by relaxing simplifications that were useful for crafting the basic theory developed in chapters 2 and 3. Although the theory developed in the previous chapters is complicated, especially compared to realist theories that focus solely on power, it includes a number of important simplifications. For example, the theory distinguishes between security seekers and greedy states, but not between security seekers that place different value on protecting what they possess, nor between greedy states that vary in the value they place on expansion. While it is productive to categorize states as either security seeking or greedy, variation within these types is possible and could influence a state's strategy. Similarly, although it is useful to envision states facing material variables that they know the value of with certainty, states will often face uncertainty about power and the offense-defense balance that should influence their decisions. And the theory has focused on how material and information variables should influence states' decisions, but not on how the possibility that these variables will change exogenously in the future should also influence their decisions. This possibility requires modifying some of the earlier arguments about cooperation and competition, as well as raising the question of preventive war.

With the foundation of the theory established, taking up these complexities is now productive. The simplifications enabled us to focus on how a relatively small number of key variables should influence a state's choice of strategy, providing a broad understanding of how states should interact with their international environment. These simplifications are what might be called "within theory" simplifications; they are not required to sustain the fundamental character of the theory—its assumptions of rational unitary actors facing anarchy; its taking of motives, initial information, and material variables as exogenous; and its strategic-choice perspective. Consequently, moving beyond these simplifications by including additional complexity is best envisioned as creating a fuller version of the existing theory, not as generating a basically new theory. Dealing with these complexities does not result in a different basic understanding of international politics. In certain cases, however, it does lay the foundation for a more nuanced assessment of states' strategy options; in other cases, dealing with the complexity provides a sounder foundation for arguments that were developed earlier.

Following this discussion of complexities, the chapter next extends the theory to a couple of major topics that the basic theory has not yet addressed. While the theory has focused broadly on competition versus cooperation and looked more closely at arming decisions, it has not yet focused on war. A short section explores how a state's decision for war should depend on the theory's variables. Also deserving attention is the question of the role and importance of international institutions, especially their importance for making cooperation feasible.

Variation within Security Seekers: Implications for Signaling and the Deterrence Model

The Logic of Communicating Resolve

Although all security seekers value their security, they may not value it equally. Security seekers could differ in the value they place on protecting their homeland, and on protecting and/or acquiring other territory that they believe would contribute to their security. The term "resolve" is frequently used to capture a state's determination to protect its interests. For a rational state, resolve measures and reflects nothing more than the state's interest in a particular territory or issue.

This variation among security seekers could be important because it should affect the behavior of both the security seeker and its adversary. A state that places greater value on its territory should be willing to invest more in the military forces required to protect it, run greater risks in bargaining over the territory, and, if conflict occurs, incur higher risks and costs in fighting. An adversary that recognizes the state's greater interest should anticipate these greater investments in arms, bargaining, and fighting and adjust its strategy accordingly. For example, because a state with greater interests at stake should be willing to invest more in arms to protect them, an adversary's decision about whether to engage in an arms race should depend on its assessment of the state's interests, as well as the state's power. Facing two states with equal power, a rational adversary could choose to compete against the state that possessed less resolve, while deciding to forgo an arms race against the state that had greater resolve.

Similarly, if the adversary believes the state places higher value on territory, it is more likely to be deterred from attacking than if it believes the state places lower value on the territory. This is simply a version of the familiar argument that the effectiveness of a state's deterrent depends on the credibility of its threats, which depends not only on a state's military capability but also on its willingness to carry out threatened actions. For a rational state, this latter factor—willingness—is directly related to the interests at stake; the greater the state's interests, the more likely it is to be willing to incur the costs and risks of fighting, and therefore the more likely that it will carry out its threat.[1]

The adversary, however, may be uncertain about the value the security seeker places on defending its territory. This incomplete information is essentially the parallel of the security seeker's uncertainty about the adversary's motives and is an important element of the international environment the adversary faces. Underestimates of the state's interest could lead the adversary to pursue a military buildup when it would otherwise prefer cooperation and to use military threats to coerce the state when it would otherwise peacefully accept the status quo. Consequently, in choosing its strategy, the state should attempt to insure that the adversary does not underestimate the extent of its interest. In other words, in commonly used terminology, the state will need to communicate its resolve.

The adversary's uncertainty about the value the state places on territory creates a challenge for the security seeker. The security seeker has incentives to exaggerate its interests—convincing its adversary that its interests are greater than they actually are would enhance the state's ability to achieve cooperation, and to succeed in bargaining and deterrence. The adversary therefore should be skeptical of the state's statements about the extent of its interests and resolve. Consequently, the state will have to rely on costly signals to communicate its resolve and convince its adversary to raise its estimate of the state's interest.

During peacetime, buying military forces can serve as a costly signal because investing in forces requires the state to forgo consumption, which it also values. Spending more resources on forces can therefore provide information about the extent of the state's interest, helping the adversary distinguish between states with greater interests and those with lesser interests at stake. This in turn improves the state's ability to bargain and deter.[2] Similarly, during peacetime a state can communicate resolve by

---

[1] In addition, however, a state's willingness to carry out a threat should also depend on the costs and risks of the action. For a given level of interest (that is, resolve), a state's willingness to carry out its threat decreases as the costs and risks increase. Thus, willingness to carry out a threat is not a characteristic of the state alone, but depends in addition on the military situation it faces and its information about the adversary's motives (because this should influence the state's assessment of how the adversary would respond).

[2] There could, however, be another important reason that security seekers choose different levels of arming—they could disagree about the military capabilities and strategy that are required to provide a given level of security—in which case investing more does not provide as much information about the extent of a state's interests. In fact, debates about spending and arms requirements are often cast in these terms, making it difficult to separate the actual reasons for divergent policies.

adopting a strategy that promises to make a future crisis more dangerous, thereby making clear its willingness to run large risks to protect a specific interest and possibly as a result avoiding a crisis or war.

Resolve also matters during crises. The understanding of its resolve that a state establishes via its peacetime policies influences not only whether an adversary will challenge the state, but also the state's initial bargaining position in a crisis. And once a crisis occurs, the state can pursue a variety of other actions—including mobilizing forces and launching a limited war—that further communicate its resolve. Theories of the causes of war have focused on the roles these actions play in bargaining; a following section of this chapter explores them briefly.

We can imagine two components to the signal of resolve. First, a state that places greater value on protecting the status quo should be willing to invest more in military forces if they will increase its ability to defend. As sketched above, this should help the adversary to distinguish between states that place different value on the status quo. Second, because buying forces has positive signaling value, a state should be willing to invest beyond the level determined narrowly by military considerations. Appreciating the signaling value of building, states that place greater value on the status quo might choose to invest still more than states with lesser interests.[3]

The extent of resolve that a policy signals will depend on the difficulty and cost of acquiring the forces required to perform a military mission and on its importance. Pursuing deterrent capabilities that are easy to achieve (that is, require relatively low investment) promises to provide the state with effective military capabilities, but will not be especially effective at communicating resolve precisely because they are easy to achieve. In contrast, determined pursuit of capabilities that are hard to achieve will be more effective at signaling resolve. And maybe ironically, pursuing capabilities that would make an already secure state still more secure can communicate more resolve than pursuing capabilities that are essential for a state's basic security. The logic underpinning each of these comparisons is that the larger the effort the state makes relative to the security it would expect to achieve, the larger the signal of resolve. A state that invests a great deal to gain a little security demonstrates that the interests it is attempting to protect are large and highly valued. In addition, how difficult it is for the state to make this investment matters—a wealthy and powerful state can make a large investment relatively easily compared to a weak state and, therefore, demonstrates less resolve by doing so.

---

[3] There is a parallel here to what Snyder, *Deterrence and Defense*, pp. 31–40, termed the "deterrent value" of a policy.

Because signaling resolve is costly, the state's strategy should depe
its estimate of the adversary's understanding of its resolve. This inf...
tion about the adversary's information is an additional element of the
international environment that the state faces. If the state believes its adversary believes the state's resolve is high, there is less need to signal its
resolve and less value in doing so. In contrast, if the state believes its adversary doubts that it has large interests at stake (but in fact the state
actually does), the state should be willing to incur larger costs to communicate the extent of its interests.

Although there will be variation across states, a basic hierarchy of interests provides some guidance on the necessity of communicating resolve. We expect that most states place high value on defending their
homelands and that their adversaries usually appreciate this. By comparison, the instrumental security value that a state places on protecting its
allies and possibly other countries varies more widely. As a result, adversaries are more likely to be uncertain about this value, which raises the
possibility that they will underestimate it. Consequently, a state will
usually have to make a greater effort to insure that an adversary appreci-
ates its resolve to protect secondary and tertiary interests than its resolve
to protect vital interests.[4]

The theory's material variables influence the difficulty of acquiring
military capabilities and therefore have direct implications for the extent
to which strategies communicate resolve. For example, offensive capabilities are harder to acquire when the offense-defense balance favors
defense; consequently, while a security seeker should anchor its strategy
on a defensive capability, supplementing this with an offensive capability
could be particularly effective for communicating its resolve. Looking at
power provides a parallel example: a weaker state can communicate
more resolve by investing a given amount in a defensive force than can a
more powerful state because the weaker state would find the opportunity
cost of the investment to be larger. On the flip side, a more powerful state
that adopts a cooperative policy that denies it an offensive capability that
could have been acquired by competing and would have been useful for
defending an ally could signal a lack of resolve.

An argument that hawkish analysts frequently used during the Cold
War provides a nice example of the logic of competing to communicate
resolve. Although achieving the United States' basic requirement for nuclear deterrence—an assured destruction capability—was relatively easy,
hawks argued that the United States needed in addition to acquire a damage-limitation capability. For example, Stephen Rosen argued that "the

[4] See Schelling, *Arms and Influence*, for discussion of how credibility varies with types of interests.

Soviet Union may miscalculate and challenge the United States in an area where it expects no American response. . . . This is the danger that makes a new nuclear strategy necessary. A doctrine making it abundantly visible that the United States is taking seriously the problems of limiting the damage resulting from a nuclear war would demonstrate to the Soviet Union that the United States would in fact take all necessary steps to stop Soviet advances. The present doctrinal confusion does not communicate any resolve to prevent war."[5] In fact, the United States had virtually no chance of acquiring such a capability. But this did not completely undermine the argument because the United States would have had to make a tremendous effort to have even the slightest prospect of acquiring a significant damage-limitation capability, and this effort might have indicated the great extent of U.S. resolve. Designing U.S. policy based on this argument would have shifted U.S. policy from a potentially restrained nuclear policy to one characterized by intense ongoing competition. Explained in offense-defense terms, damage limitation is an offensive mission; because nuclear weapons create a large advantage for the defense, acquiring a damage-limitation capability requires a large investment that can be easily offset by a major power, which would in turn require continuing large investments by the United States. Moreover, if the doctrine was really designed to protect areas in which the Soviet Union might not expect a U.S. response, the Soviet Union must have believed the areas were of relatively little value; an enormous U.S. investment should have changed this assessment.

Integrating with the Theory: A Still Broader Understanding of the Security Dilemma

Having included variation among security seekers—by allowing for differences in the value they place on security—and laid out the basic logic of communicating resolve, we can now integrate these arguments with the theory developed in previous chapters. While the importance of communicating resolve can favor a competitive strategy, a state should not always adopt a competitive strategy, nor will signaling resolve necessarily be its most important reason for competing. Rather, including uncertainty about the state's resolve and the state's estimate of the adversary's information about its resolve adds to the already complicated balance that a state must sometimes strike between cooperative and competitive strategies. Put another way, a state's need to communicate resolve adds

---

[5] Stephen Peter Rosen, "Foreign Policy and Nuclear Weapons: The Case for Strategic Defenses," in Samuel P. Huntington, ed., *The Strategic Imperative: New Policies for American Security* (Cambridge, MA: Ballinger, 1982), p. 149. For other examples, see Glaser, *Analyzing Strategic Nuclear Policy*, pp. 63–67.

an element to the state's security dilemma, increasing its incentives to compete, which needs to be balanced against its incentives to cooperate.

Up to this point, the theory has formulated the security dilemma as a trade-off between, on the one hand, acquiring the military capabilities required for deterrence and defense; and, on the other hand, avoiding military capabilities that reduce its adversary's ability to defend and/or that signal that the state is motivated by greed, not only security. Including the potentially positive signaling benefits of competing in military forces rounds out this picture. Now both building (competing) and restraint (cooperating) have implications for signaling, as well as for the state's military capabilities. Whereas restraint can signal that the state is a security seeker, building and competing can signal that the state places greater value on protecting the status quo.[6]

To better understand the interplay of these variables, we can consider a number of different situations. Consider first cases in which the state can acquire an adequate deterrent capability with relative ease—that is, when defense has the advantage and/or the state has a power advantage. Because it is easy, acquiring effective defensive capabilities does not communicate much resolve; thus, signaling a high level of resolve would require the state to build forces beyond those required for an adequate deterrent. Whether this is the state's best strategy depends on a number of additional variables. A key variable would be whether offense and defense are distinguishable. If they are not distinguishable, then building "extra" forces to communicate resolve would also be provocative because the state would be increasing its offensive capability as well as its defensive capability. This trade-off would then depend on the state's information about its adversary's motives: if likely to be a greedy state, then competing to communicate resolve is more attractive; if likely to be a security seeker, then restraint designed to avoid reducing the adversary's security is more attractive. And, as discussed above, the trade-off will also depend on the importance of communicating resolve—if the state is confident that the adversary has not underestimated its interests, the case for competition is weaker.

The argument quoted above made by hawks during the Cold War helps to illustrate this logic. Because nuclear weapons provide defense (retaliation) with a large advantage, a dedicated effort to acquire a damage-limitation capability (offense) could communicate extensive resolve. Hawks, believing that the Soviet Union was a highly greedy state, worried relatively little that U.S. policies might be provocative and decrease

[6] It is also possible that building would signal that the state places greater value on expansion and is a greedier state, in which case the signal would have a negative effect. The proper balance between these effects would depend on the state's estimate of the adversary's type.

Soviet security, and instead placed much greater weight on communicating U.S. resolve. In contrast, doves placed greater weight on increasing Soviet security and less weight on communicating U.S. resolve. As a result, they opposed offensive nuclear damage-limitation policies.[7]

In contrast, if offense and defense are distinguishable, then the trade-off between increased capability and provocation is essentially eliminated: the state can build up its forces to communicate resolve and further enhance its deterrent capabilities without reducing the adversary's security. How much "extra" to build would then depend on the effectiveness of the state's defensive capability; its estimate of the value the adversary places on expansion (which depends on both the state's understanding of adversary's beliefs about the state's type, which influences the adversary's insecurity, and the state's estimate of the adversary's greed[8]); and the state's preference for security relative to consumption.

The U.S. Cold War decision to build diversified and redundant nuclear retaliatory capability provides an example of this configuration of variables. The substantial investment required for forces that were larger than necessary for assured destruction and were deployed on a variety of survivable delivery systems (in a nuclear triad) should have been sufficient to eliminate any Soviet uncertainty about the great importance the United States placed on maintaining its nuclear retaliatory capability. In turn, this should have eliminated any Soviet doubts about the extent of the interests these U.S. capabilities were dedicated to defending. At the same time, larger and more diverse forces could be deployed without threatening the Soviet retaliatory capability and, therefore, did not need to be provocative. This explains why hawks and doves did not disagree strenuously about this aspect of U.S. nuclear policy.

By comparison, situations in which the state would need to try much harder simply to acquire an adequate deterrent pose a different set of challenges, but dedicated efforts to communicate resolve would not rank among the top priorities. These situations are characterized by offense advantage and/or power disadvantage. Because acquiring an adequate deterrent capability would be difficult, requiring the state to adopt a competitive policy and likely to dedicate a substantial portion of its resources to military capabilities, a state that pursues an effective deterrent capability would simultaneously communicate its resolve. When offense and defense are distinguishable, the state has the option of pursuing qualitative arms control, thereby shifting deployed forces toward defense. This strat-

---

[7] This example does not entirely match the logic, however, because offense and defense were largely distinguishable; because the U.S. policy would have required choosing offense, it would have been provocative, arguably more so than if offense and defense were indistinguishable.

[8] Variation in the greediness of adversaries is discussed in the following section.

egy could increase the state's ability to defend[9] but would not communicate resolve. Any state that valued its security would prefer this agreement, so it would not send a costly signal of resolve. The agreement, however, would signal that the state was not very greedy (that is, it placed much greater value on its security than on nonsecurity expansion).

The Security Dilemma, and the Spiral and Deterrence Models

Including variation in the decision-making state's value for security enables the theory to more fully capture a key feature of the deterrence model. As noted in chapter 3, the deterrence model, as described by Jervis, prescribes a strategy that is appropriate for dealing with greedy states and lays the foundation for competitive strategies. Under uncertainty about an adversary's type, the security dilemma requires a state to balance the strategic demands of the deterrence and spiral models. Although the security dilemma is commonly understood to drive the spiral model, in fact the security dilemma also captures much of the deterrence model: a state faces a security dilemma when it not only needs to reassure its adversary but also needs simultaneously to maintain the military capabilities required to deter its adversary, at least partly because the adversary might be a greedy state.

However, while the security dilemma captures key features of the deterrence model, the theory developed in earlier chapters is not capable of fully capturing it. The deterrence model emphasizes not only that the state must maintain the military capabilities required to deter, but also that the state must communicate its resolve to protect its interests. The deterrence model highlights the importance of communicating resolve because a state's security depends more on being understood to be highly resolved (that is, have vital or at least large interests at stake) when it is facing a greedy state, especially a very greedy one, than when facing a security seeker. But, as explained above, the need to communicate resolve is only an issue if the adversary is uncertain about the value that the state places on its interests. Consequently, including this variable enables the theory to fully capture the key arguments that lie at the heart of the deterrence model. Importantly, the theory also simultaneously captures the key elements of the spiral model.

In its most full-blown version, the deterrence model argues essentially that a state needs to worry only about acquiring deterrent capabilities and communicating resolve, and not about its adversary's security and therefore about the potentially provocative nature of its competitive pol-

---

[9] As discussed in chapter 3, to increase the state's overall ability to defend, the agreement would have to be robust in the face of cheating and breakout.

icy. In this view, there is not a trade-off between cooperative and competitive strategies; the security dilemma ceases to exist. This is because the deterrence model, in addition to applying when the state knows its adversary is a greedy state, also assumes that this greedy adversary knows the state will not attack it. My theory makes clear that the deterrence model must make two further assumptions to reach this conclusion. First, the adversary must be certain that it faces a security seeker, not a greedy state. Second, the adversary must believe that the security seeker is in fact secure; otherwise, the state's insecurity could lead it to adopt expansionist policies that could threaten the greedy state.

These are quite demanding assumptions. The greedy state might believe the state is a security seeker even though it is pursuing the competitive arming policies prescribed by the deterrence model; these reasons could be related to beliefs about regime type or a long history of the state choosing to forgo the use of force when the costs of expansion would have been low. It is harder to see how the adversary could also believe that the state was secure—if secure, why would a secure security seeker adopt a highly competitive military policy? The theory suggests, therefore, that the signature version of the deterrence model is internally inconsistent.

However, a less extreme version of the deterrence model is not internally problematic and highlights the importance of communicating resolve. Broadening the theory to include uncertainty about the extent of the state's security interests enables it to capture this central feature of the deterrence model. At the same time, the theory reminds us that when facing uncertainty about the adversary's type, the state needs to search for a balance between the policies prescribed by the deterrence model and those prescribed by the spiral model. In the end, how to strike this balance depends on the nature and the severity of the security dilemma. Fully appreciating this richness of the security dilemma requires including an adversary that is uncertain about the extent of the state's interests. By adding this variable, the theory fully integrates the security dilemma with both the deterrence and spiral models, and provides guidance for how a state should balance their sometimes opposing demands.

Variation within Greedy States

Greedy states can vary along two dimensions—the depth of greed and the breadth of greed. Depth refers to the nonsecurity value that a greedy state places on acquiring territory. Depth of greed can vary—some greedy states may be willing to pay only a small amount to expand, while others may value expansion so highly that they are willing to run grave risks to their security.[10] A state's strategy could depend on where along this spectrum it believes its potentially greedy adversary lies. Consider, for example, the choice that a state faces between cooperating to signal its benign motives and competing to avoid falling behind in an arms race when uncertain about whether it faces a security seeker or a greedy state. As argued in chapter 3, cooperating with a security seeker is often preferable to cooperating with a greedy state both because the latter is less likely to reciprocate cooperation and because failed cooperative efforts are more dangerous. The basic logic extends to variation in depth of greediness. A greedier state is likely to see greater value in not reciprocating restraint or cheating on an agreement because this is more likely to provide military capabilities it requires to achieve its goals at acceptable costs. Although the military impact of these actions does not vary with greediness, the costs the greedier state is willing to pay to achieve its objectives do. Therefore, a military advantage that would be too small to make a war of expansion acceptable to a less greedy state could be large enough to make it acceptable to a greedier state.

Consequently, when facing the trade-off created by uncertainty about the adversary's type, a state should be less willing to cooperate when the greedy type is greedier. More precisely, for cooperation to be a state's preferred option, the probability that the adversary is a security seeker will have to be higher when the greedy type is greedier. The Cold War provides a familiar example: American hard-liners believed not only that the Soviet Union was likely to be a greedy state, but further that it was a very greedy state, willing to pay tremendous costs to conquer Western Europe. As a result, they called for the United States to adopt highly competitive military policies designed both to avoid the risks of arms control and to acquire military advantages.[11]

The extent of an adversary's greediness can also influence a state's choice between offensive and defensive strategies. A very greedy state may see the costs of fighting a war as small compared to the value of expansion. Deterrence can then require offensive capabilities that

[10] States at the very low greed end of the continuum resemble security seekers in that they are willing to pay very little for nonsecurity expansion and in many ways may be well approximated as security seekers. One could argue that there may not be any states that are truly pure security seekers, but that the similarity between security seekers and these slightly greedy states is sufficient that the type "security seeker" captures what is essential.

[11] For an extreme view, see Colin S. Gray, "Nuclear Strategy: A Case for a Theory of Victory," *International Security* 4, 1 (Summer 1979): 54–87, who argued that the Soviet Union might be willing to accept massive nuclear destruction of its homeland to acquire Western Europe. For reviews of how beliefs about the Soviet motives played out in the nuclear debate, see Glaser, *Analyzing Strategic Nuclear Policy*, chaps. 2 and 3; and Douglas Seay, "What Are the Soviets' Objectives in Their Foreign, Military, and Arms Control Policies?," in Eden and Miller, eds., *Nuclear Arguments*.

threaten the greedy state's homeland and other vital interests. However, greedy states that place great value on expansion and also value expansion much more than protecting the status quo are most likely to pursue revisionist policies and are especially hard to deter; in this case, offensive threats will add little to deterrence, so maintaining defensive capabilities designed to defeat an attack (as opposed to deter it) could be especially important.

The implications of variation in depth of greed are maybe more familiar and straightforward when considering decisions from the perspective of a greedy state. For the reasons summarized above, the greedier a state is, the wider the range of conditions under which attempting to change the status quo through coercive bargaining, and if necessary war, will be its best option. Hitler is often characterized as placing great value on nonsecurity expansion and possibly little value on maintaining only the territory that Germany already controlled; this combination of preferences is in turn seen to be the key to Germany's revisionist policies.[12]

The second dimension of variation in greed is breadth—a greedy state can have limited aims, possibly interested in acquiring a small amount of adjacent territory; or instead can have essentially unlimited aims, aspiring to regional or even global hegemony. A greedy state with limited aims could be willing to pay a great deal to acquire a specific territory but then place no inherent value on further expansion. A state's preferred policy could depend on the breadth of its greedy adversary's aims. Cooperating with, and making concessions to, a limited-aims greedy state could be a state's best option, whereas competing could be its best option for dealing with an unlimited-aims greedy state. Once a limited-aims greedy state achieves its limited expansionist objectives, it is no longer a greedy state. Consequently, concessions that raise doubts about a state's resolve or risk allowing the adversary to gain military advantages are less dangerous.[13] Similarly, territorial concessions that would result in allowing the greedy state to increase its power are less dangerous because the adversary is less likely to use these resources for further expansion. In other words, "appeasement" can be an effective strategy if a greedy adversary has limited aims, but not if it has unlimited aims.

The benefits of making territorial concessions may be especially large if, in addition to satisfying the adversary's territorial desires, they also increase its security and thereby moderate or eliminate a broader and potentially more dangerous competition. Specifically, if the limited-aims

---

[12] These are the states that Schweller, *Deadly Imbalances*, p. 89, characterizes as wolves. Also on Hitler's preferences, see Jervis, *Perception and Misperception*, p. 51.

[13] For this reason, the limited vs. unlimited aims distinction plays an important role in Jervis's broad characterization of the spiral and deterrence models; see *Perception and Misperception*, chap. 3.

greedy state also highly values the territory it already possesses, and if defending the limited additional territory requires the defender to threaten the adversary's security in the status quo, then cooperative policies are especially likely to be the defender's best option.

China may be an example of such a limited-aims greedy state—it places great value on integrating Taiwan into China (although may accept the status quo as long as Taiwan does not declare independence) but may not have other significant territorial ambitions.[14] U.S. policy could depend on this judgment. Some of the capabilities that the United States might want to enhance its ability to deter a Chinese attack could reduce China's security. Most obviously, efforts to deny China a secure nuclear retaliatory capability, which could enhance U.S. threats to join a crisis or conventional war over Taiwan, could fuel Chinese insecurity and generate broader military competition that could strain political relations. Forgoing this capability could, therefore, increase U.S. security, even though this would reduce its ability to defend Taiwan. The case for restraint would be weaker both if China had unlimited aims, because nuclear advantages would be more valuable, and if China placed lower value on preserving control of its current territory, because this would reduce the security benefits of U.S. restraint.

Uncertainty about the breadth of an adversary's greed weakens the case for cooperation because making concessions to an unlimited-aims greedy state would rarely be a state's best option. British and French concessions to Germany in the 1930s were based partially on the bet that German aims were limited, and they had disastrous consequences when this turned out not to be the case.[15]

UNCERTAINTY ABOUT MATERIAL VARIABLES

The theory has focused on the implications of uncertainty about the opposing state's type but has said little about uncertainty about material variables. Although maybe less central to the theory's core arguments, uncertainty about material variables is important both because it influences the deductive logic that underpins some of my earlier arguments about these variables and because states often face uncertainty about their material situation.

[14] M. Taylor Fravel, "Regime Insecurity and International Cooperation: Explaining China's Compromises in Territorial Disputes," *International Security* 30, 2 (Fall 2005): 46–83; and Alastair Iain Johnston, "Is China a Status Quo Power?," *International Security* 27, 4 (Spring 2003): 5–56.

[15] Evan Luard, "Conciliation and Deterrence: A Comparison of Political Strategies in the Interwar and Postwar Periods," *World Politics* 19, 2 (January 1967): 167-189.

Uncertainty about power can influence a state's incentives to compete and cooperate in arming in a variety of ways. Certainty about states' power can eliminate key incentives to arm. If certainty about power enables states to foresee the outcome of an arms race, then both states' best option could be to forgo the arms race altogether. Looking down the road at the outcome of the arming, and understanding the bargaining implications of changes in their military capabilities, states could skip the arms buildup and instead negotiate the diplomatic deal that the new capabilities would produce. This could be their preferred outcome as it saves the costs of arming, while producing the same political result.[16]

Even with certainty about power, however, states can still have incentives to engage in buildups: for example, if unable to cooperate to make strategically significant cheating infeasible, states might prefer to build up to levels of arms that reduce the risks of being cheated; if states hoping to forgo an arms race cannot credibly commit not to build after reaching a diplomatic bargain, the bargain may be infeasible; and if the offense-defense balance shifts toward defense at higher force levels, states might prefer to enhance their deterrent capabilities by engaging in a mutual buildup instead of retaining smaller forces. Nevertheless, the basic point stands—certainty about power would reduce the incentives to engage in a race that one state pursued with the goal of winning because under some conditions the political benefits should be achievable without the expense.

For similar reasons, uncertainty about power can fuel military competition. A state that wants to change the status quo and is uncertain about its adversary's ability to keep up in a military competition may prefer to arm instead of accepting a diplomatic bargain, believing that the available bargain does not adequately reflect the military capabilities it could acquire in an arms race. Uncertainty can persist because an adversary that is in fact weaker can have an incentive to bluff about its ability to compete, because successful bluffing would provide a favorable political bargain. Bluffing could succeed because the stronger state might prefer avoiding the cost of arming, and thereby forgo the possibility of winning the race, to engaging in a competition that might not provide a military advantage. However, the result could also be an arms race that demonstrates the adversary's weakness and would have been avoided if the states had been certain about each other's power. This should occur when the stronger state believes its adversary is relatively likely to be unable to respond effectively to its buildup.[17]

---

[16] This logic is laid out and supported with a formal model in Andrew Kydd, "Arms Races and Arms Control."

[17] Ibid. Disagreements about the probable outcome of an arms race can also result from the complexity of power and states' abilities to compete. Although a fully rational account

At the same time, uncertainty can create incentives for states to cooperate. Consider two security seekers that already possess adequate deterrent capabilities and face uncertainty about which state has greater power and would therefore win an arms race. More specifically, consider a case in which both states believe they are equally likely to win (and that this would undermine their adversary's deterrent) and to lose the race (and that this would undermine their own deterrent). It is reasonable to assume that in most cases a security seeker will see the benefits (in additional deterrent value) of undermining the adversary's deterrent to be smaller than the costs of having its own deterrent undermined. Consequently, this uncertainty creates incentives for both of these states to cooperate to avoid this arms race. Moreover, these incentives could be larger than in the case of certainty in which the states knew that the arms race would leave their deterrent capabilities unchanged—the security risk in the former of having one's deterrent undermined could be much larger than the economic cost in the latter of an inefficient race.

The results can vary with states' beliefs about power, their motives, and their information about others' motives. As the probability of winning increases, and if there are deterrent benefits to winning, a security seeker will be more inclined to race, even though there is some risk of losing. If states disagree about the probability of winning, competition is more likely. Greedy states will be more willing to risk losing because they place greater value on acquiring offensive capabilities; this will vary, however, with the greedy state's type, with (all else being equal) less greedy states being less willing to jeopardize their security. And a security seeker that is concerned about its adversary's beliefs about its own motives will have additional incentives for restraint because this may signal benign motives, which will tend to offset the forgone possibility of winning the race.

Uncertainty about the offense-defense balance can also influence states' arming decisions by creating uncertainty about the outcome of war.[18] For example, consider a case in which states believe the offense-defense balance is most likely to moderately favor defense, but is also equally but less likely to favor neither and to strongly favor defense. Although the balance is likely to favor defense, maybe strongly, states would have to worry about the possibility that it did not. To hedge against this possibil-

---

requires that states with access to the same information will reach the same conclusions, complexity combined with different analytic capabilities for dealing with it can lead to divergent estimates of the probability of winning an arms race, which can fuel competition.

[18] States' overall uncertainty about the outcome of a war could also depend on variables that are not built in to the theory, including scenarios—states do not know who will attack first and whether they will be caught by surprise—and the skill and will of the states' militaries. These uncertainties will create incentives similar to those created by uncertainty about the offense-defense balance, although states may have some different options for dealing with them.

ity, a state with a power advantage would have greater incentives to compete to achieve an advantage in force ratios, an advantage that would be less valuable if the balance were known to favor defense. This competition comes with risks—signaling malign motives and decreasing the adversary's security by reducing its military capabilities—but the possibility that the balance does not favor defense could nevertheless make competition the powerful state's best option.

This uncertainty should not, however, fuel arms competition under all conditions. For example, equally powerful states cannot expect to gain sustainable advantages in forces; as argued above, security seekers should therefore be willing to forgo competitive buildups, if sufficiently confident that cooperation can insure parity. The possibility of offense advantage would make this more difficult because states would be more concerned both that the measurement/counting of forces provided them with (at least) equal forces and that cheating could be detected quickly enough to render it strategically insignificant. However, even if this type of cooperation is feasible, uncertainty over the offense-defense balance, and specifically the possibility of offense advantage, will leave states less secure, which could fuel other types of competition—for example, over territory, resources, and allies—designed to provide security, but potentially leading to conflict.

Dynamic Considerations

All of the theory's key variables could change over time; consequently, a state assessing its policy choices needs to consider not only the international situation it currently faces, but also the situation it might face in the future. International relations theory and analyses of national security policy have addressed many of the issues raised by the possibility that these variables could change. For example, shifts in power can create incentives for preventive war; the possibility of changes in technology that shift the offense-defense balance can fuel competition in weapons systems that reduce the feasibility and significance of cooperation in limiting current systems; and the possibility of changes in beliefs about an opposing state's motives can make cooperation more difficult. This brief section sketches how these arguments follow the basic outlines of my theory and discusses a few points of disagreement with common arguments.

A state whose power is declining can face incentives to launch a preventive war because its prospects in a war would be better now than later; war will not improve the state's position relative to the status quo, but instead relative to future outcomes, whether a diplomatic bargain or war. Standard descriptions of preventive war are based in deterrence logic and describe the declining state's choice as between war now or later.[19] Bargaining theories of war explain preventive war as a commitment problem in which a rising state cannot credibly commit not to use its improved power position later; they emphasize that a state compares war now to the concessions that it would have to accept later when it is weaker.[20]

The benefits of preventive war depend on the magnitude of the anticipated power shift—larger shifts make war now more attractive because the future looks worse. However, whether preventive war is a state's best option depends on many variables beyond power. The offense-defense balance influences the military implications of a negative shift in power and therefore the incentives for preventive war: for a given loss of power, the larger the advantage of defense, the smaller the negative impact on a state's deterrent capabilities and therefore the smaller the incentives for preventive war. So, for example, the loss of unipolarity would matter much less for the United States given the defense dominance it enjoys—created by nuclear weapons and distance, reinforced by oceans—than for a prenuclear continental hegemon.

The probability that the rising power would attack (or use its increased power coercively) also matters. The less likely coercion or war is in the future, the weaker the case for preventive war. States' information about each others' motives should play a central role in this judgment: a state that believes its adversary is likely to be a security seeker would find the probability of future coercion or war to be lower and, therefore, the incentives for preventive war to be smaller. In the simplest comparison, a state will find a rising security-seeking ally to be much less threatening than a rising greedy adversary. The belief that the United States is uninterested in challenging their vital interests (reinforced by defense advantage) is probably the key factor explaining the lack of reaction by major powers to growing U.S. power following the end of the Cold War.[21] Be-

[19] On preventive war, see Copeland, *The Origins of Major War*, who makes many of the points in this paragraph; Van Evera, *Causes of War*, chap. 4 and pp. 129–131, on how the offense-defense balance influences preventive incentives; and Dong Sun Lee, *Power Shifts, Strategy and War: Declining States and International Conflict* (New York: Routledge, 2007). A helpful review of the earlier literature is Jack S. Levy, "Declining Power and the Preventive Motivation for War," *World Politics* 40, 1 (October 1987): 82–107. For a broad analysis of the sources of changes in power and the implications for states' strategies see Robert Gilpin, *War and Change in World Politics* (Cambridge: Cambridge University Press, 1981).

[20] See Fearon, "Rationalist Explanations for War," pp. 404–408; Powell, *In the Shadow of Power*, chap. 4, who models both a commitment problem and the problem created by asymmetric information, and finds in the latter case that power transitions are not more dangerous than other phases of the power shift; and Powell, "War as a Commitment Problem," *International Organization* 60, 1 (Winter 2006): 169–203.

[21] There is a debate on the extent of states' reactions and the purposes behind them; see the following articles: Robert A. Pape, "Soft Balancing against the United States"; T. V. Paul,

cause information about motives matters, a rising state has incentives to pursue cooperative/conciliatory policies that signal its type, thereby reducing the danger posed by its growing power. A common criticism of this line of argument is that states' motives can change, so a declining state must focus on the shift in capabilities, essentially discounting motives. The counterpoint is that because preventive war is costly, states need to consider the probability and extent of change in motives, as well as the military implications of the shift in capabilities.

A state's own motives also influence the implications of declining power. A security seeker could find decline less worrisome than would a greedy state because it is more concerned with defense and deterrence, whereas the greedy state is more concerned with offense and expansion. If defense has an advantage, decline might leave the security seeker confident in its ability to deter, while it could undermine the greedy state's ability to take territory. As a result, the greedy state would face a closing window of opportunity and might use force coercively, and start a war if necessary, to take advantage of it.

States need to worry also that the offense-defense balance could change. Related, a state needs to worry that its adversary will achieve technological breakthroughs before it does, thereby undermining the military capability of the forces the state has deployed.[22] A state that is secure today because defense has the advantage could be insecure in the future if the balance shifts toward offense or if its adversary acquires new military systems that it cannot quickly match or counter. Consequently, states may be less secure than a static picture suggests. This will be especially likely if important technological advances cannot be limited by arms control agreements, which will often be the case. Many technologies are developed for civilian purposes and others reflect advances in basic research, which places them beyond the reach of cooperation on military capabilities. In addition, improvements in military forces can reflect numerous incremental technological advances that occur between generations of systems; these can be difficult to identify ahead of time and to characterize and measure, which makes them difficult or impossible to limit as states replace and modernize aging forces.[23] The combination and integration of these advances can lead to significant improvements in capa-

---

"Soft Balancing in the Age of U.S. Primacy"; Stephen G. Brooks and William C. Wohlforth, "Hard Times for Soft Balancing"; and Keir A. Lieber and Gerard Alexander, "Waiting for Balancing," all in *International Security* 30, 1 (Summer 2005); and Owen, "Transnational Liberalism and U.S. Primacy."

[22] A state that acquires a lead in a new technology will be able to fight better on both the offense and defense; the offense-defense balance is not well defined during the transition to both states being able to employ the new technology or weapons system. See Glaser and Kaufmann, "What Is the Offense-Defense Balance and Can We Measure It?," pp. 56–57.

[23] Barry Buzan, *Introduction to Strategic Studies: Military Technology and International*

bilities.[24] The results can be an arming dynamic that creates concern about the adequacy of future capabilities and that if misunderstood signals malign motives. More dramatically, the possibility of militarily significant technological breakthroughs can rarely if ever be dismissed, which leaves open the possibility of unanticipated shifts in military capabilities. The overall result of these possibilities is that existing defense advantages may leave states less secure, or at least less confident in their security, than the static theory suggests. This said, large defense advantages, as created by nuclear weapons (and to a lesser extent by distance), will moderate these dynamic concerns by greatly increasing the magnitude of change that is required to undermine a state's deterrent and defense capabilities.

The possibility of changes in the adversary's motives, captured in the theory by changes in the state's information about its adversary's motives, should also influence a state's current decisions. As explained in chapter 3, cooperation will sometimes be a state's best option if it is likely facing a security seeker, while competition will be its best option if likely facing a greedy state. Consequently, because the state's decision today will influence not only its current capabilities, but also its future capabilities, the state's decisions about cooperation should incorporate the possibility that the adversary's motives could change. In situations in which cooperation would otherwise be a state's preferred option, this possibility tends to make cooperation less attractive. Less frequently noted is that the opposite possibility—that an adversary that is (believed likely to be) greedy could become more benign—could make competition (and preventive war) less attractive.

A common argument is that the possibility that a state's motives could change (especially combined with uncertainty about its current motives) requires states to ignore information about motives entirely—states should assume the worst and, closely related, focus entirely on capabilities, which greatly reduces or eliminates the prospects for cooperation.[25] Such a strong conclusion, however, is unwarranted for a number of reasons. First, the state needs to consider how likely a negative shift in motives is to occur. If unlikely, although possible, then the impact on the state's decision should be smaller than if the shift is believed to be likely. Although judgments about future motives are difficult to make (even more so than for current motives), states can and do make them. For

---

Relations (New York: St. Martin's Press, 1987), part 2, on the complexity of the process of arming.

[24] The so-called revolution in military affairs may be best described as the result of these types of advances; see Michael O'Hanlon, *Technological Change and the Future of Warfare* (Washington, DC: Brookings, 2000).

[25] For further discussion of this issue, see chapter 5 on offensive realism.

example, most observers believe that the European Union, if it adopts an integrated foreign policy and deploys a powerful military, is less likely to become a greedy state than is China. Second, cooperation can sometimes be designed to insulate a state from changes in its adversary's motives. For example, if cooperation entails mutual restraint in the deployment of forces and if the state can monitor its adversary's compliance with the agreement and react to violations in a timely fashion, a negative shift in the adversary's motives is less dangerous. Although the possibility that the adversary's motives will become more malign does mean that the adversary is more likely to break out of the agreement, the overall risk of cooperation could nevertheless be smaller than the expected benefits. Third, as I discuss in the following chapter, assuming the worst ignores the danger posed by the security dilemma and can therefore be self-defeating.

WAR

My theory is cast in terms of the broad categories of cooperation and competition, and most of the more fine-grained discussion has focused on a state's choice between arming and some form of restraint, whether formal arms control or unilateral restraint. This section briefly discusses how the theory's variables affect the probability of war. I draw on a variety of arguments, including offense-defense theory and formal theories of war, which emphasize the process of bargaining, to assess how war compares to a state's other options.

Motives

A state's motives influence the value it places on acquiring additional territory. All else being equal, greedy states place greater value on acquiring territory than do security seekers.[26] As a first cut, we might expect that the greater the value a state places on territory, the harder it will be to deter; all else being equal, war would then be more likely. However, as emphasized by the formal literature on war, this line of argument overlooks the willingness of states to make concessions to avoid war:[27] a state that knows its adversary places greater value on acquiring territory, and is therefore more willing to accept the costs of war, should be willing to

[26] However, the extent of the difference depends on how much a security seeker could increase its security by taking territory; I address this issue below.

[27] For reviews of this literature, see Robert Powell, "Bargaining Theory and International Conflict," *Annual Review of Political Science* 5 (2002): 1–30; and Dan Reiter, "Exploring the Bargaining Model of War," *Perspectives on Politics* 1, 1 (March 2003): 27–43.

make larger concessions to avoid war, which would tend to reduce its probability. To assess the net effect of these countervailing factors requires looking more closely at states' decisions, which the bargaining models help us do.

The bargaining models identify a central role for uncertainty about the opposing state's power and/or resolve in creating the conditions under which a rational state's decision can result in war.[28] This uncertainty results from the combination of states' private information about their power and resolve, and their incentives to misrepresent them. A state has incentives to exaggerate them because misleading its adversary will enable the state to achieve better outcomes during crisis negotiations. Without this uncertainty, rational states would reach a negotiated agreement that avoids the cost of fighting a war.[29] However, when uncertain about resolve or power, a state faces a trade-off: offering a more generous concession decreases the probability of war but also reduces the value of the bargained outcome. War can result when a state's best option is to risk some probability of war instead of making larger concessions that would drive the probability to zero.

When this uncertainty exists, greedier states can be more likely to start wars, but the logic is somewhat different than that of the simpler deterrence argument. When facing a greedier adversary, a state needs to make a larger concession to preserve a given probability that the greedier state will accept its offer and thereby avoid war. A larger concession is required because the greedier state sees greater net benefits in war, so it is willing to forgo war only if it can achieve greater concessions diplomatically. In the standard bargaining models, the probability of winning a war depends on power, but not on the value of winning a war. Therefore, the state's expected value of war does not decrease with increases in its adversary's greediness. As a result, facing a trade-off between concessions and war, the state is unwilling to increase its concession enough to keep the probability of war from increasing with increases in the adversary's greed.[30]

---

[28] Resolve is formulated as the extent of the benefits that are being bargained over compared to the costs of war.

[29] Fearon, "Rationalist Explanations for War," who argues that there are two other basic rationalist mechanisms that can lead to war—commitment problems and indivisibility of the issue being bargained over, which he argues is likely to be less important than the other two; and Powell, *In the Shadow of Power*, chap. 3. But see Powell, "War as a Commitment Problem," pp. 176–180, who argues that indivisibility is best understood as resulting from a commitment problem, not as an independent source of war.

[30] This argument parallels, but is distinct from, arguments that model the case of changes in technology that reduce the costs of war, thereby making war relatively more appealing; see Powell, *In the Shadow of Power*, pp. 110–113. Variation in greediness is similar in that it can be captured in the cost of war, but different because the change applies to one state, not both.

If, however, we assume instead that the state's probability of winning against a greedy state does decrease with increases in the adversary's greediness, a different result is possible. This assumption seems reasonable because a greedier adversary is willing to incur larger losses to achieve its expansionist goals; therefore, it should be willing to fight longer or adopt more costly strategies, if these will increase its probability of winning. If the state believes a greedier adversary is more likely to win, then two factors should lead it to make larger concessions—in addition to recognizing that larger concessions are required to avoid war, the state also recognizes that the greedier adversary is more likely to win, which reduces the state's value for fighting. The result could be concessions that are large enough to keep the probability of war from increasing with greed.

If we go a step further and let the state change its military policy in response to its belief about whether it faces a greedier adversary, the interaction becomes still more complicated. Most of the bargaining models assume that the outcome of war is determined by a state's power. This is actually a large and potentially problematic assumption because the military forces that states have deployed may not be proportional to their (potential) power, that is, their overall potential to deploy effective military forces. The outcomes of wars, at least wars fought with forces deployed before the war starts, will depend on actual military power—that is, deployed military forces—not potential power.[31] The investment that a state makes in military forces should depend not only on its power, but also on its assessment of the adversary's type and the extent of its greed. A state that cares more about protecting its security than its adversary cares about taking its territory should be able to invest a larger percentage of its wealth in military forces. In this case, a state's prospects for deterring and winning a war would not be adequately captured by its power. Related, a state's choice of military doctrine could depend on this assessment of its adversary. For example, deterring a very greedy adversary might require an offensive doctrine to threaten punishment as well as denial, while a less greedy adversary could be deterred with a more defensive doctrine.[32] As a result, a state that believes it faces a greedier adversary and sees the political concessions required to avoid war as too costly should invest more than it would otherwise in military forces. It should trade more consumption for security. As explored in the preceding discussion of the deterrence model, this increased investment has the po-

[31] This said, the assumption is consistent with the way power is used in most structural theories.

[32] For example, this judgment plays out in the divergent conclusions over the requirements of NATO's conventional doctrine; compare Huntington, "Conventional Deterrence and Conventional Retaliation in Europe," with Mearsheimer, *Conventional Deterrence*.

tential not only to increase the state's military capability but also to communicate its resolve to protect its interests. The overall result could be that the probability of war is not higher when facing a greedier state.

Material Variables

POWER

Discussions of the impact of power on the probability of war from a deterrence perspective have provided (maybe surprisingly) indeterminate results. If two states are equally powerful, then neither has a clear advantage and each has substantial capability to deter the other (although this depends on the offense-defense balance), which makes the probability of war low. By comparison, when power is unequal, one state's ability to deter is greater, while the other's is reduced relative to the case of equal power. The probability of war depends on the probability that either state will choose to start a war. Thus, it is indeterminate in which case war is more likely. Both positions are represented in the IR debate, with balance-of-power arguments seeing a lower probability of war when power is equal and the power-preponderance school when power is unequal. But, on its own terms, neither position can be fully defended without additional assumptions or variables.

Specifying the state's motives helps to reach a clearer conclusion under certain conditions. If the more powerful state is a security seeker, the probability of war will be lower than if the states were equally powerful.[33] The security seeker does not need to be deterred, and therefore the opposing state's weakness does not make war more likely;[34] and the state's power advantage does enhance its ability to deter (assuming this is necessary). This understanding of a benign hegemon is reflected in the common view that U.S. power preponderance reduces the probability of major-power war. In contrast, if the state with a power advantage is a greedy state, this advantage increases the probability of war.

Bargaining logic can improve our understanding of how the probability of war varies with power, but it does not resolve the dispute over its impact. In contrast to the deterrence-style arguments, which take the actions to be deterred as fixed, the bargaining arguments envision states'

---

[33] This argument is actually not as simple as I imply in the text: if we take the value of territory to be endogenous, both states' interest in expansion will vary with changes in power. I address this issue later in this section.

[34] This statement actually requires further specification of the international situation: if the offense-defense balance favors offense, then the security seeker might not be secure in the status quo; if the more powerful state's power is declining, it could have incentives for preventive war; etc. In the text I am overlooking this conditionality to emphasize the point about the combination of motives and power.

demands and concessions as reflecting their understanding of the probability of winning a war, which is assumed to depend on their power. According to these arguments, the more powerful a state is, the more it will demand; and the weaker a state is, the larger the concessions it will offer. These demands and concessions reflect the probability of winning a war: the more powerful state has a greater probability of winning and therefore must be able to achieve more diplomatically to prefer accepting concessions to fighting a war. The more powerful state's larger demand tends to increase the probability of war, but the weaker state's willingness to make larger concessions tends to decrease it. The combined effect of these countervailing factors determines how changes in power influence the probability of war.

Formal models of this interaction under incomplete information have not produced a single result, reflecting different assumptions about states' bargaining options. One finding is that the probability of war does not vary with the distribution of power: [35] the countervailing factors simply offset each other. Power matters—it influences the outcomes that states can achieve by threatening to use force, with the more powerful state gaining more—but it does not influence the probability of war. A different model gives greater weight to the importance of the existing political status quo, thereby better capturing the nature of the choice that states actually face, and produces a different result: the probability of war does depend upon power, but only in relation to how the status quo is currently divided. When a state's power is close to its proportion of benefits in the status quo (for example, the distribution of territory), war should not occur. The expected benefits of war are too small to warrant the costs of war, and neither state can credibly threaten to use force to coerce concessions. As the gap between a state's power and its share of the distribution of benefits increases, war becomes more likely. The state that has more power than benefits in the status quo becomes willing to risk war because war now promises sufficient gains to warrant the costs of fighting. As described earlier, with incomplete information war can then occur because the weaker state now faces a trade-off between larger offers that do more to reduce the probability of war and smaller ones that do more to preserve the state's interests if the offer is accepted. [36] As the formal

[35] Fearon, "Threats to Use Force"; also Donald Wittman, "How a War Ends: A Rational Model Approach," *Journal of Conflict Resolution* 23, 4 (December 1979): 743–763, who explains that the probability of war termination does not change with shifts in power and that there are significant similarities between war termination and war initiation. The results for variation in greed and power are different because in the former the value of war for the opposing state does not go down (if we assume that the probability of winning does not vary with greed), while in the case of power the value of war does go down because the state is less likely to win.

[36] Powell, *In the Shadow of Power*, pp. 104–110, 257.

theorists note, these conclusions about the impact of power on the probability of war diverge from both balance-of-power and power-preponderance theories.[37]

These incomplete information bargaining arguments, however, exaggerate states' willingness to make concessions to avoid war under some conditions. If concessions shift the power that states would have in the future, which giving up territory often would, negotiations are less likely to avoid war. The state that would become more powerful will be unable to credibly commit not to use its increased power to demand a still better deal in the future; as a result of this commitment problem, the opposing state becomes less willing to make concessions relative to fighting.[38] The impact of this unwillingness to make concessions moves the relationship between power and war back toward the simpler deterrence conclusion: if the challenged state is unwilling to negotiate concessions, the probability of war increases with the challenging state's power, if it values changing the status quo.[39]

OFFENSE-DEFENSE BALANCE

The offense-defense balance influences the probability of war in a variety of ways. Its most direct impact is on the value of attacking and of striking first. As the advantage of offense increases, the state that attacks and fights on the offense is more likely to win (than when the probability of winning is proportional only to power, which means the offense-defense balance is implicitly neutral and equal to 1), and the costs of war will tend to be smaller. As a first cut, both of these effects make war more likely by making deterrence more difficult—a state that values acquiring territory will be harder to deter because the expected benefits of attacking will be larger and the costs will be smaller.[40] The logic from a bargaining

[37] However, for a formal result that is more in line with the second of these theories, see William Reed, "Information, Power, and War," *American Political Science Review* 97, 4 (November 2003): 633–641.

[38] See Fearon, "Rationalist Explanations for War," pp. 408–409, who explains that these situations might appear to be cases of indivisibility but in fact reflect commitment problems. For more extensive analysis that shows states can avoid war when small concessions result only in small changes of power, see James D. Fearon, "Bargaining over Objects That Influence Future Bargaining Power" (University of Chicago, 1996); and Powell, "War as a Commitment Problem," pp. 185–188. Another condition that could reduce the prospects for negotiated settlement returns to issues of private information. If fighting would communicate information about a state's power (military capabilities), a state might prefer war, even if there is a negotiated outcome that it preferred to war, because the state would be able to negotiate a better outcome following some fighting; see Fearon, "Rationalist Explanations for War," pp. 401–402; and Harrison Wagner, "Bargaining and War," *American Journal of Political Science* 44, 3 (July 2000): 469–484.

[39] As discussed below, although the formal literature assumes that states value acquiring more territory, this need not be true, in which case the result is different.

[40] Van Evera, *Causes of War*, pp. 123–124. For qualifications that result when defense

perspective is somewhat different. Offense advantage increases the probability that the attacking state will win and therefore narrows the range of outcomes that both states are willing to accept because war is now more attractive. Given uncertainty about power or resolve, this requires a state to make a larger concession to preserve the probability of a negotiated outcome, which increases the value of war relative to negotiation. The result is an increase in the probability of war.[41]

Offense advantage also makes war more likely by creating advantages to striking first that fuel preemptive war—if striking first is better than striking second, a state that prefers a negotiated outcome might nevertheless attack first to avoid the still worse outcome of being attacked first.[42] The probability of preemptive war becomes greater once states are in a crisis; the crisis reflects the failure to resolve issues diplomatically and indicates that war is more likely, leading the states to believe that the other may attack first, making striking first more attractive. The pressures created by first-strike advantages are a common explanation for World War I, and concern about preemptive attacks played an important role in the planning of nuclear forces during the Cold War. Formal theory explains the dangers of preemptive war in terms of a commitment problem—a situation in which an otherwise desirable deal cannot be sustained because states have incentives to break the deal. First-strike incentives can be envisioned as creating a single-play prisoners' dilemma in which both states prefer to attack first but would be willing to forgo war if confident that they would not be attacked.[43]

---

advantage interacts with economic dependence, see Peter Liberman, "The Offense-Defense Balance, Interdependence, and War," *Security Studies* 9, 3 (Autumn 1999–Winter 2000): 59-91.

[41] Powell, *In the Shadow of Power*, pp. 111–113; see also Fearon, "Rationalist Explanations for War," pp. 402–404, who argues that this narrower bargaining range can lead to an increase in the probability of war. Powell's argument captures offense advantage as separable from power, adding an increased probability of winning from striking first to the probability of winning without offense advantage, which is linear in power; in contrast, the theory developed here understands military capability as the product of power and the offense-defense balance.

[42] Van Evera, *Causes of War*, chap. 3; Schelling, *The Strategy of Conflict*, chap. 9; but see Robert Powell, *Nuclear Deterrence Theory: The Search for Credibility* (Cambridge: Cambridge University Press, 1990), chap. 5, who argues that first-strike incentives do not result in war. It is also true, however, that states that recognize the preemptive dangers posed by a crisis should be less willing to engage in one and more willing to make concessions to reach a diplomatic solution; the net result could be a reduction in the probability of war. The flip side of this logic is captured in the "stability-instability" paradox. See also Dan Reiter, "Exploding the Powder Keg Myth: Preemptive Wars Almost Never Happen," *International Security* 20, 2 (Autumn 1995): 5–34, who argues that preemptive wars have been rare.

[43] Fearon, "Rationalist Explanations for War," pp. 402–404; see also Powell, "War as a Commitment Problem," esp. pp. 184–185.

Offense-defense variables could also influence the probability of war in a variety of less direct ways. First, and most basic, the offense-defense balance could influence the value that states place on additional territory, which influences the probability of war. When defense has a large advantage, a security seeker will tend to be secure and will place little or no value on additional territory. Under these conditions, variations in the distribution of power might not influence the demands a state would make—a more powerful state might not make more ambitious demands than a less powerful state. In fact, they both might be uninterested in making any territorial demands and war should not occur, even if there is uncertainty about power and resolve. In contrast, as the advantage of offense increases, security seekers will value additional territory more if it increases their ability to defend and/or deter. This endogenous shift in the value of territory would increase the benefits of war relative to the costs, which tends to make war more likely. This indirect impact would reinforce the direct impact of offense advantage on the probability of war that was described above—in addition to making war more attractive by increasing the probability of winning, offense advantage makes it more attractive by increasing the value of winning.[44]

Put more broadly, the theory developed here makes the value of territory (and more generally the value of reducing an adversary's military capability) at least partly endogenous to the international situation that states' face. This key feature of the theory (and at least implicitly of the entire family of structural-realist and security dilemma theories) is missing in the formal models summarized above. These formal models assume that states want to acquire more territory and that its value is unrelated to the international situations they face. A related point is that the formal theories have not adequately incorporated different types of states—implicitly, the models deal with purely greedy states, those whose value for territory is independent of the international situation they face and who therefore have fundamental conflicts of interest, but not with security seekers.[45]

This basic point brings us back to the arguments about the relationship

[44] Variation in the states' value for territory is captured in the states' "utility for the cost of war": as Fearon, "Rationalist Explanations for War," p. 387, explains, these variables "capture not only the states' values of the costs of war but also the value they place on winning or losing the issues at stake." See also Powell, *In The Shadow of Power*, p. 98. Translating the argument in the text into this formulation, large defense advantage would make the value of additional territory small (or zero), making the utility of the costs of war large, which would reduce the probability of war.

[45] Powell does define satisfied and dissatisfied states; see *In The Shadow of Power*, pp. 91–92, 98–99. However, these types are defined in terms of their willingness to use force to change the status quo, not in terms of their fundamental interests and motives separate from the situation they face. In my terminology, his satisfied states are greedy states that are

between power and bargaining demands, and yields a potentially different relationship between power and the probability of war. As with greater defense advantage, all else being equal, a more powerful state will be more secure; this could reduce its value for territory, which could result in a reduction (not an increase) in the demands it would make. Combined with its improved probability of winning a war, this smaller demand could reduce the probability of war, even though the weaker state's value for territory is increased by its weakness.

Second, offense-defense variables could influence the political conditions under which states enter a bargaining situation in ways that influence the probability of war. In the diplomatic and military interactions that form peacetime relations and precede the crisis bargaining that could lead to war, states develop and revise their assessments of each other's type. As described in chapter 3, offense-defense variables could influence the evolution of states' beliefs about others' motives; more specifically, they influence the probability of negative spirals—in which interaction leads states to believe the opposing state is more likely to be greedy—and of positive spirals—in which interaction has the opposite effect. Defense advantage, as well as the distinguishability of offense and defense, increase a security seeker's prospects for communicating that it has benign motives or at least reduce the probability of requiring policies that signal malign motives.[46] As discussed below in the section on information about motives, the impact of these assessments on the probability of war depends on a number of countervailing factors.

Third, the offense-defense balance, and military technology more generally, could influence the uncertainty that states have about their military capabilities, which in turn influences the probability of war. Van Evera argues that offense advantage leads states to adopt more secretive military policies because small advantages in force size, quality, or mobilization can provide larger advantages in military capabilities.[47] The result is an increase in the private information that states hold, which can increase the probability of war. More generally, the extent of military complexity can influence a state's assessment of the probability of winning a war. Although not a strictly rational explanation, but instead a boundedly rational one, greater complexity can result in states reaching divergent assessments of the probability of winning a war, which in turn

---

willing to accept the status quo because the costs of expansion are too high. As discussed in chapter 2, this is a very different way to define types of states.

[46] For critiques of this argument, see Evan Braden Montgomery, "Breaking Out of the Security Dilemma: Realism, Reassurance, and the Problem of Uncertainty," *International Security* 31, 2 (Fall 2006): 151–185; for responses, see chapter 5.

[47] Van Evera, *Causes of War*, pp. 137–142, identifies a number of other interactions between offense advantage and war.

makes war more likely.[48] This explanation is quite different from the prevailing rationalist one that focuses on private information. Uncertainty resulting from complexity does not reflect incentives to misrepresent but instead reflects a lack of experience with, and interaction between, the military forces the states have deployed. War may be the only way for states to learn about their prospects for winning. Changes in technology that result in greater complexity and, related, in a lack of experience with the deployed forces therefore make war more likely.[49]

Information about Motives

A state's information about its adversary's motives could affect the probability of war directly by influencing its negotiating position during a crisis. This information could also influence states' interactions before a crisis in ways that change the probability of crises and the factors that states consider once bargaining in a crisis.

In a crisis, a state that is uncertain about its adversary's motives and is considering making concessions to avoid war should make an offer that balances the concessions it would make to a greedy state with the concessions it would make to a security seeker. A state should offer more to a greedy state than to a security seeker because larger concessions are required to avoid war. These larger concessions are not the best offer if facing a security seeker, however, because a diplomatic solution would then give up more than was appropriate for trying to avoid war. Because the size of concessions differs, the state needs to balance the offers that would be best for the two different types of states. In striking this balance, the state would weigh the outcomes for greedy and security-seeking states by the probabilities that it faces these types of states. The larger the probability that the adversary is a greedy state, the larger the concession it should make. Uncertainty about the other state's type (of motives) is not included in standard bargaining models of war but could be added.[50] Instead of facing a single type of adversary, the state would be envisioned as facing two different types, with some probability that it faces a greedy state and the remaining probability that it faces a security seeker. For both types of adversaries, the state could remain uncertain about the

[48] Fearon, "Rationalist Explanations for War," pp. 392–393, on this distinction. Of course, if the states underestimate the capability of their forces, this can reduce the probability of war.

[49] The argument here parallels the common argument that uncertainties about power can require war to resolve them; for related arguments, see Geoffrey Blainey, *The Causes of War* (New York: Free Press, 1973).

[50] An exception is Rui J. P. de Figueiredo Jr. and Barry R. Weingast, "The Rationality of Fear: Political Opportunism and Ethnic Conflict," in Barbara F. Walter and Jack Snyder, eds., *Civil Wars, Insecurity and Intervention* (New York: Columbia University Press, 1999).

costs of war, with the cost distribution for the greedy opponent shifted toward lower costs.

Higher estimates that the adversary is greedy would result in a lower probability of war. At first this seems counterintuitive, as high probabilities that one's adversary is greedy are typically understood to reflect more strained political relations, higher probabilities of confrontation, and so forth. However, all else being equal, once a state is bargaining over concessions, higher probabilities that the adversary is greedy lead to larger concessions, which reduces the probability of war regardless of whether the adversary is a security seeker or a greedy state. At least taken narrowly, this means that a negative political spiral between security seekers before they enter into crisis bargaining could reduce the probability of war between them.

Part of the issue (or problem) here is that the focus of the analysis is too narrow—estimates that the adversary is likely to be greedy could have a number of effects that are not captured in this type of basic bargaining model. First, as discussed above, the value the state places on territory could grow with its insecurity, which could increase the probability of war; and a greater probability that the adversary is greedy would increase the state's insecurity. On the flip side, a security seeker that believes its adversary is likely to be a security seeker will place less value on acquiring additional territory; under a range of conditions this could reduce the probability of crises, as well as the probability that crisis would lead to war. Second, the greater probability that the adversary is greedy could lead the state to adopt more competitive, offensive military policies during the period that precedes a crisis; for the reasons discussed above, these policies could increase the probability of war once involved in bargaining. Third, making concessions to a greedy state could be more dangerous, reducing the state's willingness to make larger concessions and possibly eliminating its willingness to make any concessions. A state will be more concerned about shifts in power if facing a greedy state, thereby making concessions less acceptable for the reasons discussed above. Closely related, if a state comes to believe that its adversary has unlimited, as opposed to limited, greedy aims, concessions will be less attractive. This greater reluctance to make concessions would make war more likely. The net result could be an increase in the probability of war, in which one or a combination of these effects offsets the bargaining implications of a greater probability that the adversary is greedy.

In addition, we should remember that the information that a state has at the time of a crisis results partly from interactions that precede it. More specifically, a state's information about its adversary's motives in periods before a possible crisis can influence the probability that states ever enter a crisis, as well as the factors that influence the probability of war once a crisis occurs. As explained in chapter 3, a state's information about the opposing state's motives can influence its choice between cooperative and competitive policies, which can influence the opposing state's choice of policies, which can in turn influence the state's information about its adversary. An initial belief that the opposing state is likely to be a security seeker supports cooperative policies, which if feasible have the potential to generate reactions that reinforce this belief, leading to higher estimates that the adversary is a security seeker. This positive spiral, which reflects a less severe security dilemma, has a logic that parallels the potential impact of defense advantage on states' interactions, which was summarized above. High estimates that the adversary is a security seeker in turn tend to reduce the probability of war, for the reasons discussed in the previous paragraph.

In sum, a broad point that flows from this assessment is that the bargaining models of war have not yet adequately captured some of the key ways in which my theory (and neorealism more narrowly) understands the impact of states' motives and their international environment on the probability of war.[51] The formal theories take the value of territory (or whatever is being bargained over) as given, whereas the theory developed here argues that the value of territory can at least partially reflect the material and information situation the state faces. In addition, the formal theories do not adequately capture states' uncertainty about the type of adversary they face. And they do not capture how a state's international situation influences key choices that precede crisis bargaining—including cooperation and competition, and more specifically strategy and force posture. These choices influence the conditions under which states enter bargaining, including the information they have about the opposing state's motives and the military capabilities they possess in the crisis, which in turn influence the probability of war.[52] The formal theories do shine a powerful light on the bargaining that could lead to war once states are in a dispute, showing among other things the limitations of simpler deterrence-style arguments.

INTERNATIONAL INSTITUTIONS

My theory focuses on a state's international environment—the material and information conditions that it faces—and shows that cooperation, and even stable peace, should occur under a range of conditions. Given

---

[51] This is interesting because key statements of the rationalist theories see them accomplishing this; see Fearon, "Rationalist Explanations for War," p. 380; and, somewhat less explicitly, Powell, *In the Shadow of Power*, pp. 4–6.

[52] Some of these interactions are addressed by Branislav L. Slantchev, "Military Coercion in Interstate Crises," *American Political Science Review* 99, 4 (November 2005): 533–547.

that neo-institutionalism identifies international institutions as the key to cooperation, offering an alternative to the standard realist assessment of the difficulty of cooperation,[53] the question naturally arises—what role does my theory see for international institutions?[54]

My theory understands security institutions as endogenous, a means available to states for achieving their goals. From this perspective, institutions are policy choices, comparable to states' choices of military forces and doctrine. Consistent with institutionalist arguments, I identify possible roles for international institutions in performing a variety of functions that could increase a state's security. These include providing information about motives, providing information about states' actions, and providing a forum for negotiating distributional issues and confronting real-world complexity.

Given its international environment, a state needs to assess its choice between competitive and cooperative policies by exploring the more specific elements that would make up these policies. In the security realm, these means include not only the military forces both sides would likely deploy under cooperative and competitive policies, but also the institutions they could establish, including negotiated agreements that limit military forces and the arrangements for monitoring and enforcing them; and agreements that commit states to aid each other in war and to coordinate military forces and planning during peacetime.[55] In other words, from the perspective of my strategic choice theory, international institutions are first and foremost policy choices to be evaluated and prescribed, not exogenous constraints.[56] Similarly, continued participation in an in-

---

[53] Keohane, *After Hegemony*. More specifically on security cooperation, see Celeste A. Wallander, *Mortal Friends, Best Enemies: German-Russian Cooperation after the Cold War* (Ithaca: Cornell University Press, 1999); and Helga Haftendorn, Robert O. Keohane, and Celeste A. Wallander, eds., *Imperfect Unions: Security Institutions over Time and Space* (Oxford: Oxford University Press, 1999). For an assessment of the institutional theory research program, see Robert O. Keohane and Lisa L. Martin, "Institutional Theory as a Research Program," in Colin Elman and Miriam Fendius Elman, eds., *Progress in International Relations Theory: Appraising the Field* (Cambridge: MIT Press, 2003). For a less benign view of the impact of institutions, see Lloyd Gruber, *Ruling the World: Power Politics and the Rise of Supranational Organizations* (Princeton: Princeton University Press, 2000), who argues that multilateral institutions can support outcomes that leave less powerful states worse off.

[54] On the definition of international institutions, see Beth A. Simmons and Lisa L. Martin, "International Organizations and Institutions," p. 194, in Walter Carlsnaes, Thomas Risse, and Beth A. Simmons, eds., *Handbook of International Relations* (London: Sage, 2002).

[55] International institutions can take a variety of forms; see Robert O. Keohane, *International Institutions and State Power: Essays in International Relations Theory* (Boulder: Westview Press, 1989), pp. 3–4. My argument applies best to the forms that at a given time are a choice for states—organizations, agreements, and certain types of regimes—and least well for conventions, which are not problematized here or by neo-institutionalism.

[56] For a different approach to bringing institutions into structural theory, see Snyder, "Process Variables in Neorealist Theory."

ternational institution is a policy choice. The same is true of deploying and maintaining military forces. Both military forces and institutions reflect states' decisions; they therefore have equal standing in the theory. The deep sources of significant cooperation are found in states' motives and their international environment, not in the international institutions that states have the choice to create and preserve.

This argument, however, does not imply that institutions are unimportant.[57] The issue here is one of perspective. From the perspective of a strategic choice theory, means—whether military forces or international institutions—can appear unimportant because it is the state's motives and international environment that generate outcomes. In contrast, from the perspective of a state designing a strategy, the choice of the best available means is not a foregone conclusion, and choosing the wrong means will leave it less secure than required by its environment. Put another way, from the perspective of the strategic choice theory, institutions are endogenous; when institutions are the best available means to achieve their objectives, states will create them. Under these conditions, failure to create the institution is a form of suboptimal behavior that can reduce a state's security.

Consistent with the neo-institutionalist argument, my theory suggests a variety of ways in which institutions can contribute to a state's security. If an arms agreement would increase a state's security, except that the possibility of the adversary cheating makes the agreement too risky, an institutional arrangement that increases the state's abilities to monitor the agreement could make the agreement acceptable. If an agreement has the potential to increase a state's security, but its desirability depends on the types of forces that will be covered, the levels at which they will be limited, the measures that will be used to define their size and quality, or the restrictions on improvements in the quality of forces, then negotiations and formal agreement on these issues will be required to enable states to choose among the set of desirable agreements. These negotiations are necessary not simply to manage the real-world complexity of policies issues, but also to resolve distributional issues among the set of mutually beneficial agreements.[58] U.S. and Soviet diplomats who were negotiating agreements on strategic nuclear forces during the Cold War

---

[57] For related observations, see Lisa L. Martin and Beth A. Simmons, "Theories and Empirical Studies of International Institutions," *International Organization* 52, 4 (Autumn 1998): 729–757. Some critics, however, come close to arguing that endogeneity goes hand in hand with insignificance; see, for example, John J. Mearsheimer, "The False Promise of International Institutions," *International Security* 19, 23 (Winter 1994/95): 7.

[58] On distributional issues, see Stephen D. Krasner, "Global Communications and National Power: Life on the Pareto Frontier," *World Politics* 43, 3 (April 1991): 336–366; and James D. Fearon, "Bargaining, Enforcement and International Cooperation," *International Organization* 52, 2 (Spring 1998): 269–305.

spent much of their time and effort dealing with these types of issues, including defining the size and type of allowed ballistic missiles (and whether they would be counted as carrying multiple warheads), the types of systems that would be limited (e.g., bombers and cruise missiles, or only ballistic missiles), and the allowed infrastructure for antimissile defense systems.[59]

In addition, like unilateral decisions about force structure and military doctrine, a state's decision to join an institution can provide information about its motives because participating in the institution requires the state to abide by restrictions that a security seeker would be more likely to accept than would a greedy state. For example, an arms control agreement that includes provisions for effectively monitoring states' compliance can, in addition to reducing the risks of cheating, also provide information about motives because a state that wanted to acquire military advantages by arms racing would be less likely to join the institution. This would not be possible via unilateral restraint if the monitoring established by the agreement was necessary to make cooperation desirable.

Beyond these basic points about the relationship between security institutions and the international environment, the theory helps identify the conditions under which security institutions are likely to have a large impact. Like arms control more generally, security institutions will be hardest to create, but make their largest contribution, when the international environment makes security hard to achieve. For example, if the offense-defense balance favors offense and states believe that their adversaries are likely to be greedy, an arms control agreement limiting offense could greatly increase a state's security. This agreement is likely to be especially important if negotiated agreement is necessary to provide monitoring capabilities that insure against significant cheating. Not only would this agreement significantly enhance the state's ability to deter, it would also send a significant signal because the cost of forgoing offense would be larger for a greedy state. This said, cooperation, and institutions more specifically, could also be valuable under less harsh conditions, especially given the implications of uncertainty about the material and information variables that define a state's international environment.

[59] On these negotiations, see Gerard C. Smith, *Doubletalk: The Story of the First Strategic Arms Limitation Talks* (Garden City, NY: Doubleday, 1980); and Strobe Talbott, *Endgame: The Inside Story of SALT II* (New York: Harper and Row, 1979). Similar issues were the focus of the naval agreements reached at the Washington Conference of 1921–22; see chapter 9 for citations.

CHAPTER FIVE

Counterarguments

THIS CHAPTER ADDRESSES a number of counterarguments that maintain that cooperation is significantly more difficult than suggested by my theory. These counterarguments include that the possibility of being cheated makes cooperation too risky; that the possibility the adversary will achieve relative gains makes cooperation undesirable; that there are serious problems with the offense-defense variables, which undermine the possibilities they create for cooperation; that signaling requires states to accept increased military vulnerability, rendering it too risky; and that states should assume the worst about their adversaries' motives, which favors competition. Most of the arguments were developed either to support the standard structural-realist conclusion that the international environment generally drives states into competition or to counterarguments that challenged this conclusion. These counterarguments apply to the more general theory I have developed in this book; examining them helps both to further develop my theory and to demonstrate its strengths. The following sections show that the counterarguments suffer serious shortcomings; none of them significantly weakens the central insights offered by the theory.

CHEATING ON COOPERATION

A major potential barrier to international cooperation is that under anarchy, because there is no authority that can enforce agreements, states will cheat when doing so serves their interests. In the military realm, the possibility that one's adversary will cheat on an arms agreement means that a state's true choice may not be between successful arms control and arms racing, but instead between risking being left behind when the adversary cheats and racing from the start to insure that the adversary fails to gain a lead. The theory developed in the previous chapters explains how cooperation, assuming it holds, compares to competition, and demonstrates that under a range of conditions cooperation should be a state's preferred option. If, however, the risks of cheating are sufficiently large, then otherwise beneficial cooperation would not increase a state's security and could undermine it.

Pessimistic structural-realist arguments have focused on the possibility of cheating, suggesting that it will usually prevent cooperation. According to these arguments, cooperation on security issues is likely to be quite difficult to achieve because states are especially reluctant to risk shortfalls in military capability.[1]

My theory recognizes that cheating is a significant danger but does not see the risks consistently outweighing the benefits of cooperation. Earlier discussion has touched on factors that influence the danger of cheating: for example, the offense-defense balance—cheating is less dangerous when defense has a larger advantage; and the quality of warning that the adversary is cheating—the better a state's ability to monitor cooperation, a task that institutions can sometimes improve, the smaller the danger of cheating. More broadly, by recognizing that competition can be dangerous—for example, a state can lose an arms race, end up militarily less capable even if it does not lose, and signal malign motives while simply trying to insure its security—the theory calls for comparing the risks of cooperation, including cheating, to the risks of competition.

Two bodies of literature help to reinforce and extend the argument that the possibility of cheating need not make cooperation undesirable. Modern arms control theory recognizes the danger posed by the adversary's cheating but does not see it as a necessarily insurmountable barrier to cooperation. These arguments explain that the risks of cheating must be weighed against the benefits an agreement would provide, assuming it holds. They explain that the danger of cheating depends on a number of factors, including the probability of detecting violations of a given size; the strategic implications of a given degree of cheating, which depends upon the level and type of forces allowed by the agreement; and the state's ability to respond to violations by joining the renewed arms race.[2]

To reduce the risks of cooperation, a formal arms control agreement could include provisions for monitoring the agreement that would improve a state's ability to detect cheating, and thereby reduce the advantage it could provide. If, however, the states' independent national monitoring capabilities already provide information that makes the benefits of

---

[1] This view of cheating in making security cooperation more difficult than economic cooperation is supported by important articles on cooperation theory; for example, Robert Jervis, "Security Regimes," in Stephen Krasner, ed., *International Regimes* (Ithaca: Cornell University Press, 1983); and Charles Lipson, "International Cooperation in Economic and Security Affairs," *World Politics* 37, 1 (October 1984): 1–23, esp. 12–18. Both articles, however, point to conditions that increase the probability of security cooperation.

[2] Schelling and Halperin, *Strategy and Arms Control*. See also Abram Chayes, "An Inquiry into the Working of Arms Control Agreements," *Harvard Law Review* 85, 5 (March 1972): 905–969, esp. 945–961; and James A. Shear, "Verification, Compliance, and Arms Control: Dynamics of the Domestic Debate," in Eden and Miller, eds., *Nuclear Arguments*.

cheating small, deals to accept the military status quo may not require extensive provisions for monitoring. And, in these cases, formal agreements may not be more promising than unilateral statements that a state plans to build only if its adversary builds. Schelling and Halperin conclude that "It cannot be assumed that an agreement that leaves some possibility of cheating is necessarily unacceptable or that cheating would necessarily result in strategically important gains."[3]

The basic point that the possibility of cheating does not necessarily make cooperation undesirable is also supported by the literature that has used game theory to explore cooperation under anarchy.[4] Cooperation theory provides insights that parallel those offered by arms control and offense-defense theories, emphasizing the importance of each state's preferences. A simple model of the choice between an arms control agreement and an arms race assumes that if an agreement is reached and cheating is then detected, the arms race begins and is not halted again by another agreement.[5] Given this assumption, the state comparing the value of an arms control agreement and the risks of being cheated faces four possible outcomes: the agreement holds (CC); the adversary cheats, leaving the state one step behind in the ensuing arms race (CD); an equal arms race ensues (DD); or the state cheats, gaining a one-step lead in the arms race (CD).[6] A state is concerned with the implications of cheating only if it prefers the arms agreement to the equal arms race, that is, CC > DD.[7] If the state prefers an arms race in which it gets a one-step lead to the arms agreement (DC > CC), and if its adversary has the same preference order-

[3] Schelling and Halperin, *Strategy and Arms Control*, p. 69.

[4] See Robert Axelrod, *The Evolution of Cooperation* (New York: Basic Books, 1984), who provides the foundation for much of this work; key works include Keohane, *After Hegemony;* and Oye, ed., *Cooperation under Anarchy.*

[5] More complex (and realistic) assumptions would allow for reestablishing an agreement at any point during the ensuing arms race. Although renegotiation would be possible, the simplified assumption seems adequate to capture the options that states would consider in joining and breaking out of a major arms control agreement. Relaxing this assumption opens up the possibility of iterated-game models of tit-for-tat type strategies, which play a central role in the literature on cooperation under anarchy, but not in my discussion.

[6] "C" stands for cooperation, which in this example means abiding by the agreement, and "D" stands for defection, which in this example means cheating on the agreement. CC refers to the outcome in which both states cooperate; DD refers to the outcome in which both states defect; and DC and CD refer to outcomes in which one state cooperates and the other defects.

[7] Some structural-realist arguments suggest that this condition is rarely met. For example, the argument that cooperation theory is flawed because it fails to take into account states' concern about relative gains amounts to saying that DD > CC for at least one state; this argument is addressed in the following section. The offensive-realist argument that states attempt to maximize power produces a similar conclusion; this argument is addressed in the following chapter.

ing, the state faces a prisoner's dilemma, and its best option is to compete. In contrast, if the state prefers the arms agreement to an arms race in which it gets a one-step lead (CC > DC), and if its adversary has the same preference ordering, the states face a "stag hunt."[8] Unlike the prisoner's dilemma, in a stag hunt it can be individually rational for two states to cooperate.[9]

However, cooperation is not assured in a stag hunt if the states are unsure of each other's preference orderings. For example, a state with stag-hunt preferences believing that it faces a state with prisoner's-dilemma preferences should defect. A state that is unsure about its adversary's preferences and, therefore, unsure about whether the adversary will abide by the arms control agreement should compare the magnitude of its payoffs.[10] This is where the magnitude of the danger posed by cheating comes into play.

To determine when the risks of cooperation are "too large," the state compares an arms race in which it starts one step behind (CD) to both an arms race started on equal footing (DD) and to the arms agreement (CC). The state's willingness to risk cooperation grows as (1) the difference between falling behind by a step and running an equal arms race (CD-DD) decreases; and (2) the difference between the arms control agreement and the equal arms race (CC-DD) increases. As discussed in the arms control and security dilemma literatures, the difference between CD and DD depends on a variety of factors, including the forces allowed by the agreement, the offense-defense balance, the quality of monitoring capabilities, and the rate at which states can build forces. For example, improving a state's ability to monitor an agreement reduces the difference between an adversary getting a lead and starting an arms race at the same time, that is, it reduces CD-DD, thereby making cooperation more desirable. The difference between an arms race and an agreement that limits offensive forces increases as the offense-defense balance shifts toward offense.

To translate this argument into the kind of model that is commonly used in cooperation theory, we can envision the arms control–arms race choice as a series of decisions made over time; each decision constitutes a

---

[8] This also requires the reasonable assumption that DC > DD > CD. For a discussion of how a stag hunt compares to other two-by-two games where cooperation is necessary for states to achieve mutual gains, see Kenneth A. Oye, "Explaining Cooperation under Anarchy: Hypotheses and Strategies," In Oye, ed., *Cooperation under Anarchy*.

[9] For a discussion of when competition will nevertheless occur in a stag hunt, see Downs, Rocke, and Siverson, "Arms Control and Cooperation," in Oye, ed., *Cooperation under Anarchy*, pp. 133–137.

[10] The state also needs to assess the probability that its adversary will cooperate. In addition to its uncertainty about the adversary's payoffs, this will depend on the adversary's understanding of the state's payoffs; uncertainty about the state's payoffs could lead an adversary to compete that would otherwise cooperate.

single play of a game, which is repeated.[11] The simplifying assumption used above—that once cheating is detected the arms race begins and is not halted again by another agreement—translates into a model in which each state's strategy is to always defect after its adversary's first defection. The prospects for cooperation depend on the states' preferences in the game. Cooperation should occur if the states believe they are playing stag hunt. However, cooperation can also be possible if the states believe they are playing prisoner's dilemma; this is because, given their strategy for dealing with defection, the overall game that results with iteration can be a stag hunt.[12] In other words, the stag hunt that was discussed in the previous paragraphs can be produced by an iterated prisoner's dilemma played under certain conditions.

In sum, the arguments presented in the arms control literature and later in the cooperation theory literature make clear that whether the dangers of cheating more than offset the potential benefits of cooperation, and arms control more specifically, depends on a variety of specific factors, including the terms of the agreement and the states' abilities to monitor it. Thus, according to the theory developed here, although the possibility of cheating could make cooperation undesirable under certain conditions, under other conditions arms control would remain preferable to arms racing.

Constraints Imposed by Concern Over Relative Gains

An influential structural-realist argument holds that international cooperation is difficult and rare because states are sensitive to relative

[11] However, the assumption of this type of model that the payoffs do not change over time can be problematic for certain arms agreements and races. For example, in an agreement that establishes low levels of forces, a given amount of cheating in the first play of the game could have implications that are quite different from the implications of cheating of the same magnitude once the renewed arms race has continued through many plays. In addition, because a war could stop the repetition of the game, a model that includes the possibility of war after each play of the game might capture more of what we care about. The probability of war after each move would depend on the states' military capabilities at that stage of the race, thereby reflecting the cumulative nature of the arms race.

[12] On this possibility and complications, see David M. Kreps, *A Course in Microeconomic Theory* (Princeton: Princeton University Press, 1990), pp. 503–515. Whether it is a stag hunt or a prisoner's dilemma depends on the cost of being cheated in a single play and on the state's discount rate. The intuition is that, assuming a prisoner's dilemma for each iteration of the game, although a state can do better than mutual cooperation by cheating on the first move, it does less well than mutual cooperation on each following move. If the first move is not valued much more than future moves (that is, the discount rate is sufficiently low), then eventually the costs suffered in all following moves will outweigh the gains of taking advantage in the first move. In effect, the prospect of restarting and prosecuting the arms race is sufficient to deter initial cheating.

gains—even if cooperation could provide absolute gains, a state might reject cooperation if it also would result in relative losses.[13] If cooperation enables a state's adversary to gain more, the adversary might be able to convert this advantage into a capability for effectively coercing the state or, in extreme cases, defeating it in war. As a result, states must be concerned about relative gains, that is, about which state gains more from cooperation. Waltz argues that states "are compelled to ask not 'Will both of us gain?' but 'Who will gain more?'"[14] States may conclude that the danger of relative losses exceeds the benefit of absolute gains, making cooperation undesirable. Relative-gains problems are generally believed to be more severe in the security realm than in the economic realm, thereby making security cooperation especially difficult.[15] If correct, many of the key arguments developed in the previous chapter are incomplete and overly optimistic about the prospects for cooperation. Instead of cooperating to avoid the risk of falling behind in an arms race, to signal benign motives, and to increase both states' defensive military capabilities, competition could be a state's preferred policy due to relative-gains concerns.

It turns out, however, that the impact of states' concern about relative gains is much exaggerated. Most important, relative-gains arguments are frequently framed incorrectly, focusing on gains in means instead of ends. Reframing the argument largely eliminates the problem for security cooperation. Moreover, under a wide range of conditions the constraints imposed by states' sensitivity to relative gains in ends will be quite mild and therefore should not significantly constrain security or economic cooperation.[16]

The Relative-Gains Problem Is Not about Relative Military Assets

The key to understanding relative gains in the security realm is to frame the issue correctly. We first must distinguish means—the instruments of

[13] Waltz, *Theory of International Politics*, pp. 105, 175; Grieco, *Cooperation among Nations*; and Grieco, "Anarchy and the Limits of Cooperation: A Realist Critique of the Newest Liberal Institutionalism," *International Organization* 42, 3 (Summer 1988): 485–507. For an application, see John C. Matthews III, "Current Gains and Future Outcomes," *International Security* 21, 1 (Summer 1996): 112–146.

[14] Waltz, *Theory of International Politics*, p. 105. In fact, a state really only needs to ask "will I gain?" to determine whether cooperation is desirable; it may, however, need to ask "will both of us gain?" to assess whether cooperation is feasible.

[15] For example, Grieco, *Cooperation among Nations*, p. 46, argues that "a state's sensitivity to gaps in gains is also likely to be greater if a cooperative venture involves security matters than economic well-being"; see also ibid., p. 14.

[16] This examination also suggests that concern about relative gains will be less constraining in security cooperation, specifically in arms control, than in economic cooperation.

policy—from ends—the value the policy produces. Concern about relative gains must be over gains in ends, not means. In the security realm, military assets are means, while security is an end. Thus, correctly formulated, in the security realm the "absolute gains" from cooperation refer to an increase in security.[17] Concern about relative gains would, therefore, compare gains in security. In the economic realm, tariffs and other barriers to trade are examples of means, while wealth is the end.[18]

This formulation helps us to correct a common mistake: analysts argue that states care a great deal about the relative impact of cooperation on their military forces and then conclude incorrectly that states are highly sensitive to relative gains. However, although states do care about relative changes in military forces, this concern does not reflect a relative-gains problem because what is being compared here is a change in means (forces), not a change in ends (security).

One way to appreciate the importance of this distinction is to notice that the formulation of relative gains that focuses on means adds nothing to standard criteria for evaluating whether security cooperation is desirable. Analysis of the military impact of security cooperation should focus on whether arms control agreements would enhance a state's military capabilities. Relative force size influences a state's military mission capabilities and therefore should play a central role in such an assessment. When cooperation would result in a relative loss in military forces, and when this loss reduces a state's mission capability and security, the state should reject cooperation. This refusal, however, would reflect the failure of cooperation to increase the state's security—that is, to provide absolute gains—not the state's concern over relative gains. If cooperation had resulted in a relative loss in forces but had nevertheless increased the state's security, the state should then have cooperated.

These arguments raise a second basic question: why should states ever care about relative gains? A common assumption about states' preferences, and one that I have used in describing types of states, is that states

---

[17] For greedy states nonsecurity expansion would also be a goal. Absolute gains could also refer to economic savings, if arms control agreements (or alliances) enable the state to reduce investment in military forces. However, although saving money is one of the three classic objectives of arms control, security is usually the priority goal of this type of cooperation. On the classic objectives of arms control, see Schelling and Halperin, *Strategy and Arms Control*, p. 2. For a dissenting view on the role of saving money, see Bernard Brodie, "On the Objectives of Arms Control," *International Security* 1, 1 (Summer 1976): 17–36.

[18] For the sake of contrast, I am using "security realm" to refer to policies that influence the size and type of forces and "economic realm" to refer to policies that influence the type and severity of trade barriers. I do not mean to imply that policies in the economic realm lack security implications and vice versa. Thus, these statements include an important simplification and therefore may exaggerate the extent to which manipulation of instruments in one realm produces only one type of value. I address the implications below.

are egoists—they are interested in maximizing their own absolute gains and are indifferent to others' gains. But then why would states ever care about relative gains? The answer lies in the possibility that ends are simultaneously means or are directly related to the production of means. For example, economic ends—wealth—can simultaneously be means in the security realm because states can use their wealth to acquire military forces. When ends are simultaneously means, states may appear to care about relative gains in ends, but in fact their willingness to cooperate should be influenced by their concern about relative gains in means that accompany gains in ends. Because a relative loss in means could reduce the state's ability to achieve absolute gains in the future, it faces a trade-off between current and future achievement of absolute gains in ends.

In short, if there is a relative-gains problem in the security realm, it must lie elsewhere. The two possibilities, discussed below, are relative gains in security and relative gains in wealth resulting from security cooperation. However, exploration of these areas casts serious doubt on whether relative-gains concerns are severe in the security realm and suggests further that states will usually not be constrained by them.

Relative Security Gains and Comparisons of Security

Because the goal of cooperation is to increase security, relative-gains logic suggests that we explore whether concern over relative gains in security should inhibit cooperation. A state is concerned about relative gains in security if cooperation would increase its adversary's security more than its own, and if this relative loss in security would in turn reduce its own security. If we narrowly equate security with military capability, this situation could arise, for example, if an arms control agreement increased both states' denial capabilities, but not equally.

However, following security-dilemma logic, all else being equal, increases in the adversary's security often increase one's own security because a more secure adversary has smaller incentives for pursuing an expansionist foreign policy and, therefore, poses a smaller threat. This argument does not depend on whether increases in the adversary's security exceed or trail the increase in one's own security because the reduction in the adversary's interest in expansion reflects its absolute security, not its relative security.[19]

In short, contrary to the issue identified by the logic of the relative-gains problem, if cooperation increases a state's security, then increases in its adversary's security are usually desirable, whether or not they ex-

---

[19] For objections and qualifications to this argument, see Glaser, "Realists as Optimists," pp. 75, 76.

ceed the increase in the state's security. In the security realm, instead of a relative-gains problem, we often have a mutual-gains benefit.

Relative Economic Savings and Economic Growth

The second line of argument shifts the focus of the relative-gains arguments from comparisons of security gains to comparisons of economic growth that are made possible by security cooperation. This argument traces the danger in security cooperation through relative increases in the adversary's wealth, which the adversary can eventually convert into superiority in military forces. More specifically, this argument holds that when security cooperation saves the adversary greater resources than it saves the defender, the adversary will be able to redirect greater resources to future security competition, which will enable it eventually to pose a greater security threat than if cooperation had never occurred.

Although this argument appears to hinge on savings, in fact it hinges on the relationship between reduced defense spending and economic growth. Assume that both states reserve their savings for a future arms race. If the agreement breaks down, the state that saved more cannot compete more effectively than if an agreement had never been reached, because it has only the resources it would have invested earlier. The agreement defers the arms race but does not advantage the state that saves more. Consequently, savings have security implications only if they generate economic growth. This could occur if defense spending crowds out private investment, which would otherwise contribute more to economic growth. In this case, the state that saves more can achieve relative gains in GNP. If the agreement then breaks down, the states' abilities to engage in an arms race would have changed.

The problem with this line of argument is that studies have not established a strong relationship between defense spending and economic growth.[20] Moreover, the difference in savings produced by an arms control agreement is unlikely to be large, which further reduces the risks of differential economic growth. An agreement that saved the United States 1 percent of GNP per year would have to be quite dramatic;[21] the difference in savings promises to be much smaller because the agreement

[20] Aaron L. Friedberg, "The Political Economy of American Strategy," World Politics 41, 3 (April 1989): 395–405; Charles A. Kupchan, "Empire, Military Power, and Economic Decline," International Security 13, 4 (Summer 1989): 40–47; and Steve Chan, "The Impact of Defense Spending on Economic Performance: A Survey of the Evidence and Problems," Orbis 29 (Summer 1985): 403–434.

[21] For example, during much of the Cold War the United States spent approximately 1 percent of its GNP per year on nuclear forces; an agreement to ban nuclear weapons might therefore have saved approximately this much per year.

would also provide the adversary with savings. In sum, although focusing on the possibility that security cooperation could generate relative gains in economic growth is analytically sound, it appears that the dangers posed by this possibility should rarely, if ever, be a major barrier to security cooperation.

Factors That Would Influence the Security Implications of Relative Economic Losses

In cases in which security cooperation would generate differential economic growth, three additional considerations influence whether the risks would outweigh the defender's direct gains in security, thereby making security cooperation undesirable. The second and third of these considerations also apply to economic cooperation and, therefore, influence the security implications of trade and other types of agreements that could produce unequal economic gains.

First, the beneficial effects of the adversary's increased security make its increased relative economic strength less threatening since it would be less inclined to use this economic potential for security-driven expansion. Thus, the state should find relative economic losses produced by security cooperation somewhat less threatening than comparable relative losses produced by economic cooperation.

Second, the magnitude of the relative gains influences the potential security threat.[22] Small relative gains, compared to GNP, would rarely pose a major threat. If cooperation breaks down, the disadvantaged state would be able to offset any increased military threat made possible by growth in the adversary's GNP by increasing the percentage of GNP it spends on defense. Thus, when the adversary's relative gains are small, the defender risks a loss of prosperity, but not of security. If a security agreement (while it holds) provides large security gains, risking this loss would usually be warranted.

Third, the offense-defense balance influences the security implications of the relative economic gains.[23] Relative gains matter less as the advantage of defense grows because acquiring effective offensive capabilities requires the adversary to make increasingly disproportionate investments

[22] In a parallel argument Liberman, "Trading with the Enemy," argues that the relative gains from economic cooperation are small and, therefore, not a significant barrier to cooperation.

[23] A second structural factor that can influence the implications of relative gains is the number of major states in the system. See Duncan Snidal, "Relative Gains and the Pattern of International Cooperation," *American Political Science Review* 85, 3 (September 1991): 701–726.

in military forces. Thus, when defense has a large advantage over offense, the possibility of relative gains should do little to inhibit security or economic cooperation.[24] Consequently, states that possess large nuclear arsenals and that rely heavily on nuclear deterrence for their security should not be inhibited from security or economic cooperation by security-related relative-gains constraints, because nuclear weapons create a large advantage for the defense.[25]

In sum, these arguments suggest that, under most conditions, states should focus on the absolute security gains offered by security cooperation because these gains would rarely be jeopardized by relative economic losses.

CRITIQUES OF OFFENSE-DEFENSE VARIABLES

Among the variables that play a central role in my theory, offense-defense variables have probably been the focus of the most controversy. Here I briefly summarize and then evaluate the key criticisms. Some are simply wrong; others, while raising important issues, turn out not to weaken the theory's foundation.[26]

A common criticism is that the offense-defense balance is a vague concept, which is reflected in the variety of ways in which this variable is

[24] Robert Powell, "Absolute and Relative Gains in International Relations Theory," *American Political Science Review* 85, 4 (December 1991): 1303–1320, reaches a similar conclusion but has cast it in terms of the costs of fighting, not the offense-defense balance. See also Helen Milner, "International Theories of Cooperation among Nations: Strengths and Weaknesses," *World Politics* 44, 3 (April 1992): 483–484. Waltz, *Theory of International Politics*, p. 195, suggests this logic but does not spell it out.

[25] For a similar point, see Kenneth N. Waltz, "The Emerging Structure of International Politics," *International Security* 18, 2 (Fall 1993): 74; Layne, "The Unipolar Illusion," pp. 44–45, appears to disagree.

[26] On this debate, see Glaser and Kaufmann, "What Is the Offense-Defense Balance?"; Stephen Van Evera, "Offense, Defense and the Causes of War," *International Security* 22, 2 (Spring 1988): 5–43; Glaser and Kaufmann, "Correspondence"; Sean Lynn-Jones, "Offense-Defense Theory and Its Critics," *Security Studies* 4, 4 (Summer 1995): 660–691; Keir A. Lieber, *War and the Engineers: The Primacy of Politics over Technology* (Ithaca: Cornell University Press, 2005); Stephen Biddle, "Rebuilding the Foundations of Offense-Defense Theory," *Journal of Politics* 63, 4 (August 2001): 741–774; Biddle, *Military Power*; and Karen Ruth Adams, "Attack and Conquer?: International Anarchy and the Offense-Defense-Deterrence Balance," *International Security* 28, 3 (Winter 2003/04): 45–83. For an early statement of offense-defense arguments and many examples of how technology changed the offense-defense balance, see George H. Quester, *Offense and Defense in the International System* (New York: Wiley, 1997). For an early critique, see Jack S. Levy, "The Offense/Defense Balance of Military Technology: A Theoretical and Historical Analysis," *International Studies Quarterly* 28, 2 (June 1984): 219–238.

defined.[27] This may have been a valid criticism of the scholarly literature at one time, but it is no longer the case. As explained in chapter 2, there is a clear rationale for defining the offense-defense balance as the ratio of the cost of the offensive forces required to take territory to the cost of the forces the defender has deployed.[28] This variable is required by a theory that understands states' decisions in terms of states' abilities to perform military missions—it captures how effectively states can convert power into different types of military capability. It is true that a number of assumptions and judgments are required to insure that the balance is well defined—including the assumption the balance should be measured assuming that states make optimal choices about strategy and force posture. Although fully developing this variable does reveal its complexity, none of the required concepts and distinctions is unmanageable.[29] Moreover, other widely used variables also turn out to be more complicated than is commonly appreciated. For example, power depends on many factors, including not only a state's population, economy, and technological sophistication, but also its human capital and ability to extract resources from its population. Determining how these factors combine, and further how this depends on the specific security challenges a state faces, can be as complex as the analysis required to adequately specify the offense-defense balance.

A second criticism is that offense and defense cannot be distinguished, which makes impossible both measurement of the offense-defense balance and the variety of policies that rely on limiting offense. For example, John Mearsheimer argues that determining the balance is problematic because "it is very difficult to distinguish between offensive and defensive weapons."[30] This criticism is flawed, however, because whether offense and defense are distinguishable does not affect our ability to measure the balance. To assess the offense-defense balance, we assume that the attacker and defender act optimally, deploying the weapons that best enable them to achieve their respective missions. The attacker's and defender's force structures may or may not include some of the same types of weapons. Either way, given these forces, measuring the balance then requires adapting net assessment tools that are designed to evaluate the outcome of military battles. The ability to perform this net assessment is

[27] For example, Mearsheimer, *The Tragedy of Great Power Politics*, p. 417. For earlier criticisms, see Levy, "The Offense/Defense Balance of Military Technology."

[28] On this point, see also Lynn Jones, "Offense-Defense Theory and Its Critics."

[29] Glaser and Kaufmann, "What Is the Offense-Defense Balance?"

[30] Mearsheimer, "The False Promise of International Institutions," p. 23. See also Lieber, *War and the Engineers*, p. 28; and Jonathan Shimshoni, "Technology, Military Advantage, and World War I: A Case of Military Entrepreneurship," *International Security* 15, 3 (Winter 1990/91): 190–191.

not impeded by having some of the same types of weapons on both sides.[31]

A closely related argument holds that because most types of weapons can be used by both attackers and defenders, offense and defense are indistinguishable, which renders infeasible key recommendations of my theory (and of the offense-defense theories on which it draws). For example, arguing along these lines, Samuel Huntington concluded that "weapons may be usefully distinguished in a variety of ways, but the offense-defense distinction is not one of them."[32] It follows, then, that arms control that limits offensive weapons to shift the balance of deployed forces and various forms of restraint that are designed to signal benign motives are infeasible. This criticism is flawed, however, because distinguishability does not depend on whether both attacker and defender would deploy the type of weapon. Instead, distinguishability depends on whether the attacker would have a more effective offensive capability if both states were allowed to deploy a specific weapon or if they were not. Thus distinguishability can be determined by comparative net assessment—by comparing the offense-defense balance when both sides deploy the weapon to the balance when neither deploys it. If deploying the weapon shifts the balance toward offense (defense), the weapon can be classified as offensive (defensive) and states will be able to implement the policy prescriptions that depend on the distinguishability of offense and defense.[33] For example, consider the impact of highly accurate nuclear missiles that have a significantly higher probability of destroying opposing missiles than do inaccurate missiles. For a variety of reasons, both defenders and attackers might deploy both types of missiles. This, however, does not render offense and defense indistinguishable: the cost to the attacker of a missile force capable of destroying a given fraction of the defender's force is higher if it deploys only inaccurate missiles than if it deploys a mix of the two types. This means that, relative to inaccurate missiles, accurate missiles favor offense, in effect making the two distinguishable.

Running through these responses is a more general point about the measurement of the offense-defense balance: the analytic tasks required

[31] This argument is developed more fully in Glaser and Kaufmann, "What Is the Offense-Defense Balance?"

[32] Samuel P. Huntington, "U.S. Defense Strategy: The Strategic Innovations of the Reagan Years," in Joseph Kruzel, ed., *American Defense Annual, 1987–1988* (Lexington, MA: Lexington Books, 1987). See also Colin S. Gray, *Weapons Don't Make War* (Lawrence: University Press of Kansas, 1993), p. 28.

[33] It is useful to remember that even if offense and defense are indistinguishable, a state can use restraint to signal benign motives because smaller forces will provide it with less offensive capability. Under these conditions, the state must increase its vulnerability to send this signal.

are the same as those required for military net assessments—analyses of the ability of a state's forces to perform military missions against the forces of an opponent. If useful net assessment is feasible, useful estimates of the offense-defense balance are also feasible. Both require analyzing the ability of a defender's forces to succeed against an attacker's forces. Standard net assessments analyze the ability of the forces deployed by the attacker to defeat the forces deployed by the defender. The same tools can be adapted to determine the offense-defense balance. Instead of focusing on deployed forces, to measure the balance we allow the attacker's forces to vary. The balance is defined where the offense is large enough to defeat the defense; the ratio of the cost of these offensive forces to the cost of the defensive forces is the offense-defense balance. Although there is debate about the feasibility of net assessments, a number of considerations suggest that net assessment techniques can be used effectively to evaluate military capabilities—military organizations and civilian experts have invested in and relied on these techniques; and, more important, the historical record suggests that reasonably reliable net assessment has often been feasible.[34] In any event, analysts who believe that net assessment has the potential to inform states about the likely effectiveness of their military capabilities should also believe that useful assessments of the offense-defense balance are feasible.[35]

A third criticism holds that the offense-defense balance does not usually vary enough to be an important factor in a state's assessments of its international situation; as a result, states should rely on other variables in assessing their potential military capabilities, especially power.[36] A related criticism is that states' assessments of the offense-defense balance tend to be quite uncertain, reflecting the complexity of military strategy and technology, leaving power a better indicator of military capabilities.

A key point to start with is that there are a couple of exceptions to this criticism that are sufficiently clear and important to undermine it. Nuclear weapons provide a large advantage to the defense. They give a weak state the possibility of deploying forces that provide an effective deterrent against much more powerful states; and they give equally powerful states the ability to deploy deterrent forces that are much more effective than the states could acquire by deploying conventional forces. The balance created by nuclear weapons is many times larger than 1, and states possess the analytic capabilities required to measure it within bounds that leave essentially no doubt about the overwhelming advantage of retaliatory capabilities over damage-limitation capabilities, that is, of defense

---

[34] I address this issue in chapter 7, under the question of whether states have the analytic capacity required to measure the offense-defense balance.

[35] Glaser and Kaufmann, "What Is the Offense-Defense Balance?," pp. 74–79.

[36] Lieber, *War and the Engineers*, pp. 151–152.

over offense.[37] The logic of the nuclear revolution flows from these basic insights.[38] Failing to include the offense-defense balance would leave nuclear weapons as a problem or major caveat to the some of my theory's central claims.

A second major exception is geography, most clearly distance, with long stretches of water maybe especially significant.[39] The potential of states that are separated by long distances to attack each other is much smaller than states that are close to each other. Greater distance, difficult-to-traverse terrain, and water all make offense more costly, shifting the balance toward defense. Although determining the extent of the impact of distance on the offense-defense balance for specific cases requires thorough analysis, the implications of distance are often easily recognized: for example, during the Cold War the United States did not face a serious conventional threat from the Soviet Union, but America's European allies were more vulnerable; similarly, a rising China will not pose a conventional threat to the United States but might to its regional neighbors.

Moreover, there are other examples of technologies that have significantly influenced the offense-defense balance and therefore further weaken this criticism. For example, starting in the mid-1800s and continuing through World War I, the technological advances that supported significant improvements in rifles, artillery, and machine guns, and resulted in large increases in firepower, favored the defense. In response, states that wanted or needed to fight on the offense had to change strategy—frontal assaults became too ineffective and costly, requiring states to adopt flanking operations that were operationally and logistically demanding. Wars would be more costly and longer, and harder to win, which military leaders recognized at the time.[40] Stephen Biddle has challenged this interpretation of the firepower revolution, arguing that an effective understanding of the offense-defense balance needs to focus on force employment, not technology.[41] However, Biddle's sophisticated analysis of the impact of force employment on states' military capabilities can be seen as largely consistent with a focus on technology—the impact of dramatic increases in firepower was so profound and long lasting that ever since only a single set of tactics can enable attackers and defenders

[37] This claim assumes states that are technologically advanced and have the resources required to invest in sophisticated survivability measures. The balance depends on the size of deployed forces, shifting more toward defense as forces become larger.

[38] Jervis, *The Meaning of the Nuclear Revolution*.

[39] See Mearsheimer, *The Tragedy of Great Power Politics*, pp. 114–128, on the stopping power of water, who argues that "large bodies of water sharply limit an army's power-projection capability."

[40] Lieber, *War and the Engineers*, chap. 3.

[41] Biddle, "Rebuilding the Foundations of Offense-Defense Theory"; and Biddle, *Military Power*.

to succeed against each other. And when two countries both have high levels of skill, and therefore are capable of implementing the necessary set of tactics, which Biddle terms the "modern system," the result is significant defense advantage.[42] In short, although the offense-defense balance may not always play a significant role in determining the military capabilities that a state can acquire, there are enough clear examples of its influence that the case for including it among the defining features of a state's international environment is compelling.[43]

A fourth set of criticisms holds that states' behavior is not predicted well by the offense-defense balance. In this vein, one criticism holds that perceptions of the offense-defense balance, not the balance itself, determine states' decisions for cooperation, arms racing, and war. Even assuming that states have the knowledge and skill required to measure the balance accurately, political, psychological, or other biases can still generate serious misperceptions. Consequently, according to this critique, the objective offense-defense balance is not useful for predicting states' behavior.[44] This criticism is especially important in light of the emphasis that Van Evera places on misperceptions of the balance in his theory of war.[45]

Although in a limited sense correct, this criticism misses the point—like all theories that address interaction between a state and its international environment, the theory recognizes that the effects of the environment are mediated through states' perceptions. Rational theories assume that states do not suffer misperceptions, and, as argued above, this is consistent with their primary purposes. Moreover, if states do misperceive the balance, the theory will be able to explain their choices using the misperceived variable. In addition, when misperceptions do occur, the theory provides a baseline against which a state's choices can be assessed. Indeed, these are the ways that offense-defense theory has been employed in the "cult of the offensive" explanation of World War I.

A related criticism holds that offense-defense theory is flawed because it does a poor job of predicting states' behavior when they do correctly

---

[42] Biddle, "Rebuilding the Foundations of Offense-Defense Theory," p. 754. I am not claiming that force employment does not have a large impact on outcomes, nor that it could not overwhelm the effects of technology; rather, I am simply pointing out that Biddle's argument applies in the context of a major and enduring technological change, from which the implications for force employment flow. Biddle's critique raises important questions about the sources of differences in skill, and about which of these can be addressed from the perspective of a rational theory and which must be understood in terms of unit-level variation that poses a deeper challenge to my theory. I address some of these issues in chapter 7.

[43] Also identifying the importance of changes in technology for the offense-defense balance is Gilpin, *War and Change*, pp. 61–66.

[44] See, for example, Levy, "The Offense/Defense Balance of Military Technology," p. 222.

[45] Van Evera, *Causes of War*.

assess the balance.[46] If, however, we consider the theory from a rationalist perspective—a theory of what states should do, not necessarily what they do do—this problem is likely much less severe. If the mismatch between the theory and states' behavior reflects suboptimality, this is not a problem for the theory. A more complete explanatory theory would combine the rational theory with a theory or explanation of suboptimality. Less fundamental, we also need to keep in mind that the theory is more nuanced than some critiques acknowledge. For example, there are situations in which a state should choose an offensive strategy, even when defense has the advantage. Thus, how well the theory does at explaining states' choices requires not only analyzing the offense-defense balance, but also a more complete analysis of their international environment.

In concluding this section, I should note that the theory's most basic understanding of why states should sometimes cooperate does not depend on offense-defense variables. The theory's basic arguments—about the incentives for restraint, as well as competition, and the value of signaling benign motives—stand whether or not states can measure the offense-defense balance. Still more clearly, the dual importance of states' motives and their international situation does not depend on offense-defense variables. I raise this point because defensive realism is often characterized as being distinguished from other structural realisms by its reliance on offense-defense variables. In fact, however, the divide is more fundamental and does not hinge on offense-defense variables, and the same is true for the more general theory developed here. Clearly, my theory holds that the possibility of variation in offense-defense variables is very important, creating a much richer menu of policy options and leading to different optimal policies. But, at the same time, even if states were unable to measure offense-defense variables (which I do not believe is generally the case), they would still face trade-offs between competitive or cooperative military policies designed to achieve their security and/or greedy goals.

STILL MORE COUNTERARGUMENTS

Signaling Is Too Risky

A recent analysis criticizes defensive realism for being too optimistic about states' prospects for overcoming uncertainty and the security dilemma.[47] Criticisms of the logic of defensive realism apply to my theory

[46] Lieber, *War and the Engineers*, chap. 3, makes this argument about the political impact of the fire-power revolution.

[47] Montgomery, "Breaking Out of the Security Dilemma."

due to the theories' parallels. This critique rests on a number of observations. First, it argues that to reduce uncertainty about their motives, security seekers must take actions that increase their vulnerability to attack. I do not disagree. As I argued at the beginning of chapter 2, this is simply another implication of the security dilemma: except when conditions eliminate the security dilemma, states interested in signaling their benign motives will in varying degrees face this trade-off. Consequently, the theory (and defensive realism) does not argue that states will always find that restraint and attempts at reassurance are their best option. Among other factors, how to make this trade-off will depend on the information the state has about the opposing state's motives.

Second, according to this critique, even when offense and defense are distinguishable, "neither offensive nor defensive advantages allow states to reveal their motives without increasing their vulnerability."[48] This is because it is inefficient to deploy forces that are at a disadvantage; doing so will lead to vulnerability. This argument, however, is overstated: for example, when offense has an advantage, a state could unilaterally forgo offense and deploy defense yet avoid increasing its military vulnerability by outspending its adversary; this should be possible if offense does not have a large advantage.[49] Moreover, if the adversary is a security seeker and responds by deploying defense, the overall cost of arming might not increase.

In short, while this critique provides a corrective to arguments that oversimplify and overstate defensive realism's optimism about states' prospects for using restraint and cooperation to overcome the dangers generated by the security dilemma, it is in fact largely consistent with a careful reading of defensive realism and the more general theory developed here. Moreover, the critique overstates how narrow the conditions are under which a state should find that cooperation and reassurance are its preferred strategies.

Competition between Security Seekers Is Not Rational

Critics of structural realism have argued that its emphasis on security seekers is misguided because these states should never compete with each other. In short, the logic of the security dilemma is inconsistent with the core assumptions of structural realism. Obviously, this critique applies to the more general theory developed in this book. Schweller argues the point forcefully: "A model based on the assumption that the central concern of states is not for power but for security, since it must rely on un-

[48] Ibid., p. 166.

[49] For an earlier statement of this argument, see Glaser, "Political Consequences of Military Strategy," pp. 527–528.

certainty to explain conflict, is inconsistent with both traditional and structural realism." The problem, according to this argument, is that relying on imperfect information to explain competition and conflict "violate[s] realism's most basic tenet that conflicts of interest among states are genuine rather than the result of misunderstanding and misperception."[50]

Part of the problem with this argument might result because Waltz fails to fully develop the role of uncertainty is his theory; uncertainty is necessary for his arguments to work, but it remains in the background as Waltz focuses on the impact of material structure. My theory clearly eliminates this part of the problem by making uncertainty about states' motives a central element defining the international situation a state faces.

The more basic problem with this critique, however, is that it misunderstands the status and implications of uncertainty in the rational theory. First, this uncertainty does not reflect a misunderstanding or misperception. Instead, the uncertainty about motives is real for the states involved. Uncertainty reflects the information that is actually available to the states; in contrast, misperceptions occur when a state's evaluation of available information is flawed. Rationalist theories do essentially rule out misperceptions, but they allow uncertainty about other states' motives, thereby allowing the security dilemma to operate.

Second, as I argued at the beginning of chapter 3, states cannot necessarily eliminate uncertainty about others' motives without running unacceptable risks. The security dilemma can prevent states from signaling that they are security seekers by making it too risky for them to exercise the necessary restraint. Interestingly, the uncertainty that is central to the existence of a security dilemma can be preserved by the security dilemma itself. States that begin their interaction with uncertainty about each other's types, and therefore can face a security dilemma, may be prevented from eliminating this uncertainty by the risks of cooperation.[51] In fact, their interactions can lead to rational negative political spirals that shift their estimates of each other's type toward higher probabilities that the opposing state is greedy.

Third, we need to appreciate that the security dilemma creates genuine conflicts of interest between states. The conflicting interests are not fundamental, in that they are not over ends—pure security seekers do not desire each other's territory, except possibly as a means of increasing their security. But, clearly, security seekers can have conflicting interests over means—the military capabilities they believe are necessary for maintaining their security can be incompatible with others' security requirements,

[50] Schweller, "Neorealism's Status-Quo Bias," quotes at pp. 119, 118.

[51] However, Schweller argues that this is incorrect; see *Deadly Imbalances*, pp. 51–52. For a different argument about the potential for signaling to eliminate uncertainty, see Kydd, "Sheep in Sheep's Clothing," pp. 116–117.

they can pursue territorial expansion to increase their own security, and they can attempt to reduce others' power for the same reason.

States Should Assume the Worst about Others' Intentions

It is frequently said that realism holds that states should assume the worst about other states' intentions and, more generally, should make worst-case assumptions.[52] This argument is explicit in offensive realism: John Mearsheimer argues that "intentions are ultimately unknowable, so states worried about their survival must make worst-case assumptions about their rivals' intentions."[53] A state that assumes that its adversary's motives are as dangerous as possible (I switch to motives here because Mearsheimer conflates motives and intentions, but his argument is really based on motives) need not worry about making its adversary more insecure, as this would not make the adversary harder to deter. Consequently, the state need not worry about signaling malign motives or undermining the adversary's military capabilities. Moreover, if the state also assumes that its adversary is working with similar worst-case assumptions, this mirror imaging further reduces its incentive to adopt cooperative policies because these policies would be unable to influence the adversary's assessment of the likelihood that the state is a security seeker. As a result, assuming the worst essentially eliminates key aspects of the security dilemma, dissolving its incentives for restraint, while leaving intact its pressures for competition. In other words, assuming the worst in effect eliminates the tradeoff that is the defining feature of the security dilemma.

The problem with this argument is that states should not employ worst-case assumptions when facing uncertainty about others' motives. As explained in chapter 3, the type of adversary that the state faces influences the risks and benefits of alternative policies—cooperative policies will often be preferable to competitive policies when facing a security seeker. Consequently, the state should use its assessment of the probability that the adversary is a security seeker to help weigh the overall merits of cooperative and competitive policies. In contrast, a state that assumes the worst fails to take into account the possible benefits of cooperation and restraint; under all information conditions it forgoes the possible benefits of signaling benign motives and of avoiding negative spirals that fuel conflict between security seekers. Similarly, by assuming the worst, and therefore competing, the state overlooks the risks of competition, which include arms races and wars that could be lost, yet under different

[52] For this characterization, see, for example, Robert O. Keohane and Lisa L. Martin, "The Promise of Institutional Theory," *International Security* 20, 1 (Summer 1995): 43–44.

[53] Mearsheimer, *The Tragedy of Great Power Politics*, p. 45.

decision-making criteria might be avoided altogether. Although the policies that flow from worst-case assumptions are optimal under certain conditions, they are not under others. In other words, states that assume the worst are not acting rationally, according to standard decision-making criteria, which violates a core assumption of this entire family of theories.[54]

---

[54] Stephen G. Brooks, "Dueling Realisms," *International Organization* 51, 3 (Summer 1997): 445–477, esp. 453–455, emphasizes this point and argues that Waltz also builds his theory on this assumption.

CHAPTER SIX

Placing the Theory in the IR Theory Landscape

THIS CHAPTER EXPLAINS how my theory compares to other leading IR theories that address essentially the same questions in broadly similar ways. The theory is a strategic choice theory that takes both states' motives and the international situation they face as given; it explores the strategic choices of rational unitary actors facing an anarchic international environment. The theory occupies a middle layer in a more complete explanatory theory: the first layer would explain the inputs to the strategic choice theory, including states' power, states' motives, and states' information about others' motives; the third layer would explain states' failure to make optimal choices, including errors resulting from misperceptions of its international environment, and biases generated by military organizations or domestic politics.[1] A number of other prominent international relations theories lie essentially in this middle layer, including Waltz's structural realism, offensive realism, defensive realism, motivational (neoclassical) realism, and neo-institutionalism. I also addresses structural constructivism—although different in significant ways from the strategic choice theory, the questions the two theories address and the answers they offer overlap more than is generally recognized.

The comparisons are valuable for gaining a better understanding of both my theory itself and some of its strengths relative to these other IR theories.[2] As already suggested in chapter 3, although Waltz's structural realism significantly advanced IR theory, its basic framing does not cap-

[1] This placement of the theory was discussed somewhat more fully in chapter 2; as noted there, some theories cut across these layers and therefore are not adequately captured by this description.

[2] Some scholars oppose labeling theories, having concluded that the labels too often generate more confusion than clarity, and are especially critical of the "isms" debates in IR that have continued over the past few decades. Although I have not labeled my theory, I'm inclined to believe that there are benefits to the labels and isms that can exceed the risks. The risks include a bundling of arguments that lack logical coherence, often tracking scholars instead of arguments (notes in this chapter point out this problem in a couple of the isms); and an oversimplifying of arguments, which supports a sort of bumper sticker mentality, in which a theory's conclusions become the focus of too much attention, at the cost of careful analysis of its deductive logic. The benefits include increased opportunities for developing an identifiable, evolving body of theory and for comparisons of key bodies of theory. The key to having the benefits exceed the risks is simply for scholars to be more careful in using this terminology.

ture key features of states' strategic interaction, and some of its key conclusions, most importantly its generally competitive view of international politics, are undermined by significant deductive flaws. Similarly, there are serious problems in the logic leading to offensive realism's conclusion that the international system is still more competitive. In contrast, defensive realism is largely consistent with the theory developed here, which is not surprising given that it can be viewed as a way station along the route to the full theory. Defensive realism is less general, lacking both variation in states' motives and information variables, but parallels the theory within the domain that it covers. Motivational realism (which is a subset of the broader, more commonly used category neoclassical realism) is also largely compatible with the theory and can be understood as complementing defensive realism by focusing on the importance of greedy states that are making strategic decisions. Neo-institutionalism is also largely compatible with my theory, which finds a variety of roles for institutions in facilitating cooperative policies. However, my theory's emphasis is quite different—it sees institutions as first and foremost a policy choice that reflects states' motives and their international environment, in contrast to neo-institutionalism, which seems to emphasize the independent role of institutions. Finally, structural constructivism, although different in fundamental respects, nevertheless shares some surprising similarities. Both theories explain that nonmaterial factors—ideas in the case of structural constructivism and information about motives in the case of my theory—can be the key to cooperation under anarchy and that interaction can lead to the updating of information and robust peace. My theory, however, provides a fuller exploration of the joint influence of material and nonmaterial variables, thereby shedding important light on the limits of cooperation.

COMPARED TO WALTZ'S STRUCTURAL REALISM

Kenneth Waltz's *Theory of International Politics* remains the defining work in the structural-realist research program and therefore is a natural place to begin the comparisons to my theory.[3] Because I have commented on Waltz throughout earlier chapters, the following comparison is quite condensed.

I start from a broad perspective that is similar to Waltz's and with many of the same basic assumptions. The strategic-choice perspective has much in common with Waltz's structural approach—it envisions states as

---

[3] Waltz, *Theory of International Politics*; see also Waltz, "Reflections on *Theory of International Politics*; and Waltz, "The Origins of War in Neorealist Theory."

separate from the international situation they face and analyzes options for achieving their goals given the constraints posed by their international situation.[4] Waltz assumes that states are unitary actors that face an anarchic international environment. And although Waltz argues that rationality is not required—states "may not see [the structure] or, seeing it, may for any of many reasons fail to conform their actions to the patterns that are most often rewarded and least often punished," the behavior he predicts does reflect essentially rational behavior. Selection then leads to the prevalence of these behaviors.[5]

Waltz also assumes that states can be characterized as security seekers. Although he notes that states may have other motives—states "at a minimum, seek their own preservation and at a maximum drive for universal domination"—according to Waltz we can understand states' strategic choices by focusing on their desire for security: "Balance-of-power politics prevail whenever two, and only two, requirements are met: that the order is anarchic and that it be populated by units wishing to survive."[6] Waltz understands power as a means to security, not an end in itself; states that are maximizing their security may choose not to maximize their power because "only if survival is assured can states safely seek such other goals as tranquility, profit, and power." He goes on to argue that "states can seldom afford to make maximizing power their goal. International politics is too serious a business for that."[7]

As explained in chapter 2, my theory identifies a number of variables, beyond Waltz's power, that are necessary to adequately characterize a state's international environment. Of these the most important is arguably information about motives. Although I will not repeat the specific arguments here, it is worth emphasizing that information about motives emerges as an organic element of my theory, not simply as an additional variable: information plays a central role both in creating a security dilemma and in generating variation in its magnitude. Largely flowing from this richer characterization of the international environment, I make three key arguments about security seekers that generate significant divergences from Waltz. Each of these modifications stands on its own and would on its own lead to conclusions that diverge from Waltz; when combined, these modifications interact to produce larger possible divergences.

[4] In certain ways, however, Waltz's theory is more ambitious than the one developed here; it addresses how structure leads to behaviors—for example imitation and selection (pp. 92–93, 127–28)—that explain features of states that my theory simply takes as given. Critics hold, however, that Waltz fails to go far enough in this effort; see chapter 2, note 5.

[5] Waltz, *Theory of International Politics*, pp. 92–93, quote on p. 92. For statements closer to this position, see Waltz, "A Response to My Critics," pp. 330–331.

[6] Waltz, *Theory of International Politics*, pp. 91–92, quotes on pp. 118, 121. Waltz appears to use the terms "survival" and "security" interchangeably, and with the meaning that I use "security."

[7] Waltz, *Theory of International Politics*, pp. 126, 127.

First, the theory corrects what I termed the "competition bias"—emphasizing the risks of cooperation under anarchy, while failing to give comparable weight to the risks of competition. The standard realist argument emphasizes that the value of military advantages combined with the risks of cooperation—which leave a state vulnerable to cheating—require even states interested only in security to choose competitive policies. This argument is incomplete, however, because it overlooks potential risks of competition. Competition can be risky because the outcome of competition is often uncertain and failed competitive policies can damage a state's military capability. Thus, even if Waltz's focus on material considerations is maintained, his argument requires that states weigh the risks of cooperation and competition, and does not predict that one approach generally dominates the other.

Second, the theory reorients structural realism by clarifying the central role of the security dilemma in the logic of competition between security seekers.[8] Although Waltz barely mentions the security dilemma, the basic logic of structural realism necessitates that it play a central role because if not facing a security dilemma, rational security seekers would not engage in competition.[9] The possibility that the severity of the security dilemma varies has dramatic implications because now, in contrast to Waltz, the theory predicts significant variation in competitive and cooperative behavior. Related, appreciating variation in the severity of the security dilemma helps to eliminate the indeterminacy that results once we recognize that a more complete treatment of risks undermines a general tendency toward competition. And the security dilemma provides a rationale for restraint that is missing in Waltz, yet may be the most important reason for a state not to try to maximize its power.

Third, the theory addresses a type of interaction that is missing from Waltz, explaining that a state's strategy can lead an adversary to change its assessment of the state's motives through a process of costly signaling. That Waltz does not address this type of interaction is not surprising, given that uncertainty about the adversary's motives does not play an important role in his structural realism. This neglect may be reinforced by the flawed belief that in third-image theories, which assume that states do not examine others' domestic characteristics, states lack the ability to learn about other states' motives. Overlooking the potential importance of signaling reinforces Waltz's competition bias.

Beyond this richer characterization of the international environment, my theory is more general, including variation in the motives of the state that is making decisions, that is, including greedy states as well as security

---

[8] For citations to the security dilemma literature, see chapter 3.

[9] Waltz does comment on the security dilemma but does not identify it as essential for competition between security seekers; see *Theory of International Politics*, pp. 186–187; and "War in Neorealist Theory," p. 43.

seekers, whereas Waltz focuses solely on security seekers. His focus is understandable because what is arguably his key finding—that the international environment consistently requires security seekers to compete—greatly reduces the importance of greedy states. Because even states with benign motives are going to adopt competitive policies, variation in states' motives is of relatively little importance; it is the international environment that is the key to competition. In sharp contrast, because I find that cooperation can be a security seeker's best option under a range of material and information conditions, greedy states matter. Under certain conditions a greedy state's best option would be competition, while a security seeker's would be cooperation.

In sum, although sharing important similarities with Waltz, my theory is very different: it includes variables that provide a more adequate description of a state's international environment, emphasizes the security dilemma and the possibility that it varies with both material and information variables, and explains the potential importance of policies that signal information about states' motives and of greedy states. The addition of information variables itself might make the distance from Waltz so great that my theory moves out of the structural-realist family. Adding variation in the motives of the decision-making state—including greedy states, as well as security seekers—rounds out the theory but puts it clearly outside the boundaries of structural realism. And, most important, I reach conclusions about the possibilities in international politics that diverge quite appreciably from Waltz's.

COMPARED TO OFFENSIVE REALISM

Offensive realism shares many key assumptions with Waltz—rational states, motivated by security, facing an anarchic international environment.[10] In addition, John Mearsheimer, who has provided the fullest statement of offensive realism, includes among his key assumptions that states are uncertain about others' intentions—states can never know others' current intentions with certainty, and moreover states' intentions can change quickly.

---

[10] Mearsheimer, *The Tragedy of Great Power Politics*, pp. 30–31, includes an additional assumption that I do not discuss: "great powers inherently possess some offensive military capability, which gives them the wherewithal to hurt . . . each other." See also Eric J. Labs, "Beyond Victory: Offensive Realism and the Expansion of War Aims," *Security Studies* 6, 4 (Summer 1997): 1–49; Fareed Zakaria, *From Wealth to Power: The Unusual Origins of America's World Role* (Princeton: Princeton University Press, 1998); and Colin Elman, "Extending Offensive Realism: The Louisiana Purchase and America's Rise to Regional Hegemony," *American Political Science Review* 98, 4 (November 2004): 563–576.

Offensive realism expects that states will be even more competitive than does Waltz. Contrary to Waltz, offensive realists conclude that in pursuit of security states should maximize their power. According to Mearsheimer, states cannot know how much power is enough to insure their survival; trying to maximize their power therefore serves as a type of insurance policy against this risk.[11] As a result, offensive realism expects states to be more inclined toward a variety of competitive policies, including arms racing, territorial expansion, and war. Mearsheimer qualifies this claim somewhat by explaining that states should not pursue competitive policies when the prospects for increasing their power are poor; they weigh the costs and benefits of offense and do not "start arms races that are unlikely to improve their overall position." However, this qualification does not actually place significant limits on states' competitive behavior. Mearsheimer argues that the desire for power maximization explains the Cold War superpower nuclear arms race.[12] In fact, this arms race had virtually no prospect of enabling either the United States or the Soviet Union to acquire significant protection from an all-out attack and, therefore, had virtually no prospect of improving their military positions.[13] If this arms race was not precluded by weighing the prospects for success, it seems unlikely that any would be.

The case for power maximization flows largely from offensive realism's handling of information about motives. To reach this conclusion, Mearsheimer holds that states must make worst-case assumptions about others' intentions.[14] If this were true, states should try to maximize their power under a wide range of conditions, and the international system would generate consistently competitive behavior.[15] As I explained in chapter 5, assuming the worst means, in effect, that a state does not face a security dilemma because competition would not make its adversary more dangerous and negative political spirals would not occur; competition becomes essentially free of military and political risks. The strategic implications of this perspective are reflected in Mearsheimer's description of why states attempt to maximize their power: "The reason is simple:

[11] Mearsheimer, *Tragedy of Great Power Politics*, p. 34. He also argues that states have difficulty predicting future changes in power, so maximizing power provides insurance against this uncertainty as well.

[12] On calculated aggression, see ibid., p. 37; this qualification reduces the gap with Waltz, who bases his argument partly on feasibility. On the nuclear arms race, see pp. 171–172, 224–232.

[13] This nuclear competition is analyzed briefly in chapter 9.

[14] Mearsheimer, *The Tragedy of Great Power Politics*, p. 45.

[15] Even with this assumption, however, states should not always try to maximize their deployed power, even when they have some chance of succeeding. For example, if offense and defense are distinguishable, a state could be better off in an arms control agreement that bans offense than in an arms race in which it gains an advantage in offense.

the greater the military advantage one state has over others, the more secure it is."[16] Employing these arguments, Mearsheimer reaches pessimistic predictions for cooperation and peace in Europe, finding that if America withdraws from Europe, "with the ever-present possibility that they might fight among themselves . . . the United Kingdom, France, Italy and Germany would have to build up their own military forces and provide for their own security."[17]

However, as I argued in chapter 5, a state should not base its strategy on worst-case assumptions. Doing so is inconsistent with standard criteria for rational decision making because the state fails to give proper weight to the benefits of cooperation that would result if its adversary is a security seeker.

This argument against power maximization can be restated in terms of the security dilemma.[18] My theory finds that states should not, as a general rule, try to maximize their power because they face a security dilemma; policies required to maximize power will often reduce others' security and therefore could be self-defeating. Even if successful in maximizing its power, the state's adversary could become harder to deter, with the overall result being a decrease in the state's security. Moreover, efforts to maximize power are still riskier because they could fail in narrow military terms: for example, launching an arms buildup to maximize power can result in an arms race that the adversary wins. Offensive realism's call for maximizing power could be correct only if competition is always the best way to balance the tensions inherent in a security dilemma. As we saw in chapter 3, this is not the case. Even worst-case assumptions about the adversary's motives do not always make competitive policies a state's best option. The implications for IR theory are stark: a state that makes worst-case assumptions about its adversary's motives would act as though it does not face a security dilemma, even when in fact it does.

Consider the implications for predictions about the future of Europe. Although states are uncertain about others' motives, if they believe the probability that others are greedy is low, the dangers of competitive arming, including the negative spiral it could generate, could easily exceed the benefits of insurance achieved via unilateral military buildups. Less important, but reinforcing, if the probability of war appears to be very low,

---

[16] Mearsheimer, "The False Promise of International Institutions," pp. 11–12; see also *The Tragedy of Great Power Politics*, p. 33.

[17] Mearsheimer, *The Tragedy of Great Power Politics*, p. 394; and his earlier "Back to the Future: Instability in Europe after the Cold War," *International Security* 15, 3 (Summer 1990): 5–56.

[18] Also criticizing power maximization are Glenn H. Snyder, "Mearsheimer's World—Offensive Realism and the Struggle for Security," *International Security* 27, 1 (Summer 2002): 149–173; and Powell, *In the Shadow of Power*, chap. 2.

European states could conclude that the direct economic costs of competitive arming were not justified. Instead of arming and trying to maximize their power, European states might integrate their militaries to deal with external threats and/or agree to limits on their forces to avoid generating security fears within Western Europe (these possibilities are discussed briefly later in this chapter). For offensive realism none of these questions is on the table because even states that are very likely to have benign motives should be dealt with as though they have malign motives.

Offensive realism makes a second argument that reinforces the divergence from my theory—it essentially dismisses offense-defense variables, thereby eliminating a variable that can facilitate cooperation and peace. Mearsheimer argues that the offense-defense balance is "an amorphous concept that is especially difficult for scholars and policy makers to define and measure."[19] However, as argued in chapter 5, the definition is not problematic and measurement is often possible. Moreover, a couple of Mearsheimer's key points are essentially offense-defense arguments: the significance that he attributes to nuclear weapons and the stopping power of water reflect their contribution to shifting the balance heavily toward defense, an impact that cannot be captured in power alone.

Offensive realism argues that the competitive history of the past couple centuries supports its arguments. However, because the central divergence between these theories results from disagreement over what follows logically from their assumptions—that is, over the theories' internal deductive integrity—the disagreement cannot be resolved by turning to states' historical behavior. Examples of competitive/power-maximizing policies cannot provide support for flawed deductions. Competitive international behavior therefore needs to be explained by a different theory.

One possibility is the theory that I have developed in this book, which would predict extensive competition between security seekers if the material and information conditions required for cooperation have simply been rare in the history of the international system. The empirical question then focuses on the values that the independent variables have taken on over time. For example, if states have usually started their interactions believing there is a high probability that others are greedy, competition is more often their best strategy. Assuming the worst about an adversary would not then be very different from utilizing the available information about the adversary's motives, so the theories' explanations and prescriptions would be less likely to diverge. Similarly, if the offense-defense balance has usually favored offense, or even if it has not favored defense, the theory predicts a tendency toward competitive policies. However, ana-

[19] Mearsheimer, *The Tragedy of Great Power Politics*, p. 417, n. 28. He has also argued that the balance cannot be measured because offensive and defensive forces cannot be distinguished; *Conventional Deterrence*, pp. 25–27.

lysts who have focused on the offense-defense balance argue it has often favored defense;[20] if this has in fact been the case, consideration of this variable would not bring the predictions of these two theories into line.

Nevertheless, even if unfavorable material or information conditions have historically generated highly competitive behavior, the theories' explanations would remain quite different. This is important because the international environment could change, and the predictions offered by these theories would then diverge. Coming back to the debate over Europe, it may be that states' information about others' motives has historically been sufficiently negative that competitive policies were the best way to manage their security dilemmas, but that conditions in Europe today are sufficiently different that U.S. withdrawal would not trigger a return to competitive policies.

Moreover, even if conditions that should generate cooperation have been prevalent, historical examples of competition do not support offensive realism. In this case, competition would have to be explained by theories that are built on assumptions that are different from offensive realism's. One possibility is that states have not acted rationally. Theories that explain states' suboptimal behavior can then be combined with a rational theory to understand competition.[21] Another possibility is that instead of being motivated primarily by security, states were motivated by greed. My theory explains that greedy states will sometimes choose to compete when facing international conditions that would lead security seekers to cooperate.

COMPARED TO DEFENSIVE REALISM

Defensive realism can be viewed as a major step toward the full theory I have developed in this book, so not much needs to be said about it here. Defensive realism, like my more general theory, includes the deductive corrections that eliminate the competition bias in Waltz, puts the security dilemma at the center of its explanation for competition, adds offense-defense variables that explain variation in the severity of the security dilemma, and explores the possibility of providing information about mo-

---

[20] Snyder, *Myths of Empire*; and Van Evera, *Causes of War*.

[21] Scholars have productively combined the rational predictions that follow from defensive realism with theories of suboptimality; for example. Van Evera, *Causes of War*; Snyder, *Myths of Empire*; Christensen and Snyder, "Chain Gangs and Passed Bucks"; and Thomas J. Christensen, "Perceptions and Alliances in Europe, 1865–1940," *International Organization* 51, 1 (Winter 1997): 65–97. More generally on the complementary nature of these types of theories, see Fearon, "Domestic Politics, Foreign Policy, and Theories of International Relations."

tives via costly signaling.[22] It does not, however, include information variables as an explicit element of a state's international environment. In addition, defensive realism does not address greedy states, focusing instead entirely on the decisions of states that are security seekers.

I am using "defensive realism" more narrowly than has become common in the literature. Some prominent scholars who are categorized as defensive realists have combined the rational theory that flows from the security dilemma with unit-level theories to explain states' suboptimal policies; the term defensive realism is used to cover both the rational foundation of their theories and their explanations of suboptimality.[23] In contrast, I am using defensive realism to refer only to the rational foundation. These unit-level theories are largely independent of this foundation; moreover there are many unit-level theories that have not yet been combined with the rational foundation, but that could be. Combining them should not make the unit-level theories part of defensive realism. We create confusion by categorizing types of theories according to the scholars that have used them.

In contrast to Waltz and offensive realism, defensive realism finds that states should adopt cooperative policies under a range of conditions. These include when uncertainty about the outcome of an arms race makes arms control less risky than racing, when defense advantage makes competition unnecessary for achieving necessary military capabilities, and when offense-defense differentiation make possible qualitative arms control.

As we saw in chapters 2 and 3, including additional variables—information about motives and variation in states' motives—follows logically from the strategic-choice perspective. Defensive realism also points in this direction, suggesting the importance of information about motives by focusing on the possibility of costly signals. However, it does not take the

---

[22] On defensive realism, see Glaser, "Realists as Optimists"; Posen, *The Sources of Military Doctrine*; Snyder, *Myths of Empire*, esp. pp. 11–12, 21–26; and Van Evera, *Causes of War*. Stephen M. Walt is frequently categorized as a defensive realist, among other reasons because his theory of alliance behavior includes perceptions of the adversary's intentions and because he finds that states balance against threats, which makes expansion more difficult and security more plentiful; see *The Origins of Alliances* (Ithaca: Cornell University Press, 1987). However, Walt's theory differs in important ways from my description of defensive realism: the adversary's intentions are not uncertain but instead vary in terms of the extent of aggressiveness; as a result, the security dilemma does not lie at the core of Walt's theory of alliance behavior. Useful assessments of defensive realism include Brooks, "Dueling Realisms"; Jeffrey W. Taliaferro, "Security Seeking under Anarchy—Defensive Realism Revisited," *International Security* 25, 3 (Winter 2000): 128–161; and Sean M. Lynn-Jones, "Realism and America's Rise: A Review Essay," *International Security* 23, 2 (Autumn 1998): 157–182.

[23] Snyder and Van Evera are the most prominent examples; their theories are multilevel theories; I am excluding their unit-level theories of suboptimality from defensive realism.

next step by explaining the role of information in determining the sever-ity of the security dilemma and in defining the international context in which states choose their strategies, including whether to send costly sig-nals. As a result, defense realism and my theory can yield divergent con-clusions. For example, when a state is not militarily secure, but its infor-mation about its potential adversary's motives suggests it is quite likely to be a security seeker, my theory finds greater opportunities for restraint and cooperation. As a result, offense advantage and disadvantages in de-ployed forces need not require a state to adopt competitive policies, and power disadvantages need not lead states to search for partners to bal-ance with. On the flip side, information that the adversary is likely to be greedy can call for competitive policies when material conditions suggest otherwise. Defensive realism also makes clear the importance of greedy states—by demonstrating that a state's international situation does not consistently make competitive strategies a security seeker's best option, it clarifies the potential importance of variation in states' motives, and spe-cifically, the role of greedy motives in making competitive policies a state's best option.

Finally, the importance of including these variables is supported by a number of important cases in which the more general theory provides a better rational explanation than defensive realism does. As discussed in the introduction, adequately understanding the end of the Cold War re-quires a theory that includes both information and material variables and addresses their combined effect. The difference between major-power re-lations in Europe and in Northeast Asia is largely explained by different assessments of states' motives, not by their material situations. A sound understanding of post–Cold War U.S. relations with other major powers hinges on information variables. Hitler's efforts to dominate Europe can-not be well explained without including his greedy motives. (Chapter 8 briefly explores these cases.) As I explained at the outset, my claim is not that the rational theory will necessarily explain the vast majority of the major-power strategic choices; states may sometimes, and I believe do, choose suboptimal policies. Nevertheless, it is useful to identify impor-tant cases that my more elaborate rational theory does better at explain-ing than defensive realism; otherwise, the trade-off in parsimony becomes harder to justify, although I believe it would still be warranted.

COMPARED TO MOTIVATIONAL (NEOCLASSICAL) REALISM

In contrast to structural realism, including defensive realism, which es-sentially assumes that all states are security seekers, motivational realism emphasizes the importance of variation in states' motives and goals.

More specifically, motivational realism focuses on the importance of greedy states and argues that it is these states, not the pressures created by the international system, that lead to competition and conflict.[24] I am using the term "motivational realism" to cover this group of arguments, instead of the more common "neoclassical realism." The latter is commonly used to also include a variety of unit-level factors, including states' perceptions of power and the ability of states to extract and mobilize resources, which are simplified away in the broad class of strategic choice theories I am comparing.[25] Related, and running parallel to my rationale for using defensive realism narrowly, these unit-level factors could be built into theories that focus on security seekers; they are not theoretically or deductively linked to a specific type of state.

Randall Schweller, who is commonly termed a neoclassical realist, argues that greedy states are the source of international competition: "At bottom, Waltzian neorealism suffers from a status-quo bias: that is, it views the world solely through the lens of a satisfied established state," and "the characteristic balancing behavior of Waltz's self-help system is triggered precisely by states that wish not simply to survive but also to weaken and destroy other states."[26] Andrew Kydd, who develops a rational theory and labels it motivational realism (as I am using here), argues that "the search for security does not lead to conflict in the absence of genuinely aggressive states ... arms races and wars typically involve at least one genuinely greedy state."[27]

Although the theory I have developed is different in significant ways from motivational realism—for example, it pays greater attention to offense-defense variables—the theories have much in common. They both address greedy states, as well as the international situation that states face. Moreover, whatever elements are further developed in my theory could be included in motivational realism; there is not a fundamental incompatibility.[28]

---

[24] A similar difference is the key to distinguishing classical realism from structural realism, although classical realism locates the source of motivation in human nature, not in states. See Keith L. Shimko, "Realism, Neorealism, and American Liberalism," *Review of Politics* 54, 2 (Spring 1992): 281–301.

[25] On neoclassical realism, see Gideon Rose, "Neoclassical Realism and Theories of Foreign Policy," *World Politics* 51, 1 (October 1998): 144–72; and more recently, Randall L. Schweller, *Unanswered Threats: Political Constraints on the Balance of Power* (Princeton: Princeton University Press, 2006).

[26] Schweller, *Deadly Imbalances*, p. 20.

[27] Kydd, "Sheep in Sheep's Clothing," pp. 153, 154.

[28] In fact, Kydd does fully address information about motives in his work; see, for example, his *Trust and Mistrust in International Relations*. And Schweller, *Deadly Imbalances*, pp. 25–26, notes that offense-defense variables could be added to his theory but believes they would unnecessarily complicate the theory because they are "generally less important than power and the interests of the units."

Given their basic similarities, the question becomes how motivational realism reaches its conclusion that greedy states are the key to international competition, while my theory sees the potential for security seekers as well as greedy states to be the source of conflict. Schweller and Kydd reach this conclusion by different routes; as I explain below, Kydd's argument is stronger and hinges on a set of empirical questions. The key to Schweller's conclusion is his argument that competition should not occur between rational security seekers; he holds that misperception is required to generate a security dilemma and, in turn, competition. However, as I explained in the previous chapter, this argument is flawed. It confuses uncertainty with misperception; rational security seekers could face uncertainty about opposing states' motives, making a security dilemma possible. Schweller's underplaying of uncertainty and the security dilemma is also evident in his argument that I quoted above about the sources of balancing behavior—balancing could reflect uncertainty about other states' motives, which is preserved by the security dilemma, not the motives of greedy states.

In contrast, Kydd argues that security seekers can reduce uncertainty about their motives to a sufficiently low level that the security dilemma ceases to operate. In contrast to Schweller, he does not challenge the rational logic of the security dilemma; in fact, Kydd's research has contributed to a deeper understanding of the security dilemma's rational foundation. His argument that security seekers can sufficiently reduce uncertainty about their motives rests upon two pillars. First, he argues that modern democracies are sufficiently transparent that their benign motives will be revealed by their policy processes. Second, Kydd argues that security seekers often have the ability to send costly signals that will reveal their motives. In addition to the military possibilities that I have focused on, he argues that states can send signals in a number of additional issue areas, including moderating their ideology and respecting the sovereignty of weaker states that they have the capability to attack. Kydd argues that the availability of multiple areas in which signals are possible ensures that security seekers will be able to communicate their benign motives. Obviously, the prospects for democracies are especially good as they can rely on both the transparency of their political systems and costly signals.

The key divide between my theory and Kydd's version of motivational realism is empirical, not in the foundation of the theories or their logical deductions.[29] Although the question warrants more sustained empirical study than I offer here, Kydd's conclusion about the ability of security

---

[29] A second difference is that I assume that the state black-boxes the opposing state—that is, does not consider its internal workings—once the states begin their strategic interaction. This choice reflects an effort to keep the theory reasonably simple, not a claim about how states actually act.

seekers to reveal their motives appears overstated. For example, the
United States' experience suggests that the security-seeking motives of a
democracy may well not be apparent to other states. During the Cold
War, the Soviet Union did fear the United States; Soviet leaders did understand the U.S. nuclear arsenal as a threat to their security and U.S. nuclear
strategy as communicating malign motives.[30] The signals that Kydd identifies may also not work as well as he suggests. For example, powerful
states may sometimes have reasons for intervening in the affairs of their
neighbors, or even invading weaker states, but not have greedy motives
and certainly not greedy motives that extend to major powers. Again, the
United States provides an illustrative example: the U.S. invasion of Iraq,
although misguided in many ways, did not reflect greedy motives on a
global scale, if at all, yet could easily lend itself to misinterpretation. My
point here is not that the foreign policies of greedy states and security
seekers will necessarily be indistinguishable, but rather the milder point
that in certain situations security seekers can find that they need to pursue aggressive policies to ensure their security, thereby creating ambiguity
about their motives.

COMPARED TO NEO-INSTITUTIONALISM

As laid out briefly in chapter 4, my theory sees a variety of roles for institutions in facilitating cooperative policies that would increase a state's
security, including helping to provide information about states' actions
and their motives. In this sense, it has much in common with neo-institutionalist arguments and can draw on insights offered by this body of
research.

At the same time, however, the emphasis in my theory is significantly
different—a state's international environment largely determines whether
cooperation would serve its interests, as well as the roles that institutions can play in supporting cooperation.[31] As a result, institutions "matter," but the theory finds a far less central role for them than does neo-
institutionalism. It finds the deep sources of security cooperation in
state's motives and international environment, not international institutions.[32] In many situations, institutions are not necessary or essential for

[30] See chapter 9 for brief discussion and references.

[31] The relationship between the literatures on regimes and institutions and that on structural realism is complex because although their assumptions are quite similar, their conno-
tations are different. See Krasner, "Global Communications and National Power," pp.
360–362, who explains that "the connotation of a research program suggests which questions are most important, what kind of evidence should be gathered, and, often tacitly,
which issues should be ignored."

[32] For a similar, still stronger, critique of neo-institutionalism, see Kenneth N. Waltz,
"Structural Realism after the Cold War," *International Security* 25, 1 (Summer 2000): 18–

cooperation; my theory's central arguments generate few distinct roles for institutions relative to the other noninstitutionalized means that are available to states. For example, the monitoring necessary to make cooperation desirable can sometimes be made possible by technologies that make unilateral monitoring of adversary's actions feasible; signaling may be achieved by unilateral restraint, and by reciprocated but nonnegotiated restraint, as well as by institutionalized restraint. And in situations in which they are necessary, institutions will often complement more basic measures by enabling states to work through the complexity that characterizes most real-world cooperation.

Given that neo-institutionalism and structural realism are usually cast as key competitors and that my theory has a realist lineage, it may be surprising that it finds a role for institutions. It should not be, however, because there is not a deep theoretical divide between neorealism and neo-institutionalism. From the beginning of his work on institutions, Robert Keohane made explicit that his analysis preserved the core of structural realism's assumptions.[33] More recently, Keohane and Martin argue that neo-institutionalism is distinguished from realism by changing what they understand to be one of the latter's key, albeit implicit, assumptions. They argue that "realism assumes that information about the intentions of other states is pertinent, but of poor quality," and "scarce information, and the inability of states to do anything to improve the situation, force states to adopt worst-case scenarios when choosing their strategies." In contrast, institutional theory "treats information as a variable that can be influenced by human action."[34] While this characterization may accurately capture Waltz's influential neorealism, it does not fit defensive realism, which is grounded in the security dilemma and rational

---

27, who makes similar points, while emphasizing the role of power and interests, but not information.

[33] Robert O. Keohane, "Theory of World Politics: Structural Realism and Beyond," in Ada Finiter, ed., *Political Science: The State of the Discipline* (Washington, DC: APSA, 1983); and Keohane, *After Hegemony*, p. 66. See also Stephen D. Krasner, "Structural Causes and Regime Consequences: Regimes as Intervening Variables," *International Organization* 36, 2 (Spring 1982): 185–206. For related arguments, see Robert Jervis, "Realism, Neoliberalism and Cooperation: Understanding the Debate," in Elman and Elman, eds., *Progress in International Relations Theory*.

[34] Keohane and Martin, "Institutional Theory as a Research Program," pp. 79–80. At least until recently, most neo-institutionalist work has focused on reducing transaction costs and monitoring behavior, not signaling motives. Reviewing this literature are Simmons and Martin, "International Organizations and Institutions," pp. 195–197. Work that does focus on signaling includes Wallander, *Mortal Friends, Best Enemies*; Alexander S. Thomson, "Coercion through IOs: The Security Council and the Logic of Information Transmission," *International Organization* 60, 1 (January 2006): 1–34; and G. John Ikenberry, *After Victory: Institutions, Strategic Restraint, and the Building of Order after Major Wars* (Princeton: Princeton University Press, 2001).

spiral model, and identifies a key role for signaling and rejects worst-case analysis. The theory I have developed in this book makes the central role of information about motives more explicit, making it a defining feature of a state's international situation and thereby providing still firmer grounding for the role of signaling.

Many of the similarities between my theory and neo-institutionalism, as well as how they differ in their attribution of causal significance, can be illustrated by considering post-Soviet Europe. I first briefly sketch neo-institutionalism's explanation of peace, then show how my theory provides a complementary explanation that places greater emphasis on the impact of the international environment. Neo-institutionalists argued that the probability of war in post–Cold War Europe depended heavily on the extent to which international institutions continued to play central roles.[35] At the end of the Cold War, a key potential problem was how other states would assess Germany's motives. NATO provided Germany with the opportunity to manage this problem by continuing to signal its benign intentions. During the Cold War, NATO's organizational structure was essential to the alliance's ability to adapt to increases in German power, thereby enabling Germany to continue accepting significant constraints on its military capabilities.[36] German acceptance of these constraints sent a costly signal to Germany's allies about its motives since a greedy state would find these constraints far more costly than would a security seeker. Following the Cold War, Germany placed great value on preserving NATO, as a hedge against a resurgent Soviet Union, but also importantly as a means to preserve good political relations within Western Europe.[37]

While recognizing a role for institutions, I give greater weight to the international environment, viewing NATO as one among a variety of means and asking how variations in the environment would have influenced the relative desirability of the alternatives. A first point to make is that Germany's willingness to continue using NATO to send costly signals largely reflected the material and information conditions it faced.

[35] See, for example, Robert O. Keohane, "Correspondence: Back to the Future II," *International Security* 15, 2 (Fall 1990): 192–194; Robert O. Keohane and Joseph S. Nye, "Introduction: The End of the Cold War in Europe," in Robert O. Keohane, Joseph S. Nye, and Stanley Hoffmann, eds., *After the Cold War: International Institutions and State Strategies in Europe, 1989–1991* (Cambridge: Harvard University Press, 1993); and Wallander, *Mortal Friends, Best Enemies.*

[36] Christian Tuschhoff, "Alliance Cohesion and Peaceful Change in NATO," in Haftendorn, Keohane, and Wallander, eds., *Imperfect Unions.*

[37] Jeffrey J. Anderson and John B. Goodman, "Mars or Minerva: A United Germany in Post-Cold War Europe," in Keohane, Nye, and Hoffmann, eds., *After the Cold War.* See also Seth G. Jones, *The Rise of European Security Cooperation* (New York: Cambridge University Press, 2007).

Because these conditions were benign—states held quite positive views of each other's motives and the offense-defense balance favored defense[38]—Germany could afford to run the limited risks involved in sending a costly signal by remaining in NATO. If the international environment had been less forgiving, then Germany would have faced greater pressures to adopt a more competitive policy. The risks of accepting the military vulnerability involved in remaining in NATO might well have been too high, so instead of relying on institutional cooperation to manage the dangers of its security dilemma, Germany would have been more likely to decide to rely on deterrent capabilities acquired unilaterally. In other words, although NATO mattered, the international environment was critical in making this cooperative, institutionalized option desirable.

Second, given the benign international environment, Germany had other promising options for managing relations with its Western European neighbors. If the United States had pulled out of Europe at the beginning of the 1990s, Germany could have worked to invigorate the Western European Union (WEU), making it the vehicle for the coordination of Western European military policies. Although the lack of American reassurance would have increased the challenge facing Germany, this option would likely have been successful.[39] Germany has a still more promising option today because the EU has developed a military and political dimension over the past decade, which could be deepened in response to U.S. withdrawal. In fact, U.S. withdrawal might contribute to advances in EU security cooperation because the signals provided by these steps would then be larger and more important.

Even if these institutions were no longer relevant, because changes in the international environment eliminated the rationale for integrating European military forces,[40] Germany would still have good prospects for developing successful policies of reassurance. Germany could continue forgoing nuclear weapons, thereby insuring that other European powers (including Russia) would have highly effective deterrent capabilities. This option would be feasible if Germany remained quite confident that its European neighbors had benign motives. Alternatively, Germany could acquire nuclear weapons but also commit itself to strict limits on its force. Although more threatening than continuing to renounce nuclear weap-

[38] This reflects most importantly the defense advantage created by nuclear weapons; although Germany lacks nuclear weapons, it could acquire them quickly and could be protected during a transition by the United States. See Stephen Van Evera, "Primed for Peace: Europe after the Cold War," *International Security* 15, 3 (Summer 1984): 7–57.

[39] Anderson and Goodman, "Mars or Minerva," p. 60.

[40] On the conditions under which this could occur, see Celeste A. Wallander, "NATO after the Cold War," *International Organization* 54, 4 (Fall 2000): 705–735.

ons, forgoing a more militarily threatening force posture would still signal the defensive nature of Germany's decision. Given the defensive advantage created by nuclear weapons, Germany could pursue this policy
unilaterally, although there would be advantages to coordinating independent force structures across Europe through a nuclear arms control
agreement.[41] In sum, while agreeing that NATO matters for peace in Europe, my theory places more weight on the international environment in
determining NATO's feasibility, how much it mattered and what the alternatives were.

In closing this section, it is important to note that I am not arguing that
my rationalist theory provides the foundation for a complete theory of
international institutions. Addressing specific questions of institutional
design requires moving beyond such a broad-gauge theory.[42] Once institutions are created, for a variety of reasons changes in the international
environment may not lead immediately to changes in institutions; when
such lags occur, institutions cannot be viewed as entirely endogenous,
and a still more elaborate theory is required.[43] A still richer theory requires integrating the rational theory with other theoretical perspectives,[44]
with the largest departure arguing that international organizations can
change states' interests.[45] Again there are parallels to military forces:
broad structural theories must often be refined or supplemented to assess
how a state should meet its offensive and defensive military requirements;

[41] Germany might have additional options, including making its willingness to forgo
nuclear weapons contingent on the formation of an integrated European nuclear force and
negotiating arms control agreements designed to limit the offensive capability of conventional forces.

[42] For example, see Barbara Koremenos, Charles Lipson, and Duncan Snidal, "Rational
International Institutions," *International Organization* 55, 4 (Autumn 2001): 761–799; and
Wallander, "NATO after the Cold War."

[43] For early work on this issue, see Arthur A. Stein, "Coordination and Collaboration:
Regimes in an Anarchic World," and Stephen D. Krasner, "Regimes and the Limits of Realism: Regimes as Autonomous Variables," both in *International Organization* 36, 2 (Spring
1982). On the features that determine whether institutions adapt to structural change, see
Wallander, "NATO after the Cold War."

[44] See, for example, Kenneth W. Abbott and Duncan Snidal, "Why States Act through
Formal International Organizations," *Journal of Conflict Resolution* 42, 1 (February 1998):
3–32; Jervis, "Realism, Neoliberalism and Cooperation," pp. 58–63; Keohane and Martin,
"Institutional Theory, Endogeneity, and Delegation"; and, on the contribution of liberal
international relations theory to institutionalist analysis, Keohane and Nye, "Introduction,"
pp. 4–6.

[45] Early examples include Ernst B. Haas, "Words Can Hurt You; or Who Said What to
Whom about Regimes," and John Gerald Ruggie, "International Regimes, Transactions,
and Change: Embedded Liberalism in the Postwar Economic Order," both in *International
Organization* 36, 2 (Spring 1982); a more recent example is Martha Finnemore, *National
Interests and International Society* (Ithaca: Cornell University Press, 1996).

the forces a state deploys can lag behind changes in its international environment for a variety of reasons; a state's forces can provide information about motives that create a path dependence that cannot be fully explained by the international situation it faces; and efforts to more fully explain states' military forces and doctrines have combined structural theory with other levels of analysis.[46]

COMPARED TO STRUCTURAL CONSTRUCTIVISM

Structural constructivism takes Waltz's neorealism as its central point of comparison and argues that a number of key differences divide the theories. My theory provides a better point of comparison, reflecting changes that are required to adequately specify a state's international environment and to make the internal logic of a rationalist, strategic choice theory work. In a variety of ways, the similarities between this rational theory and key structural constructivist arguments are as striking as the differences.

Constructivists characterize structural realism, as well as neo-institutionalism, as material theories,[47] in contrast to their own, which focuses on ideas—a broad category used to include information, norms, and causal ideas.[48] The rationalist theory I have developed, which has its roots in Waltz's structural realism, shows that information about motives is an essential component of a strategic choice theory that emphasizes the importance of a state's international environment. In addition, it highlights the possibility that states' interactions will lead them to revise their information about adversaries' motives. Consequently, the material versus nonmaterial distinction does a poor job of characterizing the difference between these theories.[49]

Moreover, many of the deductive arguments offered by these theories

[46] See, for example, Snyder, *The Ideology of the Offensive*.

[47] Wendt, *Social Theory of International Politics*, pp. 16, 30, 263; Emanuel Adler and Michael Barnett, "Security Communities in Theoretical Perspective," in Emanuel Adler and Michael Barnett, eds., *Security Communities* (Cambridge: Cambridge University Press, 1998).

[48] Bundling all nonmaterial factors under "ideas" risks creating analytic confusion because information, norms, and causal beliefs operate quite differently. However, I continue with this broad use because it is employed widely.

[49] Wendt, however, might respond that the theory remains fundamentally materialist because it continues to treat states interests as exogenous and reflecting material considerations, instead of being the product of ideas; see Wendt, *Social Theory of International Politics*, pp. 34–35. On the relationship between rationalist and constructivist theories, and their potential complementarity, see James Fearon and Alexander Wendt, "Rationalism v. Constructivism: A Skeptical View," in Walter Carlsnaes, Thomas Risse, and Beth A. Simmons, eds., *Handbook of International Relations* (London: Sage, 2002).

produce similar predictions about the possibilities for competition and cooperation. For example, Alexander Wendt, who has provided the seminal statement of structural constructivism, argues that neorealism finds that anarchy has a single logic—that is, anarchy creates a tendency toward competitive policies—but that a broader constructivist theory shows that anarchy does not have a unique logic.[50] More specifically, his theory holds that variation in structure—especially ideational structure— can result in a wide range of behaviors under anarchy, from intense competition to deep cooperation. The rationalist theory developed here, however, produces similar results, explaining that states in an anarchic environment can sometimes best achieve their goals via cooperation. Sometimes this cooperation will result from states' information about motives, and a deep cooperative peace flowing from this information is possible. As I explain below, this similarity reflects parallels in the theories: information about states' motives, which is a necessary element of the strategic choice theory, is related, albeit in a complicated way, to the ideational variable that defines Wendt's cultures of anarchy; and the costly signaling that enables states to revise their information is quite similar to the process of interaction that Wendt argues is missing in Waltz.

Before proceeding, it is important to note that there are fundamental differences between these theories. Structural constructivism addresses how interaction can change states' interests,[51] whereas my theory holds fundamental interests constant and focuses on strategic interaction.[52] This difference reflects a theoretical choice, not an empirical claim; both sets of questions are important and challenging in their own right. In addition, while both theories place importance on some ideational variables (again used broadly to include all nonmaterial factors such as information, norms, and causal beliefs), structural constructivism emphasizes norms, instead of focusing entirely on information about motives, and sees them playing an essential role in establishing states' interests, in contrast to the rationalist theory, which takes interests as exogenous, intrinsic, and separate from the international situation states face.[53] Conse-

---

[50] Wendt, *Social Theory of International Politics*, pp. 247–249.

[51] Ibid., chap. 7.

[52] Even here the differences are smaller than may be immediately apparent—although my theory does take fundamental interests as constant, changes in states' information about others do change their political relations, and therefore the roles that they adopt, which in constructivist terms means their identities also change. We should note also that strategic choice theories can address changes in states' interests by decomposing states into substate actors and exploring how interaction influences the domestic power of these substate actors, as for example in second-image reverse theories.

[53] See Wendt, *Social Theory of International Politics*, chap. 3. Part of this difference reflects a pragmatic choice—I am not arguing that the ideas that give meaning to material facts do not matter but instead bracket them, reflecting my judgment that most of these

quently, while the theory I have developed is not a purely materialist theory, it is ideationally thin compared to Wendt's constructivist theory.

The key point, however, is that these differences do not lead to different possibilities for international politics—quite the contrary, the strategic choice theory identifies similar possibilities. First, information about other states' motives has an important parallel in structural constructivism. Structural constructivists object to structural realism's focus on material structure, arguing that international structure also depends on the distribution of ideas and that ideational structure is likely more important than material structure. Wendt argues that "the most important structures in which states are embedded are made of ideas, not material forces. Ideas determine the meaning and content of power, the strategies by which states pursue their interests, and interests themselves."[54] Although not highlighted by Wendt, a key dimension of ideational structure is states' information about others' motives. The information required by my argument is narrower than the elements that comprise Wendt's ideational structure but is nevertheless sufficiently significant to shape the impact of material structure in many of the ways that structural constructivism describes. Most simply, the rationalist theory agrees with Wendt's claim that ideational factors can explain the different implications of the same military forces when possessed by different states—for example, the implications for the United States of British and Soviet nuclear weapons.[55] The theories' fundamental differences are evident: Wendt emphasizes shared understandings about the use of military force and defines the states' relationship in terms of this understanding; the rationalist theory emphasizes information about states' motives, which plays a central role in determining their political relations. Nevertheless, these concepts are closely related and do parallel work in the deductive arguments—the rationalist theory expects states with different motives to be prepared to

---

understandings are sufficiently self-evident that simply accepting them is efficient for tackling the questions the theory is designed to address. Part of the difference is more fundamental, with constructivists emphasizing the constitutive role played by these ideas and the holistic relationship between actors. Both approaches recognize the importance of causal ideas but do not problematize them; on this type of idea, see Judith Goldstein and Robert O. Keohane, "Ideas and Foreign Policy: An Analytic Framework," in Judith Goldstein and Robert O. Keohane, eds., *Ideas and Foreign Policy: Beliefs, Institutions, and Political Change* (Ithaca: Cornell University Press, 1993). On the way different theories view norms, see Jeffery T. Checkel, "International Norms and Domestic Politics: Bridging the Rationalist-Constructivist Divide," *European Journal of International Relations* 3, 4 (December 1997): 473–495.

[54] Wendt, *Social Theory of International Politics*, p. 309.

[55] Alexander Wendt, "Collective Identity Formation and the International State," *American Political Science Review* 88, 2 (June 1994): 389; and *Social Theory of International Politics*, p. 255, using North Korea in the comparison.

use force for different purposes and to different degrees, and this supports different strategies and interactions.

More broadly, as explored in chapter 3, information alone—that is, without norms and collective identities—can be sufficient, when combined with the signals generated by self-restraint, to explain the possibility of a robust cooperative major-power peace. As a result, Wendt's argument that there are "three cultures of anarchy" that yield divergent logics and tendencies—ranging from frequent wars of total conquest to deep, reliable peace—is paralleled by my strategic choice theory.[56] Wendt generates these possibilities by identifying three roles—enemy, rival, and friend—that can dominate the international system. My argument works differently; both have advantages.

A key to Wendt's argument about a deep peace (as well as collective security arrangements) is that states can be friends—have collective identities in which they value other states' security as well as their own and are therefore not pure egoists. International relations theory has spent relatively little time addressing states with collective identities because most effort has focused on explaining conflict. For this purpose, assuming that states are security seekers is ambitious because it eliminates the most obvious explanation for conflict—the incompatible motives and goals of greedy states. Addressing instead the possibilities for lasting peace, constructivists have filled this gap by emphasizing the importance of collective identities.[57]

From the perspective of the strategic choice theory, considering states that have an additional reason to cooperate is a natural move because the international environment can prevent security seekers from cooperating.

[56] Wendt, *Social Theory of International Politics*, chap. 6. The information argument also has parallels to Thomas Risse's liberal constructivist argument that social identification between democracies provides the information required to essentially eliminate the security dilemma and create peaceful relations in Europe. In addition, Risse provides an explanation for the information, which is outside the boundaries of my rationalist theory, and includes collective identities in his argument; Thomas Risse-Kappen, "Collective Identity in a Democratic Community," in Peter Katzenstein, ed., *The Culture of National Security: Norms and Identities in World Politics* (New York: Columbia University Press, 1996), pp. 367–68; and *Cooperation among Democracies* (Princeton: Princeton University Press, 1995). For a constructivist analysis of Europe that focuses on the unit level, see Ole Waever, "Integration as Security: Constructing a Europe at Peace," in Charles A. Kupchan, ed., *Atlantic Security: Competing Visions* (New York: Council on Foreign Relations, 1998).

[57] In addition to Wendt, *Social Theory of International Politics*, see Emanuel Adler and Michael Barnett, "A Framework for the Study of Security Communities," in Adler and Barnett, eds., *Security Communities*; and Risse-Kappen, "Collective Identity in a Democratic Community." Constructivists have also focused on the role of collective identities in supporting effective collective security and security communities; see Wendt, "Collective Identity Formation and the International State"; and Adler and Barnett, "A Framework for the Study of Security Communities."

A collective identity could increase a state's willingness to cooperate when facing a security dilemma. A security dilemma could exist even when states have collective identities because these states could also face uncertainty about other states' motives and about other states' beliefs about their motives. While these uncertainties would make cooperation risky, collective identities would add to the benefits of cooperation because the other state's security is now valued for its own sake. As a result, under certain conditions, collective identities could flip a state's policy choice from competition to cooperation.

While these arguments are sound, structural constructivism has exaggerated the importance of collective identities. As explained in chapter 3, information that the opposing state is very likely to be a security seeker can produce extensive cooperation and lasting peace, without collective identities. Wendt's categorization of states as friends (those with collective identities) as compared to rivals and enemies (those without collective identities) underplays the potential impact of information on the interaction of security seekers.[58] Security seekers that are confident that the opposing states are security seekers can pursue extensive cooperation and possibly a lasting peace without being friends.

The possibility of two sets of conditions that make possible stable cooperation and peace suggests a comparison of the prospects for achieving them.[59] Shared confidence that other states are security seekers is likely to be easier to achieve than becoming friends and likely to be as lasting. If confidence that other states are security seekers precedes the development of collective identities, which seems likely, then becoming "nonenemies" is a prerequisite for becoming friends. In this case, the security dilemma would be essentially eliminated before collective identities are formed, which reduces their importance. In addition, confidence in other states' benign motives may be as lasting as collective identities since information that other states are security seekers makes possible cooperative policies that reinforce this information. Although analyzing these interactions is beyond the boundaries of a theory that takes states' interests as fixed, my point here is simply that the contribution of collective identities to cooperation and peace does not clearly exceed that of information that the opposing state's motives are benign.

The second way in which the theories produce similar possibilities is by capturing the impact of interaction on states' information: like structural constructivism, my theory argues that states' interactions can provide in-

---

[58] Adler and Barnett, "A Framework for the Study of Security Communities," do emphasize an important role for information (within a broad concept of trust) but argue that both trust and collective identities are required for dependable expectations of peaceful change.

[59] They are not mutually exclusive and in combination would provide reinforcing advantages.

formation about motives and thereby change political relationships. In response to Waltz's neglect of the possible availability of information about states' motives, constructivists argue that the interaction between states can moderate or eliminate fears, thereby reducing the threat posed by other states' capabilities and making cooperation and peace possible.[60] In the theory developed here, although motives and fundamental interests are taken as fixed, a state's understanding of others' motives is not. Constructivists have blurred this distinction in their critique of realism. Structural constructivism argues that realism requires states to make worst-case assumptions,[61] which eliminate the possibility that interaction could improve assessments of others' motives. The strategic choice theory developed here (as well as defensive realism), however, agrees with Wendt that "most decisions . . . should be made on the basis of probabilities, and these are produced by interaction."[62]

Beyond these parallels, my argument provides a fuller account of the combined effect of material and information variables in constraining and producing states' choices. Constructivists have exaggerated the general potential of ideational factors to determine outcomes and, more specifically, appear overly optimistic about the ability of states to overcome dangerous material conditions. Wendt is partially correct in arguing that "*History matters.* Security dilemmas are not acts of God: they are effects of practice."[63] But states do not get to choose their history; instead, their interactions may start under information conditions that prevent them from overcoming material conditions that create pressures for competition, and these information conditions can reflect prior material conditions, as well as prior information. As a result, states can find important cooperative options too risky and, therefore, adopt policies that reduce their military vulnerability, but that also communicate malign motives.[64] As I have argued, although information variables certainly matter, states will nevertheless usually be guided by the joint implications of material and information variables, which means we should place a premium on theories that analyze their combined implications.

---

[60] Alexander Wendt, "Anarchy Is What States Make of It: The Social Construction of Power Politics," *International Organization* 46, 2 (Spring 1992): 391–425.

[61] Wendt, *Social Theory of International Politics*, p. 262. In the same spirit, Hopf argues that constructivism helps solve problems with neorealism, which treats uncertainty about other states' goals as a constant. Ted Hopf, "The Promise of Constructivism in International Relations Theory," *International Security* 23, 1 (Summer 1998): 186–188.

[62] Wendt, "Anarchy Is What States Make of It," p. 404; on the importance of this point for many realist theories, see Brooks, "Dueling Realisms."

[63] Alexander Wendt, "Constructing International Politics," *International Security* 20, 1 (Summer 1995): 77; and "Anarchy Is What States Make of It," p. 407.

[64] On this point, see Dale C. Copeland, "The Constructivist Challenge to Structural Realism: A Review Essay," *International Security* 25, 2 (Fall 2000): 201–202.

CHAPTER SEVEN

Evaluating the Theory from Within

THE STANDARD AND universally accepted approach for evaluating a social science theory is to take the theory to the data—to test whether the theory's hypotheses are supported by evidence.[1] However, a rational, prescriptive theory may have to be evaluated differently. If states sometimes do not act as they "should," that is, if they do not act rationally but instead choose suboptimal policies, then testing the theory against the data of state behavior may not tell us much about the quality of the theory. Although the data will not correlate well with the theory's prescriptions, the theory might nevertheless be identifying the best strategies that were available; the states simply failed to choose them. Put another way, the theory might be identifying the impact a state's international environment should have on its choice of strategy, but the state is not respecting or understanding these constraints; similarly, the theory might be correctly identifying the impact of variation in states' motives, but states are not acting consistently with their goals.

In fact, we have strong grounds for believing that states do frequently choose suboptimal policies. Over the past few decades, scholars have advanced a diverse range of theories to explain such suboptimal behavior. Overly competitive behavior, including unnecessary arms racing, unduly tight balancing, self-defeating expansionist grand strategies, and avoidable wars, have been explained by organization theory, theories that focus on regime type and state structure, and psychological theories.[2] Other research explores overly restrained or cooperative policies, includ-

[1] See, for example, Gary King, Robert O. Keohane, and Sydney Verba, *Designing Social Inquiry: Scientific Inference in Qualitative Research* (Princeton: Princeton University Press, 1994); Stephen Van Evera, *Guide to Methods for Students of Political Science* (Ithaca: Cornell University Press, 1997); and Alexander L. George and Andrew Bennett, *Case Studies and Theory Development in the Social Sciences* (Cambridge: MIT Press, 2005).

[2] For example, on the impact of organizations, see Stephen W. Van Evera, "Causes of War" (Ph.D. diss., University of California at Berkeley, 1984); Snyder, *The Ideology of the Offensive*; and Posen, *The Sources of Military Doctrine*. Earlier relevant work includes Graham T. Allison, *Essence of Decision: Explaining the Cuban Missile Crisis* (Boston: Little, Brown, 1971); and Morton H. Halperin, *Bureaucratic Politics and Foreign Policy* (Washington, D.C.: Brookings, 1974). On state structure, see Snyder, *Myths of Empire*; and Chaim Kaufmann, "Threat Inflation and the Failure of the Market Place of Ideas: The Selling of the Iraq War," *International Security* 29, 1 (Summer 2004), pp. 5–48. On psychological explanations, see Jervis, *Perception and Misperception*; and Robert Jervis, Richard Ned

ing underbalancing;[3] and still other research addresses how the difficulty of extracting resources to meet security requirements can lead states to distort their national security strategies.[4] Consequently, a wealth of research supports the possibility that a rational theory could be quite good but not do well at explaining states' actual behavior.

One useful approach for addressing this problem is to combine a theory of suboptimality with the rational theory, layering them together to explain outcomes. If the combined theory explains states' behavior, then this supports not only the suboptimal component, but also the rational component of the theory. Much of the work on suboptimal state behavior adopts this approach. An important example is research that explains overly competitive strategies by arguing that states made flawed assessments of the offense-defense balance, which reflected the inclinations of their military organizations, and then combining these misevaluated variables with rational offense-defense theory.[5] This approach, however, has an important shortcoming. States can and apparently do make mistakes for a variety of reasons; scholars have identified a wide range of sources of states' suboptimal policies. And we do not have, and may never have, an adequate theory of which sources of suboptimality occur when, and of how they combine and interact with each other. Consequently, although quite productive, this multilevel layering approach has significant limitations as a general approach for evaluating the quality of the rational baseline.

Instead, I adopt three different approaches to evaluating my theory. In this chapter I focus on the elements that make up the theory itself, an approach that I term evaluating the theory from "within." Instead of evaluating empirical support for the theory's predictions, we can gain some confidence in the theory's quality by scrutinizing its key components, including its assumptions, variables, and deductions. Although employing this approach does identify limitations, this chapter provides substantial confidence in the usefulness of my theory. Chapter 8 explores a few important cases that the theory does explain and shows that it does better at explaining these cases than the key alternative theories. Because we expect the theory to explain behavior when states act rationally and have little reason to expect that states never choose rational policies, finding

---

Lebow, and Janice Gross Stein, *Psychology and Deterrence* (Baltimore: Johns Hopkins University Press, 1985).

[3] For example, Schweller, *Unanswered Threats.*

[4] For example, Thomas J. Christensen, *Useful Adversaries: Grand Strategy, Domestic Mobilization, and Sino-American Conflict, 1947–1958* (Princeton: Princeton University Press, 1996).

[5] Van Evera, *Causes of War*; and Christensen and Snyder, "Chain Gangs and Passed Bucks."

important cases that the theory explains well provides additional support for my theory. Chapter 9 considers whether states are "punished" for pursuing suboptimal policies. It uses the theory as a rational baseline against which states' arming policies can be compared, then employs counterfactual analyses to assess whether states that adopted suboptimal policies would have better achieved their goals with the policies prescribed by the rational theory. The chapter finds that suboptimal arming policies did reduce states' security or their ability to achieve other goals and therefore provides further support for my theory.

There is a long-standing debate about whether a theory's assumptions need to be realistic or whether instead a theory can be judged solely by how well it explains actors' behavior.[6] Whatever its other merits may be, the effectiveness of the latter approach is greatly weakened, if not entirely undermined, if we believe that in fact states often do not act as the rational theory would prescribe.

Extending the former approach, we can try to evaluate a theory "from within," that is, by exploring not only the accuracy of its assumptions, but also its variables, decision-making requirements, and deductive logic. Our confidence in the theory should increase with (1) the accuracy of the assumptions—actually, as I explain below, the *adequacy* of the assumptions, given the theory's purpose; (2) the theory's completeness—the extent to which relevant variables are included; (3) the feasibility of its decision-making requirements—the extent to which states are capable of measuring the relevant variables and performing the analysis envisioned by the theory; and (4) the deductive strength of the theory's logic and arguments. Although not focused on explaining outcomes, this approach to evaluating the theory is nevertheless partially empirical: three of the four components—assumptions, completeness, and state capability—address the match between the theory and the real world; only the fourth component—deductive logic—might be considered purely theoretical.

All these components need to be explored within the context of the questions the theory is designed to address. As I explain below, although two of the theory's key assumptions—rational states and unitary actors—are clearly not accurate, they are for the most part well matched to the purposes of the theory. Similarly, which variables are relevant depends on the purposes of the theory. For example, grand theory questions

---

[6] See Mark Blaug, *The Methodology of Economics, or How Economists Explain* (Cambridge: Cambridge University Press, 1980), chap. 4; Terry M. Moe, "On the Scientific Status of Rational Models," *American Journal of Political Science* 23, 1 (February 1979): 215–243; and Paul K. MacDonald, "Useful Fiction or Miracle Maker: The Competing Epistemological Foundations of Rational Choice Theory," *American Political Science Review* 41, 4 (December 2005): 373–393.

about a rational state's broad basic choices between cooperative and competitive policies are unlikely to depend on the industrial structure of its arms industry; in contrast, a midlevel theory designed to explain the particulars of a state's military force structure is much more likely to depend on this variable. Likewise, a simplified characterization of a state's decision-making process that might influence the nuances of its negotiating strategy, but not its broad decision to pursue negotiated cooperation, is not problematic. Of course, even with this guidance evaluating the theory promises to be challenging—the boundary created by the guiding questions will often require judgment calls.

Moreover, a fair assessment using these criteria will undoubtedly show that the theory has limitations. Even viewed from the perspective of the theory's key questions, a theory's assumptions and variables must include simplifications. This is necessary to enable the theory to focus on what is likely most important and to make possible deductions about strategic interaction. To appreciate the range of factors that are excluded, we need to recall only that my theory assumes away many second-image/unit-level aspects of states' choices. Even the most committed structural theorists recognize that sometimes unit-level factors influence behavior.[7] At the same time, it is important to keep in mind that there are many unit-level features that, even if they do influence states' actual behavior, should be excluded from the theory. Because the theory is designed to explain and prescribe rational choices, there is no role for unit-level features that fuel suboptimal state behavior. It is also important to keep in mind that my theory does include some key unit-level features—for example, variation in states' motives, although it does not offer an explanation for this variation. Nevertheless, other unit-level features that can influence the constraints facing rational states and the effectiveness of their strategies are excluded. The following assessment strives to judge the significance of these limitations in the context of the questions the theory is designed to address.

Clarifying which simplifications and incompletenesses are potentially problematic provides a more sophisticated understanding of the theory's strengths and weaknesses. Appreciation of shortcomings enables us to analyze how the theory's central prescriptions might need to be amended in specific cases; closely related, when using the theory as a rational baseline, appreciation of these limitations enables us to ask further questions before deciding whether a state's behavior was suboptimal. As we will see below, some of these adjustments flow naturally from the theory's basic setup and perspective; they leave the theory largely intact, identifying, for example, ways to improve the specification and measurement of the the-

---

[7] Waltz, *Theory of International Politics*, pp. 122–123.

ory's variables. Other limitations do pose more fundamental challenges, but none appears to seriously reduce the value of the theory.

ARE THE THEORY'S ASSUMPTIONS *ADEQUATELY* ACCURATE AND REALISTIC?

We need to begin by asking whether the theory's assumptions are accurate. Because evaluating a theory from within is a self-contained exercise, the quality of the theory's foundation—its core assumptions—becomes a central issue. The more precise question that we need to address here is: Are the assumptions sufficiently accurate or realistic, given the type of question the theory is designed to address?[8] The rational/normative orientation of the theory has important implications; so does its grand theory perspective on states' choices.

As discussed in chapter 2, the theory's assumptions of anarchy and rationality are not problematic. Anarchy is an accurate description of the international situation that major powers face—no international institution or authority is capable of protecting states from attack by major powers and enforcing international agreements.[9] The assumption that states are rational is not generally accurate—research suggests that states often choose suboptimal strategies. But the rationality assumption is nevertheless appropriate to the central goal of the theory, which is determining which strategies a state *should* choose. It is this perspective that creates the potential gap between the theory and the outcomes data, which in turn creates a challenge for evaluating the theory, though not for the theory itself.

Adequacy of the Unitary-Actor Assumption

The theory's two other key assumptions—envisioning states as unitary actors and treating opposing states as "black boxes"—require more discussion. States are obviously not unitary actors. Loosening the unitary-actor assumption raises a host of issues that are typically bundled within the diverse family of unit-level or domestic-politics explanations,[10] which

---

[8] On the potential value of oversimplified mechanisms and assumptions, see Arthur L. Stinchcombe, "The Conditions of Fruitfulness of Theorizing about Mechanisms in Social Science," *Philosophy of the Social Sciences* 21, 3 (September 1991): 367–388.

[9] For a skeptical view, see Milner, "The Assumption of Anarchy in International Relations." For an analysis of hierarchy in international relations, see David A. Lake, "Escape from the State of Nature: Authority and Hierarchy in World Politics," *International Security* 32, 1 (Summer 2007): 47–79.

[10] On conceptual issues that determine what counts as a domestic politics explanation see

includes arguments that emphasize the nature and diversity of domestic actors' preferences; the role of institutions in aggregating preferences, and in influencing states' material and signaling capabilities; the impact of regime type and institutions on states' decision-making capabilities; and related, the processes that influence whether states reach optimal/ rational choices or instead suboptimal ones. As explained above, the purposes of the theory call for it to exclude those domestic politics arguments that focus on explaining suboptimal decisions. And the theory does integrate across levels of analysis by including variation in states' motives as well as their international situation. The theory does, however, assume away many of the other issues that are the focus of rational second-image, unit-level explanations. Once we recognize that examining the unitary-actor assumption draws us into this large portion of the levels-of-analysis debate, it becomes clear that sorting out the implications of the unitary-actor assumption is a large undertaking that cannot be completely accomplished here. I am nevertheless able to show that the assumption is productive for answering the key questions the theory is designed to address, and that some of the problems that do arise can be handled within the theory's basic strategic-choice approach.

IMPLICATIONS OF NONUNITARY ACTORS FOR MOTIVES

A key issue that is glossed over by the unitary-actor assumption is that a state may not have well-defined (uniquely defined) national motives and interests. Instead, the key actors that make up the state may have different motives and interests, creating a situation in which there is not a description of interests that adequately captures all the actors. As a result, there may not be a policy that all the actors would prefer to the alternatives; if so, it might also be unclear which motives and interests should be used in evaluating a state's strategy, and, related, which interests the rationality (optimality) of a state's strategy should be judged against. For example, evaluations of U.S. security policy that include domestic politics might identify a wide range of actors that could influence outcomes, including politicians that give priority to being reelected, militaries that give priority to increasing their budgets or implementing their preferred military strategy, defense industries that give priority to profits, and citizens that give priority to consumption. Even assuming that each of these actors values U.S. national security, trade-offs with other values could lead them to prefer different defense strategies. Some of these interests, for example consumption, are widely shared and therefore need to be included in fully characterizing a state's well-being. Others, for example

Fearon, "Domestic Politics, Foreign Policy, and Theories of International Relations," who makes a number of additional points relevant to the discussion here.

maximizing an organization's budget, can from the perspective of the state be viewed as narrow and distorting. Nevertheless, a U.S. leader facing these actors with divergent interests can be constrained by them, making otherwise preferable policies politically infeasible. From the perspective of the constrained leader, making a choice from the politically available set of options is not suboptimal, even though other options might provide the state with greater security.

Although certainly a more accurate description of the composition of the state than is offered by the unitary-actor assumption, this degree of complexity is largely unnecessary (and usually not helpful) for answering the key questions the theory is designed to address. Recall that, in broad terms, these questions include: What strategy should a state choose? And does a state's international situation create overall incentives favoring cooperative or competitive policies? Instead, adopting the perspective of a single actor with well-defined motives and interests, that is not constrained by domestic actors' divergent interests and power, is appropriate for answering these questions and, more generally, for achieving the theory's objectives. Although this unitary state does not actually exist, we are nevertheless interested in how such a state should act if it did exist. Imagining this state (and in effect therefore treating it as an individual actor) enables us to focus on the theory's key variables—the international situation and states' motives—and their interaction. And, closely related, we often want to know what strategy a state should adopt if it had specific, well-defined motives and interests. For example, if asking whether the United States during the Cold War should have pursued a cooperative or competitive policy with the Soviet Union, we primarily want to know whether there were cooperative policies that would have increased U.S. security, not whether the Senate would have refused to ratify certain types of arms control agreements or the U.S. military had the political clout to distort agreements to protect its force modernization programs. The theory with its unitary-actor assumption is well matched to answering the former type of question. Moreover, although less basic, working with the simplifying unitary-actor assumption is the first order of business even if the final objective is to develop a theory that incorporates diverse actors, and domestic institutions and constraints. Knowing which strategy each key actor or group prefers (given international constraints) is necessary for understanding how they would combine to produce a state's strategy.

This is in fact the standard approach to normative policy analysis—analysis typically starts by studying which option best achieves an actor's interests, given resource constraints. This analysis can then provide part of the foundation for addressing a different question—how the actor should bargain and compromise with other actors that have divergent preferences, given institutional constraints. Moreover, this standard apo-

then abstracting away domestic politics is arbitrary

litical policy analysis is often intended to stand on its own, providing the actor with guidance on the policies that are best matched to his/her objectives.

This perspective on the unitary-actor assumption is quite different from the one that is most common and defines the debate between levels of analysis. The standard argument is that the unitary-actor assumption is useful, maybe even sufficient, for explaining states' key decisions. If enough behavior is explained, the parsimony is worth the costs in additional explanatory power. In addition, an important realist argument holds that on vital matters of national security, especially when a state faces a large security threat, the unitary-actor assumption is usually quite accurate because decision-making power becomes concentrated in the national leadership;[11] in these cases the assumption will be especially productive for explanation. Without taking a position on this line of argument, the case I am making here for the unitary-actor assumption is quite different—I am emphasizing its utility for analyzing normative/prescriptive questions, not for explaining actual state behavior.

While this understanding of the unitary-actor assumption is analytically valuable, it does generate complications. When a state in fact contains influential actors with divergent interests, it may not adopt the strategy preferred by any of the actors, but instead a bargained compromise. Consequently, the theory may not do well at predicting the state's behavior, even though it could identify which strategy each actor should choose. As suggested above, predicting outcomes would require adding a domestic politics theory. My position is that this is not a weakness of the strategic choice theory, but rather the result of needing a different, and complementary, theory to answer a different question.

A related challenge concerns the evaluation of suboptimality. So far, the book has drawn a sharp line between rational and suboptimal international behavior—suboptimality is measured relative to a rational baseline produced by the theory and can result from a variety of domestic shortcomings, including possibly biased organizations, flawed bureaucracies and institutional decision-making structures, and cognitively biased decision makers. But divergence in motives and interests need not reflect bias or narrow interests of individuals and substate actors. Instead, it could reflect disagreements about the state's broad interests—for example, security, greedy motives (such as spreading a political ideology), and societal consumption—that may not reflect narrow interests and therefore cannot be excluded from evaluation of the state's interests simply on these grounds. As a result, although domestic politics may require compromise for many or all actors, the state's policy might not be suboptimal,

[11] Posen, *The Sources of Military Doctrine*.

even though it does not entirely match any of the actor's policy preferences over how best to achieve their interests. In these cases, evaluating suboptimality would therefore require adopting a different approach, with the possibilities including making a judgment that one actor's position within the state (for example, that held by the state's leader) is more important than others', and therefore that this actor's motives and interests should be used in determining the rational baseline; or defining a range of policies that correspond to those preferred by the key actors, with only policies outside this range judged suboptimal; or developing a model of the institutionalized state and then using its preferred strategy as the rational baseline.[12]

All of this said, when evaluating national security policy, the theory will often provide a rational baseline that is useful for evaluating whether a state's strategy is suboptimal. In cases in which all the relevant domestic actors have broad national interests that are limited to security (that is, not greed), the problem of aggregating preferences largely dissolves.[13] The theory can then be used to evaluate disagreements between these domestic actors over strategy and to assess whether the narrow interests of substate actors have distorted a state's security strategy. In addition, when a state faces strong material constraints that make certain strategies exceedingly unlikely to succeed, we may be able to judge suboptimality without fully addressing the implications of divergent motives. For example, as I argue in a following chapter, Germany's pursuit at the beginning of the twentieth century of a navy that challenged Britain's was a flawed strategy because, among other reasons, Germany lacked the power to succeed; and this judgment is robust across plausible German motives.

IMPLICATIONS OF NONUNITARY ACTORS FOR CAPABILITIES

Another key issue that is glossed over by the unitary-actor assumption is that states' capabilities may depend on unit-level features, including regime type, domestic institutions, ideology, and culture. The unitary-

---

[12] However, the latter approach has problems of its own: the preferences of this institutionalized state may depend on its international environment and therefore cannot be separated from it, as the strategic choice model requires. For example, whether a leader will propose cooperation could depend on the preferences not only of the domestic actors and institutions, but also of the opposing state; see Milner, *Interests, Institutions and Information*. An alternative designed to address this problem is to develop a theory of two-level games that models the simultaneous interactions at the domestic and international levels; see Peter B. Evans, Harold K. Jacobson, and Robert D. Putnam, eds., *Double-Edged Diplomacy: International Bargaining and Domestic Politics* (Berkeley: University of California Press, 1993).

[13] This claim is somewhat overstated because actors that place different value on security versus consumption could prefer different strategies.

actor assumption implies that all states facing the same material and information conditions have equal potential to make effective use of their resources. However, theories that focus on domestic-level variables argue otherwise. For example, domestic institutions not only aggregate preferences, they also constrain states' capabilities.[14] To the extent this is true, assuming states are unitary and therefore do not vary at the unit level risks misevaluating their potential capabilities.

Two types of arguments are particularly important in the context of the rational theory I have laid out. The first focuses on a state's potential military capabilities. A state's ability to deploy effective military capabilities depends not only on the raw-material resources that are commonly included in definitions and measures of power—including, for example, wealth, territory, and population—but also on its ability to extract resources and then convert them into effective military forces. If states differ in their ability to extract and convert resources, states that are equally powerful according to standard measures of material power may not have the same military potential. Although research on extraction and conversion has not found a strong association with regime type,[15] it has identified other factors that matter. For example, a state's extraction potential is found to be lower when elites disagree about the threat the state faces, when society is fragmented, and when the government is weak.[16] A military's will/determination to fight is found to depend on the cohesion of both the society from which it is drawn and the military itself.[17] Variations in military skill may depend on whether a state is a democracy, but there does not appear to be a strong relationship.[18] Stephen Biddle, who emphasizes the role of military skill in producing battle outcomes, argues that the quality of a state's force employment depends on a range of domestic political and organizational variables.[19] In line with these argu-

---

[14] A good overview of this perspective is Ronald Rogowski, "Institutions as Constraints on Strategic Choice," in Lake and Powell, eds., *Strategic Choice and International Relations*.

[15] Dan Reiter and Allan C. Stam, *Democracies at War* (Princeton: Princeton University Press, 2002), chap. 5.

[16] Schweller, *Unanswered Threats*; Rose, "Neoclassical Realism and Theories of Foreign Policy," identifies attention to extraction as a key feature of the works he classifies as neoclassical realism.

[17] Castillo, "The Will to Fight."

[18] Reiter and Stam, *Democracies at War*, chap. 3, do find that democratic armies are more effective, benefiting among other things from a superior ability to take the initiative; in Reiter and Stam, "Understanding Victory: Why Political Institutions Matter," *International Security* 28, 1 (Summer 2003): 168, they characterize this finding as "democratic armies enjoy a small advantage on the battlefield." For a critique of their analysis, see Michael Desch, "Democracy and Victory: Why Regime Type Hardly Matters," *International Security* 27, 2 (Fall 2002): 5–47.

[19] Biddle, *Military Power*, pp. 48–51.

ments, a recent thorough analysis concludes that assessments of a state's ability to produce effective military power should include "the aptitude of the populace for innovation, the nature of its domestic and social institutions, the constitution of its state-society relations, the quality of its knowledge base, and the character of its ideational ethos."[20]

This leaves us with the question of whether and how to incorporate these possible sources of variation in states' military potential. The theory conceives of power broadly—as the resources that a state can employ to produce effective military forces relative to its adversary's resources—and therefore its central logic does not suggest that power should be restricted to the standard raw-material factors. Including a state's institutional and domestic political assets would be consistent with this broad understanding of power.[21] And related, a state that was able to incorporate these considerations into its assessment of power would be prepared to make better strategic choices.

If we envision power as an exogenous input to the strategic choice theory, then this "correction" leaves the theory essentially intact. A state would be making a correction to the theory's simpler characterization of power, for example, by scaling raw material assets by extraction potential. When we understand power to depend on one, or even a small number of easily combined material factors, then a theory of power may seem unnecessary—all that is required is to measure the material factors and then combine them. In fact, however, this characterization actually rests on an understanding of power that identifies which material factors to include and how to weight and combine them. If we move to a fuller characterization of power, then the need for a theory of this input to the strategic choice theory becomes more evident. This move does, however, require a narrower conception of the unitary-actor assumption than is common; although states would still be envisioned as unitary decision makers (for the reasons described above), their power could depend on factors that vary across types of states. Whether in practice states (and analysts using this type of theory) will frequently be able to make these adjustments is a different matter. Material factors are more easily mea-

---

[20] Ashley J. Tellis et al., *Measuring National Power in the Postindustrial Age* (Washington, DC: RAND, 2000), p. 6.

[21] In fact, although usually viewed as a material theory, Waltz's frequently referred to list of factors that influence power includes some of these types of nonmaterial factors, specifically political stability and competence; Waltz, *Theory of International Politics*, p. 131. Waltz goes on to say, "States have different combinations of capabilities which are difficult to measure and compare, the more so since the weight to be assigned to different items changes over time. We should not be surprised if wrong answers are sometimes arrived at." On the case for a "softer" definition of international structure, which would allow the inclusion of certain unit-level features, see Glaser and Kaufmann, "Correspondence," pp. 200–201.

sured than many (possibly all) of the state capacity variables noted above, which might in practice leave more standard measures of material factors as the better indicators of power. Moreover, some important nonmaterial components of power can change relatively quickly, for example, states' skill can change during a long war, which creates additional uncertainty about these measures and should sometimes encourage states to discount them.

The second type of domestic-level argument about capabilities focuses on a state's ability to communicate information. If, for example, a state's ability to signal its type or resolve, or to make credible commitments to cooperate, varies with its regime type, otherwise similar states may have unequal capacities for bargaining and cooperation. Much of the work on this question has focused on the advantages that democracies have in signaling their resolve during crisis bargaining.[22] According to these arguments, the key cost of engaging in a crisis are domestic "audience costs"— the costs that a state's leader faces if he or she backs down once publicly engaged in a crisis. Backing down is argued to be more costly for democratic leaders than for authoritarian leaders; consequently they tend to engage in crises when they have high resolve, which in turn means that a democracy can send a more effective costly signal by engaging in a crisis than can other types of states. This argument depends on audience costs being large compared to the other types of costs that could be generated by a crisis. If other possible costs of crisis actions—which include the financial and organizational costs of mobilizing troops, and the increased risks of war generated by diplomatic and military action—were a state's principal concern, regime type would then have relatively little impact on a state's ability to signal.

This latter point is important for considering the communication that is central in my theory—the provision via costly signals of information about states' basic motives and interests during peacetime. For this communication the costly signals are embedded in the size and types of forces that states build, the arms control agreements they negotiate, the alliances they enter, and, more broadly, the foreign policies they pursue. Under certain conditions, it is quite costly for a security seeker to pursue the policy preferred by a greedy state and vice versa. The costs reflect a reduction in the states' abilities to achieve their central interests, whether security or nonsecurity expansion. Given its motives, the costs a state incurs from adopting these policies are not sensitive to its regime type.

[22] See James D. Fearon, "Domestic Political Audiences and the Escalation of International Disputes," *American Political Science Review* 88, 3 (September 1994): 577–592, which has generated a large literature on audience costs. See also Kenneth A. Schultz, *Democracy and Coercive Diplomacy* (Cambridge: Cambridge University Press, 2001), which focuses on a different mechanism.

Another strand of argument connects signaling and regime type by focusing on a state's ability to make credible commitments. As already discussed, a state's best option for cooperation will sometimes be a formalized arms control agreement.[23] A state's willingness to enter into such an agreement can depend upon the opposing state's credibility for keeping its commitments. According to these arguments, this credibility can depend on a state's regime type and domestic institutions—both high transparency of a state's arming policies and clear domestic rules for adopting and withdrawing from agreements could increase a state's credibility, in ways that favor democracies.[24] There are, however, strong reasons for questioning whether domestic institutions are likely to be the key to making otherwise desirable cooperation/arms control agreements feasible. A state's assessment of the probability that its adversary will abide by an agreement should depend on its assessment of the adversary's motives: greedy states are less likely to comply because they have larger incentives to cheat. Probably more important, to compensate for a lack of confidence that the adversary will abide by an agreement, the state can insist that the agreement be adequately verifiable, attempting to insure its ability to respond effectively to strategically significant violations. In effect, adequate verification reduces the danger if the adversary decides to cheat, which reduces the confidence the state requires that the adversary will meet its commitment.[25] In short, other sources of credibility and approaches for making it less important reduce, but do not necessarily eliminate, the significance of domestic institutions in determining the desirability of this type of cooperation.

Overall, then, the unitary-actor assumption is far less problematic than one might initially expect. Most important, although not accurate, viewing a state's decisions from the perspective of a single actor is well matched to the theory's central purpose. When evaluating what strategy a state should choose, considering the relatively simple interests of a single actor, instead of the combined interests of many substate actors, is the first

[23] Recall that cooperation can also take the form of unilateral restraint, tacit reciprocal restraint, and explicit reciprocal restraint that is not codified and ratified as an official agreement.

[24] On transparency and information about motives, see Kydd, "Sheep in Sheep's Clothing," esp. pp. 129–139; Sebastian Rosato, "The Flawed Logic of Democratic Peace Theory," *American Political Science Review* 97, 4 (November 2003): 589–599, questions the signaling value of transparency in the related but different context of crises.

[25] States can also design agreements in ways that make the allowed forces more robust to cheating. Under some conditions, however, this will also reduce the benefits offered by the agreement. These two approaches for reducing the risks of cheating—that is, giving some weight to the robustness of the allowed forces and requiring verification provisions that further reduce the risk of cheating—mean that risk of cooperation in the security realm may not be that different from in the economic realm. For an alternative perspective, see Lipson, "International Cooperation in Economic and Security Affairs."

order of business. Moreover, although exploring the unitary-actor assumption raises many knotty issues, only a couple raise doubts about the theory's ability to effectively assess a state's strategy, and the most important of these can be corrected outside the core of the strategic choice theory. As a prime example, if states' power depends on variation in regime type or other state-specific characteristics, the key is a more nuanced theory of power that can provide more accurate inputs to the strategic choice theory, while leaving the theory itself unchanged.

Adequacy of "Black Boxing" the Adversary

The other key assumption that we need to evaluate is the theory's decision to "black box" the adversary. This means that in judging the adversary's power, motives, and responses to its strategy, the state does not consider the opposing state's internal workings, including its regime type, institutions, and domestic politics. The black-box assumption is essentially a version of the unitary-actor assumption applied to the adversary. This assumption is productive because it enables us to envision the adversary as a single decision maker that interprets and responds to the state's strategy. A variety of arguments suggest, however, that the variables the theory employs to characterize an opposing state and the reactions generated by the state's strategy could depend on unit-level features that are simplified away by the black-box/unitary-actor assumption. From the perspective of the theory, some of these simplifications appear more problematic than assuming that the decision-making state is a unitary actor.

First, the domestic-level factors that I addressed above concerning the state's power and ability to communicate also influence the adversary and raise the same issues for the theory. The adversary's power would depend on its extraction and conversion capabilities. In fact, because power reflects relative potential, it is actually the impact of these factors in both states combined with their raw-material endowments that determine their power. As explained above, this unit-level variation can be included by building a theory of power that lies outside the core of the strategic interaction theory and complements it. Regarding communication, not looking inside the black box could reduce the state's ability to interpret the adversary's signals, if signals depend on regime type. As discussed above, however, this is not a problematic simplification for the types of interactions on which the theory focuses. The adversary will not have significant signaling advantages or disadvantages as a result of its regime type, for the same reasons that the state does not. Again, this is because the cost of policies to compete or cooperate will be largely contained in the direct military implications of a strategy and force posture, not in domestic reactions to it.

Second, and possibly more problematic, not looking inside the black box could limit the information a state has about its adversary's motives and interests. As discussed in chapter 2, available research suggests that states look at a variety of unit-level factors—including regime type, political ideology, domestic institutions, and political coalitions and specific leaders—to assess an opposing state's motives. My theory takes the information that states have at the beginning of their strategic interaction as given—not explained by the theory and thereby allows for incorporating the insights provided by these unit-level factors. However, any revisions of this initial information then result only from costly signals sent by the opposing state. In effect, this assumes that new unit-level information does not become available once the strategic interaction begins. If, however, changes do occur within the opposing state once strategic interaction begins, then the state could improve its future decisions by taking them into account. For example, while Soviet military and foreign policy actions starting in the mid-1980s provided information about the country's motives, changes in leadership and governance also informed U.S. assessments; overlooking these changes would have reduced the U.S. ability to appropriately adapt its strategy. A more complete theory would therefore allow the state to update its assessment of motives based on changes within the opposing state, as well as incorporating signaling information as interaction proceeds. Of course, the importance of including this type of updating is reduced when a state's unit-level characteristics are relatively stable and most information is therefore exchanged via signaling.

In an important sense, this more complete theory would be largely consistent with the perspective of the strategic choice theory that I have presented—it does not change the role of information about motives in influencing the state's decision but rather adds to the ways in which this information is updated. In addition, the theory already depends on an initial assessment of the adversary's motives, which could be informed by unit-level factors. At the same time, however, incorporating unit-level information throughout the process of interaction would require a further mixing together of different layers of theory, integrating them more fully and giving greater emphasis to unit-level considerations.

Third, black boxing the adversary overlooks the possibility that the state's policy/strategy could influence the adversary by shifting its balance of domestic power, instead of providing information that enables opposing leaders to learn about the state and revise their beliefs.[26] In this type

---

[26] For analysis of this possibility and historical examples, see Snyder, "International Leverage on Soviet Domestic Change"; and Glaser, "Political Consequences of Military Strategy," pp. 519–525. On the related point that the international system can influence domestic political structures, see Gourevich, "The Second Image Reversed."

of process, the state's policy increases the influence of some actors or groups relative to others; for example, hard-liners might gain influence, while moderates lose it. Arguments based on this type of interaction are common—for example, arguments during the late 1980s that cooperative U.S. policies would support Gorbachev, and more recent arguments that cooperative policies would support Iranian moderates in their domestic competition with more radical factions.[27] Different groups in the adversary's state can hold opposing views of the state—for example, hard-liners tend to see the state as having greedy motives, while moderates see it as having benign motives. As a result, shifts in the balance of domestic power can shift the adversary's view of the state.[28] In contrast to the unitary-actor theory, however, elites in the different groups need not learn from the state's policy but instead simply gain or lose influence. Consequently, unlike the other amendments explored above, which can be layered onto the theory, capturing this type of interaction clearly goes beyond the strategic choice theory I have developed.[29]

Whether a state's policy influences its adversary's beliefs through signaling or shifting the balance of domestic power is not an either-or choice. Instead, both types of interaction could generate changes, and there is evidence suggesting that both have been important in major-power relations. At a minimum, therefore, recognizing this second-image interaction provides a more complete description of how states' interactions can influence their beliefs about others' motives. In addition, although they appear to prescribe the same broad policies under a wide range of conditions, there are cases in which their prescriptions diverge. For example, a competitive policy that in a unitary model might be undesirable because it would signal greedy motives might in a second-image model be desirable because it would undermine the adversary's hard-liners by discrediting their competitive policies. It is also possible, however, that the competitive policy would have the opposite effect, supporting hard-liners by enabling them to argue convincingly that their hostile view of the state was accurate. In fact, one potential shortcoming of these second-image reversed models is their complexity—the impact of the state's policy can depend on an array of domestic-level variables, including whether the adversary's regime has a liberal or imperial orientation, whether the ad-

[27] On the latter, see, for example, Kenneth Pollack and Ray Takeyh, "Taking on Iran," *Foreign Affairs* 82, 2 (March/April 2005): 20–34.

[28] These shifts can also generate changes in the adversary's motives, if, for example, hard-liners are more interested in nonsecurity expansion than are soft-liners. It is also possible that the state's policies could influence the evolution of institutions in the opposing state, for example, supporting or undermining movement toward democracy.

[29] This is not to say that this interaction cannot be modeled as a strategic interaction in which the opposing state is decomposed in a number of different actors.

versary is weakly or strongly institutionalized, and whether the quality of the adversary's evaluative capabilities and its international policy debate is high or low. As a result, the state may often be unable to determine the likely impact of its policies on its adversary's domestic politics, which then leads back toward a unitary actor model of the adversary.

To close this subsection, it is useful to put the above critiques in perspective. Relaxing the black-box assumption would make the theory's foundation more accurate (at the cost of parsimony), but neither looking inside the black box to update assessments of motives nor including interactions with the adversary's domestic politics would weaken the theory's central findings. Cooperation would remain a state's best option under a range of international conditions, and competition would as well; a state's motives continue to matter, with greedy motives increasing the range of conditions under which competition is best. Updating from inside the black box could make cooperation more attractive—if domestic changes suggest that the adversary is more likely to be a security seeker—or less attractive—if domestic changes suggest the opposite. And as noted above, this additional information could be incorporated into the theory's model of strategic interaction. Although including domestic political interactions is harder to accommodate within the theory, these too would not alter the theory's broad conclusions.

Overall, then, this analysis of the adequacy of the theory's assumptions finds that the theory begins from a strong foundation. The assumption of international anarchy is accurate and captures an essential feature of the international environment. In contrast, the rationality and unitary-actor assumptions are not accurate but are well matched to the theory's central purposes and create few, if any, problems for the theory. Although the unitary-actor assumption does risk overlooking some variation in state capabilities, much of this (for example, variation in power) can be handled as an adjustment to the inputs to the strategic choice theory, without requiring changes to the theory itself. Black boxing the adversary is more limiting because this assumption prevents the theory from capturing changes in the adversary's balance of domestic power, which could influence its international policy. Relaxing this assumption to explore second-image reversed interactions is a natural direction for extending the theory.

ARE IMPORTANT VARIABLES LEFT OUT?

If important variables are left out of my theory, its analysis of a state's choice of strategy could be flawed. From one perspective, assessing whether important variables are left out is a formidable challenge—the standard approach for determining the importance of variables is to assess their addition to a theory's explanatory power. Because all theories simplify, many variables can be added and compared. And because the rational theory might not do well at explaining a state's actual behavior, since states sometimes adopt suboptimal policies, implementing this approach faces the more general problem that I have described above.

The task, however, is more feasible than it might initially appear. International relations theory has long grappled with these issues and likely provides an efficient guide to the main contenders. Moreover, the theory is already cast broadly and its purpose is limited, both of which make the task of assessing the importance of missing variables more manageable.

It is useful to distinguish between three categories of variables that are not included in the theory: (1) variables that lie outside the theory's boundaries; (2) variables that lie within the theory's boundaries and follow naturally from its key variables and analytic perspective; and (3) variables that lie within the theory's boundaries but are not a natural extension of its key variables. Of these, in principle only the third type is potentially a major problem; however, even these variables turn out not to create serious shortcomings.

Variables Outside the Theory's Boundaries

Many of the variables that might be included in a complete explanatory theory of state behavior are not included in the strategic choice theory because they lie outside its boundaries, in a different layer of theory. As discussed elsewhere (including below), theories of inputs to the strategic choice layer—for example, theories of greedy motives and states' interests more generally, of state power and of information about motives—include a variety of unit-level variables that have received attention from international relations theorists. These include regime type, ideology, state strength, and domestic institutions.[30] These variables influence state choices through their impact on the strategic choice theory's key variables. For example, a democracy might believe that an opposing state is more likely to be a security seeker because it too is a democracy. The strategic choice theory incorporates this information but does not attempt to explain it. Even farther from the central purpose of the theory, but potentially important for explaining state behavior, are variables that belong in the layer of theories that attempt to explain suboptimal behav-

---

[30] In addition to these, on the role of sectoral interest in forming states' interests, see Peter Trubowitz, *Defining the National Interest: Conflict and Change in American Foreign Policy* (Chicago: Chicago University Press, 1998); and Kevin Narizny, "The Political Economy of Alignment: Great Britain's Commitments to Europe, 1905–1939," *International Security* 27, 4 (Spring 2003): 184–219.

ior, including theories of cognitive misperception, flawed state decision-making processes and institutions, and organization theories.

Not including these variables—whether variables that help explain the inputs to the strategic choice theory or suboptimality—reflects the theory's partial nature, not shortcomings of the theory itself. These variables simply lie outside the boundaries of the strategic choice theory. Theories in these other layers can incorporate these variables and then be combined with the strategic choice theory.

Variables That Flow from the Theory's Analytic Perspective

Of possibly greater concern here is the second category of variables—those that are not identified as part of the core theory but follow naturally from the theory's basic variables and analytic perspective. The theory is already cast broadly, capturing variation along what are arguably the most important and obvious dimensions of a state's choice of strategy—a state's type, and the material and information conditions that define its international situation and constrain its choices. This basic setup guides us to a number of possible extensions of the theory that follow rather directly. These could include, for example, uncertainty about variables that are included in the theory and changes in the value of these variables over time. They could also include variables that are implicit in the theory, but whose role has not been sufficiently spelled out. In chapter 4 I termed these "within theory" extensions and suggested that adding these variables is best viewed not as creating a new theory, but instead as developing a fuller version of the existing theory. I explored the implications of variation in the value that security seekers place on the status quo, of variation in the depth and breadth of a state's greed, of uncertainty about power and offense-defense variables, and of changes in states' power.

One other variable clearly falls into this category and deserves more attention: polarity—the number of major powers in the system—or, more generally, the number of states and the distribution of power between them.[31] The theory I have developed focuses on a state that faces only one

[31] A couple of other variables that fall in this category should also be mentioned. First, the value a state places on the future compared to the present can influence its arming decision; see Powell, *In the Shadow of Power*, chap. 3; his formulation is different—with consumption as the end, and security as the means; however, the same trade-off could exist for a formulation that includes both security and consumption as ends. Second, interaction capacity—a state's ability to interact militarily—influences international relations; see Buzan, Jones, and Little, *The Logic of Anarchy*; and Ruggie, "Continuity and Transformation in the World Polity"; some aspects of interaction capacity are captured in the offense-defense balance. One variable that cannot be captured in the theory, given its unitary-actor assumption, is the distributional implications of alternative strategies; see, for example,

other state; limiting the analysis to this case enables the theory to identify a number of key incentives and trade-offs facing a state. Using this as a foundation, making the number of states a variable would enable the theory to address issues of alliance choices that have received a great deal of attention and debate.[32] Although I do not develop the arguments in this book, the basic outlines of how the extended theory would map onto those debates is reasonably clear: states will balance against threats—the combination of military capability, which is determined by power and the offense-defense balance, and information about opposing states' motives—not power alone; a state's type will influence its propensity to balance or bandwagon, with greedy states more inclined to bandwagon; and the intensity of balancing will increase with offense advantage.

In addition to appreciating that such a theory of alliance choices would fall within an extended version of the theory, a second point to emphasize here is that adding polarity will not overturn any of the theory's key conclusions regarding states' choices of cooperative and competitive strategies. As with the other "within theory" extensions that were considered earlier, the fuller version could make more nuanced prescriptions in particular situations but appears unlikely to be at variance with the theory's general conclusions and prescriptions.

Variables That Are Not a Natural Extension

The third category of variables—those that lie within the strategic choice theory's boundaries but do not follow from its core variables or basic analytic perspective—is the most challenging. The IR theory literature suggests a number of important possibilities in this category. States could have *motives other than security and greed* that my theory does not capture. For example, states could have humanitarian interests in preventing the suffering of people in other countries that results from war, disease, starvation, and natural disasters.[33] The theory does not address this set of motives/interests; there could therefore be cases in which it cannot be used effectively to analyze whether a state should launch a peacemaking

Kevin Narizny, "Both Guns and Butter, or Neither," pp. 203–220, who argues that economic class considerations influence whether a government will pursue an arms buildup, an alliance, or concessions.

[32] Important works include Stephen M. Walt, *The Origins of Alliances* (Ithaca: Cornell University Press, 1987); Schweller, *Deadly Imbalances*; Powell, *In the Shadow of Power*, chap. 5; Glenn H. Snyder, *Alliance Politics* (Ithaca: Cornell University Press, 1997); and Christensen and Snyder, "Chain Gangs and Passed Bucks."

[33] On the role of norms in establishing these interests, see Martha Finemore, "Constructing Norms of Humanitarian Intervention," in Peter Katzenstein, ed., *The Culture of National Security: Norms and Identities in World Politics* (New York: Columbia University Press, 1996).

mission to save lives, provide foreign development aid to increase prosperity, and offer disaster assistance. This limitation is not a serious problem for my theory, however, as these issues lie beyond its substantive focus. It does, however, remind us that the theory is not complete, even within the realm of evaluating and prescribing a state's international policies. A more general theory could add humanitarian motives and explore connections between the "high politics" security issues and this different set of issues. To enable the theory to address trade-offs between these motives, it would require assumptions (or evaluation) of their relative importance. We might expect that a state would rarely trade much security to accomplish humanitarian objectives, and this is certainly the impression that realist theories create;[34] nevertheless, a more general rational theory could allow this trade-off to vary.

Closer to the theory's substantive focus, but not included, is the possibility that states have *collective identities*. States with collective identities value other states' security as well as their own; this interest is fundamental—the other state's security is valued for its own sake—not instrumental, that is, valued because it increases the state's own security. As I discussed in chapter 6, collective identities play an important role in Wendt's structural constructivism. Contrary to at least the spirit of Wendt, my theory shows that the possibility of collective identities is not necessary for states to find that deep cooperation is their best strategy. But this is not to claim that collective identities could not change a state's choices. For example, as the value a state places on another's security increases, it would become more likely to balance with that state than pass the buck, more likely to form a collective security organization, and more willing to run cooperative risks to overcome the insecurity generated by the security dilemma. The importance of this type of altruism is reduced, however, by two considerations. In terms of political process, states are likely to choose extensive cooperation before they form collective identities, which makes the eventual impact of their collective identities less important. Moreover, with the possible exception of recent Western European relations, collective identities have been scarce and appear to have played little role in international politics. Consequently, while it is valuable to appreciate their potential importance because collective identities might become more common in the future, not including them does little to limit my theory's applicability to the past or to current international politics.

Finally, *norms* could influence a state's choice of means in ways that are not addressed by my strategic choice theory. Norms can influence the

---

[34] Charles L. Glaser, "Structural Realism in a More Complex World," *Review of International Studies* 29, 3 (July 2003): 412–413.

means that a state finds appropriate and should therefore influence its choice between alternative means.[35] Two norms are especially relevant to my theory: the nuclear taboo and the norm against targeting noncombatants. Examination of a number of cases of nuclear nonuse provides support for the argument that there is a norm against the first use of nuclear weapons: the United States has not used nuclear weapons in a number of cases in which its adversary lacked the capability to retaliate and in which nuclear use would have had military and/or coercive value.[36] Nevertheless, the implications of the norm for the theory are quite limited. This is because there is little evidence that the norm applies to cases in which states' truly vital interests are at stake, which are the type of case the theory focuses on.

For example, during the Cold War the United States relied on nuclear weapons primarily to deter a Soviet invasion of Western Europe and Soviet nuclear attacks against the U.S. homeland. Although evidence of a developing taboo comes from important U.S. cases—for example, the Korean and Vietnam wars—truly vital U.S. interests were not at stake in these conflicts, and nuclear weapons played a far less central role in U.S. plans for defending these interests. As a result, the norm did little to inform the core of U.S. nuclear strategy and force requirements and, closely related, did nothing to reduce the potential danger the United States saw in Soviet nuclear forces. Although the norm developed during the Cold War, the United States continued to maintain a first-nuclear-use doctrine and developed a sophisticated strategy and force structure to make its threats credible and escalation likely.[37] In addition, the United States worried a great deal about extremely improbable Soviet first strikes, reflecting its belief that the Soviet Union would not be constrained by a norm against the first use of nuclear weapons. And the United States acquired advanced nuclear forces that would be increasingly effective for attacking

[35] See Katzenstein, ed., *Culture of National Security*, especially Ronald L. Jepperson, Alexander Wendt, and Peter J. Katzenstein, "Norms, Identity and Culture in National Security," and Paul Kowert and Jeffrey Legro, "Norms, Identity, and Their Limits: A Theoretical Reprise."

[36] Nina Tannenwald, "The Nuclear Taboo: The United States and the Normative Basis of Nuclear Non-Use," *International Organization* 53, 3 (Summer 1999): 433–468, who emphasizes that the norm has constitutive effects, as well as regulative effects. See also T. V. Paul, "Nuclear Taboo and War Initiation in Regional Conflicts," *Journal of Conflict Resolution* 39, 4 (December 1995): 696–717. Somewhat ironically, the case for first use of nuclear weapons can be stronger in cases in which the adversary possesses nuclear weapons, if the state can use its nuclear weapons to significantly reduce the adversary's ability to inflict damage; consequently, cases in which the adversary lacks nuclear weapons are not the hardest test for the nuclear taboo. On the taboo against the use of chemical weapons, see Richard M. Price, *The Chemical Weapons Taboo* (Ithaca: Cornell University Press, 1997).

[37] See, for example, Paul J. Bracken, *The Command and Control of Nuclear Forces* (New Haven: Yale University Press, 1983).

Soviet forces, partly reflecting its desire to preserve the option of attacking first (or at least a close second). For its part, the Soviet Union felt threatened by the enhancements in U.S. counterforce capabilities, reflecting its lack of confidence that the United States would not use them first.[38] In short, the nuclear taboo failed to significantly influence U.S. nuclear doctrine and did not slow the arms race; nor did it increase the superpowers' security in the face of sophisticated nuclear forces. This is especially telling given that nuclear weapons created defense advantage that should have moderated competition and insecurity, which could have been reinforced by the nuclear taboo, if it had much influence.

The implications for the theory of the norm against targeting noncombatants is similarly small, for similar reasons—states that face a costly war of attrition have been willing to intentionally inflict large-scale civilian casualties once they have concluded that this might reduce their own casualties and might increase their prospects of winning the war.[39] Consequently, states have little reason to plan their strategies or assess their vulnerabilities assuming that adversaries will likely be restrained in the use of large-scale conventional force.

ARE STATES CAPABLE OF ASSESSING THE THEORY'S VARIABLES?

If states are unable to assess some of my theory's variables, the theory would need to be adapted. The revised theory might prescribe different strategies, and, as a result, the overall findings of my theory regarding cooperation and competition might then also need to be revised. In fact, doubts about whether states can measure the offense-defense balance and information about motives do play an important role in the debate over grand international relations theories. Concerns about measuring power are raised less frequently. This section argues briefly that states have the ability to measure the theory's key variables sufficiently well that the theory remains intact, and that each variable under a range of conditions can significantly influence a state's preferred strategy.

Among the theory's variables, *power* is generally considered the least problematic—none of the structural theories or their critics argues that power should not be included because states cannot measure it. While this may simply reflect the obvious importance of power, it may also reflect the belief that power is relatively easy to assess, requiring the mea-

[38] Raymond L. Garthoff, *Détente and Confrontation: American-Soviet Relations from Nixon to Reagan* (Washington, DC: Brookings, 1985), pp. 796–800.

[39] Alexander B. Downes, "Desperate Times, Desperate Measures: The Causes of Civilian Victimization in War," *International Security* 30, 4 (Spring 2006): 152–195; and Downes, *Targeting Civilians in War* (Ithaca: Cornell University Press, 2008).

surement of a number of observable features of states, including the standard list of population, territory, and GNP. To some degree this is certainly correct—for example, major powers are rarely confused with minor powers.[40] However, comparisons of states that are more similar are not so straightforward. In part, this is because power is far more complex than is suggested by a list of various types of material resources. Which resources are most important and how they combine depends on the nature of technology and of warfare, and a state's geopolitical setting. For example, is a wealthy state with a small population more powerful than a less wealthy state with a larger population? The elements of power that are most important can depend on whether a war is likely to be long or short, and on whether land or sea power is more important in determining its outcome; a state's prospects in an arms race can depend on whether it is likely to last years or instead decades. And states' abilities to assess deployed military forces will depend on the monitoring technologies that are not captured directly in measures of power. Moreover, as suggested above, power depends not only on material resources, but also on state capacity, including a state's ability to extract resources and convert them into effective military capabilities.

Estimates of future power promise to be more uncertain than estimates of current power. Future power is not observable, so states need to be able to analyze economic growth and technological innovation. State capacity may be especially important in determining future power, so the difficulty of measuring its elements adds to the uncertainty states will face. The range for error is suggested by prominent analyses in the 1980s that argued the United States was going to be a declining power.[41]

While expecting modern states to have the ability to measure at least many of the elements of power seems reasonable, research that has explored states' actual measurement of power identifies many challenges and finds a mixed record.[42] Major powers have exaggerated the importance of simplifying indicators, suffered from bureaucratic compartmentalization of assessments, and reached divergent conclusions about their power.[43] At other times, however, they have also done well at measuring

[40] This is not to claim, however, that major powers will always win wars against minor powers; see Ivan Arreguin-Toft, "How the Weak Win Wars: A Theory of Asymmetric Conflict," *International Security* 26, 1 (Summer 2001): 93–128; and Andrew J. R. Mack, "Why Big Nations Lose Small Wars: The Politics of Asymmetric Conflict," *World Politics* 27, 2 (January 1975): 175–200.

[41] See, for example, Paul M. Kennedy, *The Rise and Fall of Great Powers: Economic Change and Military Conflict, 1500–2000* (New York: Random House, 1987).

[42] Although there is a large literature on what constitutes power, much less work has focused on states' potential to measure it.

[43] On the first two points, see Aaron L. Friedberg, *The Weary Titan: Britain and the Experience of Relative Decline, 1985–1905* (Princeton: Princeton University Press, 1998); on

key aspects of both potential and deployed military power. U.S. assessment of Soviet power at the end of the Cold War is an important example because it is often portrayed as a major analytic failure. However, although often criticized for not appreciating Soviet weakness, in fact Central Intelligence Agency evaluations of the Soviet economy were quite good. Starting in the mid-1970s the CIA predicted reduced rates of growth that would make it difficult or impossible for the Soviet leadership to pursue both its traditional military and domestic goals, and identified deep structural problems that could result in economic stagnation.[44] Although few experts predicted the coming dramatic political changes, narrower assessments of Soviet power were quite sound. U.S. assessments of Soviet nuclear forces were also usually quite good—projections that turned out to be wrong often reflected the limits of available information; and, maybe especially important to the question of states' potential analytic capabilities, disagreements and mistakes often reflected organizational biases and the politicization of the estimating process, not limitations of the estimation process itself.[45]

Evaluations of power prior to World War I also provide useful examples. Instead of simply looking at the size of Russia's large population and army, states' estimates of Russia's power took into account two factors that reduced the significance of the raw numbers. Russia lacked social cohesion, which made sheer size less important. And, because the war was expected to be short, states believed that Russia's large population would have less impact than if the war was going to be long. As a result, although Russia's power was overrated, the gap was much smaller than would have been suggested by size alone.[46] Regarding Germany's assessment, Holger Herwig concludes that "On the whole, however, the General Staff and the Admiralty Staff seem to have been able to gauge the forces and probable disposition of the Entente powers with high accu-

the latter, see William Curti Wohlforth, "The Perception of Power: Russia in the Pre–1914 Balance," *World Politics* 39, 3 (April 1989): 353–381; and Wohlforth, *The Elusive Balance*. There is a tricky issue here that I am glossing over: states decide on how much to invest in analytic capabilities and how to design them; therefore, whether a failure of analysis reflects suboptimal investment or instead the inherent difficulty of the analysis is complicated to determine. How effectively states have evaluated power, therefore, tells us something about their potential but may well underestimate it, especially if the time frame for creating improved analytic capabilities is sufficiently long.

[44] Daniel M. Berkowitz et al., "An Evaluation of the CIA's Analysis of Soviet Economic Performance, 1970–90," *Comparative Economic Studies* 35, 1 (Summer 1993): 33–57; among other points, the authors argue that the CIA did at least as well as academic specialists in evaluating both the economy and the possible domestic political scenarios generated by these problems.

[45] Lawrence Freedman, *U.S. Intelligence and the Soviet Strategic Threat,* 2nd ed. (Princeton: Princeton University Press, 1986).

[46] Wohlforth, "The Perception of Power," pp. 369–371.

racy. . . . the German sense of peril in 1914 is clearly not ascribable to defects in the system of collecting or appraising intelligence."[47]

While this brief discussion does not raise serious doubts about including power in the theory, it does make clear that power is sufficiently complex that states will sometimes find it difficult to measure. Three implications follow. First, states may often have to make decisions facing uncertainty about power. Chapter 4 addressed some of the implications of this uncertainty for arms competition and war, and they may deserve more attention. Second, and related, small advantages or disadvantages in measured power should rarely, if ever, significantly influence a state's decisions: given the complexity of power, small differences in measured power will often not reflect real differences.[48] Third, power is sufficiently complex that rational states may reach different conclusions about their power without making analytic mistakes or holding private information.[49] This possibility adds to the potential sources of competition and war.

In contrast to their treatment of power, critics have argued that the *offense-defense balance* should not be included as a defining element of a state's international environment because states lack the analytic capability required to measure it.[50] Not including the offense-defense balance means in effect setting the balance to 1, reflecting states' inability to judge whether offensive missions are more difficult or costly than defensive ones. In chapter 5 I addressed some criticisms of the offense-defense balance—including the impact of the indistinguishability of offense and defense and the closeness of the offense-defense balance to 1—that bear on the feasibility of measurement and found them wanting. One point that I emphasized there is that the analytic tasks required to measure the balance are the same as those required to perform military net assessments; states that can perform net assessments can measure the offense-defense balance. Here I provide additional support for the position that states often have the capability to perform net assessments or related calculations that can be used to estimate the balance.

The easiest case concerns nuclear weapons. Detailed examinations of

---

[47] Holger H. Herwig, "Imperial Germany," in Ernest R. May, ed., *Knowing One's Enemies: Intelligence Assessment before the Two World Wars* (Princeton: Princeton University Press, 1986), pp. 70, 72; he argues instead that Germany's errors reflected the perceptual framework of its leaders.

[48] Possibly more important, even real differences in power will not translate into outcomes because power does not translate directly into military capability.

[49] These states may not be strictly rational but could be boundedly rational, doing as well as highly capable states facing real-world complexity can be expected to do. See chapter 4 for more on this issue.

[50] See chapter 5 for a discussion of this and other criticisms of the offense-defense balance.

possible U.S.–Soviet nuclear exchanges showed that neither country could get close to acquiring a significant damage-limitation capability, demonstrating that defense had a large advantage.[51] Although there was extensive debate about the adequacy of the U.S. nuclear deterrent, this debate was driven by disagreements about the requirements of deterrence, not by disagreements over the capability or interaction of U.S. and Soviet forces.

During the Cold War, net assessments performed by civilian analysts established the foundation for extensive debate over NATO's prospects for defeating a possible Soviet offensive in Central Europe. The "3 to 1" rule played an important role in many of these assessments, reflecting a belief that the offense-defense balance, at least at the tactical level, was much greater than 1. The overall result of these net assessments was to make clear that simply comparing the size of NATO and Warsaw Pact forces—that is, actual deployed power—was misleading. Instead, NATO needed to analyze its ability to defeat a Soviet blitzkrieg, and the finding was that its prospects for successfully defending were much greater than suggested by simply looking at the ratio of forces.[52] In other words, at least at the force levels that were relevant, defense had a significant advantage in the European theater. This advantage not only influenced the capabilities of deployed forces but also made clear that to gain an effective offensive conventional capability the Soviet Union would require power much greater than NATO's.

Although there has been extensive criticism of the quality of certain past net assessments, much of this criticism finds that the flaws were politically and/or bureaucratically motivated, not due to the inherent infeasibility of the task.[53] The most famous net assessment failures are probably the overestimates before 1914 of the French, German and other European militaries of their prospects for successful offensives against

[51] Important examples include Alain C. Enthoven and K. Wayne Smith, *How Much Is Enough? Shaping the Defense Program, 1961–1969* (New York: Harper and Row, 1971), which describes calculations done in the Pentagon during the 1960s; Congressional Budget Office, *Counterforce Issues for the U.S. Strategic Offensive Forces* (Washington, DC: U.S. Government Printing Office, 1978); Michael M. May, George F. Bing, and John Steinbruner, "Strategic Arsenals after START: The Implications for Deep Cuts," *International Security* 13, 1 (Summer 1988): 90–133; and Salman, Sullivan, and Van Evera, "Analysis or Propaganda?"

[52] John J. Mearsheimer, "Why the Soviets Can't Win Quickly in Central Europe," *International Security* 7, 1 (Summer 1982): 3–39; Barry R. Posen, "Measuring the European Conventional Balance: Coping with Complexity in Threat Assessment," *International Security* 9, 3 (Winter 1984–85): 47–88; and Stephen D. Biddle, "The European Conventional Balance: A Reinterpretation of the Debate," *Survival* (March–April 1988): 99–121.

[53] This discussion draws on Glaser and Kaufmann, "What Is the Offense-Defense Balance and Can We Measure It," pp. 76–77.

each other, generally known as the "cult of the offensive."[54] While all of the European militaries recognized that increased firepower and higher force densities would make frontal assaults drastically more expensive, certain militaries, because of a combination of bureaucratic incentives, class interests, and domestic political threats, chose to believe that "morale" would somehow overcome bullets. In fact, however, not only was this escape from the structural constraint infeasible, but its infeasibility was knowable in advance. The evidence from the American Civil War, Franco-Prussian War, Russo-Turkish War, Boer War, and Russo-Japanese War was already in. Unbiased observers, both civilians and some junior officers, correctly predicted that frontal assaults would be impossible, as did the German military.[55]

The German Army, recognizing that frontal assault would be infeasible, but motivated by bureaucratic and political needs to find an offensive solution to a two-front war against France and Russia, chose to pin its hopes on a wide flanking maneuver through Belgium (the Schlieffen Plan). This, however, was logistically impossible, given the distances that advancing Germans and their supplies would have to cover by foot and horse-drawn wagon, while the French and the British defenders could react by rail. This too was knowable, and in fact it was known to the General Staff. Chief of Staff Helmuth von Moltke, who was maligned for weakening Schlieffen's original commitment to an overly strong "Right Wing," was only recognizing logistic reality.[56] In addition, German planners recognized that defense had the advantage for the mission required by the Schlieffen Plan. Although German forces significantly outnumbered French forces, German generals believed they were nevertheless too small for the flanking operation; their estimates suggest a balance of 2 to 1 or greater, not including the further defensive impact of logistical constraints. In fact, Germany did not choose an offensive strategy because it believed that offense had the advantage; instead, this decision reflected either a suboptimal decision or a high-risk strategy for dealing with its geopolitical position.[57] Thus, the errors of 1914 were avoidable; accurate net assessments, and therefore accurate estimates of the offense-defense balance, were feasible, and Germany actually performed much of this analysis. It seems likely that unbiased net assess-

[54] Stephen Van Evera, "The Cult of the Offensive and the Origins of the First World War," *International Security* 9, 1 (Summer 1984): 58–107.

[55] Michael Howard, "Men against Fire: Expectations of War in 1914," *International Security* 9, 1 (Summer 1984): 41–57; William McElwee, *The Art of War: Waterloo to Mons* (Bloomington: Indiana University Press, 1974), pp. 147–255.; and Lieber, *War and the Engineers*, pp. 80–88.

[56] Martin Van Crevald, *Supplying War: Logistics from Wallerstein to Patton* (Cambridge: Cambridge University Press, 1977), pp. 109–141.

[57] See chapter 9 for a more detailed discussion of this case.

ment before World War I would have shown that the advantage of the defense was so large that no European major power could attack another with much chance of success.

States have also used estimates of the offense-defense balance in developing requirements for naval forces. In the period before World War I, Germany judged that the offense-defense balance when facing a close blockade imposed by the British was 3 to 2 and defined its force requirements in terms of this ratio. Germany also understood that the ratio would be less favorable to the defense if instead of a close blockade Britain imposed a distant blockade, which it did during the war. Fighting during the war was consistent with these estimates, with the German Navy essentially unwilling to challenge the British blockade, although given the force ratios this provides limited information about the actual balance. During the interwar period, Japan also judged that it enjoyed a naval defensive advantage, in this case against a U.S. attack across the Pacific, such that its defensive force needed to be 70 percent as large as the attacking force. This reflected both an assessment of the nature of naval battles and the attrition that the Japanese Navy believed it could impose on U.S. forces crossing the Pacific.[58]

As with the offense-defense balance, a possible concern about including *information about motives* as a variable is that states cannot measure it; if so, then the information variable would not provide much analytic leverage because states would always face such great uncertainty about others' motives. There is no doubt that motives—both their type and extent—are complex and difficult to evaluate. Motives are less directly observable than are material variables, and there is even less agreement on how states do, or should, evaluate them. The potential difficulty of the task is suggested by the U.S. experience during the Cold War—although a extensive effort was devoted to the task, American experts nevertheless continued to disagree quite substantially about Soviet motives;[59] serious disagreement about Soviet power and forces was much narrower.

We need, however, to keep in mind that states do not need to eliminate uncertainty for their estimates of the adversary's motives to be valuable; consequently, it is important not to exaggerate the standard for variation in information. Under a variety of material conditions, being able to put

---

[58] David C. Evans and Mark R. Peattie, *Kaigun: Strategy, Tactics, and Technology in the Imperial Japanese Navy, 1887–1941* (Annapolis: Naval Institute Press, 1997), pp. 141–144: and Stephen E. Pelz, *Race to Pearl Harbor: The Failure of the Second London Naval Conference and the Onset of World War II* (Cambridge: Harvard University Press, 1974), pp. 41–44. There are reasons to question the quality of this estimate, however, because the navy did not adjust as technology changed significantly.

[59] For a review of the debate, see Seay, "What Are the Soviets' Objectives in Their Foreign, Military, and Arms Control Policies?"

the probability that an opposing state is greedy within a wide range (to be distinguished from precise probabilities)—for example, high, medium (that is, roughly as likely to be greedy as security seeking), or low—can be quite useful, playing a significant role in the state's choice between cooperative and competitive policies.

From this perspective, the empirical claim that states cannot make useful distinctions about others' motives seems obviously false. A few current examples illustrate the point. The United States currently believes that Russia is less likely to be a greedy state (and if greedy, is less greedy) than the Soviet Union was during the Cold War. The United States does not view North Korean nuclear weapons (or future Iranian ones) and British nuclear weapons as equally threatening, largely because it is confident that British motives are benign.[60] And, while not as confident about current and future Russian motives, the United States is nevertheless much less worried by the large nuclear arsenal that Russia continues to deploy than by the possibility that North Korea might have built a handful of crude nuclear weapons. The United States does not now worry about a future threat from the European Union but does from China, which largely reflects different assessments of their motives, given that the EU now possesses much greater wealth and more advanced technology, and has the potentially to integrate politically in the time frame that will be required for China's power to be comparable to America's. Moreover, studies that have focused on states' understanding of others' motives have identified a number of cases in which this information significantly influenced states' policies: for example, revised Russian assessments of German motives in the 1890s contributed to Russia's decision to form an alliance with France;[61] and Hitler's negative assessment of Russia's motives increased Germany's insecurity and contributed to its decisions for expansion.[62]

Although the preceding assessments could include information provided by costly signals, the key issue here is states' abilities to assess others' motives prior to (or at least separate from) their strategic interaction. Once states interact, costly signals, which are an integral part of the strategic choice theory, help to explain changes in assessments of motives. Theories of how states initially judge others' motives focus on states' internal characteristics. I briefly review these arguments because they help

---

[60] Wendt, "Constructing International Politics," p. 73.

[61] Edelstein, "Managing Uncertainty," pp. 19–24; Edelstein focuses on intentions, but much of his analysis includes assessments of motives.

[62] Mark L. Haas, *The Ideological Origins of Great Power Politics, 1798–1989* (Ithaca: Cornell University Press, 2005), pp. 105–120; see also John W. Owen IV, *Liberal Peace, Liberal War: American Politics and International Security* (Ithaca: Cornell University Press, 1997), which focuses on U.S. decisions.

to understand the empirical finding that states can make meaningful assessments of motives, and support it.[63] There is full agreement neither on
which state characteristics are most important, nor on the extent to which
states will ever be able to be confident that they do not face a greedy
state.[64]

One family of arguments focus on states' ideology. One strand of these
arguments holds that politically liberal states find each other to be relatively unthreatening. For example, politically liberal states have found
U.S. power unthreatening because their liberal elite leaders share key interests with the United States.[65] A related, more general strand of argument holds that states see each other as less threatening as the ideological
difference between them decreases. According to this argument, the clash
of ideologies between the United States and the Soviet Union contributed
to their Cold War competition, forming and supporting beliefs on both
sides that the other harbored malign motives, and the end of the Cold
War is partly explained by changes in Soviet ideology.[66] A related but different set of arguments focuses on regime type, explaining that democracies have created a collective identity, based on beliefs about shared
norms, motives, and interests, that leads them to expect that they will not
fight each other.[67] Still another argument focuses on the transparent policy processes that characterize modern democracies—according to this
argument, an opposing state can tell whether a democracy is a security
seeker by observing its electoral, legislative, and bureaucratic politics.[68]
More broadly, many of the arguments that make up democratic peace
theory include arguments about the information that democracies have
about other democracies' motives, whether flowing from beliefs about
values, normative and institutional constraints, evaluative capabilities,
and/or identity. Much of the democratic peace can be understood as flowing from this information about motives. Finally, a different process-
based argument holds that states garner information about others' motives by observing how they remember and acknowledge their history: a
state that distorts or whitewashes its violent past leads former enemies to
fear that it harbors greedy motives.[69]

---

[63] For review of many of these arguments see Edelstein, "Choosing Friends and Enemies,"
chap. 2.

[64] Compare, for example, Kydd, "Sheep in Sheep's Clothing," and Edelstein, "Managing
Uncertainty."

[65] Owen, "Transnational Liberalism and U.S. Primacy."

[66] Haas, *The Ideological Origins of Great Power Politics.*

[67] Risse-Kappen, "Collective Identity in a Democratic Community"; and Risse-Kappen,
Cooperation among Democracies.

[68] Kydd, "Sheep in Sheep's Clothing," pp. 129–139.

[69] Jennifer M. Lind, *Sorry States: Apologies in International Relations* (Ithaca: Cornell
University Press, 2008).

Another potential source of information about motives may lie in the economic value of territorial expansion. A range of arguments holds that territory is now less valuable and, with the exception of critical natural resources, may not be valuable at all for increasing a state's wealth. Key arguments address the implications for states' wealth of the importance of knowledge-based production versus industrial production and of the globalization of production.[70] States that understand the reduced economic value of territory are less likely to be greedy; from this perspective, motives are partly endogenous to the structure of economic production. In turn, states that understand this relationship will have grounds for judging other states to be less likely to be greedy and/or less greedy. And examinations of the lack of recent major-power war suggest that states are capable of making these assessments.

In short, although not a great deal of research has focused on these issues, this section finds that modern states appear capable of making useful assessments of my theory's key variables. This is not to say states will always make these assessments effectively, but only that making them is not usually beyond their potential analytic capabilities.

ARE THE THEORY'S DEDUCTIONS LOGICALLY SOUND?

The final step in evaluating my theory from within is to consider whether its deductions are logically sound. Needless to say, I believe they are. Efforts to critique and confirm the deductions will have to fall to other scholars. Here I briefly note the existing support; in chapter 5, I have already addressed a number of challenges to the theory's logic.

Some of the theory's basic deductions find support in game-theoretic models, which provide a check on the internal logic of the theory's arguments.[71] In particular, Andrew Kydd's work on signaling and information produces similar results. One of the theory's less intuitive findings is that interaction between rational security seekers can lead each to conclude that the other is more likely to be greedy; in other words, the security dilemma can generate a negative spiral in political relations without either state suffering misperceptions. Kydd's analysis supports this finding. It also supports the finding that a state's decision to cooperate should depend on its initial beliefs about the adversary's type—that is, whether a

---

[70] On the former, see Van Evera, "Primed for Peace," pp. 14–16; and Carl Kaysen, "Is War Obsolete: A Review Essay," *International Security* 14, 4 (Spring 1990): 48–57; on the latter, see Stephen G. Brooks, "The Globalization of Production and the Changing Benefits of Conquest," *Journal of Conflict Resolution* 43, 5 (October 1999): 646–670. For a different perspective, see Liberman, *Does Conquest Pay.*

[71] On this benefit of formal models, see Powell, *In the Shadow of Power,* pp. 29–31.

security seeker should cooperate depends on its prior belief about whether its adversary is a greedy state; and that costly signals can reassure the adversary—that is, lead it to positively revise its estimate that the state is a security seeker.[72]

Other game-theoretic models provide support for the basic offense-defense argument that military spending will increase as the balance moves toward offense. In a model in which states value consumption and must invest in military forces to defend themselves, Robert Powell shows that a shift toward offense advantages leads both states to spend more—for any ratio of investment in military forces, the shift toward offense increases the probability that the attacking state will win, which leads states to invest more to deter attack.[73] Powell also finds that offense advantage increases the probability of war, but he argues that there are countervailing effects that are not captured in the standard intuition, which is that war becomes more likely because the state fighting on the offense has a greater probability of winning. He argues that while offense advantage does increase a dissatisfied state's probability of winning and thereby its value for starting a war, offense advantage also leads the defender to offer more in prewar negotiations because it recognizes that the potential attacker values war more highly. Although these effects push in opposite directions, the model finds that war becomes more likely.[74]

In closing, having worked though a wide spectrum of detailed arguments, it is useful to summarize the bottom line. Although it does not replace the need for extensive empirical testing, exploring the theory from within provides substantial confidence. First, I have argued that my theory's core assumptions are sufficiently accurate to provide a strong foundation on which to build the deductive theory. The anarchy, rationality, and unitary-actor assumptions are well matched to my theory's central goals. The primary caution concerns black boxing the adversary—when a state's policy might influence the balance of domestic power in an opposing state, the theory's prescriptions might need to be modified. Second, given its focus on strategic interaction, the theory either includes the variables that are required to address its central questions about competition and cooperation, or points the way to a more elaborate theory that in-

---

[72] Kydd's models differ in certain respects from the arguments I have laid out but capture the interactions and possibilities I have focused on. Our work on these issues has evolved over the past decade. For early statements, see Glaser, "The Security Dilemma Revisited"; Kydd, "Game Theory and the Spiral Model"; and more recently, Kydd, *Trust and Mistrust*.

[73] Powell, *In the Shadow of Power*, chap. 2.

[74] Ibid., chap. 3, esp. pp. 110–113. Powell also builds a different model that shows offense advantage increases the probability of war; in this model building arms reduces the value of living in the status quo but increases a state's deterrent; see chap. 2.

cludes additional variables that flow directly from those already included, for example, adding uncertainty about power as a natural extension of having already included power. Most of what is not included in my strategic choice theory lies in different layers of theory—either a prior layer that explains the theory's independent variables or a following layer that explains divergences from the rational baseline—and therefore does not raise concerns about the completeness of the theory's variables. These layers necessarily stand largely separate from each other, although they are complementary and can be combined into a more complete theory. Third, based on available research, states are found to be capable of assessing the theory's variables, which is required for the theory to be valuable in providing a rational baseline and prescriptive guidance. Finally, the theory appears to be deductively sound, although confidence here will have to await the scrutiny of other scholars.

CHAPTER EIGHT

Evaluating the Theory—Important Cases and Useful Comparisons

ALTHOUGH RESEARCH ON states' flawed decisions—regarding arming, doctrine, and war—does provide grounds for doubting that states always act rationally, it does not suggest that states always, or even usually, adopt suboptimal military strategies. In cases when states act rationally, my theory should do well at explaining their behavior. To illustrate the theory's ability to explain states' choices and its strengths compared to key alternative theories, this chapter briefly analyzes three important cases— the end of the Cold War, post–Cold War security politics in Europe and Asia, and Germany's decisions for expansion under Hitler.[1]

Beyond providing additional confidence in my theory, exploring cases in which it does explain state behavior provides the opportunity to compare the theory to similar theories that contain fewer variables. If a simpler theory does as well at explaining these cases, my theory's additional complexity might be unwarranted. The standard argument is that the simpler theory would be preferable, explaining as much but with greater parsimony.[2] Exploring these important cases lends support to the basic intuition that information variables and variation in motives, as well as material variables, are required for an adequate rational theory.

This chapter first explores the end of the Cold War, demonstrating the importance of the combined effect of material and information variables

---

[1] Chapter 9 evaluates cases of arms racing and cooperation and finds a number—including the intrawar naval agreements between the United States and Japan, the U.S. nuclear buildup to an assured destruction capability, and the ABM Treaty—in which the theory does explain state behavior, as well as others in which states' strategies are judged suboptimal.

[2] Although a bit of a digression, I should add that I do not entirely accept this argument—if the intuition for including a basic variable is strong, and deductive arguments show that it should influence a state's behavior under some conditions, then including the variable can have value, even if the variable does not increase the theory's current explanatory power. If there are reasons to believe that the variable has not taken on its full range of possible values, then the variable may be important in explaining the future, if not the past. And from the perspective of a normative/prescriptive theory, including the variable can identify possibilities that would otherwise be overlooked. For example, excluding information variables from grand IR theories reduces the prospects for peaceful great-power relations. Of course, this argument for including variables that lack explanatory power raises difficult issues concerning which variables have the standing to be included.

on Soviet decisions and the role of costly signals in influencing U.S. decisions. The chapter then compares current major-power relations in Europe and East Asia, arguing that information about motives is the key to appreciating why policies are more competitive in Asia. The chapter ends with an analysis of Hitler's Germany, arguing that greedy motives are necessary to explain Germany's expansionist policies.

One way to read this chapter is as a comparison of defensive realism to the more general theory presented here. The central role of information about motives in the Cold War and post–Cold War cases demonstrates advantages of my theory compared to defensive realism. At the same time, the importance of material variables—on their own and in interaction with information variables—supports the need for including both types of variables and weighs against developing a theory built entirely on information variables. The central role of greedy motives in the case of Hitler's Germany shows the theory's advantages compared to theories built entirely on the interaction of security-seeking states, including defensive realism.

End of the Cold War

The introduction briefly discussed the importance of U.S. estimates of Soviet motives in explaining the end of the Cold War; this short section extends that discussion, first addressing the role of international situational variables in influencing Soviet decisions and then reviewing the role of costly Soviet signals in U.S. assessments of Soviet motives.

Why the Soviet Union changed its security policy dramatically during the second half of the 1980s has received a great deal of attention. Although analysts have emphasized a variety of factors, power appears to be an essential ingredient of the answer. By the beginning of the 1980s, Soviet leaders were increasingly worried about declining Soviet economic growth and the growing gap with the United States. We now know that Soviet leaders were well informed about not only the problems with their economy, but also the burden posed by high military spending and the priority that the military received in the allocation of resources required for economic growth.[3] Soviet GNP was much smaller than U.S. GNP throughout the Cold War. By the late 1980s, recognition of declining growth rates and growing gaps in high technology led Soviet leaders to conclude that effective military competition was becoming increasingly beyond their reach. Reflecting his understanding of these resource con-

[3] Brooks and Wohlforth, "Power, Globalization and the End of the Cold War," esp. pp. 28–33.

straints, in 1986 Gorbachev argued to his Politburo colleagues, "Our goal is to prevent the next round of the arms race. If we do not accomplish it, the threat to us will only grow. We will be pulled into another round of the arms race that is beyond our capabilities, and we will lose it."[4] Consistent with the theory, a state that expects to lose an arms race because it lacks the power to compete should try to avoid it.[5]

Although there is a lag between Soviet economic decline and shifts in Soviet policy, some analysts conclude that the timing is sufficiently close and the constraints sufficiently severe that power had a direct and possibly dominant effect on Soviet decisions. Others argue that although important, declining Soviet power is best understood as opening a "window" that created the opportunity for essential arguments about restraint and cooperation to gain traction in the Soviet debate. Either way, power played an important role in Soviet decisions.[6]

The Soviet willingness to adopt a cooperative strategy was also influenced by other situational variables. Nuclear weapons, which greatly favored defense (via deterrence), made it relatively safe for the Soviet Union to cap or reduce its investment in military forces, and even to unilaterally reduce its conventional forces and then to give up the territorial buffer provided by Eastern Europe. At the same time, nuclear weapons made competitive solutions to decline unattractive. A standard possibility for a declining state is to launch a preventive war, taking advantage of its current capabilities before they decay. But nuclear weapons precluded the preventive war option—the defense advantage that they provide the United States meant that the Soviet Union could not reasonably hope to stop its decline by launching a conventional preventive war against U.S. allies or a nuclear preventive war against the United States; in both cases the likelihood of potentially massive nuclear retaliation made this path

---

[4] Quoted in ibid., p. 29. But see Robert English, "Power, Ideas, and New Evidence on the Cold War's End," *International Security* 26, 4 (Spring 2002): 81, who argues that Brooks and Wohlforth fail to consider the political context of this statement; and Brooks and Wohlforth, "From Old Thinking to New Thinking in Qualitative Research," *International Security* 26, 4 (Spring 2002): 93–111, for responses.

[5] Soviet recognition of their deteriorating economic situation also convinced them of the value of gaining access to the global economy, which required improving relations with the West.

[6] On the former, see Brooks and Wohlforth, "Power, Globalization and the End of the Cold War"; on the latter—second-image reversed type arguments about power and ideas—see, for example, Matthew Evangelista, *Unarmed Forces*, who emphasizes the impact of transnational movements on Gorbachev's thinking (p. 290) and domestic policy windows (pp. 330–331); and Jeff Checkel, "Ideas, Institutions, and the Gorbachev Foreign Policy Revolution," *World Politics* 45, 2 (January 1993): 271–300, who emphasizes the role of institutionalized expertise. See also Mark Kramer, "Ideology and the Cold War," *Review of International Studies* 25, 4 (October 1999): 563–576, who emphasizes the importance of including ideological change for understanding Gorbachev's decisions.

far too risky. Soviet leaders did not discuss preventive war, but this is not a problem for my theory—the reality of massive nuclear vulnerability was sufficiently clear that the option was simply not on the table.

This does leave open the question of why the Soviet Union adopted these more competitive policies in the first place—that is, why did not nuclear weapons lead it to adopt more cooperative geopolitical, conventional, and nuclear policies sooner? An important part of the answer appears to lie in changes in Soviet information about the United States— both its motives and its view of Soviet motives. Into the mid-1980s Soviet leaders continued to see the United States as inherently aggressive, reflecting the natural inclination of capitalist systems. The views held by the Soviet leadership began to change under Gorbachev, who started to argue that the United States did not pose a threat to the Soviet Union, which reflected a reassessment of the foreign policies of capitalist systems.[7] This more benign view of U.S. motives made cooperation more attractive to Soviet leaders because they now believed that Soviet restraint was more likely to be reciprocated and/or because concessions were less risky.[8] Distinct, but related, Soviet leaders came to appreciate that the United States was threatened by Soviet military forces, reflecting the belief that the United States believed the Soviet Union had malign motives. Closely related, Gorbachev and Soviet civilian reformers came to appreciate that "one side cannot be secure at the expense of the other side's security."[9] This understanding laid the foundation for Soviet efforts to change the U.S. image of the Soviet Union, including unilateral concessions, a shift to more defensive conventional forces, and efforts to continue with arms control agreements even as the United States pursued the Strategic Defense Initiative (SDI). All these efforts were fueled by this Soviet appreciation of their security dilemma.[10]

Given that all these variables—power, the offense-defense balance, and

[7] Checkel, "Ideas, Institutions, and the Gorbachev Foreign Policy Revolution," pp. 288–291. This changed understanding of capitalism also included a positive assessment of its long-term economic prospects, which further supported the case for Soviet retrenchment.

[8] There is a difficult question about whether Soviet recognition of their own decline fueled the change in their understanding of the U.S. motives and of the offense-defense balance; if it did, these other variables are endogenous to power and have less explanatory power than analyses that focus on them might suggest. For alternative perspectives, see, for example, Brooks and Wohlforth, "Power, Globalization and the End of the Cold War," compared to Checkel, "Ideas, Institutions, and the Gorbachev Foreign Policy Revolution," and Matthew Evangelista, "Norms, Heresthetics, and the End of the Cold War," *Journal of Cold War Studies* 3, 1 (Winter 2001): 5–35.

[9] Evangelista, *Unarmed Forces*, pp. 184, 305–306. It is interesting that a parallel understanding was developing in the United States; see Melvyn P. Leffler, *For the Soul of Mankind: The United States, the Soviet Union and the Cold War* (New York: Hill and Wang, 2007), pp. 356–365, on the evolution of Reagan's understanding of the Soviet Union.

[10] On Soviet new thinkers, see Robert D. English, *Russia and the Idea of the West* (New

information about motives—point in the same direction, the end of the Cold War might appear to be somewhat overdetermined, raising the possibility of a simpler, more parsimonious theory.[11] However, all these variables contribute to the explanation, and different values on any single variable could have led to different Soviet policies. For example, if other international situational variables had taken different values, declining power might well have led to different outcomes: if offense had had the advantage, the Soviet Union might have decided to fight from its position of declining strength instead of making concessions that increased its military vulnerability; if Soviet leaders were convinced that American motives were highly malign and that the United States was bent on expansion, cooperative policies would have looked much riskier and they might have tried to compete for longer and rejected domestic liberalization; and if Soviet leaders believed that the United States believed the Soviet Union was a security seeker and therefore was not a threat, the case for unilateral reductions, shifting to more defensive conventional forces, and continuing to pursue arms control would have been much weaker. In sum, not only does each of these three variables contribute to a fuller explanation of the Soviet decisions that brought about the end of the Cold War, but excluding any of them would mean overlooking an important ingredient of this outcome.[12]

My theory also helps to understand the end of the Cold War from the U.S. side. In the introduction I argued that a theory that focuses only on material factors cannot explain why the Cold War ended as early as it did. The capability of Soviet deployed forces had not declined significantly; Soviet actions that reduced their capability or reflected a willingness to adopt cooperative policies could have been reversed; and although the United States knew that the Soviet economy was experiencing increasing difficulties, there was little reason to believe that the Soviet Union could not maintain large nuclear and conventional forces well into the future. Therefore, information about Soviet motives must be a key

---

York: Columbia University Press, 2000); and Michael MccGwire, *Perestroika and Soviet National Security* (Washington, DC: Brookings, 1991).

[11] In this spirit, see Stephen G. Brooks and William C. Wohlforth, "Economic Constraints and the End of the Cold War," in William C. Wohlforth, ed., *Cold War Endgame: Oral History, Analysis, Debates* (University Park: Pennsylvania State University Press, 2003), who argue that although many factors contributed to the end of the Cold War, this should not be allowed to cloud our understanding of the far-reaching implications of Soviet economic decline. For an analysis that identifies still more factors, see Daniel Deudney and G. John Ikenberry, "The International Sources of Soviet Change," *International Security* 16, 3 (Winter 1991–1992): 74–118.

[12] The explanation I have sketched does, however, leave open important questions about the process by which Soviet leaders came to understand these variables, especially the initial values of the information variables, which are not explained by U.S. signaling.

factor in understanding U.S. reactions. Here I add to this explanation by reviewing the role of costly Soviet signals in contributing to the U.S. reassessment.[13]

Starting in 1987 the Soviet Union made a series of changes in its military and foreign policy—including negotiating the Intermediate-range Nuclear Forces (INF) Treaty, withdrawing from Afghanistan, and making large unilateral reductions in conventional forces—that led the United States to favorably change its assessment of Soviet motives.[14] In the INF Treaty both countries gave up their intermediate-range missiles. Arguably the United States traded away the strategically more important systems because its missiles could quickly hit militarily valuable targets in the Soviet Union. However, the United States considered the treaty a significant success because Soviet deployment of SS-20s had started this round of arms competition and NATO had adopted its "dual track" strategy—deploying new missiles and simultaneously negotiating—with the goal of offsetting and ideally eliminating the Soviet intermediate-range systems.[15] Maybe most significant here, the Soviet Union's increased cooperation, which included allowing verification of the treaty with unprecedentedly intrusive on-site inspection, sent a costly signal because this policy was more likely to be pursued by a security seeker that was willing to accept the status quo than by a greedy state that was determined to change it.

Soviet unilateral cuts in conventional forces provided a still clearer and more significant indication of Soviet motives. In late 1988 Gorbachev announced large cuts in Soviet conventional forces—reductions of 500,000 men facing Western Europe, including six tank divisions in Eastern Europe—to be carried out over two years. These reductions would greatly reduce, if not eliminate, the possibility of a short-notice surprise attack; the feasibility of surprise attack was reduced not only by the size of the cuts, but also by elimination of specific equipment required to sup-

---

[13] For an alternative explanation, see Mark L. Haas, "The United States and the End of the Cold War: Reactions to Shifts in Soviet Power, Policies, or Domestic Politics?," *International Organization* 61, 1 (Winter 2007): 145–179, who argues that liberal ideological change was the key to changes in U.S. assessments of Soviet motives.

[14] See Kydd, *Trust and Mistrust*, for an analysis of these actions in terms of costly signals, as well as discussion of some earlier policies—including a nuclear test moratorium and the Reykjavik summit—that were not sufficiently costly to dramatically influence U.S. assessments; see also Alan R. Collins, "GRIT, Gorbachev and the end of the Cold War," *Review of International Studies* 24, 2 (1998): 201–219; and Richard A. Bitzinger, "Gorbachev and GRIT, 1985–89: Did Arms Control Succeed Because of Unilateral Actions or in Spite of Them?," *Contemporary Security Policy* 15, 1 (April 1994): 68–79.

[15] See Thomas Risse-Kappen, "Did 'Peace through Strength' End the Cold War: Lessons from INF," *International Security* 16, 1 (Summer 1991): 162–188, for analysis of the debate on why NATO succeeded.

port a Soviet offensive.[16] NATO was able to observe the reinforcements that would be required before the Soviet Union could launch an offensive, which insured that it would have the time required to respond effectively. Throughout the Cold War, Soviet forces and doctrine for launching a conventional invasion of Western Europe were likely the clearest signal of Soviet greedy motives.[17] The offensive orientation of Soviet doctrine was highlighted by comparisons to NATO's much more defensive doctrine for protecting its side of the inter-German border. By launching an initiative that significantly reduced Russia's offensive conventional capabilities, Gorbachev provided a costly signal that enabled the United States to favorably revise its assessment of Soviet motives.

In sum, analyzing the end of the Cold War demonstrates the importance of the full range of international situational variables—material and information—as well as the role of strategic interaction in providing states with information about others' motives. Although theories that include fewer variables can explain aspects of this case, they fail to provide a balanced understanding, overlooking not only variables that played a significant role in producing the end of the Cold War, but also the conditional nature of the impact of the variables that they do identify.

Post–Cold War Europe and Northeast Asia

This section uses the theory to explain the difference between post–Cold War major-power politics in Europe and Northeast Asia. While there is wide (although not complete) agreement that Europe is likely to remain peaceful, assessments of Northeast Asia are more pessimistic or at least uncertain.[18] The security differences between the two regions are reflected in changes that have occurred in key alliances since the end of the Cold War. The United States has greatly reduced its conventional and

---

[16] By the fall of 1989 the National Intelligence Council, "Status of Soviet Unilateral Withdrawals," NIC M 89-10003, October 1989, concluded that the overall result would be "a very significant reduction in the offensive combat capability of Soviet forces in Eastern Europe," https://www.cia.gov/library/center-for-the-study-of-intelligence/csi-publications/books-and-monographs/at-cold-wars-end-us-intelligence-on-the-soviet-union-and-eastern-europe-1989-1991/16526pdffiles/NIC89-10003.pdf. See also Richard A. Falkenrath, *Shaping Europe's Military Order: The Origins and Consequences of the CFE Treaty* (Cambridge: MIT Press, 1995).

[17] Lebow, "The Soviet Offensive in Europe."

[18] For a pessimistic exception on Europe, see Mearsheimer, *The Tragedy of Great Power Politics*, chap. 10. For a review of the theoretical debate over Asia, see Aaron L. Friedberg, "The Future of U.S.–China Relations: Is Conflict Inevitable?," *International Security* 30, 2 (Fall 2005): 7–45.

nuclear forces deployed in Europe, and many experts question whether NATO has a continuing security purpose within Europe.[19] In contrast, the U.S.–Japan alliance has intensified its military cooperation, and Japan is beginning to grapple with becoming a more "normal" military power.[20] And the United States is pursuing a broad regional strategy designed to offset China's growing power.[21] Moreover, the differences between the two regions are likely larger than suggested by current behavior because although U.S. security guarantees reduce incentives for competition in both regions, they likely have a much larger moderating effect in Asia than in Europe. Although most concern about Asia now focuses on China's growing power, my theory suggests that information about states' motives is necessary to explain much of the difference between the two regions.

The theory provides two reinforcing lines of argument for why Europe is currently not only peaceful, but also noncompetitive, and why it is likely to remain so, even if the United States ends its security commitment to the region. One argument emphasizes information, the other material factors. However, the more fully convincing and satisfactory explanation considers the potentially reinforcing impact of information *and* material conditions that both support cooperation.

The information argument focuses on the possibility that all Western European powers are convinced of each other's benign motives, and all know that this information is widely shared.[22] Given this information, even following an American withdrawal these countries would not view each other's military forces, and more broadly their power and military potential, as threatening. Germany is not threatened by British and French nuclear forces, and German power does not pose a threat to Germany's neighbors. As a result, Germany can afford to remain nonnuclear, and France can afford not to exercise its military advantage even though Germany has the potential to match and exceed its military capabilities.

[19] For discussions of NATO's new purposes, see James B. Steinberg, "An Elective Partnership: Salvaging Transatlantic Relations," *Survival* 45, 2 (Summer 2003): 113–146; and Ivo Daalder and James Goldgeier, "Global NATO," *Foreign Affairs* 85, 5 (September/October 2006): 105–113.

[20] Christopher W. Hughes, "Japanese Military Modernization: In Search of a 'Normal' Security Role," in Ashley J. Tellis and Michael Wills, eds., *Strategic Asia 2005–06: Military Modernization in an Era of Uncertainty* (Seattle: National Bureau of Asian Research, 2005).

[21] Daniel Twining, "America's Grand Design in Asia," *Washington Quarterly* 31, 3 (Summer 2007): 79–94.

[22] As I discussed in chapter 6, this information argument at least partially parallels an argument that has been made by constructivists: see, for example, Adler and Barnett, "Security Communities in Theoretical Perspective"; Thomas Risse-Kappen, "Collective Identity in a Democratic Community," pp. 367–368; and Risse-Kappen, *Cooperation among Democracies*.

In addition, because both are confident that the other knows its assessment, both countries are confident the other is secure and therefore neither will compete to increase its own security. Similar arguments explain why Britain and France would not feel the need to balance against Germany's greater economic power and military potential, even if nuclear weapons did not exist. Moreover, having been freed by their initial information from the imperative to compete, the Western European powers have adopted cooperative, integrative policies that reinforce their assessments of each other's motives, thereby making peaceful relations still more robust. The fact that none of these countries is now hedging against an American withdrawal from Europe—which is a reasonable possibility given the lack of clear major-power threats, questions about the importance of NATO's remaining missions, and quite large reductions in U.S. troops deployed in Europe—indicates the extent of their confidence in each other's benign motives. In other words, in Europe the security dilemma is greatly moderated, not by material factors—like the offense-defense balance—but instead by information that leaves virtually no uncertainty about benign European motives.

Focusing instead on the material variables provides a complementary conclusion from a quite different perspective. Defensive realists have provided a partial application of this theory to post-Soviet Western Europe, arguing that Western Europe is primed for peace because the offense-defense balance now greatly favors defense.[23] The nuclear revolution, which enables developed countries to deploy massive retaliatory capabilities relatively cheaply and therefore creates an overwhelming advantage of defense over offense, has largely eliminated the security dilemma and the accompanying pressures for security competition and war. Although Germany lacks nuclear weapons, it could acquire them if necessary, and the United States could help insure stability during the transition. Taking this argument a step further, these material conditions would enable Germany to safely signal its benign motives by rejecting nuclear capabilities that would threaten its neighbors' nuclear capabilities, while still providing a highly effective deterrent. And defense advantage is reinforced both by the reduced value of territory (which requires that offense be relatively more effective to make expansion desirable) and by the high costs of conventional war.[24]

Although both the information and material explanations indepen-

---

[23] Van Evera, "Primed for Peace." See also Eugene Gholtz, Daryl Press, and Harvey M. Sapolsky, "Come Home, America: The Strategy of Restraint in the Face of Temptation," *International Security* 21, 4 (Spring 1997): 5–48.

[24] On these issues see Kaysen, "Is War Obsolete?"; for different but related arguments, see John Mueller, *Retreat from Doomsday: The Obsolescence of Major War* (New York: Basic Books, 1989).

dently provide powerful insights, my theory emphasizes the importance of addressing the combined effect of material and information variables. A closer look at the European case illustrates this point. Because Western European countries have developed very good political relations, the pure information argument is plausible. However, at the end of the Cold War confidence in Germany's benign goals was not complete,[25] and although relations have continued to improve, uncertainty probably still exists, if not about the present then about the future. Therefore, if military technology favored offense and territory were valuable for increasing security, Germany and its European neighbors would face greater pressures to return to competitive policies. An offense-defense balance that favored offense would provide Germany, as the most powerful state on the continent, with the potential to deploy military forces capable of extensive territorial expansion. Combined with its knowledge that other major powers had doubts about its long-term willingness to accept the status quo, Germany would worry that others viewed it as a potential military threat. It might fear that other major powers would therefore try to weaken it, which could create greater incentives to pursue unilateral and competitive military policies, including rejecting multilateral European security arrangements. Although Germany would be pursuing these policies to reduce its military vulnerability, shifting to unilateralism would likely damage relations within Europe, fueling competitive reactions by others.

This does not mean, however, that competition would clearly be Germany's best option. Given high estimates of each others' benign motives, and Germany's recognition of the security dilemma and desire to signal its benign motives, Germany might chose cooperative policies in the hope of maintaining peace by reinforcing these estimates.[26] The point here is simply that difficult material conditions would create incentives for competitive policies, even when initial information pushed in the opposite direction. Then, along any number of paths, a rational negative spiral could start that would further increase tensions on the European continent.

The material argument that peace in Europe could be sustained by nuclear weapons because they essentially eliminate the material foundation of the security dilemma is also plausible but would be weakened if states believed their neighbors were probably greedy states. If the countries of Western Europe believed that each was likely willing to run great risks to expand, their standards for adequate nuclear deterrence could become so demanding that the nuclear forces they believed were required

---

[25] Robert Art, "Why Western Europe Needs the United States and NATO," *Political Science Quarterly* 111, 1 (1996): 1–39.

[26] Arguing that this explains recent cooperation in Europe is Seth G. Jones, "The European Union and the Security Dilemma," *Security Studies* 12, 3 (Spring 2003): 114–156.

for deterrence would pose a threat to other states' nuclear forces. The demanding nuclear capabilities that the United States believed were necessary during the Cold War can be understood partly as an effort to hedge against extremely risky Soviet behavior that could not be fully ruled out on logical grounds. If following the American withdrawal these planning requirements were accepted by European states, the offense-defense balance would not so fully favor defense,[27] nuclear weapons would not eliminate the security dilemma, and cooperation within Europe would be less certain. Similarly, doubts about the effectiveness of nuclear deterrence would create requirements for highly effective conventional forces, which would further exacerbate the security dilemma. War would probably remain quite unlikely, but European relations would be strained, policies would be competitive, and the possibility of war would color diplomatic interactions.

In short, both information about motives and material variables in today's Europe have rather extreme values and might be sufficient on their own to explain continued security cooperation if the United States ended its security involvement in Europe. It is also possible, however, that neither would be sufficient on its own and that their combined effect would make a robust peace significantly more likely.

The security dynamics in Northeast Asia are quite different from those in Europe, and the impact of U.S. withdrawal from the region would likely be much larger. China's economic growth is the focus of much attention. Although its GNP is currently comparable to Japan's, China's significantly higher rate of economic growth and much larger population mean that China's power will eventually dwarf Japan's. China's and Japan's military policies look significantly more competitive than do Europe's, and assessments of insecurity are higher. China's military spending has been increasing rapidly for over a decade and is now estimated to be more than twice Japan's.[28] China is modernizing its forces, including deploying short-range ballistic missiles, improved fighter aircraft, and submarines.[29] Since the end of the Cold War, Japan has significantly revised its security policy, including tightening its alliance with the United States, expanding its area of security responsibility, increasing its power

[27] Glaser, *Analyzing Strategic Nuclear Policy*, pp. 94–99.

[28] "Appendix: Strategic Asia by the Numbers," in Ashley J. Tellis and Michael Wills, eds., *Strategic Asia 2007–08: Domestic Political Change and Grand Strategy* (Seattle: National Bureau of Asian Research, September 2007), http://www.nbr.org/publications/strategic_asia/pdf/xs0708/appendix.pdf. It is useful to keep in mind that Japan's defense spending, at approximately 1 percent of GNP, is a much lower percentage than that of other major powers, especially the United States.

[29] David Shambaugh, "China's Military Modernization: Making Steady and Surprising Progress," in Tellis and Wills, eds., *Strategic Asia 2005–06*.

projection capability, and preparing to deploy ballistic missile defenses.[30] Arguably, Japan is reducing its emphasis on reassurance of China, which it pursued by restricting its offensive capabilities,[31] and instead is placing greater weight on acquiring military capabilities required to play a broader role in regional security.

My theory helps clarify why Northeast Asia is more competitive and dangerous than Europe. Although growth in China's power is now frequently identified as the defining feature of the region, the theory draws attention to the important role that information about states' motives plays in distinguishing these regions, while also addressing the impact of greater Chinese power.[32]

With respect to homeland defense, material conditions in Asia favor defense, much as they do in Europe. Unlike Europe, geography provides Japan and China with some protection from direct conventional attack because their separation by hundreds of miles of water significantly increases the difficulty of invasion. Nuclear weapons also create defense advantage in the region. The United States provides Japan with an extended nuclear deterrence guarantee; assuming this commitment is credible, Japan benefits from the overwhelming defense advantage provided by nuclear weapons. In addition, Japan has the ability to build quickly a large survivable nuclear force of its own, which would meet the requirements for effective deterrence of a Chinese nuclear attack, and likely a conventional attack, against its homeland.[33] At the nuclear level, the extent of defense advantage will offset future Chinese advantages in power; even without U.S. support, Japan would be able to maintain effective nuclear forces.

The situation, however, is more complicated regarding other military missions, including protection of sea lines (which are vital to the flow of oil to both countries), China's ability to invade and coerce Taiwan, Ja-

---

[30] Christopher W. Hughes, "Japanese Military Modernization: In Search of a 'Normal' Security Role," in Tellis and Wills, eds., *Strategic Asia 2005–06*; and Nicholas Szechenyi, "A Turning Point for Japan's Self-Defense Forces," *Washington Quarterly* 29, 4 (Autumn 2006): 139–150.

[31] Paul Midford, "The Logic of Reassurance and Japan's Grand Strategy," *Security Studies* 11, 3 (Spring 2002): 1–43.

[32] To put concern about Chinese power in perspective, it is useful to recall that prominent pessimistic analyses from the mid-1990s, while identifying the potential danger of rising Chinese power, included this as one among many dangers, and not necessarily the most significant. See, for example, Aaron L. Friedberg, "Ripe for Rivalry: Prospects for Peace in a Multipolar Asia," *International Security* 18, 3 (Winter 1993/94): 5–33; and Richard K. Betts, "Wealth, Power and Instability: East Asia and the United States after the Cold War," *International Security* 18, 3 (Winter 1993–94): 34–77.

[33] Gholtz, Press, and Sapolsky, "Come Home, America," pp. 21–23, 31–32; and Jennifer M. Lind, "Correspondence: Spirals, Security, and Stability in East Asia," *International Security* 24, 4 (Spring 2000): 190–192.

pan's ability to aid the United States in the defense of Taiwan, and the power projection capabilities that could be relevant in disputes between China and Japan over island territories. The role of nuclear weapons in deterring these conflicts is likely to be limited; at a minimum, both countries will worry about the possibility of conventional conflict in the shadow of nuclear weapons. The offense-defense balance for these limited conventional missions will not favor defense as strongly as it does for invasion, and although there is disagreement about their difficulty, China and Japan are concerned about their abilities to perform these missions.[34] Consequently, both Japanese and Chinese assessments of their conventional capabilities, and their security, will be sensitive to increases in the size and quality of the other's conventional forces.

The information conditions and political relations in Asia are quite different from those in Europe. China's beliefs about Japan's motives are far less positive than the beliefs that European powers hold about each other. Rooted in history, and exacerbated by Japan's failure to adequately deal with its expansionist past and by China's nationalism, China is far from confident that Japan is motivated only by a desire to preserve the status quo.[35] In fact, many Chinese officials believe that Japan is interested in regional domination and that Japanese militarism could return.[36] Consequently, China worries about increases in Japan's military capabilities, as well as changes in the U.S.–Japan alliance that give Japan a more significant or far-reaching military role.[37] An indication of China's assessment of Japan's motives is reflected in its view of this alliance. Although the alliance enables the United States—which is much more powerful than Japan—to maintain large forces and a major foothold in its region, and even though China lacks confidence that U.S. motives are benign, China has preferred the alliance to American withdrawal from the region.[38] This

[34] See Lind, "Correspondence," and the response, Thomas J. Christensen, "Correspondence," pp. 197–98; and Christensen, "China, the U.S.–Japan Alliance, and the Security Dilemma in East Asia," *International Security* 23, 4 (Spring 1999): 49–80. See also Michael A. Glosny, "Strangulation from the Sea: A PRC Submarine Blockade of Taiwan," *International Security* 28, 4 (Spring 2004): 125–160, on the difficulty of effectively blockading Taiwan; blockading Japan would be still more difficult.

[35] For a recent discussion, see Yang Bojiang, "Redefining Sino–Japanese Relations after Koizumi," *Washington Quarterly* 29, 4 (Autumn 2006): 129–137; see also Christensen, "China, the U.S.– Japan Alliance, and the Security Dilemma in East Asia," pp. 52–55.

[36] Richard J. Samuels, "Japan's Goldilocks Strategy," *Washington Quarterly* 29, 4 (Autumn 2006): 112. See also Ming Wan, *Sino-Japanese Relations: Interaction, Logic and Transformation* (Stanford: Stanford University Press, 2006).

[37] Christensen, "China, the U.S.–Japan Alliance, and the Security Dilemma in East Asia," esp. pp. 49–55; and Wu Xinbo, "The End of the Silver Lining: A Chinese View of the U.S.–Japanese Alliance," *Washington Quarterly* 29, 1 (Winter 2005–06): 119–130.

[38] On China's concerns about the United States, see Avery Goldstein, *Rising to the Chal-*

is because the alliance has greatly moderated Japanese defense spending and helped sustain a limited set of roles and missions for Japan's force.[39]

Though less discussed, Japan lacks confidence in China's motives and willingness to accept the status quo.[40] Compared to Chinese beliefs, current Japanese beliefs about China's motives reflect less long-standing and deeply etched problems, but are nevertheless negative, and have been influenced by China's use of force to crush the Tiananmen Square protests, its launching of missiles during the mid-1990s crisis over Taiwan, its sending of naval forces into disputed areas, and recent anti-Japanese protests.[41] Combined with growth in Chinese power and military capabilities, Japan has experienced growing questions about the adequacy of its military forces and is enhancing its forces in response.[42]

This combination of material and information conditions—uncertainty about motives, even approaching high estimates of greedy goals, plus some relevant conventional missions in which defense dominance is not large and the possibility of Japan becoming a nuclear power, all backed by overwhelming defense-dominance in a future nuclear equilibrium[43]—results in a moderate security dilemma.[44] Both China and Japan have been aware of the security dilemma and have restrained their military policies in recognition of the dangers it can create. Regarding China, Avery Goldstein concludes that "the experience of the early 1990s has also taught them that even the modest improvements in the PLA's capa-

---

lenge: *China's Grand Strategy and International Security* (Stanford: Stanford University Press, 2005), esp. chaps. 5 and 7.

[39] China's view of the alliance appears to be shifting somewhat, however, due to U.S. efforts to expand the roles Japan will play, including explicitly identifying Taiwan as a contingency in which Japan would contribute to U.S. efforts, and to Japan's deployment of theater missile defense in cooperation with the United States. See Wu, "The End of the Silver Lining."

[40] For an early discussion, see Gerald Segal, "The Coming Confrontation between China and Japan?," *World Policy Journal* 10, 2 (Summer 1993): 27–32.

[41] See Richard J. Samuels, *Securing Japan: Tokyo's Grand Strategy and the Future of East Asia* (Ithaca: Cornell University Press, 2007), esp. pp. 136–143; Kent E. Calder, "China and Japan's Simmering Rivalry," *Foreign Affairs* 85, 2 (March/April 2006): 129–139; and Hughes, "Japanese Military Modernization," p. 108.

[42] Hughes; "Japanese Military Modernization"; and Samuels, *Securing Japan*, pp. 166–171. See also Michael Jonathan Green, *Japan's Reluctant Realism: Foreign Policy Challenges in an Era of Uncertain Power* (New York: Palgrave, 2001).

[43] On why acquisition of nuclear weapons, although favoring defense, could be threatening and fuel security competition, see Charles L. Glaser, "Why NATO Is Still Best: Future Security Arrangements for Europe," *International Security* 18, 1 (Summer 1993): 43–44.

[44] Another factor influencing the importance of these missions is disagreements about the political status quo. This complexity does not fit neatly into the basic theory, which assumes agreement on the existing status quo, whereas there is disagreement over Taiwan and a couple of island groups. As a result, neither uncertainty about types nor strictly greedy states are required to generate competition and insecurity.

bilities they now seek may trigger concerns in Washington as well as among neighboring countries. . . . Beijing's interest in minimizing the risk of provoking such a dangerous deterioration in its international environment as it gradually builds its strength within the constraints of a unipolar world is an important reason it is likely to adhere to its present approach—a grand strategy that aims to increase China's influence, but without relying on methods, such as rapid armament, that would alarm potential military rivals."[45] Japan has engaged in even more extensive restraint. Paul Midford explains that "Japan has recognized that 'normal' great power behavior could fan a spiral of suspicion by its neighbors, producing counterbalancing and an arms race. Japan has engaged in an iterated series of unilateral and noncontingent conciliatory measures that significantly limit Japan's offensive capabilities, entail risk to Japanese security, and benefit others."[46]

Nevertheless, over the past decade, military competition has increased, reflecting a shift in the security dilemma. The redefinition of the region during the transition from the Cold War raised Japanese concerns about the continuation of the U.S. commitment and generated American concerns about Japan's contribution to regional security, which made Japanese restraint both militarily and politically riskier. China's growing power, which supported its increasing ability to challenge the seas around Japan, reinforced the case for Japan to deal with its security dilemma by adopting somewhat more offensive, competitive policies. Predictably, China has found the changes in Japan's security policy, as well as the expanding scope of the U.S.–Japan alliance, threatening.

If the United States were to withdraw from East Asia, Japan would face much greater pressure to expand its military forces in response to China's growing power combined with the material security dilemma outlined above. Material conditions would enable Japan to adopt relatively unthreatening military policies, including possibly maintaining a "recessed," but not actually deployed, nuclear deterrent;[47] Japan's enhanced conventional forces would appear more threatening to China's regional interests, although not to its homeland. However, both Japan's willingness to restrain its deployments and their prospects for success in managing Japan's security dilemma would be reduced by the prevailing information conditions. The prediction for Northeast Asia if the United States withdraws from the region is not that a major war would be likely, but rather that military relations would be competitive, which would in turn further

---

[45] Goldstein, *Rising to the Challenge*, p. 202; see also his chapter 6 on China's shift to multilateral policies and its efforts at regional reassurance.

[46] Midford, "The Logic of Reassurance and Japan's Grand Strategy," p. 33.

[47] Barry Buzan, "Japan's Defense Problematique," *Pacific Review* 8, 1 (March 1995): 25–44.

strain political relations—that is, shift the countries' information to a higher probability that the other is greedy—which would increase the importance of maintaining highly effective military capabilities and of bargaining hard if crises occur. Peace would likely prevail, but it would not be the relatively easy, cooperative peace that would likely follow the U.S. withdrawal from Europe. Instead, the more likely outcome would be a competitive peace supported by defense advantages and strained by unresolved territorial disputes, possibly resembling the dangerous major-power relations of the Cold War. Therefore, a continuing American military commitment makes a larger contribution to regional security in Northeast Asia than in Europe.

HITLER'S GERMANY

There is little disagreement over whether Hitler's Germany started World War II and was a highly expansionist state.[48] The more controversial question is whether German expansion reflected greedy motives or instead insecurity. Put more precisely, even if Germany did have greedy motives, were its security motives sufficient to explain its expansionist policies? If so, a security-based explanation can be considered adequate, and more parsimonious, even if not entirely accurate. Another possibility is that rational explanations built on either (or both) of these motives are inadequate and, instead, suboptimal explanations are required. Although my brief discussion cannot resolve this debate, it does suggest that greedy motives are essential for explaining World War II.[49]

Under Hitler, Germany was driven by a mixture of security and nonsecurity motives. Security concerns were partly the result of the settlement of World War I. The Treaty of Versailles greatly restricted the German military—limiting its army to 100,000 men, banning tanks and an air force, and requiring the demilitarization of the Rhineland.[50] In the early 1930s the French Army was much larger and Germany viewed it as a seri-

---

[48] There is not, however, a consensus on Hitler's role; see PMH Bell, *The Origins of the Second World War in Europe* (London: Longman, 1986), chaps. 2 and 3, who summarizes the contending views on whether the situation created by World War I would have led to World War II under almost any German leadership; see John Mueller, *Retreat from Doomsday: The Obsolescence of Major War* (New York: Basic Books, 1989), pp. 64–68, for a brief statement of the argument that World War II would not have occurred without Hitler.

[49] For contending positions in the political science debate, see, on greedy motives, Schweller, *Deadly Imbalances*; on security motives, Mearsheimer, *The Tragedy of Great Power Politics*, and Copeland, *The Origins of Major Power War*, chap. 5, who focuses on preventive war logic; and on state-based suboptimality, Snyder, *Myths of Empire*, chap. 4.

[50] Bell, *The Origins of the Second World War in Europe*, pp. 17–21, summarizes the arguments about the harshness of the treaty.

ous threat, especially if combined with the forces of France's allies (Poland and Czechoslovakia) that bordered Germany.[51] However, Hitler's security concerns went well beyond the limits imposed by the treaty. Germany's traditional security fears reflected its central location in Europe, which left it potentially vulnerable to attack from both the east and the west. Considering basic measures of power suggests that Germany faced the possibility of major powers banding together to overwhelm it.[52] Britain and France combined had a population larger than Germany's and an economy of comparable size. Russia alone had almost three times Germany's population and many more times its territory; Dale Copeland argues that Hitler's policy was guided by a "rational fear of a rapidly industrializing Russia."[53] According to Norman Rich, Hitler believed "it was only a question of time before these eastern masses would overrun the insignificant area to which the Germans were restricted."[54] Germany was still more vulnerable because it lacked resource autonomy, depending on others for raw materials—including petroleum and iron—and food supplies, which left it vulnerable to a wartime blockade.[55] One potential explanation, therefore, for Germany's expansionist policies is that these structural sources of insecurity made attempting to conquer all of Europe Hitler's best option for achieving Germany security.[56]

In addition to these security concerns, Hitler was guided by a number of nonsecurity motives. Hitler's ideology called for the acquisition of land, which he argued was necessary for the survival of the racially superior Aryan race, and more narrowly the German people.[57] Although it is

[51] Gerhard L. Weinberg, *The Foreign Policy of Hitler's Germany: Diplomatic Revolution in Europe, 1933–36* (Chicago: University of Chicago Press, 1970), pp. 41–42. Hitler's concern reflected his beliefs about French goals, as well as its capabilities; Norman Rich, *Hitler's War Aims: Ideology, the Nazi State and the Course of Expansion* (New York: Norton, 1973), pp. 4–5: "Only through the obliteration of Germany could France maintain its world importance. French policy would always be one of waiting to engage in the final destruction of the Germans." On the racial dimension to Hitler's views of France, see Weinberg, *The Foreign Policy of Hitler's Germany*, pp. 4–5.

[52] See, for example, the measures in Schweller, *Deadly Imbalances*, appendix, pp. 203–208.

[53] Copeland, *The Origins of Major Power War*, chap. 5, quote on p. 119.

[54] Rich, *Hitler's War Aims*, p. 5, who also explains that Hitler believed a country's "security was in direct proportion to its territorial dimensions"; and p. 65. But see Weinberg, *Foreign Policy of Hitler's Germany*, p. 13, who argues that Hitler actually believed that Russia did not pose a serious threat but argued otherwise for its propaganda value.

[55] Willamson Murray, *The Change in the European Balance of Power, 1938–1939* (Princeton: Princeton University Press, 1984), chap. 1, esp. pp. 4–12.

[56] See Mearsheimer, *The Tragedy of Great Power Politics*, pp. 181–82; Copeland, *The Origins of Major Power War*, chap. 5; and David Calleo, *The German Problem Reconsidered: Germany and the World Order, 1870–Present* (Cambridge: Cambridge University Press, 1978), p. 6.

[57] On the historical development and political uses of Germany ideology see Woodruff D.

possible to interpret this desire for territorial expansion in traditional security terms, Hitler's motivation was not the territorial security of Germany. Instead he believed that Germany could not "feel itself secure until it was able to give each citizen his own bit of earth. To possess his own land and to till his own soil was the most sacred right of man."[58] He believed that vast amounts of land were required, far exceeding the land that Germany had lost in World War I; as a result, Hitler had little interest in simply restoring Germany to its 1914 borders. The required land was in Russia; to conquer Russia, Germany would have first to defeat France.[59] In addition, Hitler was driven by a radical anti-Semitism that reinforced his determination to conquer Russia. And Hitler offered other nonsecurity reasons for expansion into specific areas. For example, regarding Austria he wrote, "Common blood belongs in a common Reich."[60] According to Gerhard Weinberg, the racial and spatial logics of Hitler's expansion had a "potentially limitless quality . . . if space is to be adjusted to an expanded population by conquest, and such conquest enables the population to expand and facilitates further conquest, the only possible limitations are utter defeat on the one hand or total occupation of the globe on the other."[61] And this conclusion was reinforced by Hitler's racial theories: Rich explains that "because they were universal in a cultural sense, it followed that they had the moral right to be universal in a territorial sense as well; in other words, that they had a moral right to world territorial domination."[62]

These two types of motives were potentially reinforcing. Satisfaction of the greedy/nonsecurity motives required competitive and expansionist policies, and, given Germany's international situation, security motives could push toward these policies as well.

Nevertheless, a variety of arguments suggest that explaining Germany's behavior requires greedy motives—arguments based entirely on security seeking are not compelling[63] and ideology-based nonsecurity motives are essential for explaining Hitler's decisions. First, Germany's prospects for achieving continental hegemony were poor. Reflecting the key lesson of World War I, Hitler knew that Germany had little chance of winning a war if opposed by both Russia and England, and clearly the

---

Smith, *The Ideological Origins of Nazi Imperialism* (Oxford: Oxford University Press, 1986).

[58] Rich, *Hitler's War Aims*, p. 8.

[59] Bell, *The Origins of the Second World War in Europe*, chap. 6; and Weinberg, *Foreign Policy of Hitler's Germany*, pp. 5–7, 12–14.

[60] *Mein Kampf*, p. 3; quoted in Rich, *Hitler's War Aims*, p. 90.

[61] Weinberg, *The Foreign Policy of Hitler's Germany*, p. 7.

[62] Rich, *Hitler's War Aims*, p. 4.

[63] Snyder, *Myths of Empire*, pp. 70–75, offers a somewhat different set of arguments in reaching the same conclusion.

prospects were still worse if the United States opposed it.[64] This judgment was consistent with a broad reading of the states' power and an appreciation of their geography. Not only did this potential opposition greatly exceed Germany's power, but it also enjoyed access to resources that Germany lacked. Even Germany's success in conquering Western Europe "did not change the fact that Britain and the United States controlled the oceanic world economy and that the Soviet Union controlled the raw material and economic potential of European and Asiatic Russia."[65] Consequently, Hitler believed that avoiding a two-front war was essential, especially because Germany lacked the ability quickly to defeat England. Thus, his overall vision for success on the continent entailed an alliance with England, or at least a bargain that would keep England out of the war. In explaining why Germany could succeed, Hitler developed arguments for why England should and would stay out of the war, emphasizing that Germany's continental ambitions did not threaten Britain's empire.[66]

Although Germany's early successes may have suggested otherwise, British decisions showed that these arguments were flawed. Having reluctantly accepted the initial stages of German expansion, England was unwilling to accept Germany's bid for hegemony. This became clear following Germany's declaration of war on Poland, when Britain declared war against Germany, and still clearer following the fall of France. In addition, Germany had increasing reasons to doubt that the United States would stay out the war and instead support England, which further reduced its prospects. Nevertheless, although it violated a principle that had guided his thinking, Hitler continued his expansion of the war. Whether or not he wanted to acknowledge it, his own analysis showed that Germany's prospects for achieving continental hegemony were very poor. In other words, Hitler's goals were beyond his means. Barry Posen asks the question, "Could German means, qualitatively or quantitatively, ever be reconciled with such grandiose ends?" and concludes that although Hitler made substantial progress toward achieving his hegemonic goals, the answer to the question is no.[67]

We now need to consider why the low probability of achieving continental hegemony, let alone global dominance, supports the conclusion

[64] Andreas Hillgruber, *Germany and the Two World Wars* (Cambridge: Harvard University Press, 1981), pp. 51–55.

[65] Williamson Murray, "Net Assessment in Nazi Germany in the 1930s," in Williamson Murray and Allan R. Millett, eds., *Calculations: Net Assessment and the Coming of World War II* (New York: Free Press, 1992), p. 91.

[66] See Calleo, *The German Problem Reconsidered*, pp. 94–95, who also explains the flaws in Hitler's argument and why Hitler's worldview should have made them clear to him, pp. 112–115.

[67] Posen, *The Sources of Military Doctrine*, p. 179.

that Hitler was motivated by greed and not insecurity. If motivated by security, hegemony must be compared to the alternative approaches for achieving it. In contrast, if motivated by nonsecurity considerations that required the acquisition of massive amounts of territory, there is no alternative to expansion—territory is the end, not the means. If valued highly enough, even a very low probability of success does not necessarily make an effort to pursue this expansion undesirable. Arguably, given his expansionist ideology, any chance of success was sufficient to make launching his quest for continental hegemony Hitler's best bet.

By comparison, the case for pursuing hegemony to achieve security cannot be rescued so simply—showing that Germany had some chance of succeeding is insufficient; instead, hegemony must be compared to Germany's other options for increasing its security. Although achieving regional hegemony might well have maximized Germany's security, whether this was Germany's best option depended also on its probability of success. Less ambitious strategies that had a higher probability of success, even if less satisfactory, were arguably preferable. Among the possibilities were a number of limited gains that Hitler might have achieved through renegotiation of the Versailles Treaty and gains that he did achieve without fighting, including remilitarization of the Rhineland, rearmament, and acquisition of Austria and Czechoslovakia. The first two of these significantly increased Germany's ability to defend against France. The latter two added significantly to Germany's manpower and resources, and improved its access to other resources, although they did not provide sufficient power and autonomy to fight an offensive coalition of major powers.[68] But Hitler had no interest in building German security on this improved status quo and saw his initial successes as only paving the way to his continental objectives. After conquering France, Germany did have short-term security reasons that influenced its decision to attack Russia, most importantly its dependence on resources that Russia either possessed or controlled access to.[69] However, these risks were smaller than the risks of attacking Russia and certainly of confronting a two-front war that Hitler had long known was almost certainly beyond Germany's capabilities.

Hitler's lack of interest in changes to the status quo that significantly improved Germany's security strongly suggests that security was not in fact his key motive. For Hitler the choice was either "world power or decline." Even when it became clear that Germany had little or no chance of victory, Hitler refused to pursue more limited goals. "And so his alternative—the resolve not to capitulate but instead to bring about the delib-

---

[68] On the resource value of this expansion, see Rich, *Hitler's War Aims*, pp. 100–101, 109–110, 118.

[69] Rich, *Hitler's War Aims*, pp. 204–211.

erate destruction of Germany—led to that inferno of a war in which not only the Reich's great power position was lost but, in the end, German national unity itself was placed in peril."[70]

A final point that reinforces the conclusion that security was not Hitler's primary goal is that Germany diverted significant resources to implementing his racial policies that could have been productively used to advance its war aims.[71] If security had been Germany's driving motive, these policies could have been delayed until the war was won. In addition, Germany's policy of extermination following the occupation of Russian territory fueled Russia's determination to resist, thereby undermining Germany's invasion in a second way.[72]

In short, Germany's effort to conquer Europe cannot be well explained in terms of security alone—Hitler's racial and ideological goals appear necessary to explain his willingness to pursue such an ambitious, risky expansionist policy. Andreas Hillgruber concludes that "Hitler . . . in the decisive phase of the war in 1940–1941, despite an alignment of powers different from that foreseen in his program, abandoned Machiavellian methods of 'grand policy' in favor of the immediate realization of his ultimate racial-ideological aim."[73] David Calleo concludes that "To observe that the race policy was fatally impolitic or seriously interfered with conducting the war is to miss the point. Racial policy was the object of the war."[74] Williamson Murray argues that "From that moment [when Hitler gained power], German foreign policy ran risks that neither its military nor its diplomatic experts imagined possible. The level of those risks and Hitler's drive become understandable only when one recognizes his long-term ideological goals."[75]

The harder question may be whether Hitler's policies were suboptimal—even given the great value that he placed on achieving these nonsecurity goals, it is possible the prospects for achieving hegemony were too low and/or the security risks were too high.[76] Although beyond the scope

---

[70] Hillgruber, *Germany and the Two World Wars*, p. 96.

[71] Rich, *Hitler's War Aims*, pp. 55–58.

[72] Hillgruber, *Germany and the Two World Wars*, pp. 92–93;

[73] Ibid., p. 82.

[74] Calleo, *The German Problem Reconsidered*, p. 119; he argues further that "Hitler's solution to the German Problem flowed with terrible logic, not merely from that geopolitical analysis that he shared with his imperial predecessors, but also from his own peculiar racist doctrine"; this does not, however, seem to match easily with the emphasis in his introduction, cited above.

[75] Murray, "Net Assessment in Nazi Germany in the 1930s," p. 64.

[76] There is also some question about the value that Hitler placed on security—for example, Jervis, *Perception and Misperception*, p. 51, argues that Hitler seemed to place little value on preserving what Germany already possessed; if this were the case, then there was not even a trade-off between security and greedy goals.

of this discussion, Germany did underestimate both Russian and American power, and Hitler was overly optimistic about Britain and the United States staying out of the war.[77] The key point here, however, is that the rational baseline supporting an explanation of suboptimal behavior would have to include substantial greed among Germany's motives.

[77] On underestimation of Russian power, see Murray, "Net Assessment in Nazi Germany in the 1930s," pp. 84–85, 94–95.

CHAPTER NINE

Applying the Theory to Arms Races; Testing It with Counterfactuals

THIS CHAPTER HAS two related purposes. First, it uses my theory to analyze the question of whether arms races are dangerous. Although the danger of arms races has usually been explored by looking at the correlation between arms races and war, a proper framing of the question requires a theory of when a state should arm, and race if necessary. Therefore, the strategic choice theory is required to provide a rational baseline against which states' actual arming behavior can be judged. Second, the chapter provides a partial test of the theory. If the theory does in fact offer good prescriptive guidance, a state that chose an arming policy that diverges from the one prescribed by the theory should be "punished," that is, do worse than if it had chosen the optimal arming policy. Judging whether the policy a state chose was in fact suboptimal requires a counterfactual analysis. We need to ask: if the state had not armed, would the various negative consequences (including possibly strained political relations, counterbalancing alliances, and war) not have occurred? The chapter analyzes this counterfactual question for the arms races that it finds were suboptimal.

"Are arms races dangerous?" is among the most basic questions of international relations theory and has received extensive attention.[1] A large quantitative empirical literature addresses the consequences of arms races by focusing on whether they correlate with war, but it remains divided on the answer.[2] The theoretical literature falls into opposing camps—(1)

---

[1] The pioneering study is Samuel P. Huntington, "Arms Races: Prerequisites and Results," *Public Policy* 8 (1958): 41–86. Historical treatments include Paul Kennedy, "Arms-Races and the Causes of War, 1850–1945," in Paul Kennedy, *Strategy and Diplomacy, 1870–1945* (London: George Allen and Unwin, 1983); and Grant T. Hammond, *Plowshares into Swords: Arms Races in International Politics, 1840–1991* (Columbia: University of South Carolina Press, 1993). Reviews of the literature include George W. Downs, "Arms Races and War," in Philip E. Tetlock et al., eds., *Behavior, Society, and Nuclear War*, vol. 2 (New York: Oxford University Press, 1991), pp. 73–109; and Charles L. Glaser, "The Causes and Consequences of Arms Races," in Nelson W. Polsby, ed., *Annual Review of Political Science* 3 (2000): 251–276.

[2] Susan G. Sample, "Arms Races and Dispute Escalation: Resolving the Debate," *Journal of Peace Research* 34, 1 (February 1997): 7–22; Michael D. Wallace, "Arms Races and Escalation: Some New Evidence," *Journal of Conflict Resolution* 23, 1 (March 1979): 3–16;

arms races are driven by the security dilemma, are explained by the rational spiral model, and decrease security, or (2) arms races are driven by revisionist adversaries, are explained by the deterrence model, and increase the security of status quo powers.[3] These theories support divergent policy guidance—arms control versus arms competition.[4] Neither body of literature, however, succeeds in isolating the causal impact of building arms.

To solve this problem, this chapter proposes a new perspective for assessing the consequences of arms races.[5] Scholars need to ask whether an arms buildup was a state's best option for achieving its motives and goals—security and possibly other vital interests. Consistent with the perspective of the strategic choice theory, I argue that a sharp distinction must first be made between, on the one hand, the factors that influence a state's decision—its motives and its international environment—and, on the other hand, the state's decision to build arms. If a security seeker's international environment necessitates an arms buildup, arming, as well as the competition that ensues if its adversary responds, is rational and the security seeker's best policy option. Even if arms races correlate with war, they do not cause it. Instead, the state's international environment causes the arms race and in turn war. In contrast, if a security seeker's decision to launch a buildup is poorly matched to its international environment, the military buildup and the arms race that it provokes reduce the state's security. It is these suboptimal races that are dangerous, that is, they make war *unnecessarily* likely. They reflect distortions generated by domestic politics.

Implementing this approach requires addressing two questions. First, under what conditions is an arms buildup a state's best option? The stra-

---

Michael D. Wallace, "Armaments and Escalation: Two Competing Hypotheses," *International Studies Quarterly* 26, 1 (March 1982): 37–56; Paul F. Diehl, "Arms Races and Escalation: A Closer Look," *Journal of Peace Research* 20, 3 (September 1983): 205–212; Paul F. Diehl and Jean Kingston, "Messenger or Message? Military Buildups and the Initiation of Conflict," *Journal of Politics* 49, 3 (August 1987): 801–813; and Suzanne Werner and Jacek Kugler, "Power Transitions and Military Buildups: Resolving the Relationship between Arms Buildups and War," in Jacek Kugler and Douglas Lemke, eds., *Parity and War: Evaluations and Extensions of the War Ledger* (Ann Arbor: University of Michigan Press, 1996).

[3] On these models, see Jervis, *Perception and Misperception*, chap. 3; and Glaser, "Political Consequences of Military Strategy." Hedley Bull, *The Control of the Arms Race: Disarmament and Arms Control in the Missile Age* (New York: Praeger, 1961), pp. 3–12, identifies both types of causes.

[4] For example, Schelling and Halperin, *Strategy and Arms Control*; George W. Rathjens, "The Dynamics of the Arms Race," *Scientific American* 220 (April 1969): 15–25; and Colin S. Gray, *House of Cards: Why Arms Control Must Fail* (Ithaca: Cornell University Press, 1992).

[5] The term "arms race" is itself controversial; for a helpful discussion, see Buzan, *Introduction to Strategic Studies*, pp. 69–75.

tegic choice theory I have developed provides the foundation for answering this question, focusing on when a rational state should build up arms instead of pursuing restraint and cooperation. A state's arming policy should reflect its own motives and the constraints and opportunities created by its international environment, which is determined by material variables—power and offense-defense variables—and information variables, with the most important being the state's information about its adversary's motives. Second, have states engaged in arms races when they should not have? Using the theory to evaluate many of the past century's key arms races, as well as cases of cooperation, I find that a number of these races were suboptimal.

For the cases that are found to be suboptimal, the chapter uses counterfactual arguments to assess whether the state would have been better off if it had adopted the alternative policy prescribed by my theory. A state would be better off if it avoids wasting resources, damaging political relations, increasing the probability of war, and/or otherwise impairing its ability to achieve its goals. According to my theory, a state that adopts policies that diverge from its prescriptions should do worse than if it had followed the strategy identified by the rational theory. Thus, finding that a state would have been better off if it had followed the prescribed strategy lends support to the theory. Turning to counterfactual analysis is a necessary move because, as already explained, the more standard approach of testing the theory's ability to explain states' actual behavior does not work well for testing a rational theory when we have reasons to doubt that states consistently choose optimal policies.

The chapter first develops the rationale for reformulating the arms race question and identifies a number of significant implications of doing so for studying the consequences of arms races. The second section briefly reviews the strategic choice theory of arming and addresses a few related questions that should influence a state's decision, including how dangerous falling a step behind in the arms race would be and how likely its adversary is to respond if the state builds. The chapter then uses the theory to evaluate most of the key arms races of the past century, including the Anglo-German naval race before World War I, the German buildup of ground forces before World War I, Japanese and U.S. naval cooperation and then competition during the interwar years, and U.S. Cold War decisions concerning the size and modernization of its nuclear forces. A number of these arms buildups are found to be suboptimal, meaning specifically that states chose arming policies that diverged from the rational baseline provided by my theory.

This leaves open the question, however, of whether these states would actually have been better off if they had pursued a different, more cooperative, nonracing policy. The other possibility is that the theory is somehow flawed and that states in fact chose the correct arming strategy. To explore this possibility and, closely related, to perform a partial test of my theory, the chapter uses counterfactual analysis to examine the cases that diverge from the theory's prescriptions—German naval policy before World War I, Japan's naval policy during the 1930s, and the U.S. decision to pursue deployment of MIRVed missiles in the 1970s. This counterfactual analysis finds that in these cases the states would have been better off if they had pursued more cooperative arming policies. This finding supports the theory because we expect that if it is sound, states that adopt policies that diverge from its rational baseline would suffer as a result. Especially when combined with the analysis in chapter 7—which explored the theory's foundations from within—and chapter 8—which demonstrated the theory's explanatory capability in key historical cases—these results provide substantial confidence in the theory's overall quality.

REFORMULATING THE ARMS RACE QUESTION

Research on the consequences of arms races has failed to distinguish between the impact of a state's motives and international environment, on the one hand, and the impact of its arming policy, on the other. When a state chooses the best available military policy, it is making a rational decision that reflects, and is largely determined by, its motives and international environment. In explaining outcomes, analysts should credit them to these key factors, not to the state's arming policy. More specifically, when a state's best option is to launch a buildup (and engage in an arms race if necessary) and the probability of war increases when it does so, the increased probability of war should not be attributed to the arms race. Rather, for a security-seeking state, its security environment causes both the arms race and the increased probability of war. The state's international environment is dangerous, but the arms race is not.[6] In contrast, if a buildup and arms race result because a state fails to choose the best military policy available, the arms race is suboptimal, has independent effects, and becomes part of the problem. Suboptimal arms races unnecessarily decrease the state's security relative to other available options.[7] Research on the consequences of arms races therefore must separate rational arming decisions from suboptimal ones.

[6] Arms races may, however, have an independent causal effect that is not captured in this formulation, if they change the state by influencing domestic politics, for example, by increasing militarism; see Van Evera, *Causes of War*, pp. 144–145.

[7] A suboptimal buildup/race, however, might simply result in wasted resources, but not a reduction in security.

Figure 9.1 captures this framing of the arms race question. In the upper-left quadrant are rational arms buildups—cases in which the combination of the state's motives and its international environment made an arms buildup the state's best option, and the state did build up. In the lower-right quadrant, like the upper-left, the state's military policy was optimal. In this category, not arming was the state's best option and the state correctly chose restraint. This restraint could be achieved by unilaterally forgoing a military buildup or by negotiating an arms control agreement. The other two quadrants cover suboptimal arming policies. In the upper-right quadrant are cases in which a state chose to engage in an arms buildup that was not well matched to its international environment. These "dangerous" races decreased the state's security unnecessarily or reduced its ability to achieve other goals (or at best simply wasted its resources). These, therefore, are the arms races that should have been prevented. Finally, in the lower-left quadrant are cases in which a state should have engaged in an arms buildup but did not. A state could have increased its security by being the first to build up arms or by responding to an adversary's buildup but failed to do so.

The probability of war tends to be higher in the upper-left quadrant than in the lower-right quadrant because the international environments that require states to engage in military competition are also more likely to generate insecurity and war than are those that allow states to pursue more cooperative arming policies.[8] First, and perhaps most important, arms races can be optimal, yet still be associated with an increased probability of war, when a state faces a security dilemma. For example, a shift in the offense-defense balance toward offense can force all states to launch arms buildups, yet reduce their capability to thwart an attack and increase the probability of dangerous windows of opportunity and vulnerability; uncertainty about adversaries' motives can require states to compete, yet this competition can reduce their security by signaling malign motives.[9] Second, a declining security seeker that can still build arms faster than its rising adversary could rationally decide that its best option is to launch a buildup that yields military advantages and supports a preventive war policy. This logic can be used to explain Germany's rapid buildup of land forces before World War I.[10] Third, a technological advance that makes existing weapons obsolete can require the state that enjoyed a lead in deployment of the earlier technology to engage in an arms race that leaves it less secure. For example, starting in the mid-

[8] Van Evera, *Causes of War*; and chapter 4.

[9] Chapter 3 explores this interaction in some detail; earlier discussions include Jervis, "Cooperation under the Security Dilemma"; Glaser, "The Security Dilemma Revisited," pp. 174–185; and Kydd, "Game Theory and the Spiral Model."

[10] Copeland, *The Origins of Major War*, pp. 56–78.

State Should Have Armed/Raced

		Yes	No
State Did Arm/Race	Yes	Optimal arming: necessary races	Suboptimal arming: "dangerous" races
	No	Suboptimal restraint: dangerous cooperation	Optimal restraint: desirable cooperation

Figure 9.1. Quality of Arming Decisions

1900s, Britain had to compete in deployment of Dreadnought-type battleships, even though the ensuing arms race would reduce Britain's margin of naval superiority over Germany.[11] In addition to these examples, in which the international environment drives the arms race, greedy motives could also lead a state to choose competition. For example, a greedy state that enjoys a power advantage might launch a buildup to acquire military advantages that would make the costs of war acceptable, thereby improving its bargaining position and possibly increasing the probability of war.

Although the probability of war will tend to be higher for cases of optimal competition than for cases of optimal cooperation, it would be a mistake to conclude that arms races increase the probability of war and therefore that as a general rule states should avoid them. States in the upper-left quadrant of figure 9.1 are pursuing the best available policies; not engaging in an arms race would provide less security or other, nonsecurity objectives than racing and, in many cases, result in a higher probability of war.

This approach to analyzing the consequences of arms races yields three key insights. First, the extensive research program that has focused on the correlation between arms races and the probability of war is of little help in assessing the consequences of arms races. Starting in the late 1970s, scholars working with the Correlates of War data began investigating the correlation between arms races and the escalation of crises to war. A substantial literature revolves largely around how to code the occurrence of arms races and how to handle multiple arms races that were associated with a single conflict.[12] As challenging as these issues are, their basic framework is inadequate. Finding a correlation between arms races and the probability of war may say little about the impact of arms races be-

---

[11] Robert J. Art, "The Influence of Foreign Policy on Seapower: New Weapons and Weltpolitik in Wilhelminian Germany," in Robert J. Art and Kenneth N. Waltz, *The Use of Force*, 2nd ed. (New York: University Press of America, 1983), p. 186.

[12] Sample, "Arms Races and Dispute Escalation."

cause the correlation could simply reflect the causal impact of dangerous international environments and/or greedy motives on the incidence of both arms races and war.[13] Instead of comparing all arms races (those in both upper quadrants in figure 9.1) to nonraces (those in both bottom quadrants), rational and suboptimal cases need to be separated, comparing whether states that adopt suboptimal arming policies do worse than those that adopt optimal ones.

Second, whether an arms race increases the probability of war does not hinge on whether the spiral model or the deterrence model applies to a given race. Rational arms races are possible in both spiral model and deterrence model situations, but they are not the fundamental cause of conflict in either. Much of the arms race literature casts the question of the consequences of arms races as a debate between the "preparedness model," in which preparing for war by arming reduces its probability, and the "arms race model," in which building arms and engaging in an arms race to avoid war increases its probability. Both models have more developed versions. The deterrence model is the more developed version of the preparedness model; it explains competition and conflict as the result of greedy adversaries, that is, states interested in expansion for nonsecurity reasons. The spiral model is the more developed version of the arms race model; it assumes that an adversary is motivated by security concerns and emphasizes the potential of a security dilemma, especially uncertainty about other states' motives, to generate rational international competition.[14] In this standard framing of the arms race question, if war occurs when the deterrence model applies, fundamental political disputes, not the arms race, caused it; if war occurs when the spiral model applies, the arms race is the cause of the war. In contrast, I am arguing against attributing causation to the arms race in the spiral model cases because states are responding rationally to the incentives created by their international environment.

Third, although the literature tends to treat the causes and consequences of arms races as separate topics, in fact they are intimately related.[15] Causes are typically divided into two categories: external and internal. External causes are essentially the international factors that define a

[13] For other criticisms of this literature, including that it lumps together different types of rational arms races, see Downs, "Arms Races and War," pp. 82–84; and Glaser, "The Causes and Consequences of Arms Races." See also Paul F. Diehl and Mack J. C. Crescenzi, "Reconfiguring the Arms Race-War Debate," and Susan G. Sample, "Furthering the Investigation into the Effects of Arms Buildups," *Journal of Peace Research* 35, 1 (1998): 111–118 and 122–126, respectively.

[14] Jervis, *Perception and Misperception*, chap. 3; Glaser, "The Political Consequences of Military Strategy"; and Kydd, "Game Theory and the Spiral Model."

[15] Glaser, "The Causes and Consequences of Arms Races."

state's international environment and guide its rational behavior; internal causes are unit-level factors—for example, organizational interests and bureaucratic politics—that can distort a state's arming policy. Given this categorization, the type of cause determines the nature of the consequences—an arms race has consequences of its own only when the causes of the arms race are internal to the state, resulting in a suboptimal arms buildup.

EVALUATING ARMS RACES AND COOPERATION

Decisions about whether to engage in an arms buildup rest on three related but separable questions about the impact of an arms race. First, would an arms race enhance the state's military capabilities—that is, its ability to perform military missions? Second, would the state's increased military capabilities decrease the adversary's security? Third, would the benefits of the increased capabilities more than offset the dangers created by the adversary's insecurity? The easiest cases to judge involve races that do not promise to increase the state's military capabilities—as a rule, states should avoid these races.[16] Reaching judgments is more complicated when an arms race would produce countervailing effects.

The theory developed in earlier chapters addresses these questions,[17] focusing on whether a state is more secure if both it and its adversary launch buildups or if neither does.[18] If a state would be better off if both states build up their arms than if neither does, the state should launch an arms buildup. If, however, the state reaches the opposite conclusion—that it would be worse off if both states build up their arms than if neither does—it needs to address additional questions before reaching an arming decision.

To start, a state must consider how dangerous falling a step behind in the arms race would be. If the state is better off in the military status quo than if both states launch buildups, but would be greatly disadvantaged if its adversary is the first to do so, the state's best option could be to

[16] Because the adversary might build even if the state does not, this category does not include cases in which the state should build simply to prevent an erosion of capabilities it already possesses.

[17] Other analyses of when states should arm include Downs and Rocke, *Tacit Bargaining, Arms Races and Arms Control*; Downs, Rocke, and Siverson, "Arms Races and Cooperation"; Powell, *In The Shadow of Power*, chap. 2; and Ido Oren, "A Theory of Armament," *Conflict Management and Peace Science* 16, 1 (Spring 1998): 1–29.

[18] For analysis that focuses on binary choices about specific types of weapons, see Thomas C. Schelling, "A Framework for Evaluation of Arms-Control Proposals," *Daedalus* 104, 3 (Summer 1975): 187–200.

launch a buildup before its adversary does. The danger of waiting to respond to the adversary's buildup depends on a number of factors. First, the offense-defense balance influences the impact of the adversary's first move: the greater the advantage of defense, the less sensitive the state's capabilities are to the adversary's buildup and, therefore, the smaller the danger of building second. Second, the forces that are deployed in the military status quo will influence the implications if the adversary launches a buildup first. Larger forces tend to be more robust than smaller ones. For example, building a small number of nuclear weapons would have huge implications in a disarmed world but be virtually irrelevant when countries had already deployed thousands of nuclear weapons. Finally, the better the state's monitoring capability, the smaller the lead its adversary could achieve by launching a buildup first and, therefore, the smaller the danger in cooperating.[19] Therefore, technologies and arms control agreements that enable states to improve their monitoring capabilities make mutual cooperation more attractive. As a result, even when the offense-defense balance leaves the state's military capability sensitive to relatively small changes in force size, good monitoring arrangements could make cooperation in the military status quo preferable to launching an arms buildup.

In addition, the state needs to consider how likely its adversary would be to launch an arms buildup if the state does not. In deciding whether or not to launch a buildup, the state needs to assess the probability that its adversary would reciprocate restraint and, in the case of explicit cooperation, abide by an arms control agreement. If virtually certain that its adversary would build up, the state has little reason to accept the dangers of falling a step behind in an arms race. The adversary's motives are a key variable: greedy states place greater value on military advantages and therefore would be willing to run larger risks to acquire them. For example, during the Cold War, hard-liners in the United States opposed arms control agreements with the Soviet Union partly because they were convinced that the Soviets would cheat. A second consideration influencing the adversary's decision to launch an arms buildup is the benefit of gaining a jump in an arms race: the larger the benefits, the more likely an adversary will build. The benefits are simply the flip side of the dangers of falling behind, which were discussed above. Even an adversary pursuing only security will feel greater pressure to launch an arms buildup as the benefits increase, if only to avoid the greater danger of falling behind.

Finally, the state should ask how likely its adversary is to respond if the state builds. A state that preferred the military status quo to an arms race

---

[19] Similarly, the slower the rate at which the adversary could build, the smaller the danger posed by its first move.

might nevertheless prefer to launch a buildup if its adversary would not respond. As the theory emphasizes, the adversary might not respond because it lacks the resources. In addition, an adversary that has the necessary resources might not respond if the state's buildup does not pose a serious threat. This could occur if the buildup does not jeopardize the adversary's ability to protect its vital interests. The adversary would also see a smaller threat and therefore be less likely to respond if its information about the state's motives made it confident that the increased military capabilities would not be used against its interests. Under most other conditions, the state should expect its adversary to react to its arms buildup.

This section applies the strategic choice theory to many of the key major-power arms races of the past century to determine whether states' arming decisions were well matched to their international environments or were instead suboptimal.[20] To explore the range of possibilities captured by the theory, this section also evaluates important cases in which states cooperated when this was their best option, and in which states did not build up arms when this was not their best option.[21] I compare a state's actual behavior to the policies that my rational theory prescribes under the conditions the state faced.[22] States should be judged in light of the uncertainties they faced at the time of their decisions.

For those cases that are judged to be suboptimal, I use brief counterfactual analyses to assess whether the state would have been better off if it had adopted the alternative policy prescribed by my theory. Counterfactual arguments can be challenging to use for a variety of reasons, including the difficulty of manipulating only one variable at a time and of confidently assessing the outcomes that would have resulted under these changed conditions.[23] We cannot use the theory we are evaluating to generate these outcomes and then use the outcome to test the theory, as this would be entirely circular.[24] This said, using counterfactual arguments to

---

[20] For lists of these races, see Huntington, "Arms Races"; Kennedy, "Arms-Races and the Causes of War"; and Hammond, *Plowshares into Swords*.

[21] A likely example of the latter, which I do not evaluate here, is the British failure to build up its army before World War II; see Brian Bond, *British Military Policy between the Two World Wars* (Oxford: Oxford University Press, 1980); Posen, *The Sources of Military Doctrine*; Keir, *Imagining War*; and Stephen R. Rock, *Appeasement in International Politics* (Lexington: University of Kentucky Press, 2000), chap. 3.

[22] On this use of a rational model, instead of testing a model, see Moe, "On the Scientific Status of Rational Models," pp. 236–237.

[23] For a range of views, see Philip E. Tetlock and Aaron Belkin, eds., *Counterfactual Thought Experiments in World Politics: Logical, Methodological, and Psychological Perspectives* (Princeton: Princeton University Press, 1996).

[24] James D. Fearon, "Counterfactuals and Hypothesis Testing in Political Science," *World Politics* 43, 2 (January 1991): 176–177.

explore choices of strategy, and specifically choices of arming, may be easier than exploring imagined changes in the international environment. The international environment may have affected a wide array of states' choices, including choices made well in the past; understanding the impact of this type of manipulation therefore requires analyzing its impact on all of these prior choices, not only the outcome of particular interest, as well as future ones. In contrast, exploring the impact of an imagined change in strategy requires exploring only its impact on future choices.[25]

German Navy 1898–1912/14

In 1898 Germany launched a naval buildup that was intended to challenge the British Navy, which was significantly augmented four times in the years before World War I.[26] In the ensuing arms race, Germany failed to undermine Britain's naval capabilities. Britain interpreted the buildup as a signal of malign German motives,[27] which, combined with the increase in German capabilities, led Britain to increase cooperation with Russia and France.[28] Germany's sense of encirclement contributed to its growing insecurity, making war more likely.[29] The first question is whether

[25] This claim does overlook the question of feasibility—if a change in strategy would not have been possible without also altering the nature of the state itself, including its domestic politics, the counterfactual might need to include the full set of changes that would follow from this more basic alteration. For example, if a state's offensive strategy reflects it military's organizational preferences, shifting to a defensive strategy could require reducing the military's ability to determine the state's strategy. This could, in turn, require changes in civil-military relations, in the state's evaluative capabilities, and/or in domestic coalitions that have interests in military policy. Including these changes in the state to the counterfactual could generate different results from simply hypothesizing a change in strategy.

[26] On the stages of the naval buildup, see Holger H. Herwig, "*Luxury Fleet*": *The Imperial German Navy, 1888–1918* (London: George Allen and Unwin), especially pp. 33–92 and the appendices. On the early stages, see Jonathan Steinberg, *Yesterday's Deterrent: Tirpitz and the Birth of the German Battle Fleet* (New York: Macmillan, 1965).

[27] See Paul M. Kennedy, *The Rise of the Anglo-German Antagonism, 1860–1914* (London: Ashfield Press, 1980), pp. 421–423, on the security dilemma, and pp. 428–430, on its negative impact; Gerhard Ritter, *The Sword and the Scepter: The Problem of Militarism in Germany*, vol. 2 (Coral Gables: University of Miami Press, 1970), pp. 140–147; Steinberg, *Yesterday's Deterrent*, p. 18; and Arthur Marder, *From the Dreadnought to Scapa Flow: The Royal Navy in the Fisher Era, 1904–1919* (New York: Oxford University Press, 1961), pp. 119–123.

[28] On the role of the German threat, see A.J.P. Taylor, *The Struggle for the Mastery of Europe, 1848–1918* (Oxford: Oxford University Press, 1954), pp. 403–417, 442–446; and Samuel R. Williamson, *The Politics of Grand Strategy: Britain and France Prepare for War, 1904–1914* (Cambridge: Harvard University Press), pp. 1–25, who give it relatively little weight. For greater weight, see Kennedy, *The Rise of Anglo-German Antagonism*, pp. 266–267, 428, 441; and V. R. Berghahn, *Germany and the Approach of War in 1914* (New York: St. Martin's, 1973), p. 60.

[29] Snyder, *Myths of Empire*, p. 33.

this bad outcome reflected Germany's goals and the international situation it faced, or instead suboptimal arming policies.

EVALUATING DIVERGENCE FROM THE RATIONAL BASELINE

This is a case of power disadvantage and defense advantage that left Germany unable to acquire the naval capabilities it desired. Although Germany's naval policy was intended to challenge the political status quo, elevating Germany to a world power, its naval strategy was militarily defensive, designed to defeat a British blockade of Germany.[30] To achieve success on the defense, Germany judged that its fleet needed to be two-thirds the size of the British fleet attempting to impose a close blockade. In other words, when opposing a British close blockade, defense had the advantage and this 3:2 ratio worked to Germany's advantage.[31]

Although Germany's total power was more than sufficient to achieve this ratio, Germany could not focus its efforts entirely on Britain and invest solely in its navy. Instead, Germany had to devote the largest part of its military spending to its army, because its greatest security challenges were on the continent.[32] The national incomes of Britain and Germany were roughly comparable during the fifteen years before World War I.[33] Assuming that Germany could devote a third of its military budget to its navy, which is a generous estimate, Germany lacked the power to compete effectively with Britain.[34] Although Germany was able to pose a seri-

[30] Germany's strategy, however, did vary over these years; see Paul M. Kennedy, "The Development of German Naval Operations Plans against England, 1896–1914," in Paul M. Kennedy, ed., *The War Plans of the Great Powers, 1880–1914* (Boston: Allen and Unwin, 1979), pp. 171–198.

[31] This ratio was widely accepted at the time. Berghahn, *Germany and the Approach of War in 1914*, p. 50; and Herwig, "*Luxury Fleet*," pp. 36–39. If instead Britain decided to impose a distant blockade, which it did during the war and some in the German Navy started worrying about by the mid-1900s, Germany would require more than a 2:3 ratio; Ritter, *The Sword and the Scepter*, pp. 149–154.

[32] Assessing available power under multipolarity is complicated because a state that must plan to defend against multiple adversaries can allocate only a fraction of its total resources against each adversary.

[33] Britain enjoyed approximately a 20 percent advantage at the beginning of this period, and Germany enjoyed approximately a 5 percent advantage by the end. See John M. Hobson, "The Military-Extraction Gap and the Wary Titan: The Fiscal Sociology of British Defense Policy, 1870–1913," *Journal of European Economic History* 22, 3 (Winter 1993): 461–506, esp. 503, 505. In addition, Germany's population was larger than Britain's, which made it more difficult to extract a percentage of national income equal to the British percentage, and political divisions within the German federal system further reduced its potential for extracting revenues. Ibid., p. 496.

[34] At its peak (in 1911) the navy's budget was 55 percent of the army's; in 1898 it was 20 percent, and it had dropped to 33 percent by 1913. Herwig, "*Luxury Fleet*," pp. 78, 90; see also tables in David Stevenson, *Armaments and the Coming of War: Europe 1904–1914* (Oxford: Oxford University Press, 1996), pp. 4–8.

ous challenge, Britain responded with naval buildups of its own, placing German naval goals out of reach.[35]

The architect of Germany's naval policy, Admiral Alfred von Tirpitz, implicitly accepted this assessment of Germany's power but argued that Germany could nevertheless achieve the necessary ratio of forces because Britain's extensive overseas commitments would prevent it from concentrating its navy in the North Sea.[36] Britain, however, did (albeit reluctantly) redistribute its fleet, in addition to increasing its naval building, to offset the German challenge.[37]

The theory's discussion of when a state should expect its adversary to respond to a buildup provides the straightforward logic that guided the British reaction. The German buildup threatened Britain's vital interests and therefore had to be met, even if this required Britain to reduce its ability to protect lesser interests, for example, in East Asia. German leaders should have appreciated this weakness in Tirpitz's case but could have argued that Britain's reaction was uncertain.[38] However, even though this might have been a plausible argument at the time of the first two German naval bills—in 1898 and 1900—it was discredited shortly thereafter by Britain's naval reactions. In 1903 Britain announced plans to build a new North Sea naval base; in 1904 it started redistributing its fleet; and in 1905 it made public a memorandum that emphasized that changes in the international environment would result in the redistribution of its fleet.[39]

From the outset, Tirpitz's plan included a second argument—the "risk theory"—that was designed to deal with the limits of German power, but it too turned out to be flawed. The argument held that the German Navy did not need to be able to defeat Britain's naval forces to coerce political concessions; instead, it only had to be able to inflict enough damage to leave Britain vulnerable to the combined strength of the next two naval powers, France and Russia.[40] This complicated logic, however, depended

[35] Steinberg, *Yesterday's Deterrent*, p. 21; and Berghahn, *Germany and the Approach of War in 1914*, pp. 136–37. Hans-Ulrich Wehler, *The German Empire, 1871–1918* (New York: Berg, 1985), p. 169, notes that Germany almost reached the desired ratio in 1914.

[36] For a powerful criticism of Tirpitz's strategy, which identifies many problems not addressed here, see Paul Kennedy, "Strategic Aspects of the Anglo-German Naval Race," in Kennedy, *Strategy and Diplomacy, 1870–1945*.

[37] In fact, Britain began redistributing its navy before Germany became its principal challenger because of the growth of other European navies; the German buildup added to these pressures. See Friedberg, *The Weary Titan*, chap. 4.

[38] Kennedy, "Strategic Aspects of the Anglo-German Naval Race," p. 140, finds the assumption "was strategically and politically so wide off the mark that it seems incredible that Tirpitz should have based his hopes on it."

[39] Paul M. Kennedy, *The Rise and Fall of British Naval Mastery* (London: Ashfield, 1976), pp. 216–229.

[40] Steinberg, *Yesterday's Deterrent*, p. 83–84; and Kennedy, "Strategic Aspects of the Anglo-German Naval Race," pp. 132–133.

on, among other things, the likelihood that the other major naval powers would challenge Britain. British ententes with France and Russia effectively removed this possibility, thereby further reducing the coercive value of Germany's naval buildup.[41]

Although assessment of these material variables is sufficient to conclude that the buildup was suboptimal, consideration of Germany's information about British motives reinforces this conclusion. If Germany believed that Britain was a greedy state determined to greatly increase its influence on the continent and to undermine Germany's, there would have been a plausible case for redirecting Germany's military spending and acquiring an enhanced, although still inadequate, naval deterrent. However, although Tirpitz believed that war with Britain was unavoidable, other German leaders believed that an alliance with Britain was possible and that Germany's naval buildup was driving Britain to ally with its enemies.[42]

A possible counterargument is that German naval policy was motivated by greed—specifically Germany's desire for colonies—and therefore risks to its security were warranted. Colonies, however, were at most a secondary interest, whereas continental security was Germany's overwhelming vital interest, so it made little sense to trade the former for the latter.[43]

EVALUATING THE COUNTERFACTUAL

Given this divergence from the rational theory, the next question is whether Germany was actually hurt by pursuing what my theory identifies as a suboptimal naval policy. The answer depends on the counterfactual scenario that we consider, including both what alternative policy Germany is imagined to follow and what outcomes we compare. A cautious counterfactual simply manipulates Germany's naval policy—Germany forgoes a large battleship navy directed at Britain—but leaves unchanged the domestic sources of Germany's suboptimal policy and therefore other policies that were independent of its naval policy.[44] We can compare three different types of outcomes—resource allocation, in-

[41] Art, "The Influence of Foreign Policy on Seapower," p. 185.

[42] Kennedy, The Rise of the Anglo-German Antagonism, 1860–1914, pp. 224, 419.

[43] The two may not be entirely separable, however; David E. Kaiser, "Germany and the Origins of the First World War," *Journal of Modern History* 55, 3 (September 1983): 442–474, argues that Germany's ambitious continental policy was actually intended to produce concessions on colonies, not continental expansion.

[44] This is potentially problematic because Germany's naval policy had its deep sources in Germany's state-building and domestic coalitions, and therefore a plausible counterfactual might require a fundamental change in German society and institutions. For a good summary of domestic considerations, see Kaiser, "Germany and the Origins of the First World War"; for a detailed analysis, see Steinberg, *Yesterday's Deterrent*. However, although important, these factors did not determine German naval policy—it took Tirpitz's exceptional

ternational political relations and alliances, and war. These vary in their "distance" from the changed policy, measured in terms of the number of logical steps or mechanisms between the hypothesized policy change and the outcome, with resource allocation being closest and war being farthest. Confidence in the counterfactual assessment is greater when this distance is smaller because with a smaller number of steps between the changed policy and the projected outcome there are fewer judgments across which uncertainty can compound.

The most direct effect of forgoing Tirpitz's battleship navy would have been a significant saving in defense spending, which constituted a significant portion of overall German spending. Given that Germany's naval buildup failed to provide the promised capabilities, spending on the navy was essentially wasted. In addition, naval spending made it more difficult for Germany to increase spending on its army, which was much more important to its security. The trade-off between the two types of military spending became manifest when Germany decided army increases were essential; naval spending then had to be reduced.[45] Either saving the money or spending it on its army would have been better for Germany than wasting it on its navy.

Second, forgoing the naval buildup would have enabled Germany to maintain better political relations with Europe's other major powers, which would in turn have increased its security. Germany's naval buildup strained its relationship with Britain and fueled British cooperation with Germany's adversaries. At the turn of the century, Britain saw a greater threat from France and Russia than from Germany, and an alliance with Germany was a possibility that was sufficiently serious to warrant high-level discussions. Britain proposed cooperation in the Far East, and Germany proposed broader cooperation that included having Britain join its Triple Alliance (with Austria-Hungary and Italy).[46] Germany's naval buildup severely strained its relationship with Britain and not only damaged the prospects for an alliance but also contributed significantly to Britain's development of ententes with France and Russia, which in turn contributed to Germany's sense of encirclement. Although not the only factor leading to these ententes, Germany's naval buildup (and threat that it posed to Britain) was an important factor in Britain's shift from its traditional policy of isolation and especially in the tightening of these ententes as the decade continued.[47]

On the flip side, Germany's naval program was also the major barrier

---

political skills to design and sell the risk fleet; see Steinberg, *Yesterday's Deterrent*, especially chaps. 2–4.

[45] Berghahn, *Germany and the Approach of War in 1914*, chap. 6.

[46] George Monger, *The End of Isolation: British Foreign Policy, 1900–1907* (London: Nelson, 1963), chap. 2.

[47] In addition to references in note 28, see ibid.

to improving relations. Although Germany and Britain arguably reached a limited détente in the years immediately preceding World War I, the understandings were limited to relatively minor issues that were dwarfed in importance by the naval competition.[48] Germany made the price for reaching a naval agreement quite high, requiring a British commitment not to join a war in Europe. Britain was unwilling to meet this condition because it could not afford to allow any power to control the continent, so Britain wanted to retain the option of intervening in a continental war. Paul Kennedy argues that Britain might have been willing to commit to staying out of a continental war if Germany had posed a smaller threat to Britain. One key to this reduced threat would have been a significantly less capable German Navy. The second key would have been an army strategy that planned for a defensive war in the West and therefore possessed less potential to pursue continental hegemony. But the combination of Tirpitz's navy and the Schlieffen Plan meant that the threat to Britain was simply too great. As a result, German military policy made cooperation that would have increased Germany security unacceptable to Britain.[49] Given that Britain was clearly reacting to the German naval buildup, with the connection made explicit by British leaders, we can have substantial confidence in the counterfactual claims that Anglo-German relations would have been better and Germany would have been more secure if it had not launched the naval arms race.

Closely related, a third possible result of Germany not launching the naval race—avoiding World War I—is harder to project with confidence. At the same time, however, the more modest argument—that the war would have been less likely—is strong. The link between the arms race and war is not a direct one—Germany did not go to war because of the arms race, nor in the end did Britain join the war because of it. The arms race, however, did fuel German beliefs about being encircled and in turn increase its insecurity, including its belief that war was becoming inevitable. This belief interacted with other factors to make war more likely. Specifically, the case for preventive war becomes stronger as the probability of war in the future increases; and among the many explanations for World War I, preventive war is among the most frequently offered and convincing.[50] Consequently, if the naval arms race had not occurred, it seems probable that the war would have been less likely.

[48] Sean M. Lynn-Jones, "Détente and Deterrence: Anglo-German Relations, 1911–1914," *International Security* 11, 2 (Autumn 1986): 121–150.

[49] Kennedy, *The Rise of Anglo-German Antagonism*, pp. 428–430. Whether this incompatibility itself reflected an incompatibility of political goals is a trickier question, depending on whether Germany had greedy motives on the continent; if, in contrast, its ambitions were limited to colonial expansion, there was room for more compatible military policies.

[50] For example, see Copeland, *The Origins of Major War*; and Van Evera, *Causes of War*. I should note, however, that although often presented as a rational argument, the preventive war explanation itself depends on one or more German errors, including exaggeration of

German Army 1912–1914

In 1912, increasingly convinced that enemies encircled it and that war was growing more likely, Germany decided to build up its army.[51] In reaction, France and Russia strengthened their armies, and France and Britain advanced their plans for cooperating against Germany.[52] In response to these measures, and especially to the worsening balance of power created by the First Balkan War of 1912, in 1913 Germany launched a much larger buildup, which spurred Germany's opponents to accelerate their buildups.[53]

This is a case of defense advantage and German power advantage. German planning recognized that defense had the advantage in the west. In addition to appreciating the difficulty of frontal assaults, Germany recognized that flanking operations would require substantial numerical superiority. Although France and Germany had roughly equal peacetime armies, Germany planned to employ reserves with its main fighting forces and expected them to be effective in combat; as a result, in 1905 Germany planned in the initial battles to deploy thirty six corps against France's twenty one, an advantage of roughly 1.7:1.[54] Nevertheless, Chief of the German General Staff Alfred von Schlieffen believed that Germany's forces were inadequate, concluding that the flanking operation was "an enterprise for which we are too weak."[55] This ratio therefore pro-

---

Russian power, overestimates of Russia's military competence, and failure to appreciate the extent of defense advantage; thus, even given the impact of the naval race, preventive war was not Germany's optimal policy.

[51] The 1912 bill provided for roughly a 5 percent increase in manpower and more than a 10 percent increase in the army budget. For somewhat different estimates, see Herrmann, *The Arming of Europe and the Making of the First World War*, pp. 233–235; and Stevenson, *Armaments and the Coming of War*, pp. 8, 210. On the reasons for this decision, see Herrmann, *The Arming of Europe*, pp. 161–172. Stevenson, *Armaments and the Coming of War*, p. 146, suggests that the start of the race may be better attributed to Russia's decisions in 1910.

[52] Herrmann, *The Arming of Europe*, pp. 174–176; with somewhat different emphasis, Stevenson, *Armaments and the Coming of War*, pp. 216–224, who sees the French reaction as quite limited.

[53] Herrmann, *The Arming of Europe*, pp. 173–198; Stevenson, *Armaments and the Coming of War*, pp. 285–323. Germany planned to increase its manpower by roughly a sixth, over two years.

[54] Herrmann, *The Arming of Europe*, pp. 44–45; see also Snyder, *The Ideology of the Offensive*, pp. 109–110.

[55] Gerhard Ritter, *The Schlieffen Plan: Critique of a Myth* (Westport, CT: Greenwood, 1979), p. 66. Agreeing with this assessment is B. H. Liddell Hart, "Forward," in ibid. Schlieffen did little, however, to use this conclusion to support increases in German forces (ibid., p. 67), which suggests he was not exaggerating his concerns for this purpose; but see also Herrmann, *The Arming of Europe*, p. 184.

vides a conservative (biased toward offense) estimate of the German understanding of the balance.[56]

The measure of power that was relevant for gauging Germany's prospect in a land arms race was its power relative to France. This is because Germany's plan for victory on the continent relied on defeating France first and quickly. Although Germany suffered a power disadvantage relative to the combined resources of France, Russia, and possibly Britain, it had a power advantage over France that it had not fully exploited. Although Germany's population was about 60 percent larger than France's, their peacetime forces were of comparable size.[57] Even if France responded, Germany would be able to increase its advantage in force size.[58]

By 1912 German leaders viewed their adversaries' motives as quite threatening. For example, Gen. Franz von Wandel, head of the German General War Department, worried not only about growing Russian forces but also about Russia's inclination "to vent to the ever-growing anti-German mood through active participation in war" and that "we are never safe from war, but rather that our enemies will force one upon us without fear of consequences."[59] These views combined with a variety of other factors—including growing encirclement, negative shifts in the balance of power in the Balkans, and ongoing Russian efforts to rebuild their army[60]—to convince German leaders that war in the near future was quite likely, if not inevitable.

To evaluate whether under these material and information conditions Germany should have launched an arms race, it is first necessary to consider whether Germany required an offensive doctrine. As discussed in chapter 3, although defense advantage usually supports a defensive doc-

---

[56] It is still further biased because Schlieffen's assessment overlooked a number of knowable factors that worked against his strategy. Ritter, *The Schlieffen Plan*; Van Creveld, *Supplying War*, pp. 113–141; and Snyder, *The Ideology of the Offensive*, pp. 112–113. Cutting in the other direction, however, were the French reserves that might have influenced the battle's outcome, but were not included in the ratio of initial frontline forces.

[57] See Copeland, *The Origins of Major War*, table A2, p. 50; and Herrmann, *The Arming of Europe*, table A.1, p. 234. The GGS stressed this point—Germany inducted 52–54 percent of eligible men, whereas France inducted 85 percent—in calling for large increases in Germany manpower in the 1913 buildup; Herrmann, *The Arming of Europe*, pp. 184–85; and Stevenson, *Armaments and the Coming of War*, p. 292.

[58] Some German leaders, however, doubted that an arms race would benefit Germany. Stevenson, *Armaments and the Coming of War*, p. 294.

[59] Quoted in Herrmann, *The Arming of Europe*, pp. 167–168.

[60] In assessing the overall quality of German decision making, it is important to recognize that some of these factors—for example, the insecurity generated by the tightening of alliances opposing Germany—were largely the result of Germany's own policies. Other factors—shifts in the Balkan balance of power and improvements in Russian army capabilities—were not the result of Germany policies, but their significance may have been exaggerated by Germany's evaluation of its military environment.

trine, there are conditions under which a country facing a two-front war should choose an offensive doctrine to fight its adversaries sequentially. This purpose guided the Schlieffen Plan: to take advantage of Russia's slower mobilization, Germany would first launch a massive offensive operation against France, then turn the weight of its forces against Russia. The wisdom of Germany's offensive doctrine has been the focus of substantial debate, which I do not attempt to resolve here.[61]

If we assume that Germany required an offensive capability, the case for launching an arms race would be solid, although not overwhelming. Given the substantial defense advantage, Germany's decision to use its power advantage to increase the relative size of its army would have promised to improve Germany's chances against France.[62] Launching the buildup in 1912 promised to provide this capability before the completion of Russia's military modernization, which German military experts feared was going to undermine Germany's two-front war strategy. Chancellor Theobald von Bethmann Hollweg recognized that Germany faced countervailing, security-dilemma pressures, yet he concluded that a buildup was warranted. According to David Stevenson, "the bill had increased international tension, but [Bethmann] had had to choose between evils and could not leave so many able-bodied men untrained."[63] The German war minister, who favored the 1912 bill, warned that a major army buildup would be the prelude to war and therefore "a step to be taken only if such a struggle seemed inevitable and imminent."[64] With the probability of war already believed to be very high, Germany's decision to make this trade-off in favor of increasing capabilities at the cost of making war more likely was a reasonable way of managing its security dilemma. Both France and Russia appreciated Germany's security requirements and therefore, consistent with rational signaling, did not impute more malign motives.[65] War became more likely, however, because they understood the German buildup as an indication of the high probability that Germany placed on war, which in turn required them to intensify preparations.

[61] Jack Snyder, "Civil-Military Relations and the Cult of the Offensive, 1914 and 1984," and Stephen Van Evera, "The Cult of the Offensive and the Origins of the First World War," both in *International Security* 9, 1 (Summer 1984); and Scott D. Sagan, "1914 Revisited: Allies, Offense, and Instability," *International Security* 11, 2 (Fall 1986): 151–175. Copeland, *The Origins of Major War*, does not focus on doctrine, but his argument that Germany preferred a preventive war leads to a requirement for an offensive doctrine.

[62] However, there are reasons to believe that the plan's logistical problems limited the value of additional troops; see sources in note 56.

[63] Stevenson, *Armaments and the Coming of War*, p. 296

[64] Herrmann, *The Arming of Europe*, p. 165

[65] Ibid., pp. 174, 191–192.

On the other hand, if Germany could have adopted a more defensive doctrine, which German recognition of defense advantage in the west might well have made possible, then its entire strategic environment would have appeared quite different. With a defensive doctrine, a larger army would have been unnecessary to defend against a French attack, a larger fraction of German troops could have been shifted to defense in the east, and continuing improvements in the Russian army would have been understood to be less dangerous.[66] As a result, pressures for German arms buildups, and reactions by its continental adversaries, as well as Germany's incentives for preventive war, would have been smaller. Given this view of its doctrinal requirements, Germany's entire military strategy, including the arms race, was suboptimal.

In sum, whether Germany's army buildup was suboptimal depends on a still larger debate over whether Germany required an offensive doctrine: if offense was required, the arms buildup was arguably Germany's best option; in contrast, if defense was sufficient, the arms buildup was suboptimal. The counterfactual for the latter case—that is, Germany chooses a defensive doctrine instead of an offensive doctrine—has been studied extensively elsewhere, with critics arguing that Germany was punished for its failed policy and placing special blame on its "cult of the offensive," which significantly increased the probability of World War I.[67]

Japanese Navy in the Early 1920s

During World War I, the United States launched a naval buildup that had the potential to undermine Japan's defense of East Asia and spurred Japan to initiate a major buildup of its own.[68] Instead of continuing with naval competition, Japan agreed at the Washington Conference of 1921–1922 to significant limits on its naval forces, including force ratios that fell below those required by Japanese doctrine. Although the agreement was not fully satisfactory, both material and information conditions made cooperation Japan's best option.

Japan enjoyed defense advantage but suffered a power disadvantage that exceeded this defense advantage. Japan's military leaders believed that a 7:10 ratio in naval deployments was required to ensure its securi-

[66] Snyder, *The Ideology of the Offensive*, p. 119.

[67] Van Evera, *Causes of War*, chap. 7; Snyder *The Ideology of the Offensive*, chap. 4.

[68] John H. Maurer, "Arms Control and the Washington Conference," in Erik Goldstein and John H. Maurer, eds., *The Washington Conference, 1921–22* (Essex, UK: Frank Cass, 1994), pp. 268–274; and Roger Dingman, *Power in the Pacific: The Origins of Naval Arms Limitation, 1914–1922* (Chicago: University of Chicago Press, 1976).

ty.[69] As a result, Japan could satisfy its naval requirements while suffering a degree of naval inferiority. Japan, however, lacked the power to maintain this ratio in an arms race if the United States devoted itself to acquiring an offensive naval capability. For example, in 1922 Japanese production of iron and steel amounted to about only 3 percent of U.S. production,[70] and its economy was less than a tenth the size of America's. Consequently, an arms race would leave Japan far short of its defensive military requirement.

At the Washington Conference, Japan agreed to 6:10 inferiority to the United States in battleships, which was below the 7:10 ratio that Japan believed it required.[71] U.S. naval experts agreed with their Japanese counterparts that there was potentially a militarily significant difference between these ratios.[72] Japan's decision to accept this less than completely satisfactory ratio was heavily influenced by recognition of its inability to compete effectively with the United States and the U.S. ability to impose an even less desirable ratio. Naval Minister Kato Tomosaburo, who represented Japan at the conference, accepted the 6:10 ratio partly because he believed that the United States would win the naval race that would result if the conference failed.[73] In addition, Japan accepted the less favorable ratio because the United States and Britain agreed not to fortify their bases in the western Pacific, which reduced their ability to project naval power in the event of war.[74] Although controversial within the Japanese

[69] See Evans and Peattie, *Kaigun*, pp. 141–144.

[70] Correlates of War data at http://www.umich.edu/~cowproj.

[71] The countries also agreed to qualitative limits on the size of ships and their guns because otherwise a country could gain an advantage by building larger ships, while meeting the limitations on total tonnage. Stephen E. Pelz, *Race to Pearl Harbor: The Failure of the Second London Naval Conference and the Onset of World War II* (Cambridge: Harvard University Press, 1974), p. 1. Emphasizing the political dimension of the agreements is Emily O. Goldman, *Sunken Treaties: Naval Arms Control between the Wars* (University Park: University of Pennsylvania Press, 1994).

[72] James B. Crowley, *Japan's Quest for Autonomy: National Security and Foreign Policy, 1930–1938* (Princeton: Princeton University Press, 1966), p. 46.

[73] Sadao Asada, "Japanese Admirals and the Politics of Naval Limitations: Kato Tomosaburo vs Kato Kanji," in Gerald Jordan, ed., *Naval Warfare in the Twentieth Century, 1900–1945* (London: Croom Helm, 1977), pp. 151–152; and Robert Gordon Kaufman, *Arms Control during the Pre-Nuclear Era: The United States and Naval Limitation between the Two World Wars* (New York: Columbia University Press, 1990), p. 61. For a related argument, see Crowley, *Japan's Quest for Autonomy*, p. 27.

[74] Carl Boyd, "Japanese Military Effectiveness: The Interwar Period," in Allan R. Millett and Williamson Murray, eds., *Military Effectiveness*, vol. 2: *The Interwar Period* (London: Allen and Unwin, 1988), pp. 142–148. In addition, the treaty did not limit cruisers, destroyers, or submarines, which Japan believed would increase its ability to wear down U.S. forces as they crossed the Pacific, thereby helping to make up for the undesirable battleship ratio. Pelz, *Race to Pearl Harbor*, p. 3.

Navy,[75] these agreements arguably provided Japan with naval dominance in the region.[76]

The Japanese decision was further supported by the belief that the United States was not a greedy state bent on dominating East Asia, and that relations with the United States could be improved through military cooperation. Japan accepted the 6:10 ratio partly because Naval Minister Kato believed that improving U.S.–Japanese relations by stopping the naval competition deserved top priority: "Avoidance of war with America by diplomatic means is the essence of national defense."[77] Although pursuing an arms control agreement would have been Japan's best option even if Japan believed the United States was likely a greedy state, Japan's more benign view of the United States made arms control politically, as well as militarily, desirable.

U.S. Navy in the Early 1920s

The United States faced a more complicated decision than Japan did because it had the power required to gain an offensive naval capability. The naval limits agreed to at the Washington Conference reflected the U.S. decision not to acquire this capability. The U.S. Navy believed that the 10:6 ratio, combined with prohibitions on fortifying bases in the western Pacific, left it without forces adequate for winning on the offensive against Japan.[78]

Because defense had the advantage, parity in naval forces was more than sufficient to give the United States high confidence in its ability to protect its homeland. However, because the United States had interests in the western Pacific—including protecting the Philippines and its trading interests in China—it required an offensive capability to project naval

[75] An influential faction in the Japanese Navy believed that the arrangement did not meet Japan's minimum security requirements; Kaufman, *Arms Control during the Pre-Nuclear Era*, pp. 59–60, 71; Sadao Asada, "The Japanese Navy and the United States," in Dorothy Borg and Shumpei Okamoto, eds., *Pearl Harbor as History: Japanese-American Relations, 1931–1941* (New York: Columbia University Press, 1973), pp. 226–28; and Asada, "Japanese Admirals and the Politics of Naval Limitations," pp. 149, 152.

[76] Crowley, *Japan's Quest for Autonomy*, pp. 29–31; and Maurer, "Arms Control and the Washington Conference," p. 283.

[77] Sadao Asada, "From Washington to London: The Imperial Navy and the Politics of Naval Limitations, 1921–1930," in Erik Goldstein and John H. Maurer, *The Washington Conference* (Essex, UK: Frank Cass, 1994), p. 153; see also Asada, "Japanese Admirals and the Politics of Naval Limitations," pp. 146–147. For similar views held by the prime minister and foreign minister, see Dingman, *Power in the Pacific*, pp. 184, 202.

[78] The U.S. Navy actually believed that a 2:1 advantage and fortified bases were necessary; it would have been satisfied with a somewhat less favorable ratio because the U.S. fleet would have been more modern than Japan's; W. R. Braisted, *The United States Navy in the Pacific, 1909–1922* (Austin: University of Texas Press, 1971).

power into this region. As noted above, in the 1920s U.S. power was sufficiently great to overcome the defense advantage and provide an offensive capability in a naval arms race with Japan.

The United States was quite uncertain about Japan's motives—worried
that recent Japanese behavior reflected malign motives, but also hopeful
that future Japanese behavior would be guided by peaceful motives.[79] As
a result, a key factor leading to the U.S. decision to exercise extensive
restraint was the desire to avoid naval policies that would appear provocative to Japan.[80] Secretary of State Charles Evans Hughes, who led the
U.S. delegation, favored a complete halt in current building plans because
"it would serve as an ideal way to gain Far Eastern concessions because
the American fleet would not threaten Japan."[81]

Although the limits agreed to at the Washington Conference prevented
the United States from building offensive naval capabilities commensurate with its power, this cooperative policy was within the range of optimal policies, given the security dilemma views that underpinned U.S. decisions. In addition, the risks of cooperation were limited because defense
advantage ensured that the security of the U.S. homeland was not in jeopardy and because the U.S. interests that required offense for protection
were not vital ones. Although insufficient to preserve peace in the decades
ahead, the naval limits did achieve their goal of improving U.S.–Japan
relations.[82]

Japanese Navy in the 1930s

EVALUATING DIVERGENCE FROM THE RATIONAL BASELINE

In the mid-1930s Japan rejected continued arms control in favor of a
naval buildup. The Japanese Navy decided that it required parity in naval
forces and successfully demanded that Japan terminate the Washington

[79] Thomas H. Buckley, *The United States and the Washington Conference, 1921–1922*
(Knoxville: University of Tennessee Press, 1970), p. 127.

[80] Other factors included doubts in the Harding administration about whether Congress
would fund the U.S. naval buildup (which partly reflected these security dilemma views)
and doubts among some that the United States would go to war to protect its interests in
China. On the latter point, see Braisted, *The United States Navy, 1909–1922*, p. 595.

[81] Quoted in Buckley, *The United States and the Washington Conference, 1921–1922*, p.
54; and p. 15 on President Warren Harding expressing views that in broad terms are consistent with a security dilemma worldview. See also Kaufman, *Arms Control during the
Pre-Nuclear Era*, pp. 30–31, 43–53, who stresses the importance of Hughes's view of the
negative impact of arms races; and Robert H. Ferrell, *American Diplomacy in the Great
Depression: Hoover-Stimson Foreign Policy, 1929–1933* (London: Oxford University Press,
1957), pp. 28–29, more generally on the U.S. belief that arms races were potentially
dangerous.

[82] Warren I. Cohen, *Empire without Tears: America's Foreign Relations 1921–1933*
(New York: Knopf, 1987), pp. 53–55; and Thomas H. Buckley, "The Icarus Factor," in
Goldstein and Maurer, *The Washington Conference, 1921–22*, pp. 144–145.

and London naval treaties at the beginning of the upcoming Second London Naval Conference (1935–1936).[83] In 1936 Japan launched a buildup that went well beyond the treaty limits; the United States was somewhat slow to respond, then launched a buildup in 1938, two years after the arms control agreements had collapsed; Japan decided on a comparable arms increase in 1939, and the United States substantially expanded its building plans twice in mid-1940. In mid-1941 the ratio of Japanese to U.S. naval forces was 7:10, but a Japanese study projected it would fall to 3:10 in 1944.[84]

Material variables had not changed significantly since the early 1920s. Although Japan's assessment of its naval requirements changed, there was little analytic basis for this shift; Japan's understanding of naval technology and strategy had not changed dramatically.[85] Whereas an influential faction in the navy had earlier opposed the naval agreements because they denied Japan a 7:10 ratio, by 1933 Navy Minister Osumi Mineo decided that still more favorable ratios were required and by 1934 that parity was required.[86] Japan's power also had not changed significantly— U.S. potential continued to dwarf Japan's. In 1937 U.S. national income was $68 billion compared with Japan's $4 billion, the United States was spending only 1.5 percent of this on defense compared with 28 percent for Japan, and the United States produced almost ten times as much steel as did Japan.[87]

Consequently, although the Japanese Navy might reasonably have preferred naval limitations that were more favorable than the United States would accept, its prospects were nevertheless better within the naval treaty limits than in an unconstrained naval competition. David Evans and Mark Peattie conclude that "these treaties provided Japan with a security vis-à-vis the United States that the navy could not provide by its own efforts."[88] Even if Japan did require the higher ratio that the navy now claimed (with little foundation) was necessary, rejecting cooperation was still a bad idea. This was especially true because the United States

---

[83] Pelz, *Race to Pearl Harbor*, pp. 27–28, 53–55, 62; and Crowley, *Japan's Quest for Autonomy*, pp. 196–200.

[84] Pelz, *Race to Pearl Harbor*, pp. 196–211, 224; and Sadao Asada, *From Mahan to Pearl Harbor: The Imperial Japanese Navy and the United States* (Annapolis: Naval Institute Press, 2006), pp. 205–206, 240–241. In 1941 the opposing naval forces deployed in the Pacific were essentially equal in size; Pelz, *Race to Pearl Harbor*, p. 221.

[85] On the emotional and ideological arguments that were used to support the requirement for parity, see Asada, "The Japanese Navy and the United States," pp. 234–235; and Pelz, *Race to Pearl Harbor*, p. 27. The changes in technology that were potentially important were largely overlooked and did not influence this change in requirements; Evans and Peattie, *Kaigun*, p. 212.

[86] Pelz, *Race to Pearl Harbor*, pp. 19, 45–46.

[87] Evans and Peattie, *Kaigun*, p. 364, and more broadly, pp. 363–370.

[88] Ibid., p. 463.

was not building up to the treaty limits; by refusing to extend them, Japan increased the probability that the United States would compete at levels more commensurate with its power.

A possible counterargument is that Japan had solid grounds for believing that the United States would not react to its buildup. When Japan's prime minister, Hirota Koki, expressed concerns about the U.S. reaction, he was told that the United States lacked the resolve to respond—it was preoccupied with recession and was becoming more isolationist.[89] Although these arguments turned out to be incorrect, Washington's restrained naval policy could have supported the Japanese conclusion that the United States lacked resolve. These arguments, however, did not support launching an arms race: if the United States lacked interests that were sufficient to generate a U.S. reaction, then it also would not fight in Asia; therefore Japan would not need to risk an arms race to protect itself from a U.S. attack.

Another possible counterargument focuses on Japanese motives. By the 1930s Japan had become more determined to achieve control over the western Pacific.[90] An explanation for this shift is that Japan was becoming greedier, which should have made it willing to run greater risks to achieve its territorial objectives.[91] However, even more expansionist motives are insufficient to conclude that Japan's policy was rational. Given its large power disadvantage, Japan's best bet was not a naval race that it had little hope of winning and that increased the probability of U.S. intervention in the Pacific.

The naval race did provide Japan with a temporary advantage in naval forces—partly because it had been designing ships that violated the arms control agreements and partly because the United States was slow to respond—but within a couple of years the United States' naval reaction left no doubt that Japan's naval capabilities were going to decline rapidly. As a result, Japan faced a closing window of opportunity that created pressure to attack the United States before it faced overwhelming naval inferiority in the Pacific.[92]

EVALUATING THE COUNTERFACTUAL

To assess whether pursuing a suboptimal arms buildup actually hurt Japan, we need to consider the counterfactual of a continuing naval arms control agreement. Whether the arms race reduced Japan's security and increased the probability of war is complicated, maybe more so than most cases, by the extent to which the buildup is intertwined with other

[89] Pelz, *Race to Pearl Harbor*, pp. 173–174; also p. 82.
[90] Crowley, *Japan's Quest for Autonomy*, pp. 191–200.
[91] For a domestic politics explanation for this shift, see Snyder, *Myths of Empire*, chap. 4.
[92] Pelz, *Race to Pearl Harbor*, chap. 12.; and Van Evera, *Causes of War*, pp. 89–94.

elements of Japan's foreign policy.[93] The naval leaders who designed Japan's withdrawal from the arms control agreements also played a central role in defining Japan's bid for autarky and the territorial expansion that it required, and in the interservice competition that further distorted Japan's policy.[94] Sadao Asada concludes that the legacy of Admiral Kato Kanji (who was the leading opponent of naval limitations during the 1920 and early 1930s), including "negation of the Washington system, destruction of the Japanese naval tradition, decimation of Japan's finest naval leadership, supremacy of the Naval General Staff over the Navy Ministry, the obsession of a 70 percent ratio and inevitability of war with the United States, and reopening of the arms race," hung over Japanese naval leaders as they made decisions that led to Pearl Harbor.[95] Consequently, the counterfactual that preserves the naval agreements but leaves unchanged the rest of the history leading up to the decision for war is likely historically unrealistic; to change Japan's arming policy would have required different naval leaders and these leaders would likely have pursued a variety of other policies that Japan did not adopt. Nevertheless, the counterfactual enables us to isolate the impact of the arms race.

The clearest impact of the naval race on Japan's decision was the time pressure it created. When Japan's naval leaders considered war in 1940 and 1941, they were acutely aware of the shifting balance of naval forces. In September 1940 the vice chief of the Navy General Staff explained that by April 1941 the navy would have completed its planned preparations and "when this is done, we have prospects for victory, if we fight an early decisive battle," and that the United States was "rapidly building ships, and the gap in the ratio will become increasingly large in the future, and Japan cannot possibly overtake them, and, in that sense, if we go to war, today would be best." In July 1941, as Japan was deciding to launch its expansion into Southeast Asia, Admiral Nagano, who was the chief of the Navy General Staff, argued that "although at present we have prospects for victory over the United States, as time passes the probability of our success will decrease and by the latter half of next year, we will have difficulty matching them, and thereafter things will become worse and worse."[96] At a critical meeting in November 1941, the navy argued that

[93] On a different aspect of the historical complexity, in concluding his analysis of the naval race, Pelz argues that "great events in distant parts of the world followed so closely upon one another that it is difficult to sort cause from effect. But through this grey tangle ran the red thread of the naval race, which began long before these critical final years." *Race to Pearl Harbor*, p. 227.

[94] On the distorting impact of interservice competition for resources, see Michael A. Barnhart, *Japan Prepares for Total War: The Search for Economic Security, 1919–1941* (Ithaca: Cornell University Press, 1987).

[95] Asada, *From Mahan to Pearl Harbor*, p. 286; on this perspective, see also p. 161.

[96] Quotes are from Pelz, *Race to Pearl Harbor*, pp. 218, 223.

"because British and American defenses were improving and the number of enemy warships increasing, 'the time for war will not come later.'" [97] The Japanese Navy recognized that even if it took advantage of this temporary advantage, its prospects in a long war were poor, but it believed it had a chance of victory in a limited war.[98]

Although these window arguments appear to have encouraged Japan's decision for war, a number of other factors also contributed to the decision, which could raise doubts about whether Japan would have opted against war if the arms control agreements had continued into the 1940s. First, the war in Europe made the southern advance more attractive during this period by reducing the ability of the colonial powers to resist Japanese expansion. In addition, in 1941 the United States sent a quarter of its fleet to the Atlantic to help the British, which resulted in rough parity between the naval forces of the Western allies and Japan in the Pacific.[99] Second, the U.S. oil embargo, which the United States applied in August 1941 in reaction to Japan's move into southern Indochina, created its own pressures for war. The Japanese Navy could not fight a long war without importing oil and, with the embargo in effect, delaying war steadily reduced how long Japan could fight. As a result, Japan faced reinforcing time pressures created by the arms race and the embargo. Given these other factors, one could argue that Japan would have decided for war even if not engaged in a losing arms race with the United States. However, given the prominent role that the dire implications of the arms race played in naval leaders' discussions leading up to Japan's decision for war, we have grounds for being skeptical of this assessment. Moreover, if the balance of naval power had not been shifting, Japan might have decided for war in Southeast Asia to secure oil and protect its ability to transport it back to Japan but have forgone the attack on Pearl Harbor, which would have increased the possibility that the United States would not have entered the war.

In addition, the naval arms race may have increased the probability of war with the United States in other, less direct ways. During a number of critical meetings leading up to the decision for war, navy leaders who had serious doubts about Japan's ability to win a war with the United States were unwilling to provide an accurate assessment of the navy's poor

---

[97] Scott D. Sagan, "The Origins of the Pacific War," *Journal of Interdisciplinary History* 18, 4 (Spring 1988): 914, with quote from Nobutaka Ike, *Japan's Decision for War: Records of the 1941 Policy Conferences* (Stanford: Stanford University Press, 1967), p. 202.

[98] For divergent views on whether the Japan could have reasonably hoped for a limited war, see Sagan, "The Origins of the Pacific War," p. 916, who argues in the affirmative, if the Japanese attack had been limited instead of against Pearl Harbor; and Richard Ned Lebow, *Between Peace and War* (Baltimore: Johns Hopkins University Press, 1981), p. 274.

[99] Pelz, *Race to Pearl Harbor*, p. 221.

prospects in a near-term war. This unwillingness had a close connection to the naval arms race because naval leaders had promised that a naval buildup would benefit Japan and provide necessary capabilities. For example, Navy Vice Minister Sawamoto explained that the navy "after so many years of clamoring about its 'invincible fleet,' was hardly in a position to say it could not take on the United States; it would have no ground to stand on in dealing with its officers as well as the army and the public."[100] Acknowledging the navy's poor prospects required admitting that the navy had failed to meet this promise. In addition, the arms race was closely related to Japan's decision to expand into Southeast Asia. Unlike a rational strategic analysis, Japan did not first decide that its security required southern expansion and then evaluate whether it could acquire the military capabilities required to achieve this objective. Instead, southern expansion was attractive to the navy at least partly because this policy would require a large naval buildup and the accompanying shift of resources to the navy. Michael Barnhart concludes that "Japan might have avoided sanctions by forsaking the Southern Advance. But to have done so would have required a navy willing to see its steel allocations held constant, or even reduced, while the United States was building an incomparably larger fleet. The odds never favored such an outcome."[101] Thus, if a naval buildup had been precluded by an arms control treaty or by domestic political constraints, Japan would have been less likely to choose its expansionist policy, which led to war with the United States. This line of argument does, however, raise the question of levels of causation that I noted above—these barriers to a naval buildup would have required a change in Japan's domestic politics that go beyond simply hypothesizing a decision not to engage in a naval arms race.

U.S. Navy in the 1930s

Throughout the treaty period, the U.S. Navy was smaller than allowed by the naval arms control agreements. The United States moderately increased its naval building in 1934, which promised to bring the United

[100] Quoted in Asada, *From Mahan to Pearl Harbor*, pp. 270–271; see also Michael Barnhart, "Autarky and International Law: Japan's Attempt to Achieve Self-Sufficiency and the Origins of the Pacific War," (Ph.D. diss., Harvard University, 1980), who argues that if the navy's "leaders found war with America to be unacceptable, they had to confess that their fleet was worthless"; quoted in Snyder, *Myths of Empire*, p. 143. Other reasons for not expressing doubts about its capabilities were that the naval leaders feared that opposition to war could lead to a coup d'etat by the army (see, for example, Arthur J. Marder, *Old Friends, New Enemies* [Oxford: Oxford University Press, 1981], p. 254); and that this would result in a shift of resources from the navy to the army.

[101] Barnhart, *Japan Prepares for Total War*, esp. chap. 9, quote on p. 267; and Asada, *From Mahan to Pearl Harbor*, pp. 238–239.

States up to the treaty limits by 1942. The United States did not launch a naval buildup that approached its potential and requirements until 1940, and its slowness in responding fully to the Japanese naval challenge created a window of opportunity that influenced Japan's decision for war.

As described above, in the mid-1930s material variables continued to provide the United States with the option of acquiring an offensive capability—its huge power advantage far exceeded the extent of defense advantage. What had changed since the early 1920s was the U.S. assessment of Japan's motives.[102] By the early 1930s, Japan's policies had convinced key U.S. decision makers that Japan's goals for controlling East Asia were quite ambitious and not driven simply by Japan's desire for security. Both Japan's invasion of Manchuria in 1931 and its declaration in 1934 that it would oppose all Western aid to China ran counter to its Washington treaty obligations. Also fueling the revised assessment of Japan's motives was Tokyo's declaration at the end of 1934 that it would abandon the naval treaties.

As a result, the United States needed to manage its security dilemma differently. It had to place less weight on cooperative policies designed to reassure Japan, which guided U.S. policy at the Washington Conference, and more weight on competitive policies. More competitive policies would provide the military capabilities the United States required to protect its interests and, closely related, communicate its resolve. U.S. leaders understood the implications of their increasingly negative view of Japan's motives. Instead of wanting to avoid competition, now they hoped a naval arms race (combined with cooperation with Britain that would isolate Japan) would "bring the Japanese government to its senses."[103] Even Norman Davis, the lead U.S. arms control negotiator, who had a strong inclination to prefer cooperative policies, concluded by 1934 that refusing to pursue further negotiations and instead launching a naval buildup was the United States' best option.[104] President Franklin Roosevelt pursued negotiations at the Second London Conference largely with the goal of ensuring that Japan was blamed for its collapse and gaining support for a naval buildup.[105]

The United States, however, did not launch the naval buildup that

---

[102] Pelz, *Race to Pearl Harbor*, chaps. 5 and 6; and Dorothy Borg, *The United States and the Far Eastern Crisis of 1933–1938* (Cambridge: Harvard University Press, 1964).

[103] Secretary of State Henry Hull, quoted in Pelz, *Race to Pearl Harbor*, p. 142; see also p. 85.

[104] Ibid., pp. 83–85, 140, 142; and Meredith W. Berg, "Protecting National Interests by Treaty: The Second London Naval Conference, 1934–36," in B.J.C. McKercher, ed., *Arms Limitation and Disarmament* (Westport, CT: Praeger, 1992), pp. 214–215.

[105] Pelz, *Race to Pearl Harbor*, pp. 126–129; for somewhat different emphasis, see Kaufman, *Arms Control during the Pre-Nuclear Era*, pp. 176–177.

Roosevelt's advisers increasingly favored. Given the continuing influence of isolationists in Congress and the restraining impact of the recession, Roosevelt faced significant barriers to launching a major naval buildup. Because the United States waited until 1940 to launch a buildup that came closer to its potential, the years leading up to World War II saw a growing mismatch develop between U.S naval capabilities and its political commitments.[106] Whereas restraint and cooperation were well matched to the international conditions the United States faced in the early 1920s, negative shifts in U.S. assessments of Japan's motives called for a more competitive policy by the mid-1930s, but the United States failed to fully meet this challenge.[107]

U.S. Cold War Nuclear Buildups

The deployment of large, sophisticated nuclear arsenals by the United States and the Soviet Union was a defining feature of the Cold War. During this period the United States faced a number of major decisions and pursued a mix of competitive and cooperative policies, with the mix heavily weighted toward competition.[108] This section briefly assesses the U.S. buildup of a robust assured destruction capability and two of the key decisions that followed—the deployment of multiple independently targeted reentry vehicles (MIRVs) and the banning of large-scale antiballistic missile (ABM) systems.

BUILDING TO A ROBUST ASSURED DESTRUCTION CAPABILITY

By the early 1960s, the United States was in the process of deploying a survivable nuclear force that, although not initially designed as a strategically coherent package, promised to provide a diversified, redundant assured destruction capability.[109] Recognition of the limited value of still

---

[106] The United States did recognize that it could win a long war and developed plans for this possibility. Pelz, *Race to Pearl Harbor*, p. 76, 199. Nevertheless, basic requirements for the core U.S. war plan went unmet.

[107] Pelz, *Race to Pearl Harbor*; and more sharply, Kaufman, *Arms Control during the Pre-Nuclear Era*.

[108] Albert Wohlstetter questioned whether there was a nuclear arms race. See Wohlstetter, "Is There a Strategic Arms Race?" *Foreign Policy* 15 (Summer 1974): 3–20; and Wohlstetter, "Rivals, but No 'Race'," *Foreign Policy* 16 (Fall 1974): 48–81; responses in that issue; and Michael Nacht, "The Delicate Balance of Error," *Foreign Policy* 19 (Summer 1975): 163–177.

[109] Overviews of U.S. forces and planning include William Burr, "Essay: U.S. Strategic Nuclear Policy, 1955–1968: An Overview," in Burr, ed., *U.S. Nuclear History: Nuclear Arms and Politics in the Missile Age, 1955–1968* (Washington, DC: National Security Archive, 1997); and Jerome Kahan, *Security in the Nuclear Age* (Washington, DC: Brookings, 1975).

larger forces created a willingness to unilaterally limit the size of the U.S. buildup.[110] Although lagging behind the United States, the Soviet Union deployed comparable nuclear capabilities. The competition that led to a world of mutual assured destruction (MAD) capabilities generated a variety of dangers—the United States worried about becoming vulnerable to massive Soviet attack, about threats to its retaliatory capability, and about the implications of MAD for extended deterrence.[111] Nevertheless, U.S. policy was within the range of optimal options.

Nuclear weapons created a revolution for defense advantage. In the nuclear context, deterrence by retaliation is the functional equivalent of defense. During the Cold War, both the United States and the Soviet Union could build nuclear forces capable of inflicting massive retaliatory damage for substantially less than the cost of the forces required to undermine these capabilities. Therefore, assuming that the ability to retaliate (in limited as well as massive ways) provides an effective deterrent, nuclear weapons resulted in a large advantage for defense.[112] The United States enjoyed a power advantage during the first couple of decades of the Cold War, but this advantage was insufficiently large to offset the defense advantage.[113] Consequently, a nuclear arms race would not enable the United States to prevent the Soviet Union from achieving a massive retaliatory capability of its own.

The United States therefore had to choose between two broad force posture options:[114] building a nuclear force that would provide robust

[110] Richard L. Kugler, "The Politics of Restraint: Robert McNamara and the Strategic Nuclear Forces, 1963–1968" (Ph.D. diss., Massachusetts Institute of Technology, 1975), esp. chaps. 2, 3; and Desmond Ball, *Politics and Force Levels: The Strategic Missile Program of the Kennedy Administration* (Berkeley: University of California Press, 1980). Some members of the White House staff believed the force should be much smaller than planned (Ball, pp. 84–87). At the time these decisions were made, the United States enjoyed a large lead in missiles and, at least rhetorically, the need for superiority was widely accepted (pp. 179–211).

[111] Lawrence Freedman, *The Evolution of Nuclear Strategy* (London: Macmillan, 1989).

[112] This is a controversial assumption. See Robert Jervis, *The Illogic of American Nuclear Strategy* (Ithaca: Cornell University Press, 1984). On how different views of nuclear deterrence influence the offense-defense balance, see Glaser, *Analyzing Strategic Nuclear Policy*, pp. 94–99.

[113] For example, in 1950 U.S. GDP was almost three times the Soviet Union's, in 1973 it was more than two times as large, and the U.S. advantage was somewhat larger in per capita GDP; Angus Maddison, *The World Economy: A Millennial Perspective* (Paris: OECD, 2001), pp. 261, 264.

[114] The other key option was preventive war. See George H. Quester, *Nuclear Monopoly* (New Brunswick, NJ: Transaction, 2000); and Mark Trachtenberg, "American Strategy and the Shifting Nuclear Balance, 1949–1954," *International Security* 13, 3 (Winter 1988/89): 5–49. Another possibility was a cooperative transition to MAD; however, this faced many of the political and technical barriers that prevented disarmament, albeit to a lesser degree.

retaliatory capabilities, with the understanding that the Soviet Union would do the same; and negotiating an arms control agreement that would ban nuclear weapons. Because nuclear weapons had a large impact on the offense-defense balance, the transition to MAD could be dangerous—plagued by windows and transition problems—but once reached MAD would provide substantial deterrent stability. Given the clear advantage of defense, the nuclear arms race should peter out once the superpowers deployed robust assured destruction capabilities, which could provide additional security.

In contrast, banning nuclear weapons held the attraction of preserving U.S. invulnerability, but the dangers if the Soviet Union cheated on a disarmament agreement were very large because cheating would provide the Soviet Union with a nuclear monopoly. Consequently, a necessary condition for disarmament to be desirable was very high confidence that the Soviet Union was not a greedy state, and similar confidence that Soviet concerns about U.S. motives would not generate Soviet incentives to gain nuclear advantages.[115] The United States' information about the Soviet Union was not nearly this positive.[116] As a result, in nuclear disarmament negotiations at the beginning of the nuclear era, Washington insisted on highly intrusive inspections and a number of other demanding terms, which Moscow found unacceptable.[117] Whether the United States hoped the Soviets would accept these terms or instead intentionally designed its proposal to ensure Soviet rejection remains open to debate.[118] Given the clear military and political significance of nuclear weapons, however, there is a powerful case that the Soviet Union would not have accepted any realistic disarmament agreement.[119]

Although the U.S. nuclear buildup that followed was within the range of optimal policies, it is important to note that U.S. nuclear strategy was not fully consistent with the basic offense-defense and power arguments. The United States continued to place substantial importance on being able to destroy Soviet forces to reduce the damage of a Soviet attack. This partly reflected the possibility of some damage limitation during the period before the Soviet Union acquired a robust assured destruction capability. Counterforce targeting for damage limitation continued to play an important role in U.S. nuclear doctrine, however, even after the growth of Soviet forces made significant damage limitation essentially infeasible by

[115] Glaser, *Analyzing Strategic Nuclear Policy*, chap. 5.

[116] McGeorge Bundy, *Danger and Survival: Choices about the Bomb in the First Fifty Years* (New York: Random House, 1988), pp. 168–169, 175–176.

[117] Bernhard G. Bechhoefer, *Postwar Negotiations for Arms Control* (Washington, DC: Brookings, 1961), pp. 27–82.

[118] Quester, *Nuclear Monopoly*, pp. 140–144.

[119] Bundy, *Danger and Survival*, pp. 192–196.

the mid-1960s.[120] In spite of this, the types of forces the United States deployed did not heavily reflect its choice of strategy because the delivery systems then available for retaliation and counterforce were quite similar; offense and defense were largely indistinguishable.[121] The continuing U.S. interest in counterforce targeting was, however, the seed of future trouble.

U.S. MIRVS

In the late 1960s and 1970, the United States had the opportunity to try to ban the further development and deployment of MIRVs in the Strategic Arms Limitation Talks (SALT) with the Soviet Union.[122] Highly accurate MIRVs were going to increase each country's ability to destroy the other's land-based intercontinental ballistic missiles (ICBMs). However, the United States (as well as the Soviet Union) failed to pursue seriously a ban on MIRVs. The vulnerability of U.S. ICBMs increased significantly and became the most influential symbol of American insecurity during the last decade and a half of the Cold War.[123] U.S-Soviet relations were strained as both countries interpreted the other's counterforce programs as a reflection of malign motives.

Evaluating Divergence From The Rational Baseline. By reducing the difficulty of destroying the adversary's nuclear retaliatory capability, highly accurate MIRVs would shift the offense-defense balance toward offense. The overall balance would continue to favor defense because the superpowers deployed delivery systems that were not threatened by MIRVs and because even a small number of surviving nuclear weapons could threaten enormous retaliatory damage. Nevertheless, MIRVs would make preserving diversified retaliatory capabilities more difficult. Because MIRVs were more valuable for offensive (damage-limitation) missions than defensive (retaliatory) ones, offense and defense were distinguishable, which created the opportunity for qualitative arms control.

The United States still enjoyed a power advantage, but MIRV was not

---

[120] See Desmond Ball, "Development of the SIOP, 1960–1983," in Desmond Ball and Jeffrey Richelson, eds., *Strategic Nuclear Targeting* (Ithaca: Cornell University Press, 1986); and Freedman, *The Evolution of Nuclear Strategy.*

[121] This characterization does, however, underplay the importance of survivability for retaliation.

[122] On SALT, see John Newhouse, *Cold Dawn: The Story of SALT* (New York: Holt, Rinehart and Winston, 1973); Smith, *Double Talk*; Mason Willrich and John B. Rhinelander, eds., *SALT: The Moscow Agreements and Beyond* (New York: Free Press, 1974); and Garthoff, *Détente and Cooperation*, chap. 5.

[123] The danger, however, was exaggerated. See Albert Carnesale and Charles L. Glaser, "ICBM Vulnerability: The Cures Are Worse Than the Disease," *International Security* 7, 1 (Summer 1982): 70–85.

going to shift the offense-defense balance enough to make an offensive (damage-limitation) capability feasible. By the mid-1960s, the continuing Soviet buildup was leading increasingly to the conclusion within the Pentagon, at least among civilians, that significant damage limitation was going to be infeasible, primarily because the Soviet Union could react efficiently to offset U.S. efforts.[124]

Under these conditions, the United States should have pursued an arms control agreement that banned MIRVs. Banning MIRVs would have enabled the United States to retain greater confidence in the adequacy of its nuclear retaliatory forces (or, alternatively, to have invested significantly less to preserve its confidence) and to signal its benign motives to the Soviet Union. And deploying MIRVs would likely signal the opposite because a greedy state would be more willing than a security seeker to risk losing its deterrent retaliatory capability to gain military advantages, especially when the prospects for success were low. Because MIRVs could not provide the United States with a significant damage-limitation capability, it would have given up little in military capability in return for these political benefits.

Two sets of considerations, however, made the U.S. MIRV decision more complicated than suggested by these basic offense-defense arguments. First, there were a variety of other missions for MIRVs, which at least in theory created the possibility that MIRVs could favor defense, not offense. An influential argument was that MIRVs were necessary to preserve U.S. retaliatory capabilities by ensuring that U.S. warheads would penetrate Soviet ABM systems.[125] This argument suggests that the United States should have pursued a MIRV ban in combination with a ban on ABM, especially once negotiated limits on ABM appeared likely. The United States, however, failed to do this.[126] Other potential missions for MIRVs reflected U.S. strategic doctrine, which continued to require counterforce to extend deterrence to U.S. allies, to deter limited nuclear attacks against the U.S. homeland, and to control escalation if nuclear war occurred.[127] Disagreements over whether the United States required counterforce for these purposes formed the core of the Cold War debate over U.S. nuclear policy and are too extensive to explore here. In the end,

---

[124] Kugler, "The Politics of Restraint," pp. 94–108.

[125] Greenwood, *Making the MIRV*, pp. 40, 44, 76–77.

[126] A related argument—that MIRV was required to hedge against Soviet upgrading of its Tallinn air defense—was not directly affected by the ABM treaty. Freedman, *U.S. Intelligence and the Soviet Threat*, pp. 90–96; Greenwood, *Making the MIRV*, p. 116, 124, 173–176; and Newhouse, *Cold Dawn*, pp. 11–12, 72–73, 122.

[127] On these missions, as well as damage limitation, see Greenwood, *Making the MIRV*; Kugler, "The Politics of Restraint," esp. chap. 4; and Enthoven and Smith, *How Much Is Enough?*, pp. 181–183.

the case against counterforce in MAD is powerful.[128] Moreover, even if the United States required limited counterforce options, it did not require MIRVs to perform these missions because single warhead missiles would have been sufficient and even had some advantages; and its ability to perform these missions was not going to be enhanced if both countries added MIRVs to their arsenals.

Second, there was the possibility that a MIRV ban could not be verified with high confidence. Although the United States would have been better off if both states did not deploy MIRVs, if the probability of Soviet cheating was high, then an arms control agreement might not increase U.S. security. This was a salient concern because the United States believed that the Soviet Union might well have malign motives.[129] Deployment of MIRVs could not be monitored by national technical means. Consequently, proponents of banning MIRV argued for an arms control agreement that banned testing.[130] The U.S. government was split on the feasibility of monitoring a flight test ban. Agencies that favored a ban argued the Soviet Union would not deploy MIRVs without extensive testing, while those opposed argued the Soviet Union might test using a variety of deceptive techniques.[131] The critical question was whether the Soviets could develop an accurate MIRV with these techniques because inaccurate MIRVs would not pose a serious counterforce threat. Technical considerations, however, appear not to have played the key role in the U.S. decision. Instead, they were used to support broader preferences regarding MIRV.[132] Therefore, although not entirely clear cut, it appears that a MIRV ban could have effectively constrained Soviet counterforce capabilities.[133] In short, even once the risks that opponents

---

[128] Jervis, *The Illogic of American Nuclear Strategy*; and Glaser, *Analyzing Strategic Nuclear Policy*, chap. 7.

[129] Seay, "What Are the Soviet's Objectives in Their Foreign, Military, and Arms Control Policies," pp. 47–108, analyzes the spectrum of influential beliefs.

[130] Greenwood, *Making the MIRV*, pp. 111–112, 123–128; and Smith, *Double Talk*, pp. 158–165.

[131] On the controversy, see Smith, *Double Talk*, pp. 161, 173; and Alton Frye, *A Responsible Congress: The Politics of National Security* (New York: McGraw Hill, 1975), pp. 61–62.

[132] Garthoff, *Détente and Cooperation*, p. 138, focuses on divergent positions on the value of on-site inspection for verifying a MIRV ban, but the point appears to be more general; see Smith, *Double Talk*, p. 173. For a somewhat different interpretation, see Steve Weber, *Cooperation and Discord in U.S.–Soviet Arms Control* (Princeton: Princeton University Press, 1991), pp. 193–199.

[133] This conclusion is supported by the fact that opponents took flawed or exaggerated positions on a number of key issues, including the costs of delaying MIRV testing, whether the Soviets had tested a MIRV or only a maneuverable reentry vehicle, and the value of on-site inspection. See Greenwood, *Making the MIRV*, pp. 125; Smith, *Double Talk*, p. 159;

identified are considered, the U.S. decision not to pursue a MIRV ban was suboptimal.

Evaluating the Counterfactual. Did the failure to pursue a ban on MIRVs actually hurt the United States? To focus on the central issues, let the counterfactual be that if the United States had seriously negotiated a ban on MIRVs, an agreement would have been reached with the Soviet Union and this agreement could have been successfully monitored. Obviously, neither nuclear nor major conventional war occurred, so the costs of MIRV would have to be in its impact on the probability of war.[134] There are at least three possible mechanisms to consider. First, mutual deployment of MIRVs could have reduced the superpowers' deterrent capabilities and/or reduced crisis stability. At first order, this was not the case—both the United States and the Soviet Union retained assured destruction capabilities through the 1980s, and these capabilities were especially overwhelming in the politically relevant scenarios in which the countries had warning of an attack.[135] However, MIRV, and U.S. counterforce policies more generally, were dangerous in a more subtle way—they allowed and encouraged the U.S. military and some influential civilian leaders to exaggerate the potential advantages of striking first, preserving some hope that the United States could limit damage in an all-out war or favorably shift the ratio of surviving forces. Although these benefits of striking first were illusory, the belief that counterforce attacks could be valuable was nevertheless dangerous.[136] One could argue that banning MIRVs would not have eliminated the illusion, given that it had survived severe technical, analytic, and strategic challenges. Although this argument is plausible, banning MIRVs would have made the challenges still more severe because counterforce would have been still less effective. And banning MIRVs would have reflected a decision to forgo a counterforce doctrine, which should have eliminated these illusions.[137]

Freedman, *U.S. Intelligence and the Soviet Threat*, pp. 137–144; and Garthoff, *Détente and Cooperation*, pp. 138–139.

[134] In addition, MIRV and the counterforce doctrine that it supported increased the economic cost of U.S. nuclear forces. MIRV itself was not a very expensive addition to the ICBM force, although continuing to develop and deploy missiles with improved accuracy was costly. The potentially larger costs of MIRV concerned responding to the vulnerability of U.S. forces created by Soviet MIRVs; the United States considered a variety of responses but in the end did not deploy any of them.

[135] For citations on the survivability of U.S. forces, see chapter 7, note 51.

[136] Glaser, *Analyzing Strategic Nuclear Policy*, chap. 7, esp. pp. 244–249.

[137] This argument does, however, raise a question about what is being manipulated in the counterfactual: is it U.S. force posture and arms control policy or, instead, the beliefs and in turn the doctrine that drive force posture? If the latter, the impact of banning MIRV would be smaller.

Second, MIRVs in combination with other components of a nuclear counterforce strategy increased the probability of accidental and unauthorized use of nuclear weapons. In reaction to the vulnerability of their nuclear forces and command and control, the superpowers adopted launch-on-warning or related policies that increased the probability of nuclear war in response to false warning of attack. In addition, in a severe crisis or conventional war, the United States planned to predelegate launch authority to reduce the effectiveness of a combined decapitation and counterforce attack, which increased the probability of unauthorized nuclear use.[138]

Third, as predicted by the spiral model, the deployment of MIRVs, the ensuing competition in counterforce forces, and the increasing counterforce capability of opposing ICBM forces strained superpower relations by leading both states to conclude that their adversary was more dangerous. Starting in the mid-1970s, the improving counterforce capability of Soviet ICBMs become one the defining features, if not the defining feature, of the growing Soviet threat. Not only did the improving quality of Soviet forces pose a challenge to U.S. retaliatory forces, but in addition the United States imputed greedy motives to the Soviet buildup. This contributed to increasingly competitive hard-line U.S. policies, especially during the first term of the Reagan administration, which increased Soviet fears of the United States.[139]

Whether one counts this deterioration in relations as a cost depends on judgments about Soviet motives and goals, and their reactions to U.S. policies. Presenting classic deterrence model arguments, hard-line critics of U.S. policy argued that détente in general, and arms control in particular, had led the Soviet Union to question U.S. resolve. According to these arguments, the United States needed a more competitive policy, including a large nuclear buildup and a rejection of arms control, which would enable the United States to negotiate from strength and communicate its resolve to protect America's interests. From this perspective, an arms race was desirable, both because Soviet greedy motives were best dealt with by competitive policies and because the United States was better able to afford the competition, especially if in high technology weapons systems that the Soviet Union could not match. Secretary of Defense Weinberger argued that "it is neither reasonable nor prudent to view the Soviet military buildup as defensive in nature." Raymond Garthoff explains that the early Reagan buildup was "decided on before obtaining requests from the military services—it was intended to signal the strong resolve of the

---

[138] On these and related dangers, see Bruce G. Blair, *Strategic Command and Control: Redefining the Nuclear Threat* (Washington, DC: Brookings, 1985).

[139] Garthoff, *The Great Transformation*, chaps. 1–4, 12.

new administration."[140] Moreover, proponents argue that these competitive policies played an important role in bringing about the end of the Cold War.

However, the evidence supporting this position is weak. Instead of communicating resolve, competitive U.S. policies—including improved counterforce capabilities, renewed enthusiasm for ballistic missile defenses (in the form of SDI), and a massive buildup of conventional forces—did more to signal malign motives than to communicate U.S. resolve. Moreover, these buildups did little to strain the Soviet economy, and thereby contribute to the collapse of the Soviet system, because the Soviets did not increase defense spending to match U.S. spending.[141]

In sum, the counterfactual analysis suggests that the failure to ban MIRV contributed to the perpetuation of a dangerous strategic illusion, increased the probability of accidental war, and strained U.S.–Soviet relations.

ABM

During the 1960s and early 1970s, the United States also faced a major decision about whether to negotiate limits on antiballistic missile systems.[142] Proponents believed that ABM could enhance the U.S. deterrent and reduce the costs if war occurred. Opponents worried that deploying ABM would generate a costly arms race that would fail to reduce U.S. societal vulnerability to a Soviet nuclear attack, while damaging U.S.–Soviet relations and increasing the economic costs of U.S. strategic forces. The United States decided to pursue limits on ABM and succeeded in negotiating the ABM treaty with the Soviet Union.

In the context of the U.S.–Soviet nuclear competition, ABMs intended to protect cities and concentrations of economic infrastructure were a type of offense because they threatened the retaliatory capabilities that the opposing state required for deterrence. Offense and defense were therefore distinguishable. As with MIRV (although probably to a lesser extent), ABM would have made it more difficult for an opposing state to preserve its retaliatory capabilities, in effect shifting the balance of deployed forces toward offense. However, the offense-defense balance would continue to favor defense: studies of the cost-exchange ratio

---

[140] Ibid.; quotes from pp. 35, 33.

[141] Ibid., pp. 506, 516–517; and Evangelista, *Unarmed Forces*, chaps. 14 and 15.

[142] Histories include Ernest J. Yanarella, *The Missile Defense Controversy: Strategy, Technology, and Politics, 1955–1972* (Lexington: University of Kentucky Press, 1977); Edward Randolph Jayne, "The ABM Debate: Strategic Defense and National Security" (Ph.D. diss., Massachusetts Institute of Technology, 1969); and David N. Schwartz, "Past and Present: The Historical Legacy," pp. 339–342, in Ashton B. Carter and David N. Schwartz, eds., *Ballistic Missile Defense* (Washington, DC: Brookings, 1984).

showed that the Soviet forces required to defeat the U.S. ABM would cost significantly less than the U.S. ABM.[143]

Under these conditions, the United States' best option was to pursue limits on ABM. Given the continuing advantage of defense (retaliation), the Soviet Union would have been able to defeat the U.S. ABM with a combination of increases in the size of its retaliatory forces and the addition of countermeasures to its existing missile force. Because retaliatory capabilities were essential for deterrence, the Soviet Union would have had large incentives to respond. As a result, as opponents argued, superpower deployment of ABM systems would have fueled an action-reaction process that would have left the United States essentially as vulnerable as before the competition.[144] This competition, however, would have signaled malign motives because, in a world of defense advantage and offense-defense distinguishability, security seekers would be more willing than greedy states to forgo ABM. As a result, deploying ABM would have strained superpower relations and wasted resources, while not reducing U.S. vulnerability.

My theory suggests a number of possible counterpoints that support a different conclusion, but none is powerful in this case. The decision to limit ABM could have been suboptimal if the basic action-reaction argument was flawed. In fact, proponents of ABM challenged the action-reaction logic, questioning whether the Soviets measured their forces in terms of assured destruction capabilities and therefore whether they would respond to the United States' ABM. However, proponents had a difficult time making a convincing case. They argued that ABM would contribute to the preservation of U.S. nuclear superiority, but this contradicted their claim that the Soviets would lack incentives to react. Even if the Soviets were unconcerned with their ability to inflict retaliatory damage, which seemed unlikely, ABM would also have threatened their ability to perform other nuclear missions.[145] Another possibility is that the Soviet

---

[143] Jayne, "The ABM Debate," pp. 231–233, 267–268; but see David Goldfischer, *The Best Defense: Policy Alternatives for U.S. Nuclear Security from the 1950s to the 1980s* (Ithaca: Cornell University Press, 1993), pp. 168–171.

[144] This competition might have been more intense than suggested simply by the offense-defense balance because both countries were inclined to base their strategic programs on worst-case assessments of their adversary's military programs. Robert S. McNamara, "The Dynamics of Nuclear Strategy," Department of State bulletin, October 9, 1967; and Rathjens, "The Dynamics of the Arms Race."

[145] A related challenge held that ABM could be combined with limits on offensive forces, thereby reducing the importance of cost-exchange ratios; Donald G. Brennan, "Post-Deployment Policy Issues in BMD," in *Ballistic Missile Defense: Two Views*, Adelphi Paper No. 43 (London: International Institute for Strategic Studies, 1967); more recently, see Goldfischer, *The Best Defense*. For critiques of this argument see Glaser, *Analyzing Strategic Nuclear Policy*, pp. 177–180, 297–301.

Union would not react because it lacked the resources, which might have significantly increased the value of the United States' ABM.[146] However, although the Soviet economy was weaker than the U.S. economy, there were strong reasons for believing that a Soviet response was feasible: the U.S. power advantage was smaller than the extent of defense advantage; the Soviet Union was already in the midst of significantly enlarging its intercontinental missile force; and many of the reactions that could contribute to offsetting the United States' ABM were relatively inexpensive. Negotiating severe limits on ABM was therefore the United States' best option.

SUMMARY

The preceding section shows that a number of major-power arms races were dangerous—that is, states chose to build up arms when this was not their best option. Unlike the large literature on the consequences of arms races, this finding is based not on a correlation between arms races and war, but instead on a comparison of the arming options that were available to the states. My theory provides the rational baseline that is required to make this comparison. Figure 9.2 summarizes the assessments of arming decisions presented in this section.

This finding does not imply that in general states should avoid arms races. Under some conditions, arming, and if necessary competing militarily, will be a state's best option. Arms races are not always bad. As a result, failing to build up arms can sometimes reduce a state's security—the United States' slow response to Japan's naval buildup during the second half of the 1930s is an example. Nevertheless, in many of the major-power arms races of the past century, states have erred in the opposite direction.

In addition, the counterfactual analysis in the preceding section shows that states that chose policies that diverged from the theory's rational baseline—specifically states that engaged in buildups when they should not have—did worse than if they had followed the theory's prescriptions. Germany was hurt by the naval race that it launched before World War I, Japan was hurt by the naval race it initiated during the 1930s, and the United States was hurt by the nuclear competition—specifically in MIRVed missiles and improved accuracy—it engaged in during the Cold War. The costs of choosing suboptimal policies included wasted resources, unnecessarily strained political relations, decreased security, and an increased probability of war.

---

[146] Proponents made this point as well. Jayne, "The ABM Debate," pp. 329, 332, 357.

State Should Have Armed/Raced

		Yes	No
State Did Arm/Race	Yes	• German Army 1912–1914* • U.S. nuclear buildup to assured destruction	• German Navy 1898–1912/14 • Japanese Navy 1934–1936 • U.S. MIRV
	No	• U.S. Navy 1930s	• Japanese Navy 1922 • U.S. Navy 1922 • U.S. ABM

Figure 9.2. Assessment of States' Arming Decisions

*Assumes that Germany required an offensive doctrine; otherwise shifts to "should not have armed/raced."

These counterfactual tests add support to my theory because if the theory is strong, we expect states that fail to adopt its policy prescriptions to pay a price for their flawed decisions. And in combination with the analysis in chapter 7 of my theory's internal strengths, and in chapter 8 of important cases that the theory explains well, we now have a variety of reinforcing reasons for having confidence in the theory's high quality.

Finally, finding that states have frequently pursued suboptimal arming policies suggests the need for research that explains why states have made these significant military errors. A number of candidates exist in the broader literature on suboptimal decision making—including the bias of military organizations, the cognitive limits of decision makers, and the domestic structure of states.[147] A theory of suboptimal arming could have important policy implications, providing states with guidance on how to avoid choosing overly competitive military policies.

---

[147] For example, Posen, *The Sources of Military Doctrine*; Larson, *Anatomy of Mistrust*; Snyder, *Myths of Empire*; and Van Evera, "Why States Believe Foolish Ideas."

CHAPTER TEN

Summary and Policy Implications

THIS CONCLUDING CHAPTER begins by briefly summarizing a few of the book's major arguments. It then uses the theory to explore the future of major power relations over the next few decades, focusing on the implications of China's rise to full superpower status.

MAJOR ARGUMENTS

The book's introduction provides a rather full overview of the strategic choice theory I have developed. Instead of repeating that summary, here I briefly highlight a few of my book's major arguments.

First, and most broadly, the theory demonstrates that international anarchy does not create a general tendency for security-seeking states to pursue competitive strategies. Rather, under a range of conditions cooperation will be a rational state's best option. A state's choice of strategy should depend on three types of variables: the state's own motives; material factors that influence the state's military potential—power and offense-defense variables; and information about motives—both the state's beliefs about the opposing state's motives and its beliefs about the adversary's information about its motives.[1] Beyond making intuitive sense, the theory develops careful deductive arguments that demonstrate that each type of variable should influence a state's decision between cooperative and competitive strategies. The book's examination of illustrative examples and important historical cases suggests that these variables have varied substantially over time, which further supports the case for including them in a grand theory of international relations. This broad argument stands in sharp contrast to influential versions of structural realism that hold that the international system can be adequately characterized in terms of a single variable—power—and that international anarchy generates a strong general tendency toward competition.

The security dilemma plays a central role in shaping states' choices. I characterize the security dilemma in terms of both material and informa-

---

[1] In addition, in chapter 4 I argued that an adequately full characterization requires additional variables, including the value the security seeker places on protecting its interests and the state's beliefs about the adversary's beliefs about this value.

tion variables, diverging from the standard formulation that focuses on material variables. The security dilemma is less severe, and cooperation and restraint are more attractive, when a security seeker believes its adversary is likely also to be a security seeker and when defense is relatively easy compared to offense. Competition is more attractive when the opposite conditions hold.

By showing that cooperation will under a range of conditions be a security seeker's best option, my theory establishes a theoretically important role for greedy states. Greedy states take on this importance because there are conditions under which security seekers should choose cooperation, but greedy states should choose competition. Addressing only security seekers and the pressures created by uncertainty would therefore exaggerate the general prospects for cooperation and peace.

Second, the theory that I have developed is a rational normative theory. It should explain state behavior when states act rationally, but not when they act suboptimally. A substantial and diverse international-relations literature developed over the past few decades argues convincingly that states often fail to choose rational policies. Consequently, we should not expect a theory of rational international politics to do very well at explaining state behavior. A rational theory is nevertheless quite valuable. It prescribes the strategy, or at least narrows the range of strategies, that a state should pursue when facing a rational adversary. It enables us to evaluate the impact of the international system on a state's prospects for achieving security and, closely related, to understand the role of international constraints and opportunities in generating competition. It provides a rational baseline against which a state's actual behavior can be judged, which is essential for analyzing whether states have pursued suboptimal policies. And it provides the foundation for multilevel theories that combine a rational theory with a theory of suboptimal state behavior, with the goal of explaining a wider range of state behavior.

Evaluating a normative theory, when states frequently choose suboptimal policies, creates a significant analytic challenge. The standard social-science approach for testing theories—taking the theory to the historical data—is no longer effective. The theory of rational international behavior could be entirely sound but nevertheless fail to explain a high percentage of states' major strategic choices.

Third, in response to this challenge, I employ three complementary approaches to evaluate the theory. The first explores the adequacy of the theory's assumptions, the completeness of its variables, and the feasibility of its decision-making requirements. This is primarily an empirical exercise that, in light of the theory's purpose, addresses the match between the theory and the real world. Given that theories must simplify, the match turns out to be surprisingly good. The second approach identifies and analyzes important historical cases in which the theory does successfully explain state behavior. Although states frequently choose suboptimal policies, they also sometimes act rationally. Not only does the theory do well at explaining these cases, it provides better explanations than the available realist theories, demonstrating the importance of my theory's additional variables. The third approach uses counterfactual analysis to determine whether states that adopt suboptimal arming policies are punished. The theory provides the rational baseline against which states' arming decisions are compared. For cases of suboptimal arming, the question then becomes whether the state would have been better off if it had adopted the strategy identified by the theory. This counterfactual analysis demonstrates that states were in fact punished for adopting flawed arming policies—meaning that they would have done better had they followed the theory's prescriptions—thereby providing additional support for the theory. While none of these approaches is sufficient on its own, in combination they provide substantial confidence in my theory.

Fourth, the book lays the foundation for research that will extend and deepen my theory of rational international politics. I have developed the theory in layers, with the core presented in chapter 3 and a variety of extensions presented in chapter 4. The theory can be made still more comprehensive by developing additional extensions. As I argued earlier, these further developments should not be seen as creating competing theories, but instead as fuller versions of the project launched here. Many of these extensions would be strictly within the theory's boundaries. A natural next move would be to address more fully situations that include more than two major powers. I have developed the dyadic version of the theory, largely because focusing on two states is sufficient to enable the theory to explore many fundamental international issues and is necessary before exploring situations that are further complicated by larger numbers of states. However, nothing about the theory is inherently dyadic. Extending it to multipolarity would enable the theory to systematically evaluate a wider range of international environments and states' choices. A second within-theory extension would be to advance the analysis of war that I began in chapter 4. Some of this analysis might benefit from a formal game-theoretic treatment that integrated the stages of interaction—peacetime arming and signaling, adjustments in the value that states place on territory as result of these interactions, then crisis bargaining.

The theory could also be extended beyond its current boundaries. One valuable move would be to loosen the black boxing of the adversary, shifting from a unitary-actor assumption to a formulation that allows for an adversary composed of two or more domestic actors. As discussed in chapter 7, a richer characterization of the adversary would allow the rational theory to address the interaction between the state's strategy and the balance of domestic power within the opposing state. An important extension that moves beyond the rational framework would address the decisions of a rational state that believes it faces a state that may not be rational, that is, one that may be making suboptimal choices. This would broaden the prescriptive/normative reach of the theory.

POLICY IMPLICATIONS

As we look to the future, the key question for the United States about major power relations is whether China's rise to full superpower status will be peaceful. A number of leading realist scholars argue that China's rise will generate major-power competition, with war not unlikely. John Mearsheimer holds that "China cannot rise peacefully, and if it continues its dramatic economic growth over the next few decades, the United States and China are likely to engage in an intense security competition with considerable potential for war."[2] Somewhat less pessimistic, Kenneth Waltz, in discussing the achievement of great power status by Japan and China, explains that "Fortunately the changing relations of East to West . . . are taking place in a nuclear context. The tensions and conflicts that intensify when profound changes in world politics take place will continue to mar the relations of nations, while nuclear weapons keep the peace among those who enjoy their protection."[3] Arguments that contradict these gloomy expectations tend to come from unit-level theories that focus on specific features of states' domestic politics and institutions, and from liberal theories that emphasize the pacifying effect of trade and wealth.[4]

In contrast, my theory offers a more optimistic structural prediction and explains how the outcome of China's rise will be responsive to U.S. policy. First, the theory does not find a general tendency for intense security competition between a rising power and a declining power. And more specifically, this finding applies to the shift from unipolarity—which many analysts believe U.S. power has now established—to a bipolar world in which the United States and China have roughly comparable power.[5]

During the transition from unipolarity to bipolarity, the declining/uni-

---

[2] John J. Mearsheimer, "Better to Be Godzilla Than Bambi," *Foreign Policy* 146 (January/February 2005): 46–49.

[3] Waltz, "Structural Realism after the Cold War," p. 36.

[4] A good review of these arguments is Friedberg, "The Future of U.S.–China Relations."

[5] On the United States as a unipolar power, see Stephen G. Brooks and William C. Wohlforth, *World Out of Balance: International Relations and the Challenge of American Primacy* (Princeton: Princeton University Press, 2008).

polar power will need to consider whether to launch a preventive war. As sketched in chapter 4, the key question for a declining security seeker is whether it will be insecure following the other's rise. This in turn depends on its power, the offense-defense balance, and its information about the rising state's motives. Incentives for preventive war are smaller when the future power disadvantages will be small, when defense will have a large advantage, and when the adversary's future motives are expected to be benign. Defense advantage has the potential to essentially wash out the implications of changes in polarity—if the declining power will retain its essential deterrent capabilities, the shift in polarity should not have large implications for its security. Pressures for war that are generated by uncertainty about future motives will be smaller if the declining power is confident that the combination of its power and the offense-defense balance will enable it to retain effective deterrent capabilities.

Judged through this lens, China's rise should not generate pressures for preventive war. The United States will remain very secure, enjoying multiple defense advantages. Maybe most important, the large defense advantage generated by nuclear weapons will insure the United States' ability to maintain nuclear forces that meet even highly conservative requirements for deterrence. Although this argument overlaps with Waltz's argument that I quoted above, the implications are rather different—if both the United States and China are secure during the transition to bipolarity, there is no reason that relations between these states need to be damaged by the shift in power. In addition, the Pacific Ocean makes large-scale conventional attacks against the U.S. homeland virtually impossible, reflecting the defense advantage created by the combined effects of distance and water. No foreseeable increase in China's power would be large enough to offset this defense advantage. As a result, even given doubts about China's motives, the United States will not face security pressures either to launch a preventive war or to pursue policies designed to slow China's economic growth.[6]

Moreover, information about China's motives is likely to further reduce these already small incentives to prevent China's rise. The United States has virtually no reason to believe that China has grand expansionist objectives. China has resolved most of its border disputes;[7] only incorporation of Taiwan stands out as a clear expansionist objective (and one that China sees as simply maintaining its version of the status quo). If China's aims are limited to Taiwan, the stakes for the United States are

[6]The case of a declining greedy state is somewhat different because such a state faces a closing window of opportunity. However, the United States is not a greedy state, at least not on the scale of desiring to acquire the homeland territory of other major powers.

[7]Taylor M. Fravel, *Strong Borders, Secure Nation: Cooperation and Conflict in China's Territorial Disputes* (Princeton: Princeton University Press, 2008).

far too small to warrant efforts to slow China's rise, whether through economic means or through the direct use of force.

Skeptics will argue, reasonably, that current Chinese behavior is not a good indicator of its future motives and goals. Maybe most important, China has incentives now to pursue a restrained foreign policy precisely because it does not yet have the power to challenge the United States and is vulnerable to U.S. conventional and nuclear capabilities. Consequently, even a very greedy China would adopt a foreign policy that resembles China's current moderate policy. Moreover, China's motives could always become more malign, so today's motives (whatever they are) should provide little comfort to the United States.

Although these points are correct, the case for preventive war, and competitive policies more generally, remains quite weak. Defense advantages will enable the United States to meet its security requirements in even the worst case. And even if the United States did not enjoy such large defense advantages, the case for preventive war based on the possibility of very greedy Chinese motives would be weak—even in a nonnuclear world, the costs of preventive war against a major power are simply too high unless a future hegemonic challenge is likely.

Following the power transition, the question becomes whether the two states can meet their security requirements after the rising power has achieved equal or greater power. Whereas during the transition the focus was U.S. incentives to prevent further declines in its power, in this stage we need to consider both China's and America's security requirements and incentives. We are, in effect, asking about the requirements for security in a specific bipolarity. Will security require either country to acquire or control more territory? Will it require acquiring still greater military capability?

Again, for security seekers the key is whether they can be secure in a bipolar structure. The same variables that matter during the transition would matter once it is completed. For essentially the same reasons, under a range of conditions, bipolarity should not generate significant insecurity or competition. Both China and the United States will enjoy the benefits of double (conventional/geographic plus nuclear) defense advantage; and both states will be able to maintain the military capabilities they require for deterrence of attacks against their homelands without undermining the other's capabilities. The importance of defense advantage extends well beyond military capabilities, providing comparably important implications for U.S.–China political relations. By ensuring that the security dilemma is at worst mild, material conditions will enable the United States and China to avoid military competition that could signal malign motives and strain their political relationship. And good political relations would have the potential to be reinforcing, reducing the need to hedge against the possibility of a very greedy state by adopting conservative military requirements, thereby allowing a positive spiral to continue.

Replaying the preceding arguments from a different perspective, reflecting defense advantage, nuclear weapons can provide China with an excellent deterrent capability, while not threatening the U.S. nuclear deterrent. China could design its nuclear deterrent to avoid threatening America's nuclear deterrent, which would risk signaling malign motives. However, even if China were to choose to pursue a more offensively oriented nuclear force, the United States would be able to respond with programs that preserved high confidence in its deterrent capabilities. China will be unable to achieve a power advantage large enough to support a nuclear force that provides even a slight probability of undermining the U.S. nuclear deterrent capabilities, assuming the United States reacts to China's programs. The defense advantage created by nuclear weapons is simply so large that no foreseeable Chinese power advantage would overwhelm it. Recall that chapter 9 relied on essentially this analysis to argue that once the two Cold War superpowers had acquired high-confidence assured destruction capabilities, they should have greatly slowed, if not entirely stopped, their nuclear competition; and more broadly, they should have understood that they were much more secure than they in fact appreciated.

Contrary to some realist claims,[8] China would not need to pursue regional hegemony because it could be secure without undermining the ability of other countries in Northeast Asia to defend and deter. China's power—its size, large population, and wealth—combined with geography and nuclear weapons would provide the resources necessary for effective deterrence and defense. Within its region, China's separation by water from Japan makes defense easier for both countries; but even without this geographical barrier, China's size and wealth would enable it to maintain an effective deterrent against the major (nonsuperpower) powers located in Northeast Asia. China would not need to attempt to push the United States out of Northeast Asia, as would be required were China to pursue regional hegemony, because America's forward presence would not undermine China's core defensive capabilities. In addition, American withdrawal from Northeast Asia would be unlikely to enable China to achieve hegemony because Japan would be able to acquire an effective nuclear deterrent of its own; and South Korea might be able to as well. In short, regional hegemony would be both unnecessary and infeasible for China.

It is true, however, that China would see some benefits in a U.S. withdrawal because the United States' forward presence enhances its power projection capabilities, which pose a threat to China's ability to protect its sea lanes of communication (SLOCs) and to coerce Taiwan, two issues that I address briefly below. At the same time, however, the U.S. alliance with Japan provides some important benefits to China, enabling Japan to invest much less in defense and, as a result, reducing the threat that Japan poses to China. As described in chapter 8, although U.S. power greatly exceeds Japan's, on net China has seen the U.S. alliance with Japan as increasing its security because China believes that the United States is less likely than Japan to be a greedy state.

This optimistic analysis—both of China's transition to full superpower status and of the following period of bipolarity—needs to be tempered by a range of considerations that lay partially or entirely outside the theory's boundaries. First, attaining the benefits offered by large defense advantage requires the United States to accurately appreciate the constraints and opportunities it creates. I raise this cautionary note in part because research on states' military strategy and forces, including my examination of arms races in chapter 9, finds that states have often misevaluated material variables, especially exaggerating the potential of offense. In addition, there are specific reasons to worry that the United States will make a similar error—U.S. strategy has failed to appreciate the implications of defense advantage, holding that the United States needs to maintain military dominance and prevent the rise of peer competitors.[9] However, U.S. prospects for thwarting China's acquisition of a robust nuclear retaliatory capability are poor. The challenge facing the United States will be greatest if China continues to grow rapidly, but U.S. prospects will be poor even if China's growth slows. Although China currently has a small and vulnerable intercontinental force, it will be able to build a large force that is increasingly survivable. While China will not be able to build this force overnight, the combination of increased size and survivability will enable China eventually to undermine the United States' ability to maintain a significant damage-limitation capability.[10] In addition, although China will be unable to match U.S. conventional capabilities for the foreseeable future, China's economic growth will enable it to build a large advanced conventional military that will reduce the U.S. ability to operate conventional forces along China's periphery.

Failure to appreciate the impact of defense advantage would lead the

[9] This was a defining feature of what became known as the Bush doctrine; see George Bush, *The National Security Strategy of the United States of America* (Washington, DC: White House, September 2002).

[10] On China's nuclear force, see Robert S. Norris and Hans M. Kristensen, "Chinese Nuclear Forces, 2008," *Bulletin of the Atomic Scientists* 64, 3 (July/August 2008): 42–45, who report that China is projected to have 75–100 warheads on intercontinental missiles by 2015, with several dozen on mobile ICBMs.

United States to underestimate its security, which at a minimum would lead it to waste resources by overinvesting in military forces. The greater danger, however, is that overly competitive U.S. policies would end up reducing its security. If the United States believes incorrectly that its security requires military dominance, the prospect of losing dominance would spur the United States to adopt more competitive policies. Beyond intensifying the United States' own military buildup, more competitive U.S. policies could include other measures to contain China, including pressuring Japan to adopt a more ambitious military policy. These competitive policies risk signaling that the United States has greedy motives because the capabilities it would be pursuing are not clearly required to maintain U.S. security. In fact, China is already worried by U.S. capabilities; a recent Chinese white paper, although generally optimistic about China's security, argues: "The influence of military security factors on international relations is mounting. . . . Some major powers are realigning their security and military strategies, increasing their defense investment, speeding up the transformation of armed forces, and developing advanced military technology, weapons and equipment. . . . The U.S. has increased its strategic attention to and input in the Asia-Pacific region, further consolidating its military alliances, adjusting its military deployment and enhancing its military capabilities."[11] Competitive policies designed to maintain U.S. military advantages would almost certainly increase these concerns and damage U.S.–China relations.

Moreover, there is the danger that at the same time, the United States might see China's efforts to achieve deterrent capabilities as indicating that China has greedy motives. This would reflect U.S. insensitivity to the security dilemma, a failure to appreciate that U.S. capabilities were incompatible with China's ability to meet its own deterrent requirements. Although not necessarily logically associated with the requirement for U.S. dominance, this failure to appreciate the full implications of U.S. military capabilities is frequently coupled with it. For example, when he was secretary of defense, Donald Rumsfeld, having reviewed China's defense spending and purchases of advanced weaponry, argued that "Since no nation threatens China, one must wonder: Why this growing investment? Why these continuing large and expanding arms purchases?"[12] In this case, a classic negative political spiral would result, driven by a combination of rational and flawed arguments.

Second, the security implications of China's rise (and in turn bipolar-

---

[11] Information Office of the State Council of the People's Republic of China, *China's National Defense in 2008* (Beijing, January 2009).

[12] Associated Press, "Rumsfeld: China buildup threatens Asia: U.S. defense chief chides military growth, position on Taiwan," June 4, 2005, http://www.msnbc.msn.com/id/8091198/.

ity) will depend upon U.S. grand strategy. This grand strategy should depend heavily upon the variables on which my theory focuses, but it is not determined by them. More than one grand strategy could be consistent with the international situation the United States faces. And this turns out to be the case. Within the family of well-articulated grand strategies, two stand out as consistent with a bipolar world defined by U.S. and Chinese power, and characterized by defense advantage: neo-isolationism and selective engagement.[13] Neo-isolationists argue that U.S. security does not depend on protecting allies in Europe and Asia because defense advantages are sufficiently large that the United States would be able to protect itself even if a single state dominated Europe or Asia; even a continental hegemon would not be powerful enough to undermine U.S. deterrent capabilities. Moreover, they add that the danger posed by the possibility of a regional hegemon is reduced further because nuclear weapons would prevent a single state from dominating either region. Consequently, the United States should end these alliances and maintain only the military capabilities required to protect its homeland from direct invasion and to deter nuclear attack. My optimistic assessment of China's rise is most clearly consistent with this grand strategy and has been cast largely in these terms.

In contrast, selective engagement calls for the United States to retain its security commitments in Europe and Asia. Although it recognizes that defense dominance promises to provide the United States with effective deterrent capabilities, selective engagement argues that war between Eurasia's major powers could jeopardize U.S. security because the United States might, one way or another, get drawn into such a war. As a result, the best way for the United States to avoid a major-power war is to continue helping to keep the peace between major powers by retaining its alliance commitments. Therefore, according to this line of argument, the impact of China's rise depends on the U.S. ability to extend deterrence to Japan, when facing a Chinese conventional force that could be larger and more capable than U.S. forces deployed in the region.

In important ways the situation would be closely analogous to the challenge the United States faced in extending deterrence to Western Europe during the Cold War—both superpowers had robust assured destruction capabilities, and the Soviet Union was widely believed to have superior

[13] A clear presentation of the case for neo-isolation is Gholz, Press, and Sapolsky, "Come Home, America"; for selective engagement, see Robert J. Art, *A Strategy For America* (Ithaca: Cornell University Press, 2003). Comparing the key grand strategies are Barry R. Posen and Andrew L. Ross, "Competing Visions for American Grand Strategy," *International Security* 21, 3 (Winter 1996–97): 5–53. The grand strategy that is frequently termed "primacy" is not feasible when the United States faces a state of roughly equal or greater power; and as I have argued in the text, it is unnecessary when defense has the advantage.

conventional forces capable of invading Europe.[14] Experts disagreed about whether the United States could adequately extend nuclear deterrence in MAD and about the measures that could enhance the U.S deterrent. Analysts who concluded that extended deterrence was highly effective argued that a small probability of a large nuclear war was sufficient for deterrence, and that the U.S. doctrine of flexible response—which combined large conventional forces, theater nuclear forces, and strategic nuclear forces to support a doctrine of nuclear first use—more than met this criterion.[15] In contrast, analysts who questioned the viability of extended deterrence in MAD argued that U.S. threats to escalate were incredible, or at least lacked sufficient credibility to deter the highly motivated Soviet Union that threatened U.S. security. Possible solutions to this deterrence shortfall included a host of more competitive policies, such as increasing the ability of U.S. nuclear forces to destroy Soviet forces and adding an offensive retaliatory option to U.S. conventional forces.[16]

While further exploring this debate is beyond the scope of this discussion, we can sketch its implications. For analysts who conclude in favor of selective engagement and also conclude that extended deterrence requires the United States to pursue these more competitive military policies, China's rise will be somewhat more dangerous. The United States will have to compete more intensely to maintain an adequate deterrent, these forces may well signal greedy motives to China, and even if militarily successful the United States may lack confidence in its deterrent. At a minimum, therefore, according to these arguments, a world of Chinese-American bipolarity will be militarily competitive. In addition, if China were a greedy state willing to run large risks (which is the analogy to the Cold War hawks' view of the Soviet Union), China would be more difficult to deter and war would be more likely. In contrast, for analysts who conclude that U.S. requirements for extended deterrence are less demanding,[17] a less competitive and more defensively oriented strategy would suffice. This conclusion brings the added benefit of allowing the United States to meet its military requirements without fueling military competition that risks a negative political spiral. These analysts, even if they believe the United States requires a grand strategy of selective en-

[14] This conventional wisdom on the conventional balance was probably flawed, however; see Mearsheimer, "Why the Soviets Can't Win Quickly in Central Europe"; and Posen, "Measuring the European Conventional Balance."

[15] See, for example, Jervis, *The Meaning of the Nuclear Revolution*.

[16] See, for example, Huntington, "Conventional Deterrence and Conventional Retaliation in Europe."

[17] I would include myself in this category; for relevant arguments concerning Cold War policy that apply to this discussion, see Glaser, *Analyzing Strategic Nuclear Policy*, esp. chaps. 2 and 7.

gagement, would expect war to be quite unlikely and the world of U.S.–China bipolarity to be relatively safe and secure.

Third, a full assessment of the impact of China's rise depends on a couple of still more specific issues that lie further below the sweeping view of grand international relations theory yet could be consequential. At the top of this list is Taiwan, which is currently the most dangerous point of potential conflict between the United States and China. China believes that Taiwan is part of its own territory and places great value on Taiwan not declaring its independence; the United States maintains a somewhat ambiguous conditional commitment to defend Taiwan's independence. Rising Chinese power could have implications for this dispute. The United States currently sees a role for nuclear weapons in deterring attacks against Taiwan[18] and might therefore worry that losing nuclear superiority would reduce its ability to deter a Chinese conventional attack against or coercion of Taiwan. As discussed above, however, the United States will lack options for stopping this diminution of its nuclear capability because the advantage of defense is too large. Moreover, trying to maintain this capability would fuel competition that could signal that U.S. motives were malign, straining the overall U.S.–China relationship and diminishing the overall political and military benefits of defense advantage. The U.S. ability to protect Taiwan will be further reduced by improvements in China's conventional capabilities. At some point, the risks of continuing to protect Taiwan could become too large.[19] This is especially likely if Taiwan presses the limits of the extent of independence that China is willing to accept.

Another potential source of conflict could be the increasing importance of China's sea lanes of communication. China has only recently become a major importer of oil; however, it currently imports approximately half of the oil it consumes, and its growing demand for energy is likely to require it to import 70 percent of its oil by 2020.[20] China's SLOCs will be vulnerable to America's large and highly capable blue-water navy. This vulnerability would enable the United States to pose a major threat to China's economy and in wartime to weaken its ability to fight a long

[18] *The Nuclear Posture Review* [excerpts], January 8, 2002, http://globalsecurity.org/wmd/ library/policy/dod/npr/htm, states that "immediate contingencies involve well-recognized current dangers. . . . Current examples of immediate contingencies . . . a military confrontation over the status of Taiwan," and "due to the combination of China's still developing strategic objectives and its ongoing modernization of its nuclear and non nuclear forces, China is a country that could be involved in an immediate or potential contingency" (pp. 16–17).

[19] Arguing for ending the U.S. commitment to Taiwan is Christopher Layne, "China's Challenge to US Hegemony," *Current History* 107, 705 (January 2008): 13–18.

[20] Daniel Yergin, "Ensuring Energy Security," *Foreign Affairs* 85, 2 (March/April 2006): 69–82.

conventional war. Efforts to defend its SLOCs would require a large Chinese buildup of air and naval forces, which could spur U.S. reactions to maintain its command of the seas,[21] resulting in an intense conventional arms race. This competition would reflect a security dilemma, with both countries pursuing military capabilities that they believe are defensive, and would have the potential to strain their political relations. If, however, U.S.–China relations remain relatively good—that is, neither concludes that the other is likely to be greedy—the prospects are good for avoiding the potential Chinese insecurity generated by the vulnerability of its SLOCs. This vulnerability would be important only if there are plausible scenarios in which the United States tries to cut off China's oil supply; and these scenarios should exist only if political relations are sufficiently strained that major-power war is judged a significant possibility.

The interplay between this specific regional vulnerability and the overall U.S.–China relationship leads us back to my theory's analysis of how the broad features of the international environment should influence the impact of China's rise. The theory's optimistic analysis of the international environment becomes more important because restrained military competition, mutual security, and good political relations would significantly improve U.S. and Chinese prospects for avoiding dangerous competition that could be generated by specific features of China's regional security environment. Bipolarity coupled with overarching defense advantages would provide the United States with the opportunity to pursue policies that maintain good political relations with China. These good political relations would in turn reduce the significance of the vulnerability of China's SLOCs, as well as other regional issues that could otherwise combine to fuel more competitive, strained, and dangerous political relations. This interaction between the broad U.S. strategy that is driven by basic international variables and the United States' ability to manage regional issues adds to the overall case for choosing a more cooperative strategy for dealing with China's rise.

[21] On these U.S. capabilities, see Barry R. Posen, "Command of the Commons: The Military Foundation of U.S. Hegemony," *International Security* 28, 1 (Summer 2003): 5–46.

Bibliography

Abbott, Kenneth W., and Duncan Snidal. "Why States Act through Formal International Organizations." *Journal of Conflict Resolution* 42, 1 (1998): 3–32.

Adams, Karen Ruth. "Attack and Conquer?: International Anarchy and the Offense-Defense-Deterrence Balance." *International Security* 28, 3 (2003/2004): 45–83.

Adler, Emanuel, and Michael Barnett. "A Framework for the Study of Security Communities." In Emanuel Adler and Michael Barnett, eds., *Security Communities*. Cambridge: Cambridge University Press, 1998.

———. "Security communities in Theoretical Perspective." In Emanuel Adler and Michael Barnett, eds., *Security Communities*. Cambridge: Cambridge University Press, 1998.

Allison, Graham T. *Essence of Decision: Explaining the Cuban Missile Crisis.* Boston: Little, Brown, 1971.

Anderson, Jeffrey J., and John B. Goodman. "Mars or Minerva: A United Germany in Post-Cold War Europe." In Robert O. Keohane, Joseph S. Nye, and Stanley Hoffmann, eds., *After the Cold War: International Institutions and State Strategies in Europe, 1989–1991*. Cambridge: Harvard University Press, 1993.

"Appendix: Strategic Asia by the Numbers." In Ashley J. Tellis and Michael Wills, eds., *Strategic Asia 2007–08: Domestic Political Change and Grand Strategy*. Seattle: National Bureau of Asian Research, 2007.

Arreguin-Toft, Ivan. "How the Weak Win Wars: A Theory of Asymmetric Conflict." *International Security* 26, 1 (2001): 93–128.

Art, Robert J. "Coercive Diplomacy: What Do We Know?" In Robert Art and Patrick M. Cronin, eds., *The United States and Coercive Diplomacy*. Washington, DC: United States Institute of Peace Press, 2003.

———. "The Influence of Foreign Policy on Seapower: New Weapons and Weltpolitik in Wilhelminian Germany." In Robert J. Art and Kenneth N. Waltz, eds. *The Use of Force*. 2nd edition. New York: University Press of America, 1983.

———. "Introduction." In Robert Art and Patrick M. Cronin, eds., *The United States and Coercive Diplomacy*. Washington, DC: United States Institute of Peace Press, 2003.

———. *A Strategy For America*. Ithaca: Cornell University Press, 2003.

———. "To What Ends Military Power?" *International Security* 4, 4 (1980): 3–35.

———. "Why Western Europe Needs the United States and NATO." *Political Science Quarterly* 111, 1 (1996): 1–39.

Asada, Sadao. *From Mahan to Pearl Harbor: The Imperial Japanese Navy and the United States*. Annapolis: Naval Institute Press. 2006.

———. "From Washington to London: The Imperial Navy and the Politics of

Naval Limitations, 1921–1930." In Erik Goldstein and John H. Maurer, eds., *The Washington Conference, 1921–22*. Essex, UK: Frank Cass, 1994.

———. "Japanese Admirals and the Politics of Naval Limitations: Kato Tomosaburo vs. Kato Kanji." In Gerald Jordan, ed., *Naval Warfare in the Twentieth Century, 1900–1945*. London: Croom Helm, 1977.

———. "The Japanese Navy and the United States." In Dorothy Borg and Shumpei Okamoto, eds., *Pearl Harbor as History: Japanese-American Relations, 1931–1941*. New York: Columbia University Press, 1973.

Ashley, Richard K. "The Poverty of Neorealism." In Robert Keohane, ed., *Neorealism and its Critics*. New York: Columbia University Press, 1986.

Associated Press. "Rumsfeld: China buildup threatens Asia: U.S. defense chief chides military growth, position on Taiwan." June 4, 2005. http://www.msnbc.msn.com/id/8091198/.

Axelrod, Robert. *The Evolution of Cooperation*. New York: Basic Books, 1984.

Baldwin, David A. *Economic Statecraft*. Princeton: Princeton University Press, 1985.

———, ed., *Neorealism and Neoliberalism*. New York: Columbia University Press, 1993.

Ball, Desmond. "Development of the SIOP, 1960–1983." In Desmond Ball and Jeffrey Richelson, eds., *Strategic Nuclear Targeting*. Ithaca: Cornell University Press, 1986.

———. *Politics and Force Levels: The Strategic Missile Program of the Kennedy Administration*. Berkeley: University of California Press, 1980.

Barnhart, Michael A. *Japan Prepares for Total War: The Search for Economic Security, 1919–1941*. Ithaca: Cornell University Press, 1987.

Bechhoefer, Bernhard G. *Postwar Negotiations for Arms Control*. Washington, DC: Brookings, 1961.

Bell, PMH. *The Origins of the Second World War in Europe*. London: Longman, 1986.

Berg, Meredith W. "Protecting National Interests by Treaty: The Second London Naval Conference, 1934–36." In B.J.C. McKercher, ed., *Arms Limitation and Disarmament*. Westport, CT: Praeger, 1992.

Berghahn, V. R. *Germany and the Approach of War in 1914*. New York: St. Martin's, 1973.

Berkowitz, Daniel M., et al. "An Evaluation of the CIA's Analysis of Soviet Economic Performance, 1970–90." *Comparative Economic Studies* 35, 1 (1993): 33–57.

Betts, Richard K. "Conventional Deterrence: Predictive Uncertainty and Policy Confidence." *World Politics* 37, 2 (1985): 153–177.

———. "Wealth, Power and Instability: East Asia and the United States after the Cold War." *International Security* 18, 3 (1993–94): 34–77.

Biddle, Stephen. "The European Conventional Balance: A Reinterpretation of the Debate." *Survival* 30, 2 (1988): 99–121.

———. *Military Power: Explaining Victory and Defeat in Modern Battle*. Princeton: Princeton University Press, 2004.

———. "Rebuilding the Foundations of Offense-Defense Theory." *Journal of Politics* 63, 4 (2001): 741–774.

Bitzinger, Richard A. "Gorbachev and GRIT, 1985–89: Did Arms Control Succeed Because of Unilateral Actions or in Spite of Them?" *Contemporary Security Policy* 15, 1 (1994): 68–79.

Blainey, Geoffrey. *The Causes of War*. New York: Free Press, 1973.

Blair, Bruce G. *Strategic Command and Control: Redefining the Nuclear Threat*. Washington, DC: Brookings, 1985.

Blaug, Mark. *The Methodology of Economics, or How Economists Explain*. Cambridge: Cambridge University Press, 1980.

Bond, Brian. *British Military Policy between the Two World Wars*. Oxford: Oxford University Press, 1980.

Booth, Ken, and Nicholas J. Wheeler. *The Security Dilemma: Fear, Cooperation and Trust in World Politics*. New York: Palgrave Macmillan, 2008.

Borg, Dorothy. *The United States and the Far Eastern Crisis of 1933–1938*. Cambridge: Harvard University Press, 1964.

Boyd, Carl. "Japanese Military Effectiveness: The Interwar Period." In Allan R. Millett and Williamson Murray, eds., *Military Effectiveness*, vol. 2: *The Interwar Period*. London: Allen and Unwin, 1988.

Bracken, Paul J. *The Command and Control of Nuclear* Forces. New Haven: Yale University Press, 1983.

Braisted, W. R. *The United States Navy in the Pacific, 1909–1922*. Austin: University of Texas Press, 1971.

Brennan, Donald G., ed., *Arms Control, Disarmament and National Security*. New York: Brazilier, 1961.

———. "Post-Deployment Policy Issues in BMD." In *Ballistic Missile Defense: Two Views*, Adelphi Paper 43. London: International Institute for Strategic Studies, 1967.

Brodie, Bernard. "On the Objectives of Arms Control." *International Security* 1, 1 (1976): 17–36.

Brooks, Stephen G. "Dueling Realisms." *International Organization* 51, 3 (1997): 445–477.

———. "The Globalization of Production and the Changing Benefits of Conquest." *Journal of Conflict Resolution* 43, 5 (1999): 646–670.

———. *Producing Security: Multinational Corporations, Globalization, and the Changing Calculus of Conflict*. Princeton: Princeton University Press, 2005.

Brooks, Stephen G., and William C. Wohlforth. "Economic Constraints and the End of the Cold War." In William C. Wohlforth, ed., *Cold War Endgame: Oral History, Analysis, Debates*. University Park: Pennsylvania State University Press, 2003.

———. "Hard Times for Soft Balancing, *International Security* 30, 1 (2005).

———. "From Old Thinking to New Thinking in Qualitative Research." *International Security* 26, 4 (2002): 93–111.

———. "Power, Globalization and the End of the Cold War: Reevaluating a Landmark Case." *International Security* 25, 3 (2000–2001): 5–53.

———. *World Out of Balance: International Relations and the Challenge of American Primacy*. Princeton: Princeton University Press, 2008.

Brown, Michael E. "The Flawed Logic of NATO Expansion." *Survival* 37, 1 (1995): 34–52.

Buckley, Thomas H. "The Icarus Factor." In Erik Goldstein and John H. Maurer, eds., *The Washington Conference, 1921–22*. Essex, UK: Frank Cass, 1994.

———. *The United States and the Washington Conference, 1921–1922*. Knoxville: University of Tennessee Press, 1970.

Bull, Hedley. *The Control of the Arms Race: Disarmament and Arms Control in the Missile Age*. New York: Praeger, 1961.

Bundy, McGeorge. *Danger and Survival: Choices about the Bomb in the First Fifty Years*. New York: Random House, 1988.

Burr, William. "Essay: U.S. Strategic Nuclear Policy, 1955–1968: An Overview." In William Burr, ed., *U.S. Nuclear History: Nuclear Arms and Politics in the Missile Age, 1955–1968*. Washington, DC: National Security Archive, 1997.

Bush, George. *The National Security Strategy of the United States of America*. Washington, DC: White House, September 2002.

Butterfield, Herbert. *History and Human Relations*. London: Collins, 1951.

Buzan, Barry. *Introduction to Strategic Studies: Military Technology and International Relations*. New York: St. Martin's Press, 1987.

———. "Japan's Defense Problematique." *The Pacific Review* 8, 1 (1995): 25–44.

Buzan, Barry, Charles Jones, and Richard Little. *The Logic of Anarchy: Neorealism to Structural Realism*. New York: Columbia University Press, 1993.

Calder, Kent E. "China and Japan's Simmering Rivalry." *Foreign Affairs* 85, 2 (2006): 129–139.

Calleo, David. *The German Problem Reconsidered: Germany and the World Order, 1870–Present*. London: Cambridge University Press, 1978.

Carnesale, Albert, and Charles L. Glaser. "ICBM Vulnerability: The Cures Are Worse Than the Disease." *International Security* 7, 1 (1982): 70–85.

Castillo, Jasen J. "The Will to Fight: Explaining an Army's Staying Power." Ph.D. dissertation, University of Chicago, 2003.

Chan, Steve. "The Impact of Defense Spending on Economic Performance: A Survey of the Evidence and Problems." *Orbis* 29, 2 (1985): 403–434.

Chayes, Abram. "An Inquiry into the Working of Arms Control Agreements." *Harvard Law Review* 85, 5 (1972): 905–969.

Checkel, Jeffery T. "Ideas, Institutions, and the Gorbachev Foreign Policy Revolution." *World Politics*. 45, 2 (1993): 271–300.

———. "International Norms and Domestic Politics: Bridging the Rationalist-Constructivist Divide." *European Journal of International Relations* 3, 4 (1997): 473–495.

Christensen, Thomas J. "China, the U.S.–Japan Alliance, and the Security Dilemma in East Asia." *International Security* 23, 4 (1999): 49–80.

———. "Correspondence: Spirals, Security, and Stability in East Asia." *International Security* 24, 4 (2000): 195–200.

———. "Perceptions and Alliances in Europe, 1865–1940." *International Organization* 51, 1 (1997): 65–97.

———. *Useful Adversaries: Grand Strategy, Domestic Mobilization, and Sino-American Conflict, 1947–1958*. Princeton: Princeton University Press, 1996.

Christensen, Thomas J., and Jack Snyder. "Chained Gangs and Passed Bucks: Predicting Alliance Patterns in Multipolarity." *International Organization* 44, 2 (1990): 137–168.

Cohen, Warren I. *Empire without Tears: America's Foreign Relations 1921–1933*. New York: Knopf, 1987.

Collins, Alan R. "GRIT, Gorbachev and the End of the Cold War." *Review of International Studies* 24, 2 (1998): 201–219.

Congressional Budget Office. *Counterforce Issues for the U.S. Strategic Offensive Forces*. Washington, DC: U.S. Government Printing Office, 1978.

Copeland, Dale C. "The Constructivist Challenge to Structural Realism: A Review Essay." *International Security* 25, 2 (2000): 187–212.

———. *The Origins of Major War*. Ithaca: Cornell University Press, 2000.

Crowley, James B. *Japan's Quest for Autonomy: National Security and Foreign Policy, 1930–1938*. Princeton: Princeton University Press, 1966.

Daalder, Ivo, and James Goldgeier. "Global NATO." *Foreign Affairs* 85, 5 (2006): 105–113.

de Figueiredo Jr., Rui J. P., and Barry R. Weingast. "The Rationality of Fear: Political Opportunism and Ethnic Conflict." In Barbara F. Walter and Jack Snyder, eds. *Civil Wars, Insecurity and Intervention*. New York: Columbia University Press, 1999.

Desch, Michael. "Democracy and Victory: Why Regime Type Hardly Matters." *International Security* 27, 2 (2002): 5–47.

Dessler, David. "What's at Stake in the Agent-Structure Debate." *International Organization* 43, 3 (1989): 441–470.

Deudney, Daniel, and G. John Ikenberry. "The International Sources of Soviet Change." *International Security* 16, 3 (1991–92): 74–118.

Diehl, Paul F. "Arms Races and Escalation: A Closer Look." *Journal of Peace Research* 20, 3 (1983): 205–212.

Diehl, Paul F., and Mack J. C. Crescenzi. "Reconfiguring the Arms Race-War Debate." *Journal of Peace Research* 35, 1 (1998): 111–118.

Diehl, Paul F., and Jean Kingston. "Messenger or Message? Military Buildups and the Initiation of Conflict." *Journal of Politics* 49, 3 (1987): 801–813.

Dingman, Roger. *Power in the Pacific: The Origins of Naval Arms Limitation, 1914–1922*. Chicago: University of Chicago Press, 1976.

Downes, Alexander B. "Desperate Times, Desperate Measures: The Causes of Civilian Victimization in War." *International Security* 30, 4 (2006): 152–195.

———. *Targeting Civilians in War*. Ithaca: Cornell University Press, 2008.

Downs, George W. "Arms Races and War." In Philip E. Tetlock, Jo L. Husbands, Robert Jervis, Paul C. Stern, and Charles Tilly, eds. *Behavior, Society, and Nuclear War*, Vol. 2. New York: Oxford University Press, 1991.

Downs, George W., and David M. Rocke. *Tacit Bargaining, Arms Races and Arms Control*. Ann Arbor: University of Michigan Press, 1990.

Downs, George W., David M. Rocke, and Randolph Siverson. "Arms Control and Cooperation." In Kenneth A. Oye, ed., *Cooperation under Anarchy*. Princeton: Princeton University Press, 1986.

Doyle, Michael W. *Ways of War and Peace: Realism, Liberalism, and Socialism*. New York: Norton, 1997.

Edelstein, David M. "Choosing Friends and Enemies: Perceptions of Intentions in International Politics." Ph.D. dissertation, University of Chicago, 2000.

———. "Managing Uncertainty: Beliefs about Intentions and the Rise of Great Powers." *Security Studies* 12, 1 (2002): 1–40.

Elman, Colin. "Extending Offensive Realism: The Louisiana Purchase and America's Rise to Regional Hegemony." *American Political Science Review* 98, 4 (2004): 563–576.

———. "Horses for Courses: Why Not Neorealist Theories of Foreign Policy?" *Security Studies* 6, 1 (1996): 7–53.

Elman, Miriam Fendius. "Introduction: The Need for a Qualitative Test of the Democratic Peace Theory." In Miriam Fendius Elman, ed., *Paths to Peace: Is Democracy the Answer?* Cambridge: MIT Press, 1997.

Elster, Jon. *Solomonic Judgements: Studies in the Limits of Rationality*. Cambridge: Cambridge University Press, 1989.

English, Robert. "Power, Ideas, and New Evidence on the Cold War's End." *International Security* 26, 4 (2002): 70–92.

———. *Russia and the Idea of the West*. New York: Columbia University Press, 2000.

Enthoven, Alain C., and K. Wayne Smith. *How Much Is Enough? Shaping the Defense Program, 1961–1969*. New York: Harper and Row, 1971.

Evangelista, Matthew. "Norms, Heresthetics, and the End of the Cold War." *Journal of Cold War Studies* 3, 1 (2001): 5–35.

———. *Unarmed Forces: The Transnational Movement to End the Cold War*. Ithaca: Cornell University Press, 1999.

Evans, David C., and Mark R. Peattie. *Kaigun: Strategy, Tactics, and Technology in the Imperial Japanese Navy, 1887–1941*. Annapolis: Naval Institute Press, 1997.

Evans, Peter B., Harold K. Jacobson, and Robert D. Putnam, eds. *Double-Edged Diplomacy: International Bargaining and Domestic Politics*. Berkeley: University of California Press, 1993.

Falkenrath, Richard A. *Shaping Europe's Military Order: The Origins and Consequences of the CFE Treaty*. Cambridge: MIT Press, 1995.

Fearon, James D. "Bargaining, Enforcement and International Cooperation." *International Organization* 52, 2 (1998): 269–305.

———. "Bargaining over Objects That Influence Future Bargaining Power." University of Chicago, 1996.

———. "Counterfactuals and Hypothesis Testing in Political Science." *World Politics* 43, 2 (1991): 169–195.

———. "Domestic Political Audiences and the Escalation of International Disputes." *American Political Science Review* 88, 3 (1994): 577–592.

———. "Domestic Politics, Foreign Policy, and Theories of International Relations." In Nelson W. Polsby, ed., *Annual Review of Political Science*, Vol. 1, 289–313. Palo Alto, CA: Annual Reviews, 1998.

———. "Rationalist Explanations for War." *International Organization* 49, 3 (1995): 379–414.

———. "Threats to Use Force: The Role of Costly Signals in International Crises." Ph.D. dissertation, University of California, Berkeley, 1992.

Fearon, James, and Alexander Wendt. "Rationalism v. Constructivism: A Skeptical View." In Walter Carlsnaes, Thomas Risse and Beth A. Simmons, eds., *Handbook of International Relations*. London: Sage, 2002.

Ferrell, Robert H. *American Diplomacy in the Great Depression: Hoover-Stimson Foreign Policy, 1929–1933*. London: Oxford University Press, 1957.

Finnemore, Martha. "Constructing Norms of Humanitarian Intervention." In Peter Katzenstein, ed., *The Culture of National Security: Norms and Identities in World Politics.* New York: Columbia University Press, 1996.

———. *National Interests and International Society.* Ithaca: Cornell University Press, 1996.

Fravel, M. Taylor. "Regime Insecurity and International Cooperation: Explaining China's Compromises in Territorial Disputes." *International Security* 30, 2 (2005): 46–83.

———. *Strong Borders, Secure Nation: Cooperation and Conflict in China's Territorial Disputes.* Princeton: Princeton University Press, 2008.

Freedman, Lawrence. *The Evolution of Nuclear Strategy.* London: Macmillan, 1989.

———. *U.S. Intelligence and the Soviet Strategic Threat.* 2nd edition. Princeton: Princeton University Press, 1986.

Friedberg, Aaron L. "The Future of U.S.–China Relations: Is Conflict Inevitable?" *International Security* 30, 2 (2005): 7–45.

———. "The Political Economy of American Strategy." *World Politics* 41, 3 (1989): 381–406.

———. "Ripe for Rivalry: Prospects for Peace in a Multipolar Asia." *International Security* 18, 3 (1993–94): 5–33.

———. *The Weary Titan: Britain and the Experience of Relative Decline, 1985–1905.* Princeton: Princeton University Press, 1998.

Frieden, Jeffrey. "Actors and Preferences in International Relations." In David A. Lake and Robert Powell, eds., *Strategic Choice and International Relations.* Princeton: Princeton University Press, 1999.

Frye, Alton. *A Responsible Congress: The Politics of National Security.* New York: McGraw Hill, 1975.

Garthoff, Raymond L. *Détente and Confrontation: American-Soviet Relations from Nixon to Reagan.* Washington, DC: Brookings, 1985.

———. *The Great Transformation: American-Soviet Relations and the End of the Cold War.* Washington, DC: Brookings, 1994.

George, Alexander L., and Andrew Bennett. *Case Studies and Theory Development in the Social Sciences.* Cambridge: MIT Press, 2005.

Gholtz, Eugene, Daryl Press, and Harvey M. Sapolsky. "Come Home, America: The Strategy of Restraint in the Face of Temptation." *International Security* 21, 4 (1997): 5–48.

Gilpin, Robert. *War and Change in World Politics.* Cambridge: Cambridge University Press, 1981.

Glaser, Charles L. *Analyzing Strategic Nuclear Policy.* Princeton: Princeton University Press, 1990.

———. "The Causes and Consequences of Arms Races." In Nelson W. Polsby, ed., *Annual Review of Political Science* 3 (2000): 251–276.

———. "Political Consequences of Military Strategy: Expanding and Refining the Spiral and Deterrence Models." *World Politics* 44, 4 (1992): 497–538.

———. "Realists as Optimists: Cooperation as Self-Help." *International Security* 19, 3 (1994–95): 50–90.

———. "The Security Dilemma Revisited." *World Politics* 50, 1 (1997): 171–201.

———."Structural Realism in a More Complex World." *Review of International Studies* 29 (2003): 403–414.

———. "Why NATO Is Still Best: Future Security Arrangements for Europe." *International Security* 18, 1 (1993): 5–50.

Glaser, Charles L., and Chaim Kaufmann. "Correspondence: Taking Offense at Offense-Defense Theory." *International Security* 23, 3 (1998-99): 200–206.

———. "What Is the Offense-Defense Balance and Can We Measure It?" *International Security* 22, 4 (1998): 44–82.

Glosny, Michael A. "Strangulation from the Sea: A PRC Submarine Blockade of Taiwan." *International Security* 28, 4 (2004): 125–160.

Goldfischer, David. *The Best Defense: Policy Alternatives for U.S. Nuclear Security from the 1950s to the 1980s.* Ithaca: Cornell University Press, 1993.

Goldman, Emily O. *Sunken Treaties: Naval Arms Control between the Wars.* University Park: University of Pennsylvania Press, 1994.

Goldstein, Avery. *Rising to the Challenge: China's Grand Strategy and International Security.* Stanford: Stanford University Press, 2005.

Goldstein, Judith, and Robert O. Keohane. "Ideas and Foreign Policy: An Analytic Framework." In Judith Goldstein and Robert O. Keohane, eds., *Ideas and Foreign Policy: Beliefs, Institutions, and Political Change.* Ithaca: Cornell University Press, 1993.

———, eds. *Ideas and Foreign Policy: Beliefs, Institutions, and Political Change.* Ithaca: Cornell University Press, 1993.

Gourevich, Peter A. "The Second Image Reversed: International Sources of Domestic Politics." *International Organization* 32, 4 (1978): 881–912.

Gray, Colin S. *House of Cards: Why Arms Control Must Fail.* Ithaca: Cornell University Press, 1992.

———. "Nuclear Strategy: A Case for a Theory of Victory." *International Security* 4, 1 (1979): 54–87.

———. *Weapons Don't Make War.* Lawrence: University Press of Kansas, 1993.

Green, Michael Jonathan. *Japan's Reluctant Realism: Foreign Policy Challenges in an Era of Uncertain Power.* New York: Palgrave, 2001.

Greenwood, Ted. *Making the MIRV: A Study in Defense Decision Making.* Cambridge, MA: Ballinger, 1975.

Grieco, Joseph M. "Anarchy and the Limits of Cooperation: A Realist Critique of the Newest Liberal Institutionalism." *International Organization* 42, 3 (1988): 485–507.

———. *Cooperation among Nations: Europe, America and Non-tariff Barriers to Trade.* Ithaca: Cornell University Press, 1990.

Gruber, Lloyd. *Ruling the World: Power Politics and the Rise of Supranational Organizations.* Princeton: Princeton University Press, 2000.

Haas, Ernst B. "Words Can Hurt You; or Who Said What to Whom about Regimes." *International Organization* 36, 2 (1982): 207–243.

Haas, Mark L. *The Ideological Origins of Great Power Politics, 1798–1989.* Ithaca: Cornell University Press, 2005.

———. "The United States and the End of the Cold War: Reactions to Shifts in Soviet Power, Policies, or Domestic Politics?" *International Organization* 61, 1 (2007): 145–179.

Haftendorn, Helga, Robert O. Keohane, and Celeste A. Wallander, eds. *Imperfect Unions: Security Institutions over Time and Space*. Oxford: Oxford University Press, 1999.

Halperin, Morton H. *Bureaucratic Politics and Foreign Policy*. Washington, DC: Brookings, 1974.

Hammond, Grant T. *Plowshares into Swords: Arms Races in International Politics, 1840–1991*. Columbia: University of South Carolina Press, 1993.

Herrmann, David G. *The Arming of Europe and the Making of the First World War*. Princeton: Princeton University Press, 1996.

Herrmann, Richard K., and Richard Ned Lebow, eds. *Ending the Cold War: Interpretations, Causation, and the Study of International Relations*. New York: Palgrave Macmillan, 2002.

Herwig, Holger H. "Imperial Germany." In Ernest R. May, ed., *Knowing One's Enemies: Intelligence Assessment before the Two World Wars*. Princeton: Princeton University Press, 1986.

———. *"Luxury Fleet": The Imperial German Navy, 1888–1918*. London: George Allen and Unwin, 1980.

Herz, John H. "Idealist Internationalism and the Security Dilemma." *World Politics* 2, 2 (1950): 157–180.

———. *International Politics in the Atomic Age*. New York: Columbia University Press, 1959.

Hillgruber, Andreas. *Germany and the Two World Wars*. Cambridge: Harvard University Press, 1981.

Hoag, Malcomb W. "On Stability in Deterrent Races." *World Politics* 13, 4 (1961): 505–527.

Hobson, John M. "The Military-Extraction Gap and the Wary Titan: The Fiscal Sociology of British Defense Policy, 1870–1913." *Journal of European Economic History* 22, 3 (1993): 461–506.

Hopf, Ted. "The Promise of Constructivism in International Relations Theory." *International Security* 23, 1 (1998): 171–200.

Howard, Michael. "Men against Fire: Expectations of War in 1914." *International Security* 9, 1 (1984): 41–57.

Hughes, Chrisopher W. "Japanese Military Modernization: In Search of a 'Normal' Security Role." In Ashley J. Tellis and Michael Wills, eds., *Strategic Asia 2005–06: Military Modernization in an Era of Uncertainty*. Seattle: National Bureau of Asian Research, 2005.

Huntington, Samuel P. "Arms Races: Prerequisites and Results." *Public Policy* 8 (1958): 41–86.

———. "Conventional Deterrence and Conventional Retaliation in Europe." *International Security* 8, 3 (1983–84): 32–56.

———. "U.S. Defense Strategy: The Strategic Innovations of the Reagan Years." In Joseph Kruzel, ed., *American Defense Annual, 1987–1988*. Lexington, MA: Lexington Books, 1987.

Ikenberry, G. John. *After Victory: Institutions, Strategic Restraint, and the Building of Order after Major Wars*. Princeton: Princeton University Press, 2001.

Information Office of the State Council of the People's Republic of China. *China's National Defense in 2008*. Beijing, January 2009.

Jayne, Edward Randolph. "The ABM Debate: Strategic Defense and National Security." Ph.D. dissertation, Massachusetts Institute of Technology, 1969.

Jepperson, Ronald L., Alexander Wendt, and Peter J. Katzenstein. "Norms, Identity and Culture in National Security." In Peter Katzenstein, ed., *The Culture of National Security: Norms and Identities in World Politics.* New York: Columbia University Press, 1996.

Jervis, Robert. "Cooperation under the Security Dilemma." *World Politics* 30, 1 (1978): 167–214.

———. *The Illogic of American Nuclear Strategy.* Ithaca: Cornell University Press, 1984.

———. *The Logic of Images in International Relations.* Princeton: Princeton University Press, 1970.

———. *The Meaning of the Nuclear Revolution: Statecraft and the Prospect of Armageddon.* Ithaca: Cornell University Press, 1989.

———. *Perception and Misperception in International Politics.* Princeton: Princeton University Press, 1976.

———. "Realism, Neoliberalism and Cooperation: Understanding the Debate." In Colin Elman and Miriam Fendius Elman, eds., *Progress in International Relations Theory.* Cambridge: MIT Press, 2003.

———. "Security Regimes." In Stephen Krasner, ed., *International Regimes.* Ithaca: Cornell University Press, 1983.

———. "Was the Cold War a Security Dilemma?" *Journal of Cold War Studies* 3, 1 (2001): 36–60.

Jervis, Robert, Richard Ned Lebow, and Janice Gross Stein. *Psychology and Deterrence.* Baltimore: Johns Hopkins University Press, 1985.

Johnston, Alastair Iain. "Is China a Status Quo Power?" *International Security* 27, 4 (2003): 5–56.

Jones, Seth G. "The European Union and the Security Dilemma." *Security Studies* 12, 3 (2003): 114–156.

———. *The Rise of European Security Cooperation.* New York: Cambridge University Press, 2007.

Kahan, Jerome. *Security in the Nuclear Age.* Washington, DC: Brookings, 1975.

Kahler, Miles. "Rationality in International Relations." *International Organization* 52, 4 (1998): 919–941.

Kaiser, David E. "Germany and the Origins of the First World War." *Journal of Modern History* 55, 3 (1983): 442–474.

Kaufmann, Chaim. "Threat Inflation and the Failure of the Market Place of Ideas: The Selling of the Iraq War." *International Security* 29, 1 (2004): 5–48.

Kaufman, Robert Gordon. *Arms Control during the Pre-Nuclear Era: The United States and Naval Limitation between the Two World Wars.* New York: Columbia University Press, 1990.

Kaysen, Carl. "Is War Obsolete: A Review Essay." *International Security* 14, 4 (1990): 42–64.

Keir, Elizabeth. *Imagining War: French and British Military Doctrines between the Wars.* Princeton: Princeton University Press, 1997.

Kennedy, Paul M. "Arms-Races and the Causes of War, 1850–1945." In Paul M.

Kennedy, *Strategy and Diplomacy, 1870–1945*. London: George Allen and Unwin, 1983.

———. "The Development of German Naval Operations Plans against England, 1896–1914." In Paul M. Kennedy, ed., *The War Plans of the Great Powers, 1880–1914*. Boston: Allen and Unwin, 1979.

———. *The Rise and Fall of British Naval Mastery*. London: Ashfield, 1976.

———. *The Rise and Fall of Great Powers: Economic Change and Military Conflict, 1500–2000*. New York: Random House, 1987.

———. *The Rise of the Anglo-German Antagonism, 1860–1914*. London: Ashfield Press, 1980.

———. "Strategic Aspects of the Anglo-German Naval Race." In Paul M. Kennedy, *Strategy and Diplomacy, 1870–1945*. London: George Allen and Unwin, 1983.

Keohane, Robert O. *After Hegemony: Cooperation and Discord in the World Political Economy*. Princeton: Princeton University Press, 1984.

———. "Correspondence: Back to the Future II." *International Security* 15, 2 (1990): 192–194.

———. *International Institutions and State Power: Essays in International Relations Theory*. Boulder: Westview Press, 1989.

———. "Theory of World Politics: Structural Realism and Beyond." In Ada Finiter, ed., *Political Science: The State of the Discipline*. Washington: APSA, 1983.

Keohane, Robert O., and Joseph S. Nye. "Introduction: The End of the Cold War in Europe." In Robert O. Keohane, Joseph S. Nye, and Stanley Hoffmann, eds., *After the Cold War: International Institutions and State Strategies in Europe, 1989–1991*. Cambridge: Harvard University Press, 1993.

Keohane Robert O., and Lisa L. Martin. "Institutional Theory as a Research Program." In Colin Elman and Miriam Fendius Elman, eds., *Progress in International Relations Theory: Appraising the Field*. Cambridge: MIT Press, 2003.

———. "The Promise of Institutional Theory." *International Security* 20, 1 (1995): 39–51.

Kershaw, Ian. *The Nazi Dictatorship: Problems of Perspective and Interpretation*. 4th edition. London: Arnold, 2000.

King, Gary, Robert O. Keohane, and Sydney Verba. *Designing Social Inquiry: Scientific Inference in Qualitative Research*. Princeton: Princeton University Press, 1994.

Knorr, Klaus. *The War Potential of Nations*. Princeton: Princeton University Press, 1956.

Koremenos, Barbara, Charles Lipson, and Duncan Snidal. "Rational International Institutions." *International Organization* 55, 4 (2001): 761–799.

Kowert, Paul, and Jeffrry Legro. "Norms, Identity, and Their Limits: A Theoretical Reprise." In Peter Katzenstein, ed., *The Culture of National Security: Norms and Identities in World Politics*. New York: Columbia University Press, 1996.

Kramer, Mark. "Ideology and the Cold War." *Review of International Studies* 25, 4 (1999): 563–576.

Krasner, Stephen D. "Global Communications and National Power: Life on the Pareto Frontier." *World Politics* 43, 3 (1991): 336–366.

———. "Regimes and the Limits of Realism: Regimes as Autonomous Variables." *International Organization* 36, 2 (1982): 495–510.

———. "Structural Causes and Regime Consequences: Regimes as Intervening Variables." *International Organization* 36, 2 (1982): 185–206.

Kreps, David M. *A Course in Microeconomic Theory.* Princeton: Princeton University Press, 1990.

Kugler, Richard L. "The Politics of Restraint: Robert McNamara and the Strategic Nuclear Forces, 1963–1968." Ph.D. dissertation, Massachusetts Institute of Technology, 1975.

Kupchan, Charles A. "Empire, Military Power, and Economic Decline." *International Security* 13, 4 (1989): 36–53.

Kydd, Andrew H. "Arms Races and Arms Control: Modeling the Hawk Perspective." *American Journal of Political Science* 44, 2 (2000): 222–238.

———. "Game Theory and the Spiral Model." *World Politics* 49, 3 (1997): 371–400.

———. "Sheep in Sheep's Clothing: Why Security Seekers Do Not Fight Each Other." *Security Studies* 7, 1 (1997): 114–154.

———. *Trust and Mistrust in International Relations.* Princeton: Princeton University Press, 2005.

Labs, Eric J. "Beyond Victory: Offensive Realism and the Expansion of War Aims." *Security Studies* 6, 4 (1997): 1–49.

Lake, David A. "Between Anarchy and Hierarchy: The Importance of Security Institutions." *International Organization* 50, 1 (2001): 1–33.

———. "Escape from the State of Nature: Authority and Hierarchy in World Politics." *International Security* 32, 1 (2007): 47–79.

Lake, David A., and Robert Powell. "International Relations: A Strategic-Choice Approach," In David A. Lake and Robert Powell, eds., *Strategic Choice and International Relations.* Princeton: Princeton University Press, 1999.

Larson, Deborah Welch. *Anatomy of Mistrust: U.S.–Soviet Relations during the Cold War.* Ithaca: Cornell University Press, 1997.

Layne, Christopher. "China's Challenge to US Hegemony." *Current History* 107, 705 (2008): 13–18.

———. "The Unipolar Illusion: Why New Great Powers Will Rise." *International Security* 17, 4 (1993): 5–51.

Lebow, Richard Ned. *Between Peace and War.* Baltimore: Johns Hopkins University Press, 1981.

———. "The Soviet Offensive in Europe: The Schlieffen Plan Revisited?" *International Security* 9, 4 (1985): 44–78.

Lee, Dong Sun. *Power Shifts, Strategy and War: Declining States and International Conflict.* New York: Routledge, 2007.

Leffler, Melvyn P. *For the Soul of Mankind: The United States, the Soviet Union and The Cold War.* New York: Hill and Wang, 2007.

Legro, Jeffery W., and Andrew Moravscik. "Is Anybody Still a Realist." *International Security* 24, 2 (1999): 5–55.

Levy, Jack S. "Declining Power and the Preventive Motivation for War." *World Politics* 40, 1 (1987): 82–107.

———. "The Offense/Defense Balance of Military Technology: A Theoretical and Historical Analysis." *International Studies Quarterly* 28, 2 (1984): 219–238.

Liberman, Peter. *Does Conquest Pay?: The Exploitation of Occupied Industrial Societies*. Princeton: Princeton University Press, 1996.

———. "The Offense-Defense Balance, Interdependence, and War." *Security Studies* 9, 3 (1999): 59–91.

———. "Trading with the Enemy: Security and Relative Economic Gains." *International Security* 21, 1 (1996): 147–175.

Liddell Hart, B. H. "Forward." In Gerhard Ritter, *The Schlieffen Plan: Critique of a Myth*. Westport, CT: Greenwood, 1979.

Lieber, Keir A. *War and the Engineers: The Primacy of Politics over Technology*. Ithaca: Cornell University Press, 2005.

Lieber, Keir A., and Gerard Alexander. "Waiting for Balancing: Why the World Is Not Pushing Back." *International Security* 30, 1 (2005): 109–130.

Lind, Jennifer M. "Correspondence: Spirals, Security, and Stability in East Asia," *International Security* 24, 4 (2000): 190–195.

———. *Sorry States: Apologies in International Relations*. Ithaca: Cornell University Press, 2008.

Lipson, Charles. "International Cooperation in Economic and Security Affairs." *World Politics* 37, 1 (1984): 1–23.

Luard, Evan. "Conciliation and Deterrence: A Comparison of Political Strategies in the Interwar and Postwar Periods." *World Politics* 19, 2 (1967): 167–189.

Lynn-Jones, Sean. "Détente and Deterrence: Anglo-German Relations, 1911–1914." *International Security* 11, 2 (1986): 121–150.

———. "Offense-Defense Theory and Its Critics." *Security Studies* 4, 4 (1995): 660–691.

———. "Realism and America's Rise: A Review Essay." *International Security* 23, 2 (1998): 157–182.

MacDonald, Paul K. "Useful Fiction or Miracle Maker: The Competing Epistemological Foundations of Rational Choice Theory." *American Political Science Review* 41, 4 (2005): 373–393.

McElwee, William. *The Art of War: Waterloo to Mons*. Bloomington: Indiana University Press, 1974.

MccGwire, Michael. *Perestroika and Soviet National Security*. Washington, DC: Brookings, 1991.

Mack, Andrew J. R. "Why Big Nations Lose Small Wars: The Politics of Asymmetric Conflict." *World Politics* 27, 2 (1975): 175–200.

McNamara, Robert S. "The Dynamics of Nuclear Strategy." Department of State Bulletin, October 9, 1967.

Maddison, Angus. *The World Economy: A Millennial Perspective*. Paris: Development Centre of the OECD, 2001.

Marder, Arthur. *From the Dreadnought to Scapa Flow: The Royal Navy in the Fisher Era, 1904–1919*. New York: Oxford University Press, 1961.

———. *Old Friends, New Enemies*. Oxford: Oxford University Press, 1981.

Martin, Lisa L., and Beth A. Simmons. "Theories and Empirical Studies of International Institutions." *International Organization* 52, 4 (1998): 729–757.

Matthews, John C., III. "Current Gains and Future Outcomes." *International Security* 21, 1 (1996): 112–146.

Maurer, John H. "Arms Control and the Washington Conference." In Erik Goldstein and John H. Maurer, eds., *The Washington Conference, 1921–22*. Essex, UK: Frank Cass, 1994.

May, Michael M., George F. Bing, and John Steinbruner. "Strategic Arsenals after START: The Implications for Deep Cuts." *International Security* 13, 1 (1988): 90–133.

Mearsheimer, John J. "Back to the Future: Instability in Europe after the Cold War." *International Security* 15, 1 (1990): 5–56.

———. "Better to Be Godzilla Than Bambi." *Foreign Policy* 146 (2005): 46-49.

———. *Conventional Deterrence*. Ithaca: Cornell University Press, 1983.

———. "The False Promise of International Institutions." *International Security* 19, 23 (1994–95): 5–49.

———. *The Tragedy of Great Power Politics*. New York: Norton, 2001.

———. "Why the Soviets Can't Win Quickly in Central Europe." *International Security* 7, 1 (1982): 3–39.

Midford, Paul. "The Logic of Reassurance and Japan's Grand Strategy." *Security Studies* 11, 3 (2002): 1–43.

Milner, Helen. "The Assumption of Anarchy in International Politics." *Review of International Studies* 17, 1 (1991): 67–85.

———. *Interests, Institutions, and Information: Domestic Politics and International Relations*. Princeton: Princeton University Press, 1997.

———. "International Theories of Cooperation among Nations: Strengths and Weaknesses." *World Politics* 44, 3 (1992): 466–496.

Moe, Terry M. "On the Scientific Status of Rational Models." *American Journal of Political Science* 23, 1 (1979): 215–243.

Monger, George. *The End of Isolation: British Foreign Policy, 1900–1907*. London: Thomas Nelson, 1963.

Montgomery, Evan Braden. "Breaking Out of the Security Dilemma: Realism, Reassurance, and the Problem of Uncertainty." *International Security* 31, 2 (2006): 151–185.

Moravcsik, Andrew. "A Liberal Theory of International Politics." *International Organization* 51, 4 (1997): 513–553.

Morrow, James D. "The Strategic Setting of Choices: Signaling, Commitment, and Negotiating in International Politics." In David A. Lake and Robert Powell, eds., *Strategic Choice and International Relations*. Princeton: Princeton University Press, 1999.

Mueller, John. *Retreat From Doomsday: The Obsolescence of Major War*. New York: Basic Books, 1989.

———. "What Was the Cold War About? Evidence from Its Ending." *Political Science Quarterly* 119, 4 (2004–05): 606–631.

Murray, Willamson. *The Change in the European Balance of Power, 1938–1939*. Princeton: Princeton University Press, 1984.

———. "Net Assessment in Nazi Germany in the 1930s." In Williamson Murray and Allan R. Millett, eds., *Calculations: Net Assessment and the Coming of World War II*. New York: Free Press, 1992.

Nacht, Michael. "The Delicate Balance of Error." *Foreign Policy* 19 (1975): 163–177.

Narizny, Kevin. "Both Guns and Butter, or Neither: Class Interests in the Political Economy of Rearmament." *American Political Science Review* 97, 2 (2003): 203–222.

———. "The Political Economy of Alignment: Great Britain's Commitments to Europe, 1905–1939." *International Security* 27, 4 (2003): 184–219.

National Intelligence Council. "Status of Soviet Unilateral Withdrawals." NIC M 89-10003, 1989.

Newhouse, John. *Cold Dawn: The Story of SALT*. New York: Holt, Rinehart and Winston, 1973.

Norris, Robert S., and Hans M. Kristensen. "Chinese Nuclear Forces, 2008." *Bulletin of the Atomic Scientists* 64, 3 (2008): 42–45.

Nuclear Posture Review [excerpts]. January 8, 2002. http://globalsecurity.org/wmd/ library/policy/dod/npr/htm.

O'Hanlon, Michael. *Technological Change and the Future of Warfare*. Washington, DC: Brookings, 2000.

Oren, Ido. "A Theory of Armament." *Conflict Management and Peace Science* 16, 1 (1998): 1–29.

Osgood, Charles E. *Alternative to War or Surrender*. Urbana: University of Illinois Press, 1962.

Owen, John W., IV. *Liberal Peace, Liberal War: American Politics and International Security*. Ithaca: Cornell University Press, 1997.

———. "Transnational Liberalism and U.S. Primacy." *International Security* 26, 3 (2001–02: 117–152.

Oye, Kenneth A., ed., *Cooperation under Anarchy*. Princeton: Princeton University Press, 1986.

———. "Explaining Cooperation under Anarchy: Hypotheses and Strategies." In Kenneth A. Oye, ed., *Cooperation under Anarchy*. Princeton: Princeton University Press, 1986.

———. "Explaining the End of the Cold War: Morphological and Behavioral Adaptations to the Nuclear Peace." In Richard Ned Lebow and Thomas Risse-Kappen, eds., *International Relations Theory and the End of the Cold War*. New York: Columbia University Press, 1995.

Pape, Robert A. "Soft Balancing against the United States." *International Security* 30, 1 (2005): 7–45.

Paul, T. V. "Nuclear Taboo and War Initiation in Regional Conflicts." *Journal of Conflict Resolution* 39, 4 (1995): 696–717.

———. "Soft Balancing in the Age of U.S. Primacy." *International Security* 30, 1 (2005): 46–71.

Pelz, Stephen E. *Race to Pearl Harbor: The Failure of the Second London Naval Conference and the Onset of World War II*. Cambridge: Harvard University Press, 1974.

Pollack, Kenneth, and Ray Takeyh. "Taking on Iran." *Foreign Affairs* 82, 2 (2005): 20–34.

Posen, Barry R. "Command of the Commons: The Military Foundation of U.S. Hegemony." *International Security* 28, 1 (2003): 5–46.

———. "Crisis Stability and Conventional Arms Control." *Daedalus* 120, 1 (1991): 217–232.

———. "Measuring the European Conventional Balance: Coping with Complexity in Threat Assessment." *International Security* 9, 3 (1984–85): 47–88.

———. *The Sources of Military Doctrine*. Ithaca: Cornell University Press, 1984.

Posen, Barry R., and Andrew L. Ross. "Competing Visions for American Grand Strategy." *International Security* 21, 3 (1996–97): 5–53.

Powell, Robert. "Absolute and Relative Gains in International Relations Theory." *American Political Science Review* 85, 4 (1991): 1303–1320.

———. "Anarchy in International Relations Theory: The Neorealist-Neoliberal Debate." *International Organization* 48, 2 (1994): 313–344.

———. "Bargaining Theory and International Conflict." *Annual Review of Political Science* 5 (2002): 1–30.

———. "Game Theory, International Relations Theory, and Hobbesian Stylization." In Ira Katznelson and Helen V. Milner, eds., *Political Science: State of the Discipline*. New York: Norton, 2002.

———. *In the Shadow of Power: States and Strategies in International Politics*. Princeton: Princeton University Press, 1999.

———. *Nuclear Deterrence Theory: The Search for Credibility*. Cambridge: Cambridge University Press, 1990.

———. "Uncertainty, Shifting Power, and Appeasement." *American Political Science Review* 90, 4 (1996): 749–764.

———. "War as a Commitment Problem." *International Organization* 60, 1 (2006): 169–203.

Price, Richard M. *The Chemical Weapons Taboo*. Ithaca: Cornell University Press, 1997.

Quester, George H. *Nuclear Monopoly*. New Brunswick, N.J.: Transaction, 2000.

———. *Offense and Defense in the International System*. New York: Wiley, 1997.

Rathjens, George W. "The Dynamics of the Arms Race." *Scientific American* 220 (1969): 15–25.

Reed, William. "Information, Power, and War." *American Political Science Review* 97, 4 (2003): 633–641.

Reiter, Dan. "Exploding the Powder Keg Myth: Preemptive Wars Almost Never Happen." *International Security* 20, 2 (1995): 5–34.

———. "Exploring the Bargaining Model of War." *Perspectives on Politics* 1, 1 (2003): 27–43.

Reiter, Dan, and Allan C. Stam. *Democracies at War*. Princeton: Princeton University Press, 2002.

———. "Understanding Victory: Why Political Institutions Matter." *International Security* 28, 1 (2003): 168–179.

Rich, Norman. *Hitler's War Aims: Ideology, the Nazi State and the Course of Expansion*. New York: Norton, 1973.

Risse-Kappen, Thomas. "Collective Identity in a Democratic Community." In

Peter Katzenstein, ed., *The Culture of National Security: Norms and Identities in World Politics*. New York: Columbia University Press, 1996.

———. *Cooperation among Democracies*. Princeton: Princeton University Press, 1995.

———. "Did 'Peace through Strength' End the Cold War: Lessons from INF." *International Security* 16, 1 (1991): 162–188.

———. "Ideas Do Not Float Freely: Transnational Coalitions, Domestic Structures, and the End of the Cold War." *International Organization* 48, 2 (1994): 185–214.

Ritter, Gerhard. *The Schlieffen Plan: Critique of a Myth*. Westport, CT: Greenwood, 1979.

———. *The Sword and the Scepter: The Problem of Militarism in Germany*, Vol. 2. Coral Gables: University of Miami Press, 1970.

Rock, Stephen R. *Appeasement in International Politics*. Lexington: University of Kentucky Press, 2000.

Rogowski, Ronald. "Institutions as Constraints on Strategic Choice." In David A. Lake and Robert Powell, eds., *Strategic Choice and International Relations*. Princeton: Princeton University Press, 1999.

Rosato, Sebastian. "The Flawed Logic of Democratic Peace Theory." *American Political Science Review* 97, 4 (2003): 585–602.

Rose, Gideon. "Neoclassical Realism and Theories of Foreign Policy." *World Politics* 51, 1 (1998): 144–72.

Rosen, Stephen P. "Foreign Policy and Nuclear Weapons: The Case for Strategic Defenses." In Samuel P. Huntington, ed., *The Strategic Imperative: New Policies for American Security*. Cambridge, MA: Ballinger, 1982.

———. "Military Effectiveness: Why Society Matters." *International Security*, 19, 4 (1995): 5–31.

Ruggie, John Gerald. "Continuity and Transformation in the World Polity: Toward a Neorealist Synthesis." *World Politics* 35, 2 (1983): 261–285.

———. "International Regimes, Transactions, and Change: Embedded Liberalism in the Postwar Economic Order." *International Organization* 36, 2 (1982): 379–415.

Sagan, Scott D. "1914 Revisited: Allies, Offense, and Instability." *International Security* 11, 2 (1986): 151–175.

———. "The Origins of the Pacific War." *Journal of Interdisciplinary History* 18, 4 (1988): 893–922.

Salman, Michael, Kevin J. Sullivan, and Stephen Van Evera. "Analysis or Propaganda? Measuring American Strategic Nuclear Capability, 1969–1988." In Lynn Eden and Steven E. Miller, eds., *Nuclear Arguments: Understanding the Strategic Nuclear Arms and Arms Control Debates*. Ithaca: Cornell University Press, 1991.

Sample, Susan G. "Arms Races and Dispute Escalation: Resolving the Debate." *Journal of Peace Research* 34, 1 (1997): 7–22.

———. "Furthering the Investigation Into the Effects of Arms Buildups." *Journal of Peace Research* 35, 1 (1998): 122–126.

Samuels, Richard J. "Japan's Goldilocks Strategy." *Washington Quarterly* 29, 4 (2006): 111–127.

———. *Securing Japan: Tokyo's Grand Strategy and the Future of East Asia*. Ithaca: Cornell University Press, 2007.

Sartori, Anne E. "The Might of the Pen: A Reputational Theory of Communication in International Disputes." *International Organization* 56, 1 (2002): 121–149.

Schelling, Thomas C. *Arms and Influence*. New Haven: Yale University Press, 1966.

———. "A Framework for the Evaluation of Arms-Control Proposals." *Daedalus* 104, 3 (1975): 187–200.

———. *The Strategy of Conflict*. Cambridge: Harvard University Press, 1960.

Schelling, Thomas C., and Morton H. Halperin. *Strategy and Arms Control*. New York: Twentieth Century Fund, 1961.

Schilling, Warner R. "U.S. Strategic Nuclear Concepts in the 1970s: The Search for Sufficiently Equivalent Countervailing Parity." *International Security* 6, 2 (1981): 49–79.

Shimko, Keith L. "Realism, Neorealism, and American Liberalism." *Review of Politics* 54, 2 (1992): 281–301.

Schultz, Kenneth A. *Democracy and Coercive Diplomacy*. Cambridge: Cambridge University Press, 2001.

Schwartz, David N. "Past and Present: The Historical Legacy." In Ashton B. Carter and David N. Schwartz, eds., *Ballistic Missile Defense*. Washington, DC: Brookings, 1984.

Schweller, Randall L. "Bandwagoning for Profit: Bringing the Revisionist State Back In." *International Security* 19, 1 (1994): 72–107.

———. *Deadly Imbalances: Tripolarity and Hitler's Strategy of World Conquest*. New York: Columbia University Press, 1998.

———. "Neorealism's Status-Quo Bias: What Security Dilemma?" *Security Studies* 5, 3 (1996): 90–121.

———. *Unanswered Threats: Political Constraints on the Balance of Power*. Princeton: Princeton University Press, 2006.

Seay, Douglas. "What Are the Soviets' Objectives in Their Foreign, Military, and Arms Control Policies?" In Lynn Eden and Steven E. Miller, eds., *Nuclear Argument: Understanding the Strategic Nuclear Arms and Arms Control Debates*. Ithaca: Cornell University Press, 1989.

Segal, Gerald. "The Coming Confrontation between China and Japan?" *World Policy Journal* 10, 2 (1993): 27–32.

Shambaugh, David. "China's Military Modernization: Making Steady and Surprising Progress." In Ashley J. Tellis and Michael Wills, eds., *Strategic Asia 2005–06: Military Modernization in an Era of Uncertainty*. Seattle: National Bureau of Asian Research, 2005.

Shear, James A. "Verification, Compliance, and Arms Control: Dynamics of the Domestic Debate." In Lynn Eden and Steven E. Miller, eds., *Nuclear Arguments*. Ithaca: Cornell University Press, 1989.

Shimshoni, Jonathan. "Technology, Military Advantage, and World War I: A Case of Military Entrepreneurship." *International Security* 15, 3 (1990–91): 187–215.

Simmons, Beth A.. and Lisa L. Martin. "International Organizations and Institutions." In Walter Carlsnaes, Thomas Risse, and Beth A. Simmons, eds., *Handbook of International Relations*. London: Sage, 2002.

Singer, J. David. "The Level-of-Analysis Problem." In James N. Rousenau, ed., *International Politics and Foreign Policy*. New York: Free Press, 1969.

———. "Threat-Perception and the Armament-Tension Dilemma." *Journal of Conflict Resolution* 2, 1 (1958): 90–105.

Slantchev, Branislav L. "Military Coercion in Interstate Crises." *American Political Science Review* 99, 4 (2005): 533–547.

Smith, Gerard C. *Doubletalk: The Story of the First Strategic Arms Limitation Talks*. Garden City, NY: Doubleday, 1980.

Smith, Woodruff D. *The Ideological Origins of Nazi Imperialism*. Oxford: Oxford University Press, 1986.

Snidal, Duncan. "Relative Gains and the Pattern of International Cooperation." *American Political Science Review* 85, 3 (1991): 701–726.

Snyder, Glenn H. *Alliance Politics*. Ithaca: Cornell University Press, 1997.

———. *Deterrence and Defense: Toward a Theory of National Security*. Princeton: Princeton University Press, 1961.

———. "Mearsheimer's World—Offensive Realism and the Struggle for Security." *International Security* 27, 1 (2002): 149–173.

———. "Process Variables in Neorealist Theory." *Security Studies* 5, 3 (1996): 167–192.

———. "The Security Dilemma in Alliance Politics." *World Politics* 36, 4 (1984): 461–495.

Snyder, Jack L. "Civil-Military Relations and the Cult of the Offensive, 1914 and 1984." *International Security* 9, 1 (1984): 108–146.

———. *The Ideology of the Offensive: Military Decision Making and the Disasters of 1914*. Ithaca: Cornell University Press, 1984.

———. "International Leverage on Soviet Domestic Change." *World Politics* 42, 1 (1989): 1–30.

———. "'Is' and 'Ought': Evaluating Empirical Aspects of Normative Research." In Colin Elman and Miriam Elman, eds., *Progress in International Relations Theory: Appraising the Field*. Cambridge: MIT Press, 2003.

———. *Myths of Empire: Domestic Politics and International Ambition*. Ithaca: Cornell University Press, 1991.

Stein, Arthur A. "Coordination and Collaboration: Regimes in an Anarchic World." *International Organization* 36, 2 (1982): 299–324.

———. "The Limits of Strategic Choice: Constrained Rationality and Incomplete Explanation." In David A. Lake and Robert Powell, eds., *Strategic Choice and International Relations*. Princeton: Princeton University Press, 1999.

———. *Why Nations Cooperate: Circumstance and Choice in International Relations*. Ithaca: Cornell University Press, 1990.

Steinberg, James B. "An Elective Partnership: Salvaging Transatlantic Relations." *Survival* 45, 2 (2003): 113–146.

Steinberg, Jonathan. *Yesterday's Deterrent: Tirpitz and the Birth of the German Battle Fleet*. New York: Macmillan, 1965.

Stevenson, David. *Armaments and the Coming of War: Europe 1904–1914*. Oxford: Oxford University Press, 1996.

Stinchcombe, Arthur L. "The Conditions of Fruitfulness of Theorizing about Mechanisms in Social Science." *Philosophy of the Social Sciences* 21, 3 (1991): 367–388.

Suri, Jeremi. "Explaining the End of the Cold War: A New Historical Consensus?" *Journal of Cold War Studies* 4, 4 (2002): 60–92.

Szechenyi, Nicholas. "A Turning Point for Japan's Self-Defense Forces." *Washington Quarterly* 29, 4 (2006): 139–150.

Talbott, Strobe. *Endgame: The Inside Story of SALT II.* New York: Harper and Row, 1979.

Taliaferro, Jeffrey W. "Security Seeking Under Anarchy—Defensive Realism Revisited." *International Security* 25, 3 (2000): 128–161.

Tannenwald, Nina. "The Nuclear Taboo: The United States and the Normative Basis of Nuclear Non-Use." *International Organization* 53, 3 (1999): 433–468.

Taylor, A. J. P. *The Struggle for the Mastery of Europe, 1848–1918.* Oxford: Oxford University Press, 1954.

Tellis, Ashley J., et al. *Measuring National Power in the Postindustrial Age.* Washington, DC: RAND, 2000.

Tetlock, Philip E., and Aaron Belkin, eds. *Counterfactual Thought Experiments in World Politics: Logical, Methodological, and Psychological Perspectives.* Princeton: Princeton University Press, 1996.

Thomson, Alexander S. "Coercion through IOs: The Security Council and the Logic of Information Transmission." *International Organization* 60, 1 (2006): 1–34.

Trachtenberg, Mark. "American Strategy and the Shifting Nuclear Balance, 1949–1954." *International Security* 13, 3 (1988–89): 5–49.

Trubowitz, Peter. *Defining the National Interest: Conflict and Change in American Foreign Policy.* Chicago: Chicago University Press, 1998.

Tuschhoff, Christian. "Alliance Cohesion and Peaceful Change in NATO." In Helga Haftendorn, Robert O. Keohane, and Celeste A. Wallander, eds., *Imperfect Unions: Security Institutions over Time and Space.* Oxford: Oxford University Press, 1999.

Twining, Daniel. "America's Grand Design in Asia." *Washington Quarterly* 31, 3 (2007): 79–94.

Van Crevald, Martin. *Supplying War: Logistics from Wallerstein to Patton.* Cambridge: Cambridge University Press, 1977.

Van Evera, Stephen. "Causes of War." Ph.D. dissertation, University of California at Berkeley, 1984.

———. *Causes of War: Power and the Roots of Conflict.* Ithaca: Cornell University Press, 1999.

———. "The Cult of the Offensive and the Origins of the First World War." *International Security* 9, 1 (1984): 58–107.

———. *Guide to Methods for Students of Political Science.* Ithaca: Cornell University Press, 1997.

———. "Offense, Defense and the Causes of War." *International Security* 22, 2 (1998): 5–43.

———. "Primed for Peace: Europe after the Cold War." *International Security* 15, 3 (1990–91): 7–57.

———. "Why States Believe Foolish Ideas: Non-Self-Evaluation by Government and Society." 1998.

Waever, Ole. "Integration as Security: Constructing a Europe at Peace." In Charles A. Kupchan, ed., *Atlantic Security: Competing Visions*. New York: Council on Foreign Relations, 1998.

Wagner, Harrison. "Bargaining and War." *American Journal of Political Science* 44, 3 (2000): 469–484.

Wallace, Michael D. "Armaments and Escalation: Two Competing Hypotheses." *International Studies Quarterly* 26, 1 (1982): 37–56.

———. "Arms Races and Escalation: Some New Evidence." *Journal of Conflict Resolution* 23, 1 (1979): 3–16.

Wallander, Celeste A. *Mortal Friends, Best Enemies: German-Russian Cooperation after the Cold War*. Ithaca: Cornell University Press, 1999.

———. "NATO after the Cold War." *International Organization* 54, 4 (2000): 705–735.

Walt, Stephen M. "Keeping the World 'Off-Balance': Self-Restraint and U.S. Foreign Policy." In G. John Ikenberry, ed., *America Unrivaled: The Future of the Balance of Power*. Ithaca: Cornell University Press, 2002.

———. *The Origins of Alliances*. Ithaca: Cornell University Press, 1987.

Waltz, Kenneth N. "The Emerging Structure of International Politics." *International Security* 18, 2 (1993): 44–79.

———. "International Politics Is Not Foreign Policy." *Security Studies* 6, 1 (1996): 54–57.

———. *Man, the State and War*. New York: Columbia University Press, 1959.

———. "The Origins of War in Neorealist Theory." In Robert I. Rotberg and Theodore K. Robb, eds., *The Origin and Prevention of Major Wars*. Cambridge: Cambridge University Press, 1989.

———. "Reflections on *Theory of International Politics*: A Response to My Critics." In Robert O. Keohane, ed., *Neorealism and Its Critics*. New York: Columbia University Press, 1986.

———. "Structural Realism after the Cold War." *International Security* 25, 1 (2000): 5–41.

———. *Theory of International Politics*. Reading, MA: Addison-Wesley, 1979.

Wan, Ming. *Sino-Japanese Relations: Interaction, Logic and Transformation*. Stanford: Stanford University Press, 2006.

Weber, Steve. *Cooperation and Discord in U.S.–Soviet Arms Control*. Princeton: Princeton University Press, 1991.

Wehler, Hans-Ulrick. *The German Empire, 1871–1918*. New York: Berg, 1985.

Weinberg, Gerhard L. *The Foreign Policy of Hitler's Germany: Diplomatic Revolution in Europe, 1933–36*. Chicago: University of Chicago Press, 1970.

Wendt, Alexander. "The Agent-Structure Problem in International Relations." *International Organization* 43, 3 (1987): 335–370.

———. "Anarchy is What States Make of It: The Social Construction of Power Politics." *International Organization* 46, 2 (1992): 391–425.

———. "Collective Identity Formation and the International State." *American Political Science Review* 88, 2 (1994): 384–396.

———. "Constructing International Politics." *International Security* 20, 1 (1995): 71–81.

———. *Social Theory of International Politics.* Cambridge: Cambridge University Press, 1999.

Werner, Suzanne, and Jacek Kugler. "Power Transitions and Military Buildups: Resolving the Relationship between Arms Buildups and War." In Jacek Kugler and Douglas Lemke, eds., *Parity and War: Evaluations and Extensions of The War Ledger.* Ann Arbor: University of Michigan Press, 1996.

Williamson, Samuel R. *The Politics of Grand Strategy: Britain and France Prepare for War, 1904–1914.* Cambridge: Harvard University Press, 1969.

Willrich, Mason, and John B. Rhinelander, eds. *SALT: The Moscow Agreements and Beyond.* New York: Free Press, 1974.

Wittman, Donald. "How a War Ends: A Rational Model Approach." *Journal of Conflict Resolution* 23, 4 (1979): 743–763.

Wohlstetter, Albert. "Is There a Strategic Arms Race?" *Foreign Policy* 15 (1974): 3–20.

———. "Rivals, But No 'Race.'" *Foreign Policy* 16 (1974): 48–81.

Wolfers, Arnold. *Discord and Collaboration: Essays on International Politics.* Baltimore: Johns Hopkins University Press, 1962.

Wohlforth, William Curti. *The Elusive Balance: Power and Perceptions during the Cold War.* Ithaca: Cornell University Press, 1993.

———. "The Perception of Power: Russia in the Pre-1914 Balance." *World Politics* 39, 3 (1989): 353–381.

Wu, Xinbo. "The End of the Silver Lining: A Chinese View of the U.S.–Japanese Alliance." *Washington Quarterly* 29, 1 (2005–06): 119–130.

Yanarella, Ernest J. *The Missile Defense Controversy: Strategy, Technology, and Politics, 1955–1972.* Lexington: University of Kentucky Press, 1977.

Yang, Bojiang. "Redefining Sino-Japanese Relations after Koizumi." *Washington Quarterly* 29, 4 (2006): 129–137.

Yergin, Daniel. "Ensuring Energy Security." *Foreign Affairs* 85, 2 (2006): 69–82.

Zakaria, Fareed. *From Wealth to Power: The Unusual Origins of America's World Role.* Princeton: Princeton University Press, 1998.

Index

magnitude and security seeker's optimal strategy, 53, 72–73 (*see also under* security dilemma); structuralist-realist pessimism, summary of, 57–59, 58nn.18–20, 59nn.23–24; vs. structural realism, 15; summary/implications of, 90–92, 90–91nn.82–83; summary of major arguments, 269–72, 269n.1

—FINDING YOUR WAY AROUND: application to arms races (*see* arms race applications of theory); counterarguments (*see* counterarguments to theory); evaluated by cases/comparisons (*see* case evaluation); evaluated from within (*see* internal evaluation); extensions (*see* extensions of theory); vs. IR theories (*see* IR theories vs. the strategic choice theory); offense-defense balance (*see* offense-defense balance); power (*see* power); setup (*see* setting up theory)

Strategic Defense Initiative (SDI), 209, 265

structural constructivism: on collective identities, 169–70, 169–70nn.57–58, 192; vs. neorealism, 171n.61; vs. the strategic choice theory, 18–19, 149, 166–71, 166nn.48–49, 167–68nn.52–53, 169–70nn.56–59, 171n.61; vs. structural realism, 6; on worst-case assumptions, 171

structural level, 24–25, 24–25nn.4–5

structural realism: alliance formation predicted by, 51n.3, 59; on cheating, 128; vs. classical realism, 159n.24; on competition as best strategy, 57–59, 58nn.18–20, 59nn.23–24; vs. defensive realism, 13; on international environment as generating competition, 13, 25–26, 54; on irrationality of competition between security seekers, 144–45; vs. neo-institutionalism, 162; power as central to, 25, 43, 45, 64; on relative gains, 131–32, 132n.14; on security as central motive, 54, 54n.8; security dilemma's role in, 151, 151n.9; on self-help, 58, 58nn.18–20; vs. the strategic choice theory, 15, 148–52, 150n.4, 150n.6, 151n.9, 153n.12; vs. structural constructivism, 6, 166; on uncertainty, 145; variables in, 25n.5; on worst-case assumptions about intentions, 147n

suboptimal behavior, 15, 19, 21–22, 27, 31, 156–58, 172–74, 176, 179–80. *See also* rationality assumption

survival assumption, 37n.39

Taiwan, 105, 217–18, 219n.39, 219n.44, 273–74, 280, 280n.18

Tannenwald, Nina, 193n.36

technology: arms race fostered by advances in, 232–33; offense-defense balance affected by, 141–42, 142n.42, 143n.46; and war, 113n.30, 120–21; weapons, 141–42, 142n.42, 143n.46 (*see also* nuclear weapons)

Theory of International Politics (Waltz), 149. *See also* structural realism

Tirpitz, Alfred von, 240–43, 240n.38, 241–42n.44

Triple Alliance, 242

unilateral restraint, 67–68

unitary-actor assumption: and evaluating the theory from within, 20, 176–85, 180nn.12–13, 181n.16, 181n.18, 182n.21, 184nn.23–25, 188, 271; and setting up the theory, 31–32, 31n.25, 32n.27

United States: ideology of, 202, 210n.11; Iraq invaded by, 161; motives (theirs) as influencing nuclear threat assessment, 5–6; power of, post–Cold War reactions to, 5, 202; top dangers facing, 1

United States Navy. *See under* arms race applications of theory

United States policies: ABM Treaty withdrawal, 10n.11; toward China, future, 272–81, 276n.10, 278n, 280.18; Cold War, hawks vs. doves on, 83–84, 97–100, 100n.7, 103n.11; Cold War nuclear, 67, 71, 71n.45, 78, 97–100, 125–26, 153, 161; Japanese relations (*see under* arms race applications of theory); NATO expansion, 10n.11; nuclear deterrence, 10–11, 61, 67, 193–94, 198 (*See also under* arms race applications of theory); oil embargo, 254; peaceful major-power relations' effects on, 1; post–Cold War, 109, 109n.21, 212–13 (*see also* case evaluation, post–Cold War Europe and Northeast Asia); Soviet mo-